www.wadsworth.com

wadsworth.com is the World Wide Web site for Wadsworth and is your direct source to dozens of online resources.

At *wadsworth.com* you can find out about supplements, demonstration software, and student resources. You can also send email to many of our authors and preview new publications and exciting new technologies.

wadsworth.com
Changing the way the world learns[®]

Worlds of Music

AN INTRODUCTION TO THE MUSIC OF THE WORLD'S PEOPLES

Shorter Version / Second Edition

Jeff Todd Titon
General Editor

Linda K. Fujie
David Locke
David P. McAllester
David B. Reck
John M. Schechter
R. Anderson Sutton

SCHIRMER

THOMSON LEARNING

Australia • Canada • Mexico • Singapore • Spain
United Kingdom • United States

SCHIRMER
THOMSON LEARNING ™

Publisher: Clark Baxter
Senior Assistant Editor: Julie Yardley
Editorial Assistant: Anne Gittinger
Technology Project Manager: Michelle Vardeman
Marketing Manager: Diane Wenckebach
Advertising Project Manager: Kelley McAllister
Project Manager, Editorial Production: Catherine Morris
Art Director: Maria Epes
Print/Media Buyer: Barbara Britton

Permissions Editor: Joohee Lee
Production Service: Greg Hubit Bookworks
Text Designer: Harry Voigt
Copy Editor: Molly Roth
Cover Designer: Joan Greenfield
Cover Image: Jeff Todd Titon
Cover Printer: Coral Graphic Services, Inc.
Compositor: Stratford Publishing Services, Inc.
Printer: Courier Corporation/Kendallville

Printed in the United States of America
1 2 3 4 5 6 7 08 07 06 05 04

For more information about our products, contact us at:
Thomson Learning Academic Resource Center
1-800-423-0563

For permission to use material
from this text, submit a request online at
http://www.thomsonrights.com.

Any additional questions about permissions
can be submitted by email to
thomsonrights@thomson.com.

Library of Congress Control Number: 2004103820

ISBN 0-534-62757-9

Thomson Schirmer
10 Davis Drive
Belmont, CA 94002-3098
USA

Asia
Thomson Learning
5 Shenton Way #01-01
UIC Building
Singapore 068808

Australia/New Zealand
Thomson Learning
102 Dodds Street
Southbank, Victoria 3006
Australia

Canada
Nelson
1120 Birchmount Road
Toronto, Ontario M1K 5G4
Canada

Europe/Middle East/Africa
Thomson Learning
High Holborn House
50/51 Bedford Row
London WC1R 4LR
United Kingdom

Contents

6 India/South India 197

7 Asia/Indonesia 231

8 Latin America/Chile, Bolivia, Ecuador, Peru 265

9 Discovering and Documenting a World of Music 311

Recorded Selections

CD 1

Chapter 1

Chapter 2

Chapter 3

Preface

Why study music? There are many reasons, but perhaps the most important are pleasure and understanding. We have designed this book and its accompanying CDs to introduce undergraduates to the study of music the world over. The only prerequisites are a curious ear and an inquisitive mind.

Based on *Worlds of Music,* 4th edition (2002), this revised Shorter Version offers a textbook aimed squarely at students without prior musical training who want an entry-level appreciation course on the music of the world's peoples. In a few markedly significant ways it differs from the previous Shorter Version. First, timed listening charts keyed to the musical examples on the accompanying CD set have in all cases replaced the transcriptions in musical notation, while discussions of musical form and structure have been made more accessible to beginning students. For musical transcriptions and further discussion of many of these musical examples, students and teachers may consult *Worlds of Music,* 4th edition. Second, revised and enlarged glossaries and study questions have been moved from the online *Instructor's Manual* into the chapters themselves. Third, each chapter's case study has been shortened, while the beginning of each chapter now provides more of an overview of the regions and music cultures under examination.

Using students' everyday ideas of rhythm, meter, melody, and harmony, Chapter 1 sharpens these rudimentary concepts and shows how they may apply to many of the musics of the world's peoples that will be studied in this book. The first chapter now has many more illustrations and cross-references to musical examples in the various parts of the book/CD set. Using as illustrations the popular Ghanaian postal workers' stamp-canceling music and the song of the hermit thrush, Chapter 1 asks students how one draws the line between music and nonmusic. Our consideration of rudiments in a world music context includes not only musical sounds and structures but also a performance model as well as basic concepts of the music-culture, people's ideas about music, social activities involving music, and the material culture of music. The last chapter guides students through a fieldwork project. Each of the other chapters concentrates on music in a particular geographical and cultural area. The chapter on Latin America has been extensively rewritten with much new material, while a section on *taiko* drumming has been added to the chapter on Japan. The chapter on Europe has been dropped from this revised shorter edition. Twenty-eight of the photographs are new.

* * *

College and university courses in music of the world's peoples have increased dramatically in recent years, and the reasons are easy to comprehend. Students who love music are alive to all music. So are composers, and many use the world's musical resources in their newest works. This is an important feature of today's music, and the people who listen to it—now and in the future—will want to keep their musical horizons broad.

Another reason for the interest in all kinds of music is the upsurge in ethnic awareness. As modern people try to locate themselves in a world that is changing with bewildering speed, they find music especially rewarding, for music is among the most tenacious of cultural elements. Music symbolizes a people's way of life; it represents a distillation of cultural style. For many, music *is* a way of life.

The authors of this book are ethnomusicologists; our field, *ethnomusicology,* is usually defined as the study of music in culture. Some ethnomusicologists define the field as the study of music *as* culture, underlining the fact that music is a way of organizing human activity. By *culture* we do not mean "the elite arts," as it is sometimes used. Rather, we use the term as anthropologists do: Culture is a people's way of life, learned and transmitted through the centuries of adapting to the natural and human world. Ethnomusicology is the study of music in the context of human life.

I like to define ethnomusicology as *the study of people making music.* (Of course, music also makes [affects] people.) People "make" music in two ways: They make or construct the *idea* of music—what it is (and is not) and what it does—and they make or produce the *sounds* that they call music. Although we experience music as something "out there" in the world, our response to music depends on the ideas we associate with that music, and those ideas come from the people (ourselves included) who carry our culture. To use academic language, people "make" music into a cultural domain, with associated sets of ideas and activities. We could not even pick out musical form and structure, how the parts of a piece of music work with one another, if we did not depend on the idea that music must be organized rather than random, and if we had not learned to make music that way. (Analyzing form and structure is characteristic of some cultures, including Western ones, but in other areas of the world people do not habitually break a thing down into parts to analyze it.)

As students of music in culture, then, ethnomusicologists investigate *all* music. From the outset, therefore, *Worlds of Music* has presented case studies of Western folk, popular, and ethnic musics along with those from non-Western cultures. It may be that a future edition will include an ethnomusicological case study on Western art music.

Further, because ethnomusicologists believe there is no such thing as "the music itself"—that is, music apart from cultural considerations—we are not satisfied merely to analyze and compare musical forms, structures, melodies, rhythms, compositions, and genres. Instead, we borrow insights and methods from anthropology, sociology, literary criticism, linguistics, and history to understand music as human expression. In fact, until the 1950s ethnomusicology courses in United States' universities were more likely to be found in anthropology departments than music departments, and some nineteenth-century founders of ethnomusicology were psychologists. Ethnomusicology is therefore interdisciplinary, combining elements of the arts, humanities, and social sciences. Because of its eclectic methods and worldwide scope, ethnomusicology is well suited to students seeking a liberal arts education.

When the first edition of this textbook appeared in 1984, formal study of music of the world's peoples focused on indigenous musics of tribal peoples, classical musics of Asia and the Middle East, and the folk, ethnic and immigrant musics of the Western continents. The integrity of any curriculum in ethnomusicology today requires that a historical, geographical, cultural, and genre-based emphasis continue, and yet in the past twenty years ethnomusicologists have moved toward a more complex and nuanced picture. The older map of a world divided into markedly different human groups, each with its own distinct music, is no longer accurate, and perhaps it never was. Exchange via globalization characterizes music in the early twenty-first century just as it characterizes virtually all commerce, and many people regard music primarily as a commodity.

Musical globalization is the result of at least four major changes in the previous century. First, the enormous influence of media on contemporary musical life, not only in the largest cities but also in the most remote villages, has enabled people to hear many different kinds of music, including music that they have never heard before. Second, the migrations of peoples have engendered musical exchange and interchange. Third, modernization and Westernization throughout the world have brought with them Western musical institutions. Finally, "world music," a new category of popular, mass-mediated music based on a mix or fusion of elements associated with various musical cultures, a music with a market niche of its own, has become an intriguing path for musicians and a significant media industry commodity.

The study of the music of the world's peoples is not, and should not, be the study of a marketing category called "world music"; yet the rise of world music and a global economy challenges ethnomusicologists' categories, whether of genre or geography. It presents new challenges to fundamental concepts such as ethnicity and culture as well.

Not only is world music now important as a marketing category in the mass media, but the ideal of multicultural diversity has encouraged ethnic festivals, always featuring music. Musicians from all over the globe now appear on college and university campuses and in city auditoriums. Many younger people searching for musical roots have looked into their ethnic pasts and chosen to learn the music of their foreparents, while others view the variety of musics in the world as a vast resource to be drawn on in creating their own sounds.

Comprehensive coverage of the great variety of musics all over the globe is not possible in an introductory textbook; it is properly the subject of a multivolume encyclopedia. The best introduction to the music of the world's peoples, we think, is not a musical world tour, inevitably superficial, but an approach that explores in some depth the musics of representative human groups. This approach is not new; it adapts to ethnomusicology the case method in anthropology, the touchstone approach in literature, and the problems approach in history. Its object is not primarily to pile up factual knowledge about various musical worlds, though certainly many facts will be learned. Rather, the point is to experience something of what it is like to be an ethnomusicologist puzzling out his or her way toward understanding an unfamiliar music. This process, we believe, is the best foundation for either future coursework (including surveys and seminars) or self-directed study and enjoyment of music after college.

We decided on a small number of case studies because that is how we teach the introductory-level world-music course at our universities. We thought also that by writing about music in societies we know firsthand, we could write an authoritative book. Each chapter, then, reflects our own choice of subject. It also reflects our different ways of approaching music, for we agree that music cannot be "caught" by one method only. Most important, we have tried to present an introduction to world music that provides pleasure as well as knowledge.

We suggest that students begin with Chapter 1. The case studies, Chapters 2 through 8, can be taken in any order. In a one-semester or one-quarter course, the teacher might choose four or five case studies from the shorter edition that best suit the course's pace and purpose, perhaps adding a unit based on the teacher's own research.

Because any fieldwork project should begin well before the end of the term, we suggest that Chapter 9 be read just after the first case study and that students begin fieldwork immediately afterward. Many students say the field projects are the most valuable experiences they take away from this course, particularly when they must make sense of what they document in the field. Students find it attractive and meaningful to make an original contribution to knowledge.

I am sorry to report the death of our coauthor Linda Fujie after the publication of the 4th edition. Her unfailing grace and intelligence are much missed. For this revised Shorter Version her widower, Max-Peter Baumann, has permitted me to add to her chapter something that she wrote about *taiko* drumming only a short while before her death. And although Mark Slobin's "Europe" chapter does not appear in this Shorter Version, the echo of his voice as a co-author can still be heard in Chapters 1 and 9.

We have appreciated the assistance over the years of several editors at Schirmer—Ken Stuart, Maribeth Anderson Payne, Richard Carlin, Jonathan Wiener, and Clark Baxter. We would also like to thank Erica Haskell, for her assistance with the new listening charts, and Martin Sherry, for his help with the instructor's manuals and student study guides. We would be pleased to hear from our readers, and we may be reached by writing to the publisher or to any of us at our respective universities.

Jeff Todd Titon
General Editor

The Authors

Linda K. Fujie received the Ph.D. in ethnomusicology from Columbia University, where she was a student of Dieter Christensen and Adelaida Schramm. She conducted field research in Japan, mainly concerning urban festival and popular music, under grants from the National Endowment for the Humanities, Columbia University, and Colby College. Her interest in overseas Japanese culture also resulted in research on Japanese American and Japanese Brazilian communities, the latter funded by the German Music Council. Her research was published in the *Yearbook for Traditional Music*, in publications on popular music, and in Japanese journals. Other research interests, on which she also wrote articles and delivered papers at European conferences, included the music of the Shaker community in Maine and folk music in Germany. She taught at Colby College as Assistant Professor and at the East Asian Institute of the Free University of Berlin. She regularly wrote and delivered, on German radio, programs on topics related to traditional music. She also lectured on ethnomusicology at the University of Bamberg.

David Locke received the Ph.D. in ethnomusicology from Wesleyan University in 1978, where he studied with David McAllester, Mark Slobin, and Gen'ichi Tsuge. At Wesleyan his teachers of traditional African music included Abraham Adzinyah and Freeman Donkor. He conducted doctoral dissertation fieldwork in Ghana from 1975 to 1977 under the supervision of Professor J. H. K. Nketia. In Ghana his teachers and research associates included Godwin Agbeli, Midawo Gideon Foli Alorwoyie, and Abubakari Lunna. He has published numerous books and articles on African music and regularly performs the repertories of music and dance about which he writes. He teaches at Tufts University, where he currently serves as the director of the master's degree program in ethnomusicology and as a faculty advisor in the Tufts-in-Ghana Foreign Study Program. His current projects include an ethnomusicological study of the music-culture of Dagbon, the documentation and analysis of repertories of African music, and the preparation of multimedia materials on music and culture. He is active in the Society for Ethnomusicology and has served as the president of its Northeast Chapter.

David P. McAllester received the Ph.D. in anthropology from Columbia University, where he studied with George Herzog. A student of American Indian music since 1938, he has undertaken fieldwork among the Comanches, Hopis, Apaches, Navajos, Penobscots, and Passamaquoddies. He is the author of such classic works in ethnomusicology as *Peyote Music, Enemy Way Music, Myth of the Great Star Chant,* and *Navajo Blessingway Singer* (with coauthor Charlotte Frisbie). He is one of the founders of the Society for Ethnomusicology, and he has served as its president and the editor of its journal, *Ethnomusicology.* He is Professor Emeritus of anthropology and music at Wesleyan University.

David B. Reck received the Ph.D. in ethnomusicology from Wesleyan University, where he studied under Mark Slobin and David P. McAllester. Since 1968 he has traveled and worked in India under awards from the American Institute of Indian Studies, the Rockefeller and John Simon Guggenheim Memorial foundations, and the JDR IIIrd Fund. A senior disciple of the legendary Mme. Ranganayaki Rajagopalan, he is an accomplished musician on the Saraswati *veena* and has performed extensively in the United States, Canada, Europe, and India. His four concerts at the 2002 Madras Festival of Music and Dance were the first by a non-Indian *veena* player. As a composer, he has seen his works performed at Tanglewood, Town Hall, Lincoln Center, Carnegie Hall, and various universities and international music festivals. He is the author of *Music of the Whole Earth* and a mystery novel, *The Cobra's Song;* his scholarly publications include articles on Indian music, the Beatles, and cross-influences between the West and the Orient. Currently he is Professor of Asian Languages and Civilizations, and of Music, at Amherst College.

John M. Schechter is Professor of Music, presently also serving as provost of Merrill College, at the University of California, Santa Cruz. He received the Ph.D. in ethnomusicology from the University of Texas at Austin, where he studied ethnomusicology with Gérard Béhague, folklore with Américo Paredes, Andean anthropology with Richard Schaedel, and Quechua with Louisa Stark and Guillermo Delgado-P. Since 1985 he has taught ethnomusicology and music theory, and, up until 2000, directed the Taki Ñan and Voces Latin American Ensembles, at UC Santa Cruz. With Guillermo Delgado-P., Schechter is co-editor of *Quechua Verbal Artistry: The Inscription of Andean Voices/Arte Expresivo Quechua: La Inscripción de Voces Andinas* (2004), a volume dedicated to Quechua song text, narrative, poetry, dialogue, myth, and riddle. He is general editor of, and a contributing author to, *Music in Latin American Culture: Regional Traditions* (1999), a volume examining music-cultural traditions in distinct regions of Latin America, with chapters by ethnomusicologists specializing in those regions. He authored *The Indispensable Harp: Historical Development, Modern Roles, Configurations, and Performance Practices in Ecuador and Latin America* (1992). Schechter's other publications have explored the evolution of the UC Santa

Cruz Taki Ñan ensemble; formulaic expression in Ecuadorian Quichua *sanjuán;* recent evolution in the *bomba,* a focal African-Ecuadorian musical genre; the syncretic nature of the Andean Corpus Christi celebration; and the ethnography and cultural history of the Latin American/Iberian child's wake music-ritual.

R. Anderson Sutton received the Ph.D. in musicology from the University of Michigan, where he studied with Judith Becker and William Malm. He was introduced to Javanese music while an undergraduate at Wesleyan University, and he made it the focus of his master's study at the University of Hawaii, where he studied *gamelan* with Hardja Susilo. On numerous occasions since 1973 he has conducted field research in Indonesia, with grants from the East-West Center, Fulbright-Hays, Social Science Research Council, National Endowment for the Humanities, Wenner-Gren Foundation, and American Philosophical Society. He is the author of *Traditions of Gamelan Music in Java, Variation in Central Javanese Gamelan Music, Calling Back the Spirit: Music, Dance, and Cultural Politics in Lowland South Sulawesi,* and numerous articles on Javanese music. His current research concerns music and the media in Indonesia and South Korea. Active as a *gamelan* musician since 1971, he has performed with several professional groups in Indonesia and directed numerous performances in the United States. He has served as the first vice president and a book review editor for the Society for Ethnomusicology, and as a member of the Working Committee on Performing Arts for the Festival of Indonesia (1990–1992). He has taught at the University of Hawaii and the University of Wisconsin–Madison, where he is Professor of Music and a past director of the Center for Southeast Asian Studies.

Jeff Todd Titon received the Ph.D. in American Studies from the University of Minnesota, where he studied ethnomusicology with Alan Kagan and musicology with Johannes Riedel. He has done fieldwork in North America on religious folk music, blues music, and old-time fiddling, with support from the National Endowment for the Arts and the National Endowment for the Humanities. For two years he was rhythm guitarist in the Lazy Bill Lucas Blues Band, a group that appeared in the 1970 Ann Arbor Blues Festival. The author or editor of seven books, including *Early Downhome Blues,* which won the ASCAP–Deems Taylor Award, and the five-volume *American Musical Traditions,* named by *Library Journal* as one of the outstanding reference works of 2003, he is also a documentary photographer and filmmaker. In 1991 he wrote a hypertext multimedia computer program about the old-time fiddler Clyde Davenport that is regarded as a model for interactive representations of people making music. He developed the ethnomusicology program at Tufts University, where he taught from 1971 to 1986. From 1990 to 1995 he served as the editor of *Ethnomusicology,* the journal of the Society for Ethnomusicology. A Fellow of the American Folklore Society, since 1986 he has been Professor of Music and the director of the Ph.D. program in ethnomusicology at Brown University.

CHAPTER 1

The Music-Culture as a World of Music

Jeff Todd Titon

The world around us is full of sounds. Some are sounds you make. Some are sounds from sources outside yourself. All are meaningful. In the city you might be startled by the sound of a police siren or a car alarm. The noise of the garbage trucks for an early morning pickup or the drone of a motor in a parked truck might irritate you, but you usually block out the usual traffic noise. In the country you can more easily hear the sounds of nature. In the spring and summer you might hear birds singing and calling to each other, the snorting of deer in the woods, or the warning bark of a distant dog. By a river or the ocean you might hear the sounds of surf or of boats loading and unloading, or the deep bass of foghorns. Stop for a moment and concentrate on all the sounds around you. Become aware of the soundscape.

The Soundscape

Just as landscape refers to land, *soundscape* refers to sound: the characteristic sounds of a particular place, both human and nonhuman. The examples so far present today's soundscapes, but what about soundscapes of the past? What kinds of sounds did the dinosaurs make? With our wristwatches we can always find out what time it is, but in medieval Europe people told time by listening to the bells of the local clock tower. Today we take the sounds of a passing railroad train for granted, but people found its sounds quite arresting when first heard.

Listen now to **CD 1, Track 1**. The soundscape is a post office, but it is unlike any post office you will likely encounter in Europe or North America. You are hearing men canceling stamps at the University of Accra, in Ghana, Africa. Two of the men whistle a tune while three make percussive sounds. Each stamp gets canceled several times for the sake of the rhythm. You will learn more about this example shortly. For now, think of it as yet another example of a soundscape: the acoustic environment where sounds, including music, occur.

CD 1:1

Postal workers canceling stamps at the University of Accra, Ghana, post office (2:58). The whistled tune is the hymn "Bompata," by the Ghanaian composer W. J. Akyeampong (b. 1900). Field recording by James Koetting. Legon, Ghana, 1975.

The Music-Culture

Every human society has music. Although music is universal, its meaning is not. For example, a famous musician from Asia attended a European symphony concert approximately 150 years ago. He had never heard Western music before. The story goes that after the concert his hosts asked him how he had liked it. "Very well," he replied. Not satisfied with this answer, his hosts asked (through an interpreter) what part he had liked best. "The first part," he said. "Oh, you enjoyed the first movement?" "No, before that." To the stranger, the best part of the performance was the tuning-up period. His hosts had a different opinion. Who was right? Different cultures give music different meanings. Recall from the Preface that *culture* means the way of life of a people, learned and transmitted from one generation to the next. The word *learned* is stressed to differentiate a people's cultural inheritance from what is passed along biologically in their genes. From birth, people all over the world absorb the cultural inheritance of family, community, schoolmates, and other larger social institutions such as the mass media—magazines, movies, television, and computers. This cultural inheritance tells people how to understand the situations they are in (what the situations mean) and how they might behave in those situations. It works so automatically that they are aware of it only when it breaks down, as it does on occasion when people misunderstand a particular situation. What one person understands as a twitch of the eye might have been intended as a wink. Like the people who carry them, cultures do not function perfectly all the time.

Musical situations and the very concept of music mean different things and involve different activities around the globe. Because music and all the beliefs and activities associated with it are a part of culture, we use the term *music-culture* to mean a group's total involvement with music: ideas, actions, institutions, material objects—everything that has to do with music. In our earlier example, the European music-culture dictates that the sound made by symphony musicians tuning up is not music. But to the stranger from Asia, it was music. Within their own cultural contexts, both the stranger and his hosts were correct.

Today, because of the widespread distribution of music on radio, television, film, video, sound recordings, and computers, people in just about every music-culture are likely to have heard some of the same music. The media turn us all into musical tourists. Although the local is emphasized throughout this book, music-cultures should not be understood as isolated and untouched. Thinking about the interaction between the local and the global can help us appreciate and understand all music-cultures, including our own.

Music or Nonmusic?

Sound is anything that can be heard, but what is music? As students of people making music all over the world, ethnomusicologists have a special interest in this question. Not all music-cultures have the same idea of music. In other words, music represents different ideas to different peoples: They "make" it in different ways. If we want to understand the various musics of the world, then, we need first to understand them on their own terms—that is, as the various music-cultures themselves do. But we also need a way to think about all music, and to do so without imposing our ideas of music inappropriately. That is a tall order. Most of the readers of this book (and its authors) have grown up within the cultures of Europe and North America. Our approaches and viewpoints reflect this background. However, we must "get out of our cultural skins" as much as possible in order to view music from more than one point of view. We will even learn to view our own music-culture from new perspectives.

We can begin with a scientific approach and ask if all music-cultures have something in common, whether the people in those cultures are aware of it or not. If we determine what that something is, then we can use it to guide our study of all music.

To begin scientifically to answer the question "What is music?" we might ask whether certain sounds are music or not. The answer does not involve simple disagreements over whether something people call "music" is truly music. For example, some people say that hip-hop is not music, but what they mean is that they think hip-hop is not good or meaningful music. Rather, there are difficult cases that test the boundaries of the differences between sound and music, such as the songs of birds, dolphins, or whales—are these music?

Consider bird songs. People hear birds sing, but not everyone pays much attention to them. Try it for a moment. Step outside and listen for birds. If you cannot hear any, make a mental note to pay attention the next time you do hear them. Now listen to the song of a hermit thrush at dusk in a spruce forest **(CD 1, Track 2)**.

 CD 1:2

CD 1.2 Songs of hermit thrushes (0:25). Field recording by Jeff Todd Titon. Little Deer Isle, Maine, 1999.

Many think that the hermit thrush has the most beautiful song of all the birds native to North America. Most bird songs consist of a single short melody, repeated, but the hermit thrush's melody is more complicated. You hear some tones and then a pause, then another group of tones and pause, and so on. Each group has a similar rhythm and is composed of five to eight tones. We will call each group of tones a musical "phrase." A *musical phrase* is like a phrase in writing or speech, but it is made up of tones instead of words. The musical phrase of the thrush is a little higher or lower each time.

Is bird song music? The thrush's song has some of the characteristics of music. It has rhythm, melody, repetition, and variation. (These musical terms will be explained shortly.) It also has a function: Scientists believe that birds sing to tell other birds of the same kind that they are in a partic- ular space or territory, and that they sing to attract a mate. In some species one bird's song can tell another bird which bird is singing and how that bird is feeling. Further, bird song has inspired Western classical music com- posers. Some composers have taken down bird songs in musical notation, and some have incorporated, imitated, or transformed bird song phrases in their compositions. Bird song is also found in Chinese classical music. In Chinese compositions such as "The Court of the Phoenix," for *sona* (oboe) and ensemble, extended passages are a virtual catalog of bird calls and songs imitated by instruments.

Yet, people in the Euro-American music-culture hesitate to call bird songs music. Because each bird in a species sings the same song over and over, bird songs appear to lack the creativity of human musical expression. Bird songs do not seem to belong to the human world, whereas music is regarded in Euro-American culture as a creative human expression. By contrast, people in some other music-cultures think bird songs do belong to the human world. For the Kaluli people of Papua New Guinea, bird songs are the voices of their human ancestors who have died and changed into birds. These songs cause humans grief, which expresses itself in weeping (Feld 1990). The Kaluli give a different meaning to bird songs than Euro-Americans do. Does this mean it is impossible to find intercultural agreement over what music is? Not really. Euro-Americans may disagree with the Kaluli over whether bird songs have human meaning, but they both agree that *music* has human meaning. Our thought experiment with bird song and its meanings in different music-cultures suggests that music has something to do with the human world. We might go further and say that music is sound that is humanly patterned or organized (Blacking 1973; Figure 1.1).

Let us take another example of a sound that tests the boundary between music and nonmusic. Listen again to **CD 1, Track 1**. Throughout the life of *Worlds of Music,* listeners have found the Ghanaian postal workers' sounds especially intriguing. Recently I learned a little more about the circumstances of the recording. Henrietta Mckee Carter (personal communication to Jeff Todd Titon, July 2000) wrote as follows:

> Sometime in 1975, Bill Carter and I were sitting in Jim and Ernestina Koetting's quarters at the University of Ghana chatting with Ernestina, while awaiting dinner. Jim came in excitedly, picked up his recording equipment and disappeared, saying on his way out that he had just heard something he wanted to record. He came back a while later and described the scene.

These postal workers hand-canceling stamps at the post office of the University of Ghana are making drumming sounds, and two are whistling; but there are no drums, and the workers are just passing the time. How, exactly?

Koetting describes it this way:

> Twice a day the letters that must be canceled are laid out in two files, one on either side of a divided table. Two men sit across from one another at the table, and each has a hand-canceling machine (like the price markers you may have seen in supermarkets), an ink pad, and a stack of letters. The work part of the process is simple: a letter is slipped from the stack with the left hand, and the right hand inks the marker and stamps the letter.
> This is what you are hearing: The two men seated at the table slap a letter rhythmically several times to bring it from the file to the position on the table where it is to be canceled. (This act makes a light-sounding thud.) The marker is inked one or more times (the lowest, most resonant sound you hear) and then stamped on the letter (the high-pitched mechanized sound you hear). . . . The rhythm produced is not a simple one-two-three (bring forward the letter—ink the marker—stamp the letter). Rather, musical sensitivities take over. Several slaps on the letter to bring it down,

Jeff Todd Titon

Figure 1.1
Song leader Russell Jacobs leading the singing at the Left Beaver Old Regular Baptist Church in eastern Kentucky, 1979.

repeated thuds of the marker in the ink pad and multiple cancellations of single letters are done for rhythmic interest. Such repetition slows down the work but also makes it much more interesting.

The other sounds you hear have nothing to do with the work itself. A third man has a pair of scissors that he clicks—not cutting anything, but adding to the rhythm. The scissors go "click, click, click, rest," a basic rhythm used in [Ghanaian] popular dance music. The fourth worker simply whistles along. He and any of the other three workers who care to join him whistle popular tunes or church music that fits the rhythm. (Titon 1992:98–99)

Work song, found in music-cultures all over the world, is a kind of music whose function ranges from coordinating complex tasks to making boring and repetitive work more interesting. In this instance the workers have turned life into art. Writing further about the postal workers' recording, Koetting says,

It sounds like music and, of course, it is; but the men performing it do not quite think of it that way. These men are working, not putting on a musical show; people pass by the workplace paying little attention to the "music." (Titon 1992:98)

Even though the postal workers do not think of this activity as a musical performance, it is presented as music here because it is humanly patterned sound and the whistled melody is a hymn tune written by a Ghanaian composer. Even so, in Euro-American culture not all humanly patterned sound is music. For example, although speech sometimes has musical attributes, we do not claim that speech is music. Whether canceling stamps at the University of Ghana post office is "really" music is a philosophical question. What do you think? You will learn more about this musical example in Chapter 3.

People in various music-cultures pattern sounds differently. What patterns do musical sounds follow? Several aspects of musical sound that our music-culture recognizes and talks about in ordinary language should be familiar to most readers of this book: rhythm, meter, melody, and harmony. These are ways of describing patterns or structure (form) in sound. It will be interesting to see what happens to these Western (but not exclusively Western) ideas when for better or worse they are applied to every music-culture throughout this book. Here we briefly review these ideas. Then we turn our attention to how music becomes meaningful in performance, and we consider a performance model for musical activity. Finally we examine the four components of a music culture, which in music textbooks are not usually considered rudiments but are no less a part of humanly organized sound: ideas, activities, repertories, and the material culture of music.

Patterns in Music

Rhythm and Meter

In ordinary language we say "rhythm" when we refer to the patterned recurrence of events, as in "the rhythm of the seasons," or "the rhythm of the raindrops." As Hewitt Pantaleoni writes, "Rhythm concerns time felt as a succession of events rather than as a single span" (1985:211). In music, we hear rhythm when we hear a time-relation between sounds. In a classroom you might hear a pen drop from a desk and a little later a student coughing. You do not hear any rhythm, because you hear no relation between the sounds. But when you hear a person walking in the hall outside, or when you hear a heartbeat, you hear rhythm.

If we measure the time-relations between the sounds and find a pattern of regular recurrence, we have *metrical rhythm.* Think of the soldiers' marching rhythm: HUP-two-three-four, HUP-two-three-four. This is a metered, regularly recurring sound pattern. Recurring accents fall on HUP. Most popular, classical, and folk music heard in North America today has metered rhythm. Of course, most of those rhythms are more complex than the march rhythm. Most of the musical examples in this book, including the postal workers' canceling stamps **(CD 1, Track 1)**, are examples of metrical rhythm. In a metrical rhythm you feel the beat and move to it.

"Tsuru no sugomori," a Japanese *shakuhachi* piece **(CD 1, Track 23)**, lacks a steady, dancelike beat. Its free rhythm is flexible and related to the performer's breath. That it is unmetered does not mean that it is undisciplined, however. On the contrary, the uneven pulsation makes it harder for the

Figure 1.2
T. Viswanathan, flute, Ramnad V. Raghavan, *mridangam.*

student learning *shakuhachi* to convey the required precision in the sounds and silences that enhance one another (see pp. 163–168).

On the other hand, the rhythm of "Sarasiruha" **(CD 2, Track 2)** is intricate in another way. The opening *alapana* section has a flexible, nonmetered rhythm, but the following sections are metrically organized. This classical music of South India divides a metrical rhythm into long, complex, improvised accent patterns based on various combinations of rhythmic figures. The *mridangam* drummer's art (see Figure 1.2) is based on fifteen or more distinct types of finger and hand strokes on different parts of the drumheads. Each stroke has its own *sollukattu*, or spoken syllable that imitates the sound of the drum stroke. Spoken one after another, they duplicate the rhythmic patterns and are used in learning and practice.

Although most North Americans may not be aware of it, the music they listen to usually has more than one rhythm. The singer's melody falls into one pattern, the guitarist's into another; the drummer usually plays more than one pattern at once. Even though these rhythms are usually tied to the same overall accent pattern, the way they interact with each other sets our bodies in motion as we move to the beat. Rhythm in the postal workers' canceling stamps **(CD 1, Track 1)** emphasizes the tugs of different rhythmic patterns. (For a detailed analysis, see Chapter 3.) This simultaneous occurrence of several rhythms with a shifting beat is called *polyrhythm.* Polyrhythm is characteristic of the music of Africa and wherever Africans have carried their music on the globe. In Chapter 3 you will learn to feel yet a further layer of complexity, *polymeter,* or the simultaneous presence of two different metrical systems, as you "construct musical reality in two ways at once" while playing an Ewe (pronounced eh-way) bell pattern in *Agbekor* (see pp. 89–91).

Melody

In ordinary language we say "melody" when we want to refer to the tune—the part of a piece of music that goes up and down, the part that most people hear and sing along with. It is hard to argue that melody and rhythm are truly different qualities of music, but it helps our understanding if we consider them separately. When we say that someone has a high-pitched (shrill) or a low-pitched (deep) voice, we are calling attention to a musical quality called *pitch,* which refers to how high or low a sound is. When a sound is made, it sets the air in motion, vibrating at so many cycles per second. This vibrating air strikes the ear drum, and we hear how high- or low-pitched it is according to the speed of the vibrations. You can experience this yourself if you sing a tone that is comfortable for your voice and then slide the tone down gradually as low as you can go. As your voice goes down to a growl, you can feel the vibrations slow down in your throat. Pitch, then, depends on the frequency of these sound vibrations. The faster the vibrations, the higher the pitch.

Another important aspect of melody is *timbre,* or tone quality. Timbre is caused by the characteristic ways different voices and musical instruments vibrate. Timbre tells us why a violin sounds different from a trumpet when they are playing a tone of the same pitch. We take the timbre of our musical instrument palette for granted, but when we encounter an instrument with a timbre that we may never have heard before, such as the Australian *didgeridoo,* we sit up and take notice. Some music-cultures, like the European, favor timbres that we may describe as smooth or liquid; others, like the African, favor timbres that are buzzy; others, like the Asian, favor timbres that we might describe as focused in sound. Other important aspects of melody, besides pitch and timbre, include *volume*—that is, how melodies increase and decrease in loudness. The Navajo Yeibichai song **(CD 1, Track 6)** begins at the loudest possible volume.

Another critical aspect of melody to pay attention to in world music is *emphasis:* the way the major tones of the melody are approached (by sliding up or down to them in pitch, as some singers do; by playing them dead on, as a piano does; by "bending" the pitch, as a blues guitarist does when pushing the string to the side and back (Figure 1.3) **(CD 1, Tracks 21 and 22)**. Figure 6.7 contrasts notes and melodies on the piano with their counterparts in Indian music.

Yet another way to emphasize a point in a melody is to add *decorative tones* or what are called ornaments in classical music. These, too, occur in many of the musics of the world. See if you can find them as you listen to the CD set. Concentrate on the way the singers and musicians do not simply produce tones but play with them.

Finding out how different music-cultures organize sounds into melodies is one of the most fascinating pursuits for the student of music. If we sing the melody of the Christmas carol "Joy to the World," we hear how Westerners like to organize a melody. Try it:

Joy to the world, the Lord has come!
(do ti la   so,   fa mi re do!)

Jeff Todd Titon

Figure 1.3
Blues guitarists Johnny Winter (left) and
Luther Allison. Ann Arbor (Michigan)
Blues Festival, August 1970.

This is the familiar do-re-mi (solfège) scale, in descending order. Try singing "Joy to the World" backwards, going up the do-re-mi scale and using the syllables in this order: "come has Lord the world the to joy." You might find it difficult! But if you first sing the do-re-mi scale, and then replace do-re-me with "come has Lord," and so forth, you will be able to do it more easily.

The white keys of the piano show how most melodies in European and Euro-American music have been organized since the eighteenth century. Do-re-mi (and so forth) represent a *major scale.* Notice that these pitches are not equally spaced. Try singing "Joy to the World" starting on "re" instead of "do." You will see that it changes the tune. If you are near a keyboard, try playing it by going down the white keys, one at a time. Only one starting key (C) gives the correct melody. This indicates that the intervals between pitches represented by the white keys are not the same.

The Euro-American culture prefers the major scale, and Euro-Americans set up many instruments, such as the piano, or the flute, so that they can easily play the pitch intervals of this scale. But other music-cultures set up their instruments and their scales differently. For example, one way Javanese musical gongs are tuned organizes the octave (the musical interval between one "do" and another) into five nearly equidistant spaces (intervals) in their *sléndro* (*slayn*-dro) scale. The Javanese have a second scale, *pélog* (*pay*-log), which divides the octave into seven tones, but the intervals are not the same as those in any Western scales. As we shall see in Chapter 7, the sounds of their *gamelan* (*gah*-muh-lahn), or orchestra, reflect these different tunings (for example, **CD 2, Track 3**, is in the *pélog* scale). Japanese music also employs two scales, the *in* and *yo,* which differ from the Javanese scales and from Euro-American scales. In the classical music of South India, known as Carnatic music, each melody conforms to a set of organizing principles called a *raga* (*rah*-gah). A *raga* is an organized melodic environment inside of which the South Indian singer or musician improvises melodically in performance (see Chapter 6, pp. 212–214).

Harmony

Most readers of this book use the word *harmony* to describe something that can happen to a melody: It can be harmonized. You sing a melody and some-one else sings a harmony, a part pleasantly different from the melody, at the same time (see Figure 1.4). You hear the intervals between the tones not only in a sequence, as in a melody, but also simultaneously. These simultane-ously sounding tones are called *chords.* Western music theory is not always useful in describing music outside the Euro-American traditions, but in this case *texture,* a word borrowed from fabrics to describe the interweaving of fibers, helps describe how melody and harmony interact in various musics throughout the world. Just as threads weave together to make cloth, so melodies can intertwine to make a multimelodic musical whole. Texture refers to the nature of these melodic interrelationships.

When the musical texture consists of a single melody only—for example, when you sing by yourself, or when several people sing the same melody at the same time (in unison)—we call the texture *monophonic* ("mono" meaning "single," "phono" meaning "voice"). If you add one or more voices doing different things, the melodic texture changes, and we describe the way the voices relate. The classical music of India commonly includes a drone, an unchanging tone or group of tones sounding continuously, against which the melody moves (see Chapter 6). European bagpipes also include drones. When two or more voices elaborate the same melody in different ways at roughly the same time, the texture is *heterophonic.* Although infrequent in Western music, it is typical of melodic organization in Japanese traditional music. **CD 1, Track 24**, shows heterophony among the voice and *shamisen* parts.

When two or more distinct melodies are combined, the texture is *poly-phonic.* Polyphony can be heard in New Orleans–style jazz from the first few decades of the twentieth century: Louis Armstrong's earliest recordings offer good examples in which several melodic lines interweave. Javanese *gamelan* and other ensemble music of Southeast Asia (Chapter 7) consists of many layers of melodic activity that some scholars have described as poly-phony. Polyphony is characteristic of European classical music in the Ren-aissance period (roughly 1450 to 1600) and the late Baroque (Bach was a master of polyphony).

When two or more voices are combined in a such way that one domi-nates and any others seem to be accompanying the dominant voice—what most people mean when they say they hear a harmony (accompaniment)—the texture is *homophonic.* Homophony is typical of folk and popular music

Figure 1.4
Teenagers harmonizing gospel music.
Bristow, Oklahoma, 1938.

throughout the world. A homophonic texture characterizes country music in the United States, such as the Fenders' Navajo rendition of "Folsom Prison Blues" **(CD 1, Track 7)** and Efraín's performance of the Quichua *sanjuán* "Muyu muyari warmigu" on the harp, which is an example of an instrument that can play a melody and an accompaniment simultaneously **(CD 2, Track 9)**. Piano playing in jazz, rock, and other popular music is homophonic. The pianist usually gives the melody to the right hand and an accompaniment to the left. Sometimes the pianist plays only accompaniment, as when "comping" behind a jazz soloist. Blues guitarists such as Blind Blake and Mississippi John Hurt developed a homophonic style in the 1920s in which the fingers of the right hand played melody on the treble strings while the right-hand thumb simultaneously played an accompaniment on the bass strings. Hawaiian slack-key guitarists developed a similar homophonic technique but their music does not sound like blues at all.

Form

The word *form* has many meanings. From your writing assignments you know what an outline is. You might say that you are putting your ideas in "outline form." By form, here, you call attention to the way the structure of your thoughts is arranged. Similarly, in music, painting, architecture, and the other arts, *form* means structural arrangement. To understand form in music, we look for patterns of organization in rhythm, melody, and harmony. Patterns of musical organization involve, among other things, the arrangement of small to medium-sized musical units of rhythm, melody, and/or harmony that show repetition or variation. Just as a sentence (a complete thought) is made up of smaller units such as phrases, which in turn are made of individual words, so a musical thought is made up of musical phrases that result from combinations of sounds. Form can also refer to the arrangement of the instruments, as in the order of solos in a jazz or bluegrass performance, or the way a symphonic piece is orchestrated. Form refers to the structure of a musical performance: the principles by which it is put together and how it works.

Consider the pattern of blues lyrics. The form often consists of three-line stanzas: A line is sung ("Woke up this morning, blues all around my bed"), the line is repeated, and then the stanza closes with a different line ("Went to eat my breakfast and the blues were in my bread"). Blues melodies also have a particular form, as do the chord changes (harmony) in blues (see Chapter 4). The forms of traditional Native American melodies (Chapter 2) involve the creative use of small units and variation. These forms are not apparent to someone listening to the music for the first time or even the second, which is one of the reasons we pay careful attention to it (see p. 40).

Structural arrangement is an important aspect of the way music is organized. It operates on many levels, and it is key to understanding not only how music-cultures organize music but also how various cultures and subcultures think about time and space in general. For these reasons musical form is an important consideration in all the chapters that follow.

Our understanding of rhythm, meter, melody, and harmony is greatly enriched when we consider how these organizing principles of human sound are practiced in music-cultures throughout the world. Much of the interest in the following chapters lies in seeing how these principles work in different circumstances. But there is more to music than the structure of sounds. When people make music, they do not merely produce sounds—they also involve themselves with other people in various social activities and express their ideas about music. To ethnomusicologists, these activities and ideas are just as important as the music's structure. In fact, the activities and ideas are also part of the human organization of the sound. In other words, ethnomusicologists research and write about all the aspects of music, not just its sound. Whether musicians are true to an ideal or whether they have "sold out" to commercial opportunity is a question whose answer cannot be learned simply by studying musical sound. This book presents music in relation to individual experience, to history, to the economy and the music industry, and to each music-culture's view of the world, which includes ideas about how human beings ought to behave.

A Music-Culture Performance Model

Even when we are curious about the music of the world's peoples and want to understand more about it, confronting a new music can be daunting. When watching a live performance, for example, our first impulse might be simply to listen to it, to absorb it, to see whether we like it or whether it moves us. Our next impulse might be to let our bodies respond by moving to the music. But soon we ask questions about it: What is that instrument that sounds so lovely? How does one play it? Why are the people dancing? (Or are they dancing?) Why is someone crying? Why are the musicians in costume? What do the words mean? What kind of a life does the head musician lead? To formulate and begin to answer these questions in a comprehensive way, we need to have some kind of systematic outline,

Figure 1.5
Elements of a musical performance.

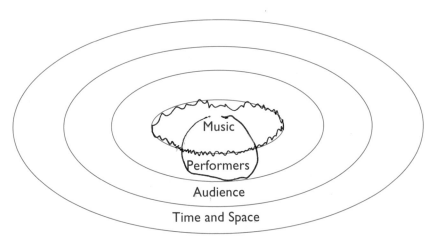

or model, of any music-culture or subculture that tells us how it might work and what its components might be.

The authors of this book propose a music-culture model that is grounded in music as it is performed (Titon 1988:7–10). To see how this model works, think back to a musical event that has moved you. At the center of the event is your experience of the music, sung and played by performers (perhaps you are one of them). The performers are surrounded by their audience (in some instances, performers and audience are one and the same), and the whole event takes place in its setting in time and space. We can represent this by a diagram of concentric circles (Figure 1.5).

Next, we transpose this diagram into four circles representing a music-culture model (Figure 1.6).

At the center of the music (as you experience it) is its radiating power, its emotional impact—whatever makes you assent, smile, nod your head, sway your shoulders, dance. That is called music's *affect*, its power to move, and which forms the center of the model.

Performance brings music's power to move into being, and so we move from performers in Figure 1.5 to performance in Figure 1.6. *Performance*

Figure 1.6
A music-culture model
(after Titon 1988:11).

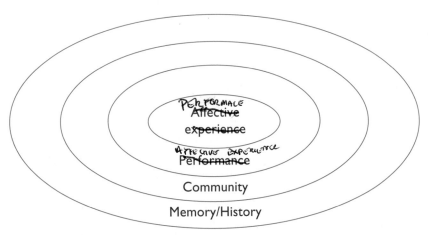

involves many things. First, people mark performances, musical or otherwise, as separate from the flow of ordinary life: "Have you heard the story about . . ." or "Now we're going to do a new song that one of the members of the band wrote while thinking about . . ." When performance takes place, people know the difference. Sammy Davis, Jr., told an interviewer, "Once I get outside my house in the morning, I'm on." We often mark endings of performances with applause. Second, performance has purpose. The performers intend to move (or not move) the audience, to sing and play well (or not well), to make money, to have fun, to learn, to advance a certain rite or ceremony. The performance is evaluated partly on how well those intentions have been fulfilled. Third, a performance is interpreted as it goes along—by the audience, who may cry out, applaud, or hiss, and by the performers, who may smile when things are going well or wince when they make a mistake.

The most important thing to understand about performance is that it moves along on the basis of agreed-on rules and procedures. These rules enable the musicians to play together and make sense to each other and to the audience. The performers usually do not discuss most of the rules; they have absorbed them and agreed to them. Starting at the same time, playing in the same key, playing in the same rhythmic framework, repeating the melody at the proper point—these are a few of the many rules that govern most of the musical performances that Westerners experience. Even improvisation is governed by rules. In a rock concert, for example, guitarists improvise melodic "breaks," but they usually do not use all twelve tones of the chromatic scale; instead they almost always choose from the smaller number of tones represented by the blues scale (see Chapter 4). Rules or accepted procedures govern the audience, too. In some situations shouting is not only permitted but expected. What to wear, what to say—these, too, are determined by spoken or unspoken rules at any musical performance. Sometimes musicians try to break these rules or expectations, as in a ritual destruction of their instruments at the close of the concert, which in turn can become an expectation.

The music-culture model presented here defines music in performance as meaningfully organized sound that proceeds by rules. Finding out those rules or principles becomes the task of analysis. These rules include (but are not limited to) what is usually covered under musical analysis: melody, rhythm, meter, and so forth. Beyond that, the task in exploring music-cultures is to discover the rules covering ideas about music and behavior in relation to music, as well as the links between these rules or principles and the sound that a group of people calls "music."

You may resist the notion that music, which you think should be free to express emotion, is best thought of as governed by rules. The point is not that musical performance is determined in advance by rules, but rather that it proceeds according to them. In this view, music is like a game or a conversation: Without rules we could not have a game, and without agreement about what words are, what they mean, and how they are used, we could not hold a meaningful conversation. Just as meaningful conversations can express emotion, so meaningful music can do so, though not, of course, in exactly the same way. Further, if a listener does not understand the rules, he or she cannot understand the composer's or musician's intention or the music's structure.

The circle corresponding to audience in Figure 1.5 becomes community in the music-culture model (Figure 1.6). The community is the group (including the performers) that carries on the traditions and norms of performance. Performance is situated in community and is part of a people's culture. The community pays for and supports the music, whether directly with money or indirectly by allowing the performers to live as musicians. Community support usually influences the future direction of a particular kind of music. In a complex society such as the United States, various communities support different kinds of music—classical, rock, hip-hop, country, jazz, gospel— and they do so in different ways. When music becomes a mass-media commodity, then packaging, marketing, and advertising are as crucial to the success of musicians as they are to the popularity of a given perfume.

How the community relates to the music makers also has a profound effect on the music. Among the folk music-cultures of nonindustrial village societies, the performers are drawn from the community; everyone knows them well, and communication takes place face-to-face. At the other end of the spectrum is the postindustrial music-culture celebrity who guards his or her private life, performs from a raised platform, offers a disembodied voice through a machine, and remains mysterious to the audience despite everything that appears in magazines or on the Internet.

How the community relates to itself is another important aspect of performance. For example, do men, women, old people, and young people experience music differently? We consider this issue later in this chapter.

Time and space, the fourth circle in Figure 1.5, becomes memory and history in our music-culture model (Figure 1.6). The community is situated in history and borne by memory, official and unofficial, whether remembered or recorded or written down. Musical experiences, performances, and communities change over time and space; they have a history, and that history reflects changes in the rules governing music as well as the effect of music on human relationships. For example, the development of radio, recordings, and television meant that music did not need to be heard in the performer's presence. This took the performer out of the community's face-to-face relationships, allowing people to listen to music without being in the presence of the performer or making it themselves. Today music is an almost constant background to many people's lives, but the musicians are largely absent.

Music historians also alter the effect of music by affecting the stock of ideas about music. When white America became interested in blues music in the 1960s and began presenting blues concerts and festivals (see Chapter 4), magazine and newspaper writers began asking blues singers questions about their music and its history. Knowing they would be asked these questions, the blues singers prepared their answers, sometimes reading and then repeating what writers had already said about blues, sometimes having fun with their questioners and deliberately misleading them, and sometimes answering truthfully based on their experiences. This history is repeating itself today with hip-hop.

Many times the subject of music is history itself. The Homeric poets sang about Odysseus; Serbian *guslars* sang about the deeds of their heroes; European ballads tell stories of nobles and commoners; African *griots* (see Chapter 3) sing tribal genealogies and history. Today, digital recorders, computers, and multimedia programs are revolutionizing community music history in the West, for they empower musicians and audience alike to record what they want to hear, represent it as they wish, and listen to it again and again; in this way they gain a kind of control over their history never before experienced. In studying the history of a music-culture, or some aspect of it, you need to know not only what that history is but also who tells or writes that history and what stake the historian has in it.

As you read through each of the case studies in the following chapters, bear this underlying music-culture performance model in mind. Because each of the case studies focuses on music and performance, you can use this model to understand how each chapter moves among experience, performance, community, memory, and history. *Musical analysis*—that is, finding patterns in the sound by breaking the music into parts and determining how the parts function in the whole—is an important part of this procedure. Unlike the analyst who investigates Western classical music by looking at the composer's written score, ethnomusicologists must usually deal with music that exists only in performance, without notation or instructions from a composer. The ethnomusicologist usually transcribes the music—that is, writes it down in musical notation—and then analyzes its structure. But it is impossible to understand musical structure fully without knowing the cultural "why" as well as the musical "what." A music-culture ultimately rests in the people themselves—their ideas, their actions, and the sound they produce (Merriam 1964:32–33). For that reason, we shall now turn to another way of talking about all these aspects of music—a component model of a music-culture. This model is divided into four parts: ideas about music, activities involving music, repertories of music, and the material culture of music (Table 1.1).

The Four Components of a Music-Culture

Ideas about Music
Music and the Belief System

What is music, and what is not? Is music human, divine, or both? Is music good and useful for humankind, or is it potentially harmful? Cultures vary enormously in their answers to these questions, and the answers often are subtle, even paradoxical; they are embodied in rituals that try to reconcile love and hate, life and death, the natural and the cultural. Even within one music-culture, the answers may change over time. For example, a medieval Christian would have trouble understanding one of today's jazz Masses.

Table 1.1   The Four Components of a Music-Culture

I.   Ideas about music
    A. Music and the belief system
    B. Aesthetics of music
    C. Contexts for music
    D. History of music
II. Activities involving music
III. Repertories of music
    A. Style
    B. Genres
    C. Texts
    D. Composition
    E. Transmission
    F. Movement
IV. Material culture of music

Throughout the book you will see many examples of how belief systems and music-cultures interact. For example, you will see in Chapter 2 that music is a major part of Navajo ceremonies to cure disease. Navajos understand the medical theories of the Euro-American world, and they use Western medicine. But they also believe that certain kinds of illness, such as depression, indicate that the person's relationship to the natural world is out of balance. Further, Navajos view nature as a powerful force capable of speaking directly to humans and teaching them the songs and prayers for the curing rituals that restore harmony. Music is so important to Native Americans that their stories of the creation of the universe are expressed traditionally in ceremonial chants (see Figure 1.7).

In Chapter 3 you will see that among the Ewe of Ghana, funerals feature singing, dancing, and drumming because the ancestral spirits, as well as their living descendants, love music and dance. The *ragas* of India, considered in Chapter 6, are thought to have musical personalities, to express particular moods. As you read through the chapters in this book, see how each music-culture relates music to its worldview.

Aesthetics of Music

When is a song beautiful? When is it beautifully sung? What voice quality is pleasing, and what grates on the ear? How should a musician dress? How long should a performance last? Not all cultures agree on these questions about what is appropriate and what is beautiful. Some people in the United States find Chinese opera singing strained and artificial, but some Chinese find the European bel canto opera style imprecise and unpleasant.

Javanese *gamelan* music (Chapter 7) is not featured in concert the way we hear classical music in the West; rather, it is usually performed to accompany dance or theater. *Gamelan* music also accompanies a family's celebration of a birth, wedding, or other event, but people are expected to mingle and talk while the music takes place in the background. The

Figure 1.7
Mr. and Mrs. Walker Calhoun, holding eagle feathers. Big Cove, near Cherokee, North Carolina, 1989. The Calhouns are leaders in preserving traditional songs and dances among the East Coast Cherokee.

Jeff Todd Titon

aesthetics of Japanese *shakuhachi* flute music (Chapter 5) revolve around the breath, which produces a variety of timbres on the same instrument. Among Zen Buddhists, the *shakuhachi* is regarded more as a spiritual tool, a means toward enlightenment, than as a musical instrument.

Contexts for Music

When should music be performed? How often? On what occasions? Again, every music-culture answers these questions about musical surroundings differently (see Figure 1.8).

In the modern world, where context can depend on the mere flip of an on-off switch and a portable MP3 player, it is hard to imagine the days when all music came from face-to-face performances. Our great-grandparents had to sing or play music or hear it from someone nearby; they could not produce it on demand from the disembodied voice of a radio, television, CD player, or computer. How attentively you would have listened to a singer or a band a hundred years ago if you had thought that the performance might be the only time in your life you would hear that music!

Even though much of the music around the globe today comes through mass media, people in music-cultures still associate particular musics with particular contexts. Navajo ceremonial music is appropriate in certain ceremonial contexts but not others. As we shall see in Chapter 2, these ceremonies have names such as Enemyway and Blessingway, and each has a specific music that must be performed properly for the ceremony to be effective. The usual context for blues is a bar, juke joint, dance hall, or blues club (Chapter 4). This is a far cry from the concert halls that provide the context

Figure 1.8
Gospel singers at a Pentecostal revival in the southeastern United States. Guitars, banjos, and camp-meeting songs that would be out place in some U.S. churches, such as the one in Figure 1.1, are appropriate in this context.

for symphony orchestra performances. For many centuries in India the courts and upper classes supported the classical music that we shall consider in Chapter 6. But concerts of classical music in India are more relaxed and informal than those in Europe, where the patronage of the courts and the aristocracy, as well as the Church, traditionally supported classical music.

Today in Europe and North America the government, the wealthy classes, and the universities supply this patronage. Classical music in various parts of the world, then, is usually associated with patronage from the elite classes, and it is performed in refined contexts that speak of its supporters' wealth and leisure.

Sometimes governments intervene to support other kinds of music. For example, during the twentieth century the Soviet Union and other Communist states encouraged a certain kind of folk music, or workers' music, thought to inspire solidarity. In the United States, the last few decades have also witnessed the rise of government-supported folk festivals (Figure 1.9). Here the diversity of ethnic musics is celebrated, and the government encourages the most traditional expressions within the music-cultures that are represented. Folk festivals provide an artificial context for traditional music, but the hope is that in a world where young people are powerfully attracted to new, mass-media, transnational popular music, folk festivals will encourage this local music in its home context.

History of Music

Why is music so different among the world's peoples? What happens to music over time and space? Does it stay the same or change, and why? What did the music of the past sound like? Should music be preserved?

Figure 1.9

Folk festivals in the United States feature traditional music from ethnic communities. Jae Sook Park plays the *gemougo*, a six-string Korean plucked lute, at the National Folk Festival, Bangor, Maine, 2003.

Jeff Todd Titon

What will the music of the future be? Some cultures institutionalize the past in museums and the future in world's fairs; they support specialists who earn their living by talking and writing about music. Other cultures pass down knowledge of music history mainly by word of mouth through the generations. Recordings, films, videotapes, CDs, DVDs, and now the Internet allow us to preserve musical performances much more exactly than our ancestors could—but only when we choose to do so. For example, one ethnomusicologist was making tapes as he learned to sing Native American music. His teacher advised him to erase the tapes and reuse them, but he decided to preserve his lessons.

Questions about music history may arise both inside and outside a particular music-culture. Most music-cultures have their own historians or music authorities, formally trained or not, whose curiosity about music leads them to think and talk about music in their own culture, ask questions, and remember or write down answers. In some music-cultures, authority goes along with being a good musician; in others, one need not be a good musician to be a respected historian. Historians usually are curious about music outside their own cultures as well, and they often develop theories to account for musical differences.

The four categories of ideas about music that we have just discussed— music and the belief system, aesthetics, contexts, and history—overlap. Though they are separated here for convenience, I do not want to suggest that music-cultures present a united front in their ideas about music or that a music-culture prescribes a single aesthetic. People within a music-culture often differ in their ideas about music. Ragtime, jazz, rock and roll, and hip-hop were revolutionary when they were introduced in the United States. They met (and still meet) opposition from some within the U.S. music-culture. This opposition is based on aesthetics (the music is thought to be loud, awful noise) and context (the music's associated lifestyles are thought to involve narcotics, violence, free love, radical politics, and so forth).

When organized divisions exist within a music-culture, we can talk about music-subcultures, worlds within worlds of music. In fact, most music-cultures in the modern world can be divided into several subcultures, some opposed to each other: classical versus hip-hop, for example, or (from an earlier era) sacred hymns versus dance music and drinking songs. Many Native American music-cultures in the northeastern United States, for example, have a subculture of traditionalists interested in older musics that are marked as Native American, while other subcultures are involved more with the music of the Catholic Church, and yet others with forms of contemporary popular music (rock, jazz, country) that they have adapted to their needs and desires. Sometimes the subcultures overlap: The performance of a hymn in a Minnesota church may involve region (the upper Midwest), ethnicity (German), and religion (Lutheranism)—all bases for musical subcultures. Which musical subcultures do you identify with most strongly? Which do you dislike? Are your preferences based on contexts, aesthetics, or a belief system?

Activities Involving Music

People in a music culture do not just have ideas about music, of course; they put those ideas into practice in a variety of activities—everything from making the sounds to putting music up on the Internet, from rehearsing in their rooms alone to playing in a band to managing a concert to making recordings and marketing them. More and more people are becoming active consumers of music, carefully selecting the music they want to experience from the great variety available.

Human activities involving music also include the way people divide, arrange, or rank themselves in relation to music. Musical ideas and performances are unevenly divided among the people in any music-culture. For example, some perform often, others hardly at all. Some musicians perform for a living, while others play for little or no payment. People sing different songs and experience music differently because of age and gender. Racial, ethnic, and work groups also sing their own songs, and each group may develop or be assigned its own musical role. All of these differences have to do with the social organization of the music-culture, and they are based on the music-culture's ideas about music. We may ask, "What is it like in a given music-culture to experience music as a teenage girl, a young male urban professional, or a rural grandmother of Swedish ethnic heritage who lives on a farm?"

Sometimes the division of musical behavior resembles the social divisions with the group and reinforces the usual activities of the culture. The Vienna Philharmonic was in the news in recent years because until 1997 it had no women in its orchestra. In many traditional ceremonies throughout the world, men and women congregate in separate areas; some ceremonies center exclusively on men and others on women. On the other hand, music sometimes goes against the broad cultural grain, often at carnival time or at important moments in the life cycle (initiations, weddings, funerals, and so forth). People on the cultural fringe become important when they play music for these occasions. In fact, many music-cultures assign a low social status to musicians but also acknowledge their power and sometimes even see magic in their work. The most important features of music's social organization are status and role: the prestige of the music makers and the different roles assigned to people in the music-culture.

Many of the musical situations in this book depend on these basic aspects of social organization. The most spiritual and meditative Japanese *shakuhachi* music was the result of *samurai* (warriors) who became Buddhist priests during the Tokugawa period (1600–1867; see Chapter 5). When blues arose early in the twentieth century, middle-class African Americans associated it with the black underclass and tried to keep their youngsters away from it. Blues musicians were assigned a low social status (Chapter 4). Neither the Argentine tango nor the Trinidadian steelband were considered respectable when they arose. Only after they gained popularity abroad and returned to their home countries did they gain acceptance to the point of becoming national symbols of music in their respective countries.

Increasingly, ethnomusicologists have turned to the ways in which race, ethnicity, class, gender, region, and identity are embedded in musical activities. When people in a music-culture migrate out of their region, they often use music as a marker of ethnic identity. Throughout North America, ethnic groups perform and sometimes revive music that they consider to be their own, whether Jewish klezmer music, Andean panpipe music, central-European polka, Portugese fado (Figure 1.10), or Peking Opera.

In the twentieth century, the music industry has played an especially important role in various music-cultures. Music is packaged, bought, and sold. How does a song commodity become popular? When is popularity the result of industry hype, and when does it come from a groundswell of consumer interest? How do new kinds of music break into the media? Why do certain kinds of music gain (or lose) popularity? What makes a hit song? Fortunes are gained and lost based on music producers' abilities to predict what will sell—yet most of the music released commercially does not sell. How should a group of musicians deal with the industry? How can they support themselves while remaining true to their musical vision? What constitutes "selling out"? The roles of musicians, consumers, and producers in the popular music industry throughout the world have drawn closer in the last few decades as markets have expanded and musicians from all over the globe now take part. Music has become an enormously important aspect of the global economy. The current struggles over the future of music delivery on the Internet alone involve profits and losses in the billions of dollars.

Figure 1.10
Ana Vinagre of New Bedford, Massachusetts, sings Portugese fado. National Folk Festival, Bangor, Maine, 2002.

Jeff Todd Titon

Repertories of Music

A *repertory* is a stock of music that is ready to be performed, and a music-culture's repertory is what most people think of as the "music itself." It consists of six basic parts: style, genres, texts, composition, transmission, and movement. Think of a music that you are familiar with and see if you can understand it using the following terms.

Style

Style includes everything related to the organization of musical sound itself: pitch elements (scale, melody, harmony, tuning systems), time elements (rhythm, meter), timbre elements (voice quality, instrumental tone color), and sound intensity (loudness/softness). All depend on a music-culture's aesthetics.

Together, style and aesthetics create a recognizable sound that a group understands as its own. For example, the fiddle was the most popular dance instrument in Europe and North America from about the eighteenth century until the turn of the twentieth. In many areas it is still popular; in others, such as Ireland, it is undergoing a revival. Old-time fiddlers in Missouri prefer their regional dance and contest tunes to the bluegrass tunes of the upper South. Old-time fiddlers in the upper South, on the other hand, prefer their own repertory of breakdown tunes. People new to these repertories do not hear significant differences between them. Are they alike? Not entirely, because each group can distinguish its own music. People learning fiddle tunes know they are getting somewhere when they can recognize the differences in national and regional styles and put those differences into words—or music.

Genres

Genres are the named, standard units of the repertory, such as "song" and its various subdivisions (for example, lullaby, Christmas carol, wedding song) or the many types of instrumental music and dances (jig, reel, waltz, schottische, polka, hambo, and so forth). Most music-cultures have a great many genres, but their terms do not always correspond to terms in other music-cultures. Among the Yoruba in the African nation of Nigeria, for example, powerful kings, chiefs, and nobles retained praise singers to sing praises to them (Olajubu 1978:685). The praise songs are called *oriki.* Although we can approximate an English name to describe them (praise songs), no equivalent genre exists today in Europe or America. In Japan, the labels identifying popular music include *gunka* (military songs), *fōku songu* (contemporary folk songs, distinguished from *minyō,* or the traditional folk songs of the countryside), *nyū myūshiku* (new music), and *pops* (see Chapter 5). In North America, blues is one genre, country music another. Subdivisions of country music include rockabilly and bluegrass. If you listen to country music stations on the radio, you will see that some identify themselves as "real country" (along with the latest hits, more of a mix of oldies and southern-oriented country music) and others as "hard country" (more of a mix of rock-oriented country music). Consider electronic dance music and some of its subdivisions; the Web site MP3.com lists the following: ambient, breakbeat, dance, down tempo, drum 'n' bass, electronica, experimental, game soundtracks, house, industrial electronic, techno, trance, and UK garage. Under hip-hop we have: alternative hip-hop, bass, beats, dirty South, east coast, freestyles, hip-hop, hip-hop cover songs, horrorcore, new school, old school, rap, shoutouts, spiritual rap, and west coast. Subgenres have proliferated as marketing has grown more sophisticated. What subgenres can you name in your favorite kind of music?

Texts

The words to a song are known as its *text.* Any song with words is an intersection of two quite different and profound human communication systems:

language and music. A song with words is a temporary weld of these two systems; for convenience we can look at each by itself.

Every text has its own history; sometimes a single text is associated with several melodies. On the other hand, a single melody can go with several different texts. In blues music, for example, texts and melodies lead independent lives, coupling as the singer desires (see Chapter 4). Certain recent Indonesian pop compositions fuse Indonesian patriotic texts, traditional Indonesian musical instruments, and electric guitars and synthesizers (see Chapter 7). Navajo ritual song and prayer texts often conclude by saying that beauty and harmony prevail (see Chapter 2).

Composition

How does music enter the repertory of a music-culture? Is music composed individually or by a group? Is it fixed, varied within certain limits, or improvised spontaneously in performance? Improvisation fascinates most ethnomusicologists: Chapters 3, 4, and 6 consider improvisation in African, African American, and South Indian music. Perhaps at some deep level we prize improvisation not just because of the skills involved but because we think it exemplifies human freedom.

The *composition* of music, whether planned or spontaneous, is bound up with social organization. Does the music-culture have a special class of composers, or can anyone compose music? Composition is related as well to ideas about music: Some music-cultures divide songs into those composed by people and those "given" to people from deities, animals, and other nonhuman composers.

Transmission

How is music learned and transmitted from one person to the next, from one generation to the next? Does the music-culture rely on formal instruction, as in South India (Chapter 6)? Or is music learned chiefly through imitation (Chapter 4)? Does music theory underlie the process of formal instruction? Does music change over time? How and why? Is there a system of musical notation? Cipher (number) notation in Indonesia did not appear until the twentieth century (Chapter 7). In the ancient musical tablature notation for the *ch'in,* the Chinese writing indicates more than what note is to be played, because the Chinese pictograms (picture writing) suggest something in nature. For example, the notation may suggest a duck landing on water, telling the player to imitate the duck's landing with the finger when touching the string. Such notation can also evoke the feeling intended by the composer.

Some music-cultures transmit music through apprenticeships lasting a lifetime (as in the disciple's relation to a *guru,* Chapter 6). The instructor becomes a parent, teaching values and ethics as well as music. In these situations music truly becomes a way of life and the apprentice is devoted to the music and the teacher. Other music-cultures have no formal instruction, and the aspiring musician learns by watching and listening, often over many years. In these circumstances growing up in a musical family is helpful. When a repertory is transmitted chiefly by example and imitation rather than notation, we say the music exists in oral tradition rather than written. Blues (Chapter 4) is an example of music in oral tradition; so is the *sanjuán* dance genre of highland Ecuadorian Quichua (Chapter 8). Music in oral tradition varies more over time and space than does music tied to a printed musical score. Sometimes the same music exists both in oral and written traditions. At gatherings called singing conventions, people belonging to Primitive Baptist denominations in the upper South sing hymn tunes from notation in tune books such as *The Sacred Harp.* Variants of these hymn tunes also exist in oral tradition among the Old Regular Baptists (see Figure 1.1), who do not use musical notation but who rely instead on learning the tunes from their elders and remembering them.

Movement

A whole range of physical activity accompanies music. Playing a musical instrument, alone or in a group, not only creates sound but also literally moves people—that is, they sway, dance, walk, work in response. Even if we cannot see them move very much, their brains and bodies are responding as they hear and process the music. How odd it would be for a rock band to perform without moving in response to their music, in ways that let the audience know they were feeling it. This oddity was demonstrated several years ago by the new-wave rock band Devo when its members acted like robots. In one way or another, movement and music connect in the repertory of every culture. Sometimes the movement is quite loose, suggesting freedom and abandon; at other times, as in Balinese dance, it is highly controlled, suggesting that in this culture controlling oneself is beautiful and admirable.

Material Culture of Music

Material culture refers to the material objects that people in a culture produce—objects that can be seen, held, felt, and used. This book is an example of material culture. So are dinner plates, gravestones, airplanes, hamburgers, pocket calculators, and school buildings. Examining a culture's tools and technology can tell us about the group's history and way of life. Similarly, research into the material culture of music can help us to understand music-cultures. The most important objects in a music-culture, of course, are musical instruments (see Figure 1.11). We cannot hear the actual sound of any musical performances before the 1870s, when the phonograph was invented, so we rely on instruments for information about music-cultures in the remote past. Here we have two kinds of evidence: instruments preserved more or less intact, such as Sumerian harps over 4,500 years old, and instruments pictured in art. Through the study of instruments, as well as paintings, written documents, and other sources, we can explore the movement of music from the Near East to China over a thousand years ago, we can trace the Guatemalan marimba to its African roots, or we can outline

Russell Lee. Courtesy of Library of Congress.

Figure 1.11
Young man playing a one-stringed diddly-bow. Missouri, 1938.

the spread of Near Eastern musical influences to Europe, which resulted in the development of most of the instruments in the symphony orchestra.

We can also ask questions of today's music-cultures: Who makes instruments and how are they distributed? What is the relation between instrument makers and musicians? How do this generation's musical instruments reflect its musical tastes and styles, compared with those of the previous generation? In the 1950s electric instruments transformed the sound of popular music in the United States, and in the 1960s this electronic musical revolution spread elsewhere in the world. Taken for granted today, electric instruments— guitars, basses, pianos, pedal-steel guitars—represented a musical revolution in the 1950s. The computer is the most revolutionary musical instrument today. Computer-assisted composition, incorporating sound sampling and other innovations, empowers a new generation of composers to do things they had otherwise been unable to accomplish, while computer-assisted distribution of music through the Internet may be the wave of the future.

Musical scores, instruction books, sheet music—these too are part of the material culture. Scholars once defined folk music-cultures as those in which people learn to sing music by ear rather than from print, but research shows mutual influence among oral and written sources during the past few centuries in Europe, Britain, and America. Because they tend to standardize songs, printed versions limit variety, but paradoxically they stimulate people to create original songs. Also, the ability to read music notation has a far-reaching effect on musicians and, when it becomes widespread, on a music-culture as a whole.

One more important part of a music's material culture should be singled out: the impact of electronic media—phonographs, radios, tape recorders, CDs, televisions, videocassettes, DVDs, MP3s (and now, AAC on the iPod), and computers. This technology has facilitated the information revolution, a twentieth-century phenomenon as important as the industrial revolution was in the nineteenth. Electronic media have affected music-cultures all over the world. They are one of the main reasons many now call our planet a global village.

Ecological Worlds of Music

Music-cultures are dynamic rather than static. They constantly change in response to inside and outside pressures. It is wrong to think of a music-culture as something isolated, stable, smoothly operating, impenetrable, and uninfluenced by the outside world. Indeed, as we shall see in Chapter 4, the people in a music-culture need not share the same language, nationality, or ethnic origin. In the early twenty-first century, blues is popular with performers worldwide. People in a music-culture need not even agree on all of the same ideas about music—as we have seen, they in fact do not. As music-cultures change (and they are always changing) they undergo friction, and the "rules" of musical performance, aesthetics, interpretation, and meaning are negotiated, not fixed. Music history is reconceived by each generation.

Music is a fluid, dynamic element of culture, and it changes to suit the expressive and emotional desires of humankind, perhaps the most changeable of the animals. Like all of culture, music is a peculiarly human adaptation to life on this earth. Seen globally, music operates as an ecological system. Each music-culture is a particular adaptation to particular circumstances. Ideas about music, social organization, repertories, and material culture vary from one music-culture to the next. It would be unwise to call one music-culture's music "primitive," because doing so imposes one's own standards on a group that does not recognize them. Such ethnocentrism has no place in the study of world musics.

In this book the authors usually describe the older musical layers in a given region first. Then we discuss increasingly more contemporary musical styles, forms, and attitudes. We all wish to leave you with the impression that the world is not a set of untouched, authentic musical villages, but rather a fluid, interactive, interlocking, overlapping soundscape in which people listen to their ancestors, parents, neighbors, and personal CD, MP3, and cassette machines all in the same day. We think of people as musical "activists," choosing what they like best, remembering what resonates best, forgetting what seems irrelevant, and keeping their ears open for exciting new musical opportunities, their choices all the while influenced by family, friends, and the media. This happens everywhere, and it unites the farthest settlement and the largest city.

In the chapters that follow, we explore the acoustic ecologies of several worlds, and worlds within worlds, of music. Although each world may seem strange to you at first, all are organized and purposeful. Considered as an ecological system, the forces that make up a music-culture maintain a dynamic equilibrium. A change in any part of the acoustic ecology, such as the invention of the electric guitar or the latest computer music technology, may have a far-reaching impact. Viewing music this way leads to the conclusion that music represents a great human force that transcends narrow political, social, and temporal boundaries. Music offers an arena where people can talk and sing and play and reach each other in ways not allowed by the barriers of wealth, status, location, and difference. This book and CD set can present only a tiny sample of the richness of the world's music. We hope you will continue your exploration after you have finished this book.

Study Questions

1. What is a soundscape? Why should we pay particular attention to it? Does it, for example, help us become better listeners?

2. Why is it important to keep an open mind when listening to unfamiliar music?

3. What is culture? What is a music-culture? What music-cultures are you involved with?

4. How can we answer the question "What is music?" when different music-cultures have different ideas of what music is?

5. *Ethnomusicology* is defined as "the study of people making music." What is meant by "making" in this definition? (*Hint:* Review the definitions of *ethnomusicology* in the Preface.)

6. According to scientists, why do birds sing? Is it possible that birds also sing for pleasure? Could scientists find out? How?

7. John Blacking defines music as "humanly organized sound." Is all music humanly organized? Is all humanly organized sound music? What is your definition of music?

8. Do you think **CD 1, Track 1** (the Ghanaian postal workers whistling and canceling stamps), is music? Why or why not?

9. What are the elements of form and structure in music? Define and discuss rhythm, melody, and harmony.

10. How does music tell us about the way a culture conceives of time?

11. Think of a musical performance that you have been a part of recently, whether as a performer or listener or dancer. Consider this performance in light of the four-part model involving affect, performance, community, and history. What

was the affective power of the performance? What rules governed it? Who constituted the musical community, and how did they interact? What is the history of this community's involvement with this music? What is the history of the music?

12. What do different music-cultures within North America think of hip-hop (or some other music that you are familiar with)? In other words, what are some of their ideas about this music? Is it music? Is it good and useful, or potentially harmful? Is it pleasing and beautiful? Is it false, or true? What are the appropriate and inappropriate occasions for this music? How is it supported? Does it have a history? What is considered "authentic" within this music, and what is considered a sellout?

13. Think of a musical ensemble you are familiar with (rock group, symphony orchestra, marching band, church choir, etc.). How are the musical roles divided? Is there a conductor? Are there sections within the group? Are there lead singers or players within the sections? Are there soloists? Do some positions carry more prestige than others? Does this ensemble reflect and embody the divisions within your society at large?

14. Are you familiar with any musical ensembles in which everyone has an equal part? What kind of society does this ensemble reflect?

15. How are ethnicity, class, gender, and region embodied in country music, hip-hop, or some other music that you know about?

16. Do you think that the mass media mostly reflects musical taste, or does it have a major role in shaping musical taste?

17. In your view, does today's music industry interfere with the natural relationship between musical artists and their audience? Do you feel that the artists and industry combine to make music mostly for profit?

18. What is a musical repertory? Explain its different parts, using a music that you are familiar with as an example.

19. What is meant by the material culture of music? Consider musical instruments as material culture. In order to understand them, how would you classify them? According to size? Shape? Sound? Power? Something else?

20. What is an ecological system? How can music-cultures be viewed as ecological systems? How does music operate as an ecological system?

Glossary

aesthetics A branch of philosophy concerned with ideas of beauty, pleasure, enjoyment, form, and affect.

affect The power in an object or experience that makes a person feel something in response.

Carnatic music The classical music of South India.

chords Tones that sound simultaneously.

context The surrounding environment.

culture The way of life of a people, transmitted from one generation to the next.

decorative tones Subordinate tones that appear to ornament, decorate, or enhance the main melody.

ecology The study of the interactions among living things and their environment. The interactions are thought to be dynamic and systematic; hence, they operate within an ecological system. The term *worlds of music* proceeds from an ecological viewpoint.

free rhythm A rhythm without a recurring accent pattern.

gamelan (*gah*-muh-lahn) An Indonesian orchestra, consisting primarily of tuned instruments made of metal, chiefly gongs and types of marimbas/xylophones.

genre A named, standard unit of the repertory. Genre can refer to types of music as well and sometimes is used to describe a musical style that is synonymous with its genre (for example, bluegrass).

harmony Music that accompanies a melody.

heterophonic texture Two or more voices or instruments elaborating the same melody in slightly different ways.

homophonic texture A dominant melody with an accompanying harmony.

improvisation Composition at the moment of performance.

interval The distance in pitch between two tones.

major scale The familiar do-re-mi-fa-so-la-ti-do scale of Euro-American music. The white keys on the piano, from C to c, yield the major scale.

material culture of music The material objects that people in a music-culture produce that can be seen, held, felt, and used in the production of music.

melody The principal tune in a piece of music, consisting of a succession of tones in a particular rhythm over a period of time.

metrical rhythm A rhythm with a recurring accent pattern.

monophonic texture A single melody.

musical analysis A procedure in which patterns in music are revealed by breaking the music into its component parts and determining how the parts operate together to make the whole.

musical community The group that carries on the traditions and norms of performance.

musical form The structure of a musical piece or performance: how it is put together (what patterns it has) and how it works.

musical performance Meaningfully organized sound that proceeds according to agreed-on rules.

musical phrase A small series of musical tones that is understood as a meaningful group or unit.

musical style The way musical sound is organized, depending on a music-culture's aesthetics.

music-culture A human group's total involvement with music: ideas, actions, institutions, material objects—everything that has to do with music.

octave Two tones, the second of which is exactly twice the frequency of the first. When men and women sing the same melody, they usually sing an octave apart.

pélog **scale** (*pay*-log) A Javanese scale that divides the octave into seven intervals.

performance model A simplified map or picture of performance that enables us to think about how it is put together, how it proceeds, and what it means.

pitch The "frequency" of a tone, depending on the vibrations of its sound waves in cycles per second.

polymeter The simultaneous presence of two or more different metrical systems.

polyphonic texture A combination of two or more distinct melodies.

polyrhythm The simultaneous occurrence of several different rhythms, with a shifting downbeat.

raga (*rah*-guh) An organized melodic matrix with a particular scale, melodic phrases, and mood, found in the classical music of India.

repertory A stockpile of music that is ready to be performed.

rhythm Time-relation among a succession of sounds.

scale An ordered, stepwise arrangement of all the principal tones in the octave within a piece of music.

sléndro **scale** (*slayn*-dro) A Javanese scale that divides the octave into five nearly equidistant intervals.

soundscape The characteristic sounds of a particular place, both human and nonhuman; the acoustic environment.

text The words to a song; its lyrics.

texture The relationship of melodies and harmony.

timbre The quality that gives voices and instruments their characteristic sound; why a trumpet sounds different from a violin even when they play the same pitch.

tone A musical sound with a definite pitch.

Resources

References

Blacking, John. 1973. *How Musical Is Man?* Seattle: Univ. of Washington Press.

Feld, Steven. 1990. *Sound and Sentiment: Birds, Weeping, Poetics and Song in Kaluli Expression.* 2nd ed. Philadelphia: Univ. of Pennsylvania Press.

Merriam, Alan P. 1964. *The Anthropology of Music.* Evanston, Ill.: Northwestern Univ. Press.

Olajubu, Chief Oludare. 1978. "Yoruba Verbal Artists and Their Work." *Journal of American Folklore* 91:675–90.

Pantaleoni, Hewitt. 1985. *On the Nature of Music.* Oneonta, N.Y.: Wellkin Books.

Titon, Jeff Todd. 1988. *Powerhouse for God: Speech, Chant, and Song in an Appalachian Baptist Church.* Austin, TX: Univ. of Texas Press.

———, ed. 1992. *Worlds of Music.* 2nd ed. New York: Schirmer Books.

Additional Reading

Barz, Gregory, and Timothy J. Cooley. 1997. *Shadows in the Field.* New York: Oxford Univ. Press.

Berliner, Paul. 1994. *Thinking in Jazz.* Chicago: Univ. of Chicago Press.

Bohlman, Philip. 2002. *World Music: A Very Short Introduction.* New York: Oxford Univ. Press.

Crafts, Susan D., Daniel Cavicchi, Charles Keil, and the Music in Daily Life Project. 1993. *My Music.* Hanover, N.H.: Univ. Press of New England.

Clayton, Martin, Richard Middleton, and Trevor Herbert, eds. 2003. *The Cultural Study of Music.* London: Routledge.

Ethnomusicology. Journal of the Society for Ethnomusicology. 3 issues/year. Urbana: Univ. of Illinois Press.

Hamm, Charles, Bruno Nettl, and Ronald Byrnside. 1975. *Contemporary Music and Music Cultures.* Englewood Cliffs, N.J.: Prentice-Hall.

Hood, Mantle. 1982. *The Ethnomusicologist.* 2nd ed. Kent, Ohio: Kent State Univ. Press.

May, Elizabeth, ed. 1981. *Musics of Many Cultures.* Berkeley: Univ. of California Press.

McAllester, David P., ed. 1971. *Readings in Ethnomusicology.* New York: Johnson Reprint Corp.

Myers, Helen. 1992. *Ethnomusicology: An Introduction.* New York: Norton.

———. 1993. *Ethnomusicology: Historical and Regional Studies.* New York: Norton.

Nettl, Bruno. 1983. *The Study of Ethnomusicology: Twenty-nine Issues and Concepts.* Urbana: Univ. of Illinois Press.

———. 1985. *The Western Impact on World Music: Change, Adaptation, and Survival.* New York: Schirmer Books.

———. 1995. *Heartland Excursions: Ethnomusicological Reflections on Schools of Music.* Urbana: Univ. of Illinois Press.

Powers, Alan. 2003. *Bird Talk: Conversations with Birds.* Berkeley, Calif.: Frog, Ltd.; North Atlantic Books.

Reck, David. 1977. *Music of the Whole Earth.* New York: Scribner.

Rice, Timothy. 1994. *May It Fill Your Soul: Experiencing Bulgarian Music.* Chicago: Univ. of Chicago Press.

Shelemay, Kay Kaufman. 1998. *Let Jasmine Rain Down.* Chicago: Univ. of Chicago Press.

Titon, Jeff Todd, and Bob Carlin, eds. 2001. *American Musical Traditions.* 5 vols. New York: Gale.

Turnbull, Colin. 1962. *The Forest People.* New York: Clarion Books.

North America/Native America

David P. McAllester

American Indian music is unfamiliar to most non-Indian Americans. Accordingly, this chapter first presents an overall perspective by contrasting three of the numerous, different, Native American musical styles. Then we shall look at some of the many types of music being performed today in just one tribe, the Navajos. Their musical life will be studied in relation to their traditional culture and their present history. Learning about the Navajos' cultural setting will greatly enhance your understanding of their music.

The essence of music is participation, either by listening or, better still, by performing. We start here with the sound likely to be the most "Indian" to the non-Indian American—a Sioux War Dance (Figure 2.1). This is also called a Grass Dance, from the braids of grass the dancing warriors used to wear at their waists to symbolize slain enemies. It is also called the Omaha Dance, after the Indians of the western plains, who originated it.

Sioux Grass Dance

Salient Characteristics of Native American Music

- From hundreds of different Native American tribes, each with a distinct culture and music.
- Accompanies most aspects of Native American life.
- Preserved through oral tradition and memory rather than written music notation.
- Usually performed vocally in unison by (usually male) choruses.
- Sometimes accompanied by percussion instruments.
- Generally in a steady duple or single meter (a series of equally emphasized beats).
- Generally short, well-defined phrases; often attacked sharply and with strong emphases.
- Prominent repetition of text phrases, vocables (meaningless syllables), and melodic/rhythmic patterns.

Figure 2.1

War dancers at a Michigan powwow.

Douglas Fulton. Courtesy of Gertrude Kurath.

 CD 1:3

Grass Dance (1:50). Traditional Sioux War Dance. Field recording by Ray Boley, n.d. Sioux Favorites. Canyon Records Productions CR-6054. Phoenix, Arizona.

Listen for a moment to the recording of a Sioux Grass Dance **(CD 1, Track 3).** When European scholars first heard this kind of sound on wax cylinder field recordings brought back to Berlin in the early 1900s, they exclaimed, "Now, at last, we can hear the music of the true savages!" For four hundred years European social philosophers had thought of American Indians as noble wild men unspoiled by civilization, and here was music that fitted the image.

Nothing known to Europeans sounded like this piercing falsetto, swooping and tumbling down for more than an octave, that seemed to come straight from the emotions. The pulsating voices with their sharp emphases, the driving drumbeat with its complex relation to the vocal part, the heavy vocal slides at the ends of phrases—what could better portray the warlike horsemen of the limitless American plains? Another feature that intrigued Europeans was the use of vocables ("nonsense" or "meaningless" syllables) for entire texts of songs, as in this Grass Dance.

From north of Mexico to the Arctic, the Native American music before European contact was almost entirely vocal and the instruments were chiefly rattles and drums used to accompany the voice. However, the varieties of rattles and drums invented by North American Indians are legion. To name a few, there are rattles made from gourds, tree bark, carved wood, deer hooves, turtle shells, spider nests, and, recently, tin cans. There are frame drums and barrel drums of many sizes and shapes; the water drum, with its wet membrane, is unique. There are a few flutes and flageolets, and one-stringed fiddles played without the voice, but these are rare. Instrumental ensembles such as Western classical orchestras are unknown in traditional North American Indian music.

In Central and South America, on the other hand, the native high civilizations did have orchestras before the Europeans came. They readily added European instruments to their ensembles and blended their music with new ideas from Portugal and Spain. Only in the last forty or fifty years has this mingling of musics begun to happen on any large scale in native North American music. The vast majority of traditional songs are still accompanied by only drum or rattle or both.

Clearly, the once-popular Euro-American theories about "savage" music did not take into account the actual diversity within Native American cultures. Survival, whatever the climate, requires encyclopedic knowledge. A language never expressed in writing may contain the most complex grammatical structures known to linguists. Unwritten music may contain melodic and rhythmic sophistication unknown in music performed from a piece of paper.

Listen again to the Sioux Grass Dance song and see if you can sing along with it. You may think it is impossible, especially if you are a man and have never tried to sing in falsetto before. You might find it easier at first to try singing the song an octave lower. After you have tried singing along, read the following listening chart as you listen to the selection once again.

Close Listening   CD 1:3

Grass Dance

Counter Number		Commentary	Form
0:00	Driving drum beat	Leader sings phrase in *vocables* (meaningless syllables) and piercing *falsetto* (artificially high pitch).	A
0:04		Male voices repeat leader's phrase.	
0:11		Leader and male voices drop to lower pitch.	B
0:19–0:22		Female voices enter at pitch above male voices and end section with *portamento* (slide).	
0:34		Leader repeats opening falsetto phrase.	A
0:37		Male voices repeat leader's phrase.	

(continued)

Counter Number	Commentary	Form
0:43	Leader and male voices drop to lower pitch.	B
0:50–0:54	Female voices enter at pitch above men and end section with *portamento* (slide).	
1:04	Leader repeats opening falsetto phrase.	A
1:07	Male voices repeat leader's phrase.	
1:14	Leader and male voices drop to lower pitch.	B
1:19–1:24	Female voices enter at pitch above male voices and end section with *portamento* (slide).	
1:29–1:33	Drum stops then resumes at faster tempo.	
	Tail or Coda	
1:37	Leader and male voices repeat opening falsetto phrase and drop to lower pitch.	A
1:42–1:48	Female voices enter at pitch above male voices and end dance with obvious *portamento* (slide).	B

On the chart, under the heading "Form," the sections of the song that sound alike have been labeled with the same letter of the alphabet to help you see where similar musical ideas are repeated. The song starts with an A phrase, sung by a leader, but before he can finish it the other male singers break in with the same phrase, repeated, and he joins them to sing it all the way through. Most of the melodic movement takes place in the B phrase, where the melody drops a full octave below the tonal center established in the A phrase. In fact, the lower part of B is almost an exact repeat of A, performed twice and an octave lower. After three repeats of the whole melody, there is a pause; then B is repeated one last time to end the song. Indian singers often call that last brief section the "tail" of the song, which is also what the European musical term *coda* means.

Although the song's overall structure is easy to understand, you will probably find it difficult to sing. It goes fast and does not have a regular meter. Most of it follows three-beat patterns, but every now and then the singers introduce a four-beat phrase. Notice that the melody makes the same downward dip wherever the meter breaks into four. Another difficulty is that the song's tempo (about 200 beats per minute) does not seem to coincide with that of the drum (about 192 beats per minute).

The best way to sing this is to listen to it again and relax and not try to reproduce it by memorizing it exactly. Concentrate on the excitement that has made this kind of music the most popular Native American style all over the country in Indian fairs, rodeos, and powwows. Like the Plains

Indians' eagle-feather war bonnet and their stately, beautifully decorated tepees, the Grass Dance, like all War Dances, symbolizes "American Indian" throughout the world. Though Indian singing styles differ from region to region, many non-Plains Indians, especially young people, have learned this style so well that they have been able to compete with Plains singers in song contests. There are non-Indians, also, who have risen to the challenge of this music and have won prizes for their singing, costumes, and dancing at powwows. In singing this song, pay particular attention to the sharp emphases, the pulsations, and the glides. These are not mere "ornamentation" but an important part of the special art of Plains singing.

The dancing that goes with this song style is based on a toe-heel movement—first with one foot and then with the other, as follows:

Foot:	left	right	right	left	left	right
Movement:	step	toe-heel,	change	toe-heel,	change	toe-heel, . . .

Each male dancer creates many personal variations and provides a solo display of his virtuosity. His body dips and bends, but his head is quite erect, sometimes nodding in time to the drumbeat and turning this way and that. His eyes are fixed on space; his expression, rapt and remote. Often he carries a decorated stick or other object in one hand. Every dancer must stop precisely on the last beat at the rhythmic break before the "tail." Then the dancing resumes with all its intensity for the last few moments and must stop exactly on the last beat of the song. One extra step disqualifies a dancer from the competition.

The movement and sound of the costume is an essential part of the Grass Dance and its music. Bells are often tied around the legs; today they are sleigh bells, often quite large, mounted on a leather strap. These resound with every step. Ribbons sway, feathers and porcupine-hair roaches quiver, beads and small mirrors gleam and flash. The costume is as elaborate as the vocal style (see Figure 2.1).

Women participate by either performing a subdued version of the dance step or simply walking around the edge of the dance area. They wear shawls with long fringes that sway in time to their movements. In recent years women's "jingle dancing" has become a competitive event. Wearing a dress decorated with scores of cone-shaped metal jingles, younger women leap and step, filling the air with glitter and tintinnabulation. Some women stand behind the male singers, who are seated around a bass drum, and enter the song an octave higher than the men.

 CD 1:4

Lullaby (0:57). Traditional Zuni. Performed by Lanaiditsa. Field recording by David McAllester. White Water, New Mexico, 1950.

Zuni Lullaby

The next song **(CD 1, Track 4)** provides a contrast with Plains singing and helps demonstrate that there is no single "Indian" musical style. It is a lullaby recorded in 1950 by a grandmother, Lanaiditsa, on the Zuni Reservation in western New Mexico (see Figure 2.2). You will have little difficulty joining in with the song. The meter is rather flexible, and the whole gentle song has only two pitches.

Close Listening   CD 1:4

Lullaby

Counter Number	Commentary	Zuni Lyrics	English Translation
0:00	The first two pitches you hear—*Hm atseki*—are the only pitches in the entire lullaby. The higher pitch is sung on "Hm atse" and the lower is sung on "ki."	1. Hm atseki, okshits'ana, pokets'ana, pokets'ana.	1. My boy, little cottontail, little jackrabbit, little jackrabbit.
0:08	The singer shows her affection for the child by repeating the word "ana" (little) and interchangeable pet names.	2. Hm atseki, okshits'ana, kochits'ana, atset s'ana, atset s'ana.	2. My boy, little cottontail, little rat, little boy, little boy.
0:18	Throughout the lullaby, words and rhythms repeat. Repetition is a prominent feature in most North American tribal music.	3. Hm atseki pokets'ana okshits'ana okshits'ana.	3. My boy, little jackrabbit, little cottontail, little cottontail.
0:25	Notice the way the singer emphasizes certain parts of each word every time she repeats the word.	4. Hm atseki pokets'ana okshits'ana kochits'ana, kochits'ana.	4. My boy, little jackrabbit, little cottontail, little rat, little rat.
0:34	Stanza 4 repeats.		
0:44	Stanza 4 repeats and closes the lullaby.		

CD 1:5

"Gadasjot" (0:47). Iroquois Quiver Dance or Warrior's Stomp Dance song. Twenty Jacobs of Quaker Ridge. Performed by Joshua Billy Buck and Simeon Gibson. Field recording by William Fenton, c. 1942. *Songs from the Iroquois Longhouse.* Archive of Folk Song of the Library of Congress AFS L6. LP. Washington, D.C.

Iroquois Quiver Dance

In this case the text is in translatable words instead of vocables. The singer's affection for the child is expressed in the repetition of the word little and pet names, which seem to be interchangeable in the first half of the song but then settle into the same sequence.

Repetition is a prominent feature in most musics of North American Indians: in the vocables, in the texts (where they occur), and in the melodic and rhythmic patterns. This is because their aesthetic taste delights in repetitions with slight variations that are sometimes too subtle for the ears of outsiders to detect. In Lanaiditsa's song each textual phrase can be used with either of the two musical phrases except for "my boy."

The Iroquois Quiver Dance song, "Gadasjot," illustrates still another of the many different musical styles in North American Indian singing **(CD 1, Track 5)**. Another name for it is the Warrior's Stomp Dance song. This was performed in 1941 by Joshua Buck and Simeon Gibson at the Six Nations Reserve in Ohsweken, Ontario, but the song was made up years before that by Twenty Jacobs of Quaker Bridge, on the Allegheny Reservation in western New York. Note the difference between the lyrics as they would be spoken and as they appear in the song.

Figure 2.2
Zuni mother and child, showing the costume and hairstyle of the early twentieth century.

Close Listening   CD 1:5

"Gadasjot"

Counter Number	Leader: The Call		Male Voices: The Response (vocables)
A Section			
0:00	Leader sings the call.	*Tga-na ho-n swe-ge** Filled is Ohsweken (Ontario)	
0:03	Leader models response.	*yo-we-hi yeye*	
0:04		*di-jod-di yak-on* With divorced women	
0:06	*yo-we-hi ye ye* (response)		
A Section repeats, call-and-response.			
0:07–0:16	*Tga-na ho-n swe-ge* *di-jod-di yak-on* *we-ya ha-no hi yo*	Filled is Ohsweken (Ontario) With divorced women With good looking ones	*yo-we-hi ye ye* *yo-we-hi ye ye* *yo-we-hi ye ye*

(continued)

Counter Number	Leader: The Call	Male Voices: The Response (vocables)
0:17	Exclamation at group's response. *hi-yo* Call at higher pitch. *wi-go hi-no hi-yo* Fine looking ones!	
0:19	*yo-we-hi ye ye* (higher pitch)	
0:21	Call *wi-go no hi yo* Fine looking ones!	
0:22	*yo-we-hi ye ye*	
Leader and male voices repeat original call and response many times.		
0:42	Leader sings *portamento.*	
0:43	Response with *portamento.*	

*Translation courtesy of William N. Fenton

The first thing that strikes the ear is the "call-and-response" form. One singer utters some words (the "call") and the other answers him with a vocable pattern: "yowehi ye ye!" This alternation continues through the song. Although quite common in the Eastern Woodlands, this pattern is rare elsewhere in North American traditional Indian singing. (Call-and-response singing can be heard in many world music-cultures, as we shall see in later chapters.) William Fenton's translation of the text shows the jocular content often found in Stomp Dance songs.

The singing in this Iroquois song is relaxed compared with Plains singing. A characteristic of Iroquois singing style is a pulsation of the voice at the ends of phrases. In Plains singing, by contrast, pulsations occur all through the song.

The Stomp Dance is a favorite recreational dance among Woodland Indians in the eastern United States and Canada. Among the Iroquois it usually takes place in the longhouse, a meetinghouse with a stove at each end of the hall and benches along the sides. The participants form a line behind the leader. They imitate his "short jog step" (Fenton 1942:31) and any other turns and gyrations he may invent as they sing the responses to his calls. More and more of the audience joins the dance until the line is winding exuberantly all over the longhouse floor. Woodland tribes other than the Iroquois may not have longhouses and often do the Stomp Dance outdoors. The singers accompany themselves with a cow-horn rattle (see Figure 2.3).

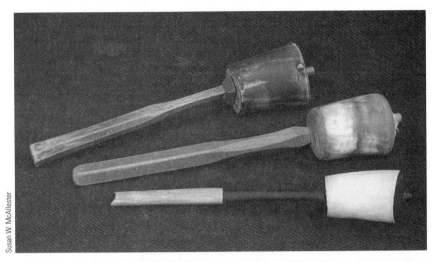

Figure 2.3
Iroquois cow-horn rattles, showing a variety of shapes and handles.

Susan W. McAllester

Music of the Navajo

Now that we have had a brief look at three of the many different North American Indian musical styles, we shall take a deeper look into the musical life of still another Indian group, the Navajos of the desert Southwest. By studying their music in some detail we can see how many different kinds of music exist in just one Indian community. Examining the cultural context of the music will show us how closely music is integrated with Indian life.

A Yeibichai Song from the Nightway Ceremony

To begin again with sound, we shall go first to one of the most exciting kinds of Navajo music, Yeibichai songs. Yé'ii-bi-chái (gods-their-grandfathers) refers to ancestor deities who come to dance at the major ceremonial known as Nightway. The masked dancers who impersonate the gods bring supernatural power and blessing to help cure a sick person.

With its shouts, ornamentation, and falsetto voices, this song **(CD 1, Track 6)** might make you think of the Plains Indians. The tense energy of the singing also resembles that of the Plains style. However, the long introduction, sung almost entirely on the basic pitch (the "tonic") of the song, differs strikingly from the Indian songs we have heard before. Then the melody leaps up an octave. In the first phrase, A, after the introduction, the song comes swooping briskly down to the tonic again. This ending appears again later on in the song in two variations. The same descent is repeated and then another acrobatic plunge takes place in B after two "false starts" that each closely resemble the first half of A. After B, another interesting variation in the use of previous motifs occurs.

The Navajos are noted for their bold experiments in artistic form. This is true in their silversmithing, weaving, sandpainting, and contemporary commercial painting. It is also true in their music, as the play of melodic and rhythmic building blocks in the passage just heard suggests. Listen again, following the pattern of this complex and intriguing song, and try

 CD 1:6

Yeibichai (2:15). Navajo dance song from Nightway. Led by Sandoval Begay. Field recording by Willard Rhodes, n.d. Archive of Folk Song of the Library of Congress AFS L41. LP. Washington, D.C.

Salient Characteristics of Navajo Music

- Closely integrated into Navajo way of life.
- Frequent use of vocalized yells or shouts and male falsetto voice, often accompanied by percussion instruments.
- Popular Navajo music heard in dance songs from ceremonials as well as in country-and-western music.
- "Classical" Navajo music made up of the great ceremonial chants that accompany religious rituals.
- Outside influences, among them country music, the Native American Church, and the Christian Missionary Movement, have impacted Navajo music.

Close Listening   CD 1:6

Yeibichai

Counter Number	Commentary	Form	Rattle
0:00	Two high shouts. *wu-wu-o-o-ho*		Shakes
Introduction			
0:04	Sung almost entirely on the basic pitch (*tonic*). *hi ye hi ye hi ye, ho ho ho ho, hi hi hi* Ending phrase or bridge. *hi ye hi ye*		Quick, insistent rhythm
Song			
0:10	A phrase begins an *octave* higher then descends. *hui yi hui-hu' i ho-e*	A	Constant rhythm
0:14	Repeat *hui yi hui hu' i ho-e* First half of A phrase sung twice. *yi 'au*	A ½A	
0:19	B phrase opens high and slowly descends. *hui hui hui hui*	B	
0:23	Melodic phrase from introduction. *ho ho hi ye, hi ye hi ye hi-i hi ho-e* Second half of A phrase sung twice. *hi-i hi ho-e hi-i hi ho-e* First half of A phrase sung twice. *yi 'u*	C ⅔A ½A	
0:35	B phrase in melody returns. *hui hui hui hu-i ho ho*	B	

Close Listening   CD 1:6

Yeibichai

Counter Number	Commentary	Form	Rattle
0:39	C phrase returns. *hi ye, hi ye hi ye ho ho ho ho hi hi hi* *hi ye hi ye* Bridge ends section. *ho ho ho ho hi hi hi* *hi ye hi ye*	C	
0:50–1:30	Shout begins song's repeat.	A	
1:48–2:00	Shout begins song's repeat. Closes with repeat of introduction. *hi ye, hi ye hi ye ho ho ho ho hi hi hi* *hi ye hi ye*	A	Rattle shakes as singing ends

to sing it yourself along with Sandoval Begay and his group of Yeibichai singers.

Entirely in vocables, this song illustrates how far from "meaningless" vocables can be. Almost any Navajo would know from the first calls that this is a Yeibichai song; these and the other vocables identify what kind of song it is. Moreover, this song includes the call of the gods themselves: *Hi ye, hi ye, ho ho ho ho!* Although there are hundreds of different Yeibichai songs, they usually contain some variation of this call of the Yei.

Yeibichai singers are organized in teams, often made up of men from one particular region or another. They create new songs or sing old favorites, each team singing several songs before the nightlong singing and dancing end. The teams prepare costumes and masks and practice a dance of the gods that proceeds in two parallel lines with reel-like figures. They also have a clown, who follows the dancers and makes everyone laugh with his antics: getting lost, bumbling into the audience, imitating the other dancers. The teams compete, and the best combination of costumes, clowns, singing, and dancing receives a gift from the family giving the ceremony. The representation of the presence of the gods at the Nightway brings god power to the ceremony and helps the sick person get well.

This dance takes place on the last night of a nine-night ritual that includes such ceremonial practices as purification by sweating and vomiting, making prayer offerings for deities whose presence is thus invoked, and sandpainting rituals in which the one-sung-over sits on elaborate designs in colored sands and other dry pigments. The designs depict the deities; contact with these figures identifies the one-sung-over with the forces of nature they represent and provides their protective power. In the course of the ceremony hundreds of people may attend as spectators, whose presence supports the reenactment of the myth on which the ceremony is based. The one-sung-over takes the role of the mythic hero, and the songs, sandpaintings, prayers, and other ritual acts recount the story of how this hero's trials and adventures brought the Nightway ceremony from the supernatural world for the use of humankind (Faris 1990). Besides the Yeibichai songs there are hundreds of long chanted songs with elaborate texts of translatable ritual poetry.

Such a ritual drama as Nightway is as complex as "the whole of a Wagnerian opera" (Kluckhohn and Leighton 1938:163). The organization and performance of the entire event is directed by the singer or ceremonial practitioner, who must memorize every detail. Such men and women are among the intellectual leaders of the Navajo communities. Most readers find the Yeibichai song difficult to learn. The shifts in emphasis, the many variations, and the difficult vocal style demand hours of training before one can do it well. But there are many other kinds of Navajo music.

CD 1:7

"Folsom Prison Blues" (2:49). Johnny Cash. Performed by the Fenders on *Second Time Roun'*. LP. Thoreau, New Mexico, 1966.

"Folsom Prison Blues"

You should be able to join in with the next song **(CD 1, Track 7)** right away, especially if you already listen to country-and-western music. This version of Johnny Cash's classic "Folsom Prison Blues" is played and sung by the Fenders, an all-Navajo country band from Thoreau, New Mexico, who were popular in the 1960s and 1970s (Figure 2.4).

Figure 2.4
Album cover of the Fenders, an early Navajo country group.

Close Listening   CD 1:7

"Folsom Prison Blues"

Counter Number	Commentary	Lyrics
Introduction		
0:00	Electric guitar, bass guitar, rhythm guitar, and drums	
1st stanza		
0:09	Soloist enters. Drums and bass guitar keep the beat.	*I hear the train a comin'* *It's rolling round the bend.* *I ain't seen the sunshine since I don't know when,* *but I'm stuck in Folsom prison, that's where I long to stay.* *When I hear that whistle blow, I hang my head and I cry.*
2nd stanza		
0:35	Soloist occasionally sings against the meter.	*When I was just a baby my mama told me. Son,* *always be a good boy, don't ever play with guns.* *But I shot a man in Reno just to watch him die.* *When I hear that whistle blowin', I hang my head and I cry.*
Break		
1:00	Electric guitar solo. Drums, rhythm and bass guitars accompany. Homophonic texture.	
3rd stanza		
1:25	Soloist occasionally sings against the meter.	*I bet there's rich folks eating in a fancy dining car* *I bet they're drinkin' coffee, smoking big cigars.* *Well I know I had it coming, I just can't be wrong.* *When I hear that whistle blow, I hang my head and I cry.*
Break		
1:50	Electric guitar solo. Drums, rhythm and bass guitars accompany.	
4th stanza		
2:16	Soloist occasionally sings against the meter.	*Well if they'd free me from this prison,* *If this railroad train was mine,* *I'd move just a little further down the line,* *far away from Folsom prison, that's where I long to stay.* *When I hear that whistle blow, I hang my head and I cry.*
2:42	Electric guitar closes. Drums, rhythm and bass guitars accompany.	

Country music has long been a great favorite with Indian people, especially in the West. There are several country and western bands on the Navajo reservation. Some, such as the Sundowners and Borderline, have issued records that sell well in Indian country. Even more popular are non-Indian country singers such as Garth Brooks and Tim McGraw. The cowboy and trucker image appeals to most people in the western states, including Indians, who identify with the open life and the excitement of the roundup and the rodeo.

The Navajo Way of Life

Who are these Navajos we have been listening to? Where and how do they live? At more than 290,000, they are the United States' largest Indian tribe. Descended from Athabascan-speaking nomadic hunters who came into the Southwest as recently as six or seven hundred years ago, they now live in scattered communities ranging from extended family groups to small towns on a reservation of 25,000 square miles (larger than West Virginia) spread over parts of New Mexico, Arizona, and Utah (see Figure 2.5). Thousands more live off the reservation in border towns such as Farmington, Gallup, and Flagstaff and such cities as Chicago, Los Angeles, and San Diego. The reason for their move is largely economic: Their population has outgrown the support afforded by the reservation.

On the reservation the Navajos' livelihood is based, to a small but culturally significant degree, on farming, raising stock, weaving, and silversmithing (see Figure 2.6). The main part of their $110 million annual income, however, comes from coal, uranium, oil, natural gas, and lumber. Much of their educational and health care funds derive from the Department of the Interior, some of it in fulfillment of the 1868 treaty that marked the end of hostilities between the Navajos and the United States Army. Personal incomes range from the comfortable salaries of tribal administrative and

Figure 2.5

Map of the Navajo Reservation and points of interest.

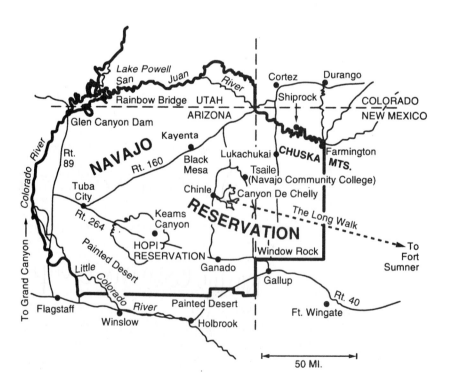

Salient Characteristics of Navajo Life ♪♪♪

- Largest Native American tribe in the United States.
- Reservation covers most of Arizona and spreads to California, New Mexico, and Utah.
- Farming, weaving, and silversmithing provide work and income.
- Western style dress preferred by men; skirts and blouses preferred by women.
- Diverse style of homes and buildings sometimes using ceremonial circular floor plans.

service jobs to the precarious subsistence of marginal farmers. Many Navajos are supported on various kinds of tribal or government relief.

Although much of traditional Navajo culture remains intact, the People (*Diné*, as the Navajos call themselves), also welcome new ideas and change. Their scholarship funds enable hundreds of young people to attend colleges and universities around the country, including their own Diné College on the reservation. A battery of attorneys and the Natural Resources Committee keep watch on the mining leases and lumber operations. The Navajos also operate motels, restaurants, banks, and shopping centers, and they encourage small industries to establish themselves on the reservation. Some Navajos jet to administrative and developmental conferences in Washington, D.C.; others speak no English and herd sheep on horseback or on foot miles from the nearest paved road.

The men dress in western style, and some of the women still wear skirts and blouses copied from the dresses worn by United States Army officers' wives in the 1860s, during the imprisonment of the Navajos at Fort Sumner, New Mexico. The skirts have shortened in recent years, and Navajo taste

Courtesy of American Museum of Natural History. (Photo: M. Raney) Neg. no. 335258.

Figure 2.6
Navajos still travel on horseback in many parts of the reservation.

has always demanded the addition of buttons, rings, bracelets, necklaces, and heavy belts of silver set with turquoise. The men wear this jewelry, too, sometimes with the added panache of silver hatbands on big cowboy hats. Young people, male and female, are now usually seen wearing blue jeans like other young people anywhere in the country. Bright blankets from the Pendleton mills in Oregon used to be worn as an overcoat in cold weather. This garment is now so identified with traditional Navajo costume that it is often worn by the protagonist in ceremonials. The Navajos' own famous rugs are woven for cash income; most of them go to the local store, sometimes still called a trading post, to pay for food and other supplies. Some of these rugs are so finely designed and woven that they have brought $20,000 or more apiece in the world market for fine arts (see Figure 2.7).

Figure 2.7
Hand weaving is a source of income for many Navajo women. This scene, from the 1920s, is still common today.

Courtesy of American Museum of Natural History. (Photo: P. E. Goddard) Neg. no. 14471.

Navajo houses range from the modern stucco ranch houses and large trailer homes of tribal officials, administrative staff, and school personnel to smaller one-room houses of every description. Some of the old-style circular log hogans (Navajo *hooghan,* "place home") can still be seen. Navajo ceremony requires a circular floor plan, and many adaptations of this well-loved and ceremonially important shape are designed into new kinds of structures. For example, the Tribal Council Building in Window Rock, Arizona, is a round sandstone structure with Navajo murals inside. It can accommodate the seventy-four council members, who gather there from all parts of the reservation. The Cultural Center at Diné College at Tsaile, Arizona, is six stories of concrete, steel, and glass, but it is octagonal, with a domed roof. Inside, at the heart of the building, stands a replica of a traditional log hogan with a dirt floor and a smoke hole that goes up four stories through a shaft to the open sky. It serves as a religious symbol and a meditation room. School buildings, chapter houses, information centers, and arts and crafts outlets exhibit other variations in size and design on the circular shape, which symbolizes the earth, and on the domed roof, which symbolizes both mountaintops and the vault of the sky.

Traditional Popular Music

Until the 1940s the most popular musics on the reservation were the different kinds of dance songs from the ceremonials. We have already studied a Yeibichai dance song from Nightway. Corral dance songs from several ceremonies were also popular, but the different kinds of *Ndáá'* (war dance) songs from Enemy-way made up the largest body of traditional popular music. These include Circle Dance, Sway, Two-step, Skip Dance, and Gift songs. Although country and western music eclipsed them in the 1960s and 1970s, the traditional songs have found a renewed popularity on the reservation today.

In the 1990s a new recreational pastime called Song and Dance emerged. It makes use of Skip Dance and Two-step songs, and it can take place in any large hall. Couples of all ages, in traditional costumes, participate. Singers or tapes provide the music, and the dancers, identified by large numbered tags, circle the hall while judges note their costumes and dancing skill. Winners receive trophies, and entry fees and donations solicited during the dancing go toward the expenses of the Song and Dance Association hosting the event or for specified benefits such as school programs.

Some traditionalists have objected to *Ndáá'* songs being used in this new, secular context; however, this is only the latest in several new uses. Radio broadcasts have featured *Ndáá'* songs since the 1930s, and they found a new wave of radio popularity in the 1990s.

The Circle Dance Song "Shizhané'é"

Ndáá' songs are the hit tunes of traditional Navajo life. Compared with the Yeibichai songs, *Ndáá'* songs are easy to sing, though for an outsider they can contain some surprises. Many of them are sung entirely with vocables, but the Circle Dance song "Shizhané'é" **(CD 1, Track 8)** contains words

CD 1:8

"Shizhané'é" ("I'm in Luck") (1:19). Navajo Circle Dance song from Enemyway. Performed by Albert G. Sandoval, Jr., and Ray Winnie. Field recording by David P. McAllester. Sedona, Arizona, 1957.

Close Listening   CD 1:8

"Shizhané'é"

Counter Number	Commentary	Form
Introduction		
0:00	Begins on tonic then leaps an octave. Vocables sung throughout. *He ne ya na*	
A and B sections		
0:03	Phrase melody starts on a high pitch, descends, rises, and descends again at end of phrase. Notice the nasal quality of the singers' voices. *Yo____ wo____ yo'o we ya he nai ya he _____*	A
0:08	Repeat. *Yo____ wo____ yo'o we ya he nai ya he*	A
0:14	New phrase melody starts at a lower pitch and descends. *A'ha ne ya 'a ha ne____ yo 'a we ya he, nai ya*	B
0:19–0:42	Repeat. *A'ha ne ya 'a ha ne____ yo 'a we ya he, nai ya*	B
C section		
0:43	Longer phrase with limited melodic movement *Shi zha ne'e shi zha ne'e ki yah si-zi-ni shi-ka no____ taV'a we ya he nai ya*	C
0:51–1:15	Repeat	C
Coda or tail		
1:16	Phrase returns to opening note *he, nai ya*	D

With the permission of Albert Sandoval Jr. and Ray Winnie.

that can be translated as well. If you play this song a few times and follow the words and music provided here, you should be able to get into the swing of this lively melody. Because you do not have to worry about producing the high falsetto sounds of the Yeibichai songs, you can concentrate on other fine points. Pay attention to the emphases. See if you can reproduce the nasal tone the Navajos enjoy in their singing. Every phrase ends with the same tones. This and the three-beat meter are characteristic of Circle Dance songs (McAllester 1954:52). As you listen with the listening chart in front of you, pay attention to the form and notice how the phrases marked A introduce the melodic elements that are more fully developed in B and then even more so in C. The whole structure is too long to include on the sound recording.

The translatable portion of the text, in the C phrases, is like a nugget in the middle of the song, framed by a vocable chorus before and after it. This is a favorite principle of design in other Navajo arts as well as music. It is the dynamic symmetry discussed by Witherspoon (1977:170–74) and illustrated in weaving and silver jewelry designs. The brief, humorous text is, like many another in Navajo song, intended to make the girls laugh and pay attention to the (male) singers. Although the dance is part of a ceremony, it also offers courtship opportunities and serves as a social dance.

The text as it is sung:

Shizhané'é, shizhané'é, kiya sizini shika nóotaaV, 'aweya he nai ya.

Free translation:

I'm in luck, I'm in luck!
She's leaning up against the store front,
Looking everywhere for me!

With the permission of Albert Sandoval Jr. and Ray Winnie.

As the Navajo is spoken, with literal translation:

shizhané	me-good luck
kíyah	house-under/against
sizíní	*standing-the one who*
shíká	me-for/after (as in running after one)
nóotááV	searching for (3rd person)

Linger for a moment on the choices of expression that make the words so witty. The song begins with foolish self-congratulation. But then we learn both from the form *"yah"* after "house" (*ki*) and from the linguistic form of *sizíní*, "the one who is standing," that the girl is really propped against the house. The suggestion is that she has had too much to drink and therefore is unable to be actively searching for ("running after") the singer at all, even though he claims she is. The irony of the situation combines with a jesting implication that women drink too much and chase after young men. Because it is actually the men who do most of the drinking and chasing after the opposite sex, the song is all the funnier. *Kiyah sizíní* also carries the meaning "prostitute." As in all clever poetry, the zest comes from the subtle shades of meaning.

The Enemyway Ceremony

Religion is one of the keys to understanding culture. We can know the Navajos better if we take a closer look at the Enemyway ceremony in which "Shizhané'é" is used. Enemyway is one of the most frequently performed rites in traditional Navajo religion. Like Nightway, it is a curing ritual. In this case the sickness is brought on by the ghosts of outsiders who have died. Enemyway is often performed for a returned Navajo member of the United States Armed Forces or for others who have been away from home among strangers for a long time. A Navajo who has been in a hospital and returns home cured, in our sense, may have an Enemyway performed because of the inevitable exposure to the spirits of the many non-Navajos who have died in such a place (see Figure 2.8).

Figure 2.8
This scene by the Navaho painter Andy Tsihnahjinnie shows drumming, singing, and dancing at the public part of an Enemyway ceremony.

Courtesy of Andy Tsihnahjinnie

The Navajos recognize the disease theory of the Euro-American world, and they gladly take advantage of hospitals, surgery, and antibiotics. In addition, however, they see bad dreams, poor appetite, depression, and injuries from accidents as results of disharmony with the world of nature. Although this view resembles Western psychiatry and psychosomatic medicine in many ways, the Navajos go still further. They see animals, birds, insects, and the elements of earth, water, wind, and sky as active potencies that directly influence human life. Each of these forces may speak directly to human beings and may teach them the songs, prayers, and ritual acts that make up the ceremonials. At the center of this relationship with the natural world is the concept of *hózhǫ́ǫ́* (beauty, blessedness, harmony), which must be maintained and which, if lost, can be restored by means of ritual. The prayers invoke this state over and over at their conclusions For example:

Hózhǫ́ǫ́ nahasdlį́į́',
Hózhǫ́ǫ́ nahasdlį́į́',
Hózhǫ́ǫ́ nahasdlį́į́',
Hózhǫ́ǫ́ nahasdlį́į́',!
Conditions of harmony have been restored,
Conditions of harmony have been restored,
Conditions of harmony have been restored,
Conditions of harmony have been restored!

The ceremony involves two groups of participants, the "home camp" and the "stick receiver's camp." Members of the latter represent the enemy and are custodians of a stick decorated with symbols of the warrior deity, Enemy Slayer, and of his mother, Changing Woman, who is the principal

Navajo deity. The decorated stick is brought from the home camp along with gifts of many yards of brightly colored yarn. The first night of the ceremony consists of singing and dancing at the stick receiver's camp. This event offers the only time in traditional Navajo life that men and women dance together—a time for fun and courtship. Before the dancing starts, a concert of Sway songs takes place. Although these may express the courtship theme, the majority of the Sway songs have texts entirely of vocables.

Heye yeye ya,
Lonesome as I am,
Lonesome as I am, *ha-i na,*
Lonesome as I am,
Lonesome as I am, *ha,*
Lonesome as I am, *na'a- ne hana. . . .*

Text, Navajo Sway song. David P. McAllester, Enemy Way Music, pp. 29, 37. Papers of the Peabody Museum of Archaeology and Ethnology, vol. 41, no. 3. Copyright © 1954 by the President and Fellows of Harvard College.

After an hour or so, the singing shifts to dance songs and the women appear, looking for partners. That the women always choose perhaps reflects the powerful position of women in Navajo society. They own the household; the children belong to the mother's clan, not the father's; and when a couple marry the husband traditionally moves in with his wife's family.

In the dance the women tend to act bashfully, but they find partners and the couples dance along together following other couples in a large circle. The dance is simply a light stepping along with a bounce on each step. When a woman wants to change partners, she lets the man know by demanding a token payment. Even some Navajos do not know that this is a symbol of the war booty brought back by Enemy Slayer from a mythical war and given away to Navajo women in the story in celebration of the victory. The song texts of the dance songs often poke fun at the women and sometimes refer to these payments.

He-ne, yane, yana-,
Yala'e-le- yado'eya 'ana he,
Yala'e-le- yado'eya ne. . . .
Your daughter, at night,
Walking around, *yado'eya yana hana,*
Tomorrow, money,
Lots of it, there will be, *yana hana,*
Yala'e-le- yado'eya na'ana,
Yala'e-le- yado'eya na'ana he. . . .

Text, Navajo Enemyway Dance song. David P. McAllester, Enemy Way Music, p. 45. Papers of the Peabody Museum of Archaeology and Ethnology, vol. 41, no. 3. Copyright © 1954 by the President and Fellows of Harvard College.

After a few hours of dancing, a Signal song indicates that the singing is to go back to Sway songs (McAllester 1954:27). The dancing stops, but the Sway songs may go on for the rest of the night. Again, the ceremony symbolizes war: The group of singers is divided into two halves, representing the home camp and the enemy, and the singers compete in vigor, repertory, and highness of pitch.

They stop at dawn, but after a rest and breakfast a new kind of singing, a serenade of Gift songs, takes place. The home camp people sing outside the main hogan of the stick receiver's camp; in exchange, small gifts such as oranges and boxes of Cracker Jack are thrown to the singers through the smoke hole. Larger gifts such as expensive blankets are brought out and handed to responsible members of the singing group; these presents will be reciprocated later in the ceremony. Most of the Gift songs are old and have text entirely in vocables, but a few of the newer ones have words concerning the hoped-for gifts.

Heye yeye yana,
Your skirts, how many? *yi-na,*
To the store I'm going, *'e hyana heye yeye ya,*
To Los Nores I'm going, *'e hya 'ena hya na.* . . .
'e-ye yeye yana,
Goats, I came for them, *yo'o'o 'ene hanena,*
Goats, I came for them, *yo'o'o 'ene hahe,*
Yo'o'o 'ena heye yeye yana. . . .

Text, Navajo Enemyway Gift song. David P. McAllester, Enemy Way Music, p. 48, songs 52, 53. Papers of the Peabody Museum of Archaeology and Ethnology, vol. 41, no. 3. Copyright © 1954 by the President and Fellows of Harvard College.

The gifts, like the payments during the dancing, represent war booty: The trip of the home party can be seen as a raid into enemy country and the gifts as the booty they take home with them. But reconciliation is symbolized at the same time, because the stick receiver's camp provides supper and camping facilities and because the meal and gifts will be returned in a similar exchange on the third morning.

After the breakfast and gift singing on the second day, the stick receiver's party prepares to move toward the home camp. Most of the home camp people leave early, but one of them remains as an official guide to lead the stick receiver to a good camping place a few miles from the home camp. They time their arrival to take place at about sundown, and another night of singing and dancing follows at this new camp.

Early the next morning the war symbolism of the ceremony is sharply emphasized with a sham battle. The stick receiver's people ride into the home camp with yells and rifle shots, raising a lot of dust and committing small depredations such as pulling down clotheslines. After four such charges they retire to a new campsite a few hundred yards away, where a procession from the home camp brings them a sumptuous breakfast. After the meal, the return gift singing takes place at the hogan of the one-sung-over.

Now comes further, heavy war drama. In a secret indoor ritual the afflicted person is given power and protection by sacred chanting and is dressed for battle. At the climax of the ceremony he goes forth and shoots at a trophy of the enemy, thus ritually killing the ghost. The songs used to prepare the warrior include long derisive descriptions of the enemy and praise of Navajo warriors (Haile 1938:276–84). If the person being sung over is a woman, a male proxy takes her place in shooting the enemy ghost.

In the late afternoon a Circle Dance is performed at the stick receiver's new camp. Men join hands in a circle, the two halves of which represent the two camps. At this point they compete with songs like "Shizhané'é" **(CD 1, Track 8).** The two sides of the circle take turns singing to see who can sing the best songs most beautifully. As the songs alternate, so does the direction in which the Circle Dance moves. Most of the songs have no translatable words, and those that do are not overtly about war; however, the presence of the two competing sides is a reminder of conflict, and it is thought that every drumbeat accompanying the songs drives the enemy ghosts farther into the ground. After a while a girl, carrying the stick, and several other women may enter the circle and walk around, following the direction of the dancing men. The symbols of Changing Woman and her warrior son incised on the sacred stick remind participants further of the dance's meaning.

After the Circle Dance, another dramatic event takes place: The secret war name of the afflicted person is revealed. Members of the stick receiver's camp walk over to the home camp, singing as they go. Four times on the way, they stop and shout out the identity of the enemy. Then the stick receiver sits down in front of the ceremonial hogan and sings four songs that mention the name of the enemy and that of the one-sung-over. In traditional Navajo life it is impolite to address anyone by name and, in particular, by his or her war name. Polite address uses a kinship term, real or fictitious. Examples of war names are "She Went Among War Parties" and "He Ran Through Warriors" (Reichard 1928:98–99).

The songs describe battle with the enemy and refer to the anguish of the enemy survivors. The death of the enemy ghost is mentioned. Then, after a serenade of Sway songs, the stick receiver's party move back to the dance ground at their camp, and the last night of the ceremony begins with a further selection of Sway songs. After an hour or so the singing changes to dance songs and dancing, which, as on the previous two nights, may go on for several hours. Again the Signal song indicates the end of dancing, and the rest of the night is spent in Sway song competition between the two camps.

At dawn the ceremony ends with a brief blessing ritual conducted while participants face the rising sun. The stick receiver's party departs, and the afflicted person, now protected by the many symbolic ways in which the ghost has been eliminated, spends four days in rest and quiet while the effect of the ceremony settles into the entire household.

The Native American Church

In their comparatively recent history the Navajos have felt the call of two highly organized religious movements from outside their traditional culture. One is evangelical Christianity. The other is the Native American Church, an Indian movement with roots in ancient Mexico and recent development in Oklahoma. This religion established itself firmly in the United States in the nineteenth century and thereafter developed different perspectives and music from that which can still be seen among the Tarahumare and Huichol Indians of Mexico. It found its way into the Navajo country in the 1930s. By the 1950s it had grown in this one tribe to an estimated membership of twenty thousand.

This music differs strikingly from traditional Navajo music. Listen to a hymn **(CD 1, Track 9)** from the Native American Church and then consider the role of this music in contemporary Navajo life.

What may strike you first is the quiet, introspective quality of the singing in this simple melody. Members of the Native American Church speak of their music as prayer. Although the text has no translatable words, the repetitive simplicity of vocables and music expresses a rapt, inward feeling.

CD 1:9

Hymn of the Native American Church (1:13). Navajo Peyote song. Performed by George Mitchell and Kaya David. Field recording by Willard Rhodes, n.d. Archive of Folk Song of the Library of Congress AFS 14. LP. Washington, D.C.

Close Listening   CD 1:9

Hymn, Native American Church

Counter Number	Commentary	Vocables	Form	Peyote Rattle
0:03	Soloist sings two cycles of phrase A, a descending melody, without harmony. All A phrases end with *he ne yo*.	*He__ yo-we no-we yu-na wu-na he ne yo* *we__ yo-we no-we yu-na wu-na he ne yo*	A	*Shaken throughout song*
0:11	Second phrase, B, begins on lower pitch and descends.	*'e __ yo-we no-we yu-na wu-na he ne yo* *he yo-we do yu-na wu-na he ne yo we*	B	
0:20	Phrase A repeats twice.	*he__ yo-we no-we yu-na wu-na he ne yo* *we__ yo-we no-we yu-na wu-na he ne yo*	A	
0:27	Phrase B repeats.	*'e __ yo-we no-we yu-na wu-na he ne yo* *he yo-we do yu-na wu-na he ne yo we*	B	
0:36	Phrase A repeats twice.	*he__ yo-we no-we yu-na wu-na he ne yo* *we__ yo-we no-we yu-na wu-na he ne yo*	A	
0:45	Phrase B repeats.	*'e __ yo-we no-we yu-na wu-na he ne yo* *he yo-we do yu-na wu-na he ne yo we*	B	
0:53	Phrase A repeats twice.	*he__ yo-we no-we yu-na wu-na he ne yo* *we__ yo-we no-we yu-na wu-na he ne yo*	A	
1:03	Phrase B repeats. This last section is always sung on the tonic and is characteristic of the Native American Church.	*'e __ yo-we no-we yu-na wu-na he ne yo* *he yo-we do yu-na wu-na he ne yo we*	B	

Transcription by David P. McAllester from field recording by Willard Rhodes. With permission of Willard Rhodes.

According to one theory, Native American Church hymns are derived from Christian hymnody. The quiet, slow movement and the unadorned voice, so unlike the usual boisterous, emphatic, out-of-doors delivery in Indian singing, support this interpretation. On the other hand, the music shows many more features that are all Indian: the rhythmic limitation to only two time values, one taking half as long as the other (a specialty of Navajo and Apache music); the descending melodic direction; the rattle and drum accompaniment; the pure melody without harmony; the use of vocables. These features are present in Native American Church music in many different tribes all across the continent to such a marked extent that one can identify a distinct, pantribal "Peyote style" (McAllester 1949:12, 80–82). In the present song, every phrase ends on *he ne yo*, anticipating the *he ne yo we* of the last phrase. This ending, always sung entirely on the tonic, is as characteristic of Native American Church music as "Amen" is to Christian hymns and prayers.

True to its Oklahoma origin, the Native American Church ideally holds its meetings in a large Plains Indian tepee. This is often erected on Saturday evening for the all-night meeting and then taken away to be stored until the next weekend. Such mobility enables the meeting to move to wherever members want a service. Meetings are sometimes held in hogans because they, too, are circular and have an earth floor where the sacred fire and altar can be built.

The members of the Native American Church use a water drum and a rattle to accompany their singing. The drum is made of a small, three-legged iron pot with a wet, almost rubbery, buckskin drumhead stretched over the opening (see Figure 2.9). The pot is half full of water, which is splashed over the inside of the drumhead from time to time by giving the drum a tossing motion. This action serves to keep the drumhead moist and flexible while in use. The player kneels, holding the drum on the ground and tipped toward his drumming hand. He controls the tone with pressure on the drumhead from the thumb of his holding hand. He strikes the membrane rapidly and rather heavily with a smooth, hard, slightly decorated drumstick. The water inside the pot most likely contributes to the strong resonance of this and other kinds of water drums, but no physical studies have yet been made to test the theory.

The peyote rattle is made with a small gourd mounted on a handle stick in much the same way as the cow-horn rattle of the Iroquois. There is no carved shelf on the handle, however: Instead, the stick is merely wedged tightly into the gourd plug. The far end of the stick protrudes two or three inches beyond the gourd, and a tuft of dyed horsehair is attached to it. This is often red to symbolize the red flower of the peyote cactus. Many Native American Church members hold a beautifully decorated feather fan during the service and use it to waft toward themselves the fragrant incense of cedar needles when these are put into the fire. The feathers of the fan are mounted in separate movable leather sleeves, like the feathers of the Plains war bonnet. This allows the user to manipulate the fan so that each feather seems to have a quivering life of its own.

Figure 2.9
Two kinds of water drum. On the left is an Iroquois drum made from a short section of hollowed-out log. On the right is a Navajo pottery water drum, used only in the Enemyway ceremony.

Susan W. McAllester

The ritual consists of long prayers, many groups of four songs each (sung in turn by members of the meetings), a special water break at midnight, and a fellowship breakfast in the morning. At intervals, under the direction of the leader of the meetings, a Cedar Chief builds up the fire, puts cedar incense on the coals, and passes the cigarettes to make the sacred smoke that accompanies the prayers. He also passes small pieces of a cactus called peyote (from the Aztec *peyotl*, "wooly," describing the fine white hairs that grow in tufts on the cactus). When eaten, peyote produces a sense of well-being and, sometimes, visions in vivid color. The peyote is eaten as a sacrament, because Father Peyote is one of the deities of the religion. The Native American Church is sometimes called the Peyote Church.

A crescent-shaped earthen altar six or seven feet long lies west of the fire, and a large peyote cactus, symbolic of Father Peyote, is placed at the midpoint of the crescent. Prayers may be directed to Father Peyote, and some members can hear him responding to their pleas for help in meeting the difficulties of life. The intense feeling of dedication and piety at Peyote Meetings is expressed through prayers and testimonies, often with tears running down the cheeks of the speakers. Prayers include appeals to Jesus and God as well as to Father Peyote. Peyotists consider the Native American Church to be hospitable to all other religions and include their ideas in its philosophy and beliefs. Members pray for friends and family members who are ill or otherwise in need of help. They also include leaders of the church, of the Navajo tribe, and of the country at large in their prayers.

In the past the Native American Church was bitterly opposed by the more tradition-minded Navajos; in the late 1940s meetings were raided by the police and church leaders were jailed. But the church constituency grew so large that the new religion had to be accepted, and today the tepees for peyote meetings can be seen in many Navajo communities. One of these tepees stands near the Cultural Center of Diné College, where participation in the Native American Church's meetings is a recognized student activity.

Another importation of a Native American religion, the Plains Sun Dance, has occurred as recently as the 1980s on the Navajo reservation. This world renewal ceremony has undergone a revival on the Plains, and Sun Dance priests have been invited to Navajo communities to perform the ceremony and teach it to Navajo participants.

Navajo Hymn Music

Christian hymns share the popularity of peyote hymns, as evidenced by the several hundred requests per week that radio stations such as WGLF in Gallup, New Mexico, receive. The Navajos who have joined the many Christian missions on the reservation appreciate them especially for their ministry. The hospitals, schools, and other services associated with the missions are a boon not only to church members but also to hundreds of other Navajos.

Navajo listeners make requests for particular hymns on the occasion of a birthday in the family, the anniversary of a death, or some other signal family event. When the request and the hymn are broadcast, the occasion is made known to hundreds of listeners. The hymns may be performed by nationally known gospel singers, but Navajo gospel singers as well have made records, and requests tend to favor these. One such group is the Chinle Galileans, a Navajo country gospel group **(CD 1, Track 10).** Their lyrics are in English, and their music is the familiar country combination of electric guitar and percussion. Listen to their recording of "Clinging to a Saving Hand."

 CD 1:10

"Clinging to a Saving Hand" (3:41). Traditional Christian hymn. Performed by the Chinle Galileans. Navajo Country Gospel LPS 909. LP. Chinle, Arizona, n.d.

Close Listening	CD 1:10
"Clinging to a Saving Hand"	

Counter Number	Commentary
Introduction	
0:00	Electric pedal steel guitar, piano, and drums.
Chorus—Lyric	
0:18	*Sing me a song of grace and glory* *Help this wondering child to understand* *So when I close my eyes in sleep eternal* *I'll be clingin' to a saving hand.*
1st verse—Lyric	
0:51	*Sing to me about the rock of ages* *Sing about eternity so sweet* *So that when I take my last breath of life* *I'll awaken at my savior's feet.*
1:21	Chorus.

(continued)

Counter Number	Commentary
Break	
1:52	Electric pedal steel guitar solo. Piano and drums accompany.
2nd verse—Lyric	
2:24	*Tell me about Paul and Matthew* *Sing about my dear savior's birth* *Tell about his trials and tribulations* *While he walked upon this heathen earth.*
2:55	Chorus.
Coda—Last line of chorus repeats	
3:25	*I'll be clingin' to a savin' hand.*

Reprinted by permission of Roland Dixon.

Interestingly, this music has few features that could be called traditionally Indian. Like the Fenders (see earlier section and Figure 2.4), the Galileans have adopted a new style of music wholeheartedly. The clues that the performers are Navajos are the singers' Navajo accent and, in the case of the Fenders' CD selection, certain melodic and rhythmic flexibility, compared with the Anglo original. This is what appeals to Navajo listeners and makes them feel that the performing groups are some of "their own."

New Composers in Traditional Modes

A recent genre of Navajo music comprises songs based musically on Enemy-way style (usually Sway songs or Dance songs) but not intended for use in that ceremony. The texts are in Navajo, because the songs are intended for Navajo listeners, but they contain a different sort of social commentary from that in the popular songs of Enemyway. The new message is one of protest. For example, we can contrast the treatment of the use of alcohol in the old songs and the new. First we have a Skip Dance song from Enemyway, probably dating from the 1920s.

'E- ne- ya,
My younger brother,
My whiskey, have some! *Nana, he, ne-ye,*
My younger brother,
My whiskey, have some! *Nana, he, ne-ye,*
Your whiskey is all gone, *ne,*
My whiskey, there's still some, *wo,*
He yo-o-wo-wo, he yo-o-wo-wo,
Heya, we, heyana, he, nai-ya.

In contrast, "Navajo Inn" speaks of the damaging effects of drinking. It is a recent song by Lena Tsoisdia, who is a social service worker at Window Rock, the headquarters of the Navajo tribal government. The title takes its name from a drive-in liquor store that used to do a thriving business a few miles from Window Rock. The store was just across the reservation's boundary and thus fell outside the jurisdiction of the tribal prohibition laws. The lyrics refer to the store and speak despairingly of women finding their husbands, unconscious, behind "the tall fence."

Such protests cover many topics, from modern problems to historical injustice. Ruth Roessel, a prominent Navajo educator, has composed a song about the "Long Walk," when the Navajos were rounded up by Kit Carson and his troops in 1864 and forcibly removed to a large concentration camp at Fort Sumner, New Mexico (see map, Figure 2.5). The hardships of the march, which preceded four years of captivity, and the Navajo love for their land are recounted here.

Long, long ago, our people,
Our grandfathers, our grandmothers,
Walking that long distance,
There was no food, there was no water,
But they were walking a long distance,
But they were walking a long distance!
At Fort Sumner, it was when they got there
They were treated badly,
They were treated badly.
"I wish I were still back in my own home,
I wish I were still back in my own home!
We shall never forget this,
The walk that we are taking now.
We shall never forget this,
The walk that we are taking now.
Even then, we still like our own land,
Even then, we still like our own land!"

With permission of Ruth Roessel. Translation by Ruth Roessel for David McAllester.

The two examples here have not been recorded commercially, but several Navajo composers of new songs in styles based on Enemyway popular songs have recorded their work on popular discs. Kay Bennett (Kaibah) produced three records on her own label. Danny Whitefeather Begay, Cindy Yazzie, and Roger McCabe have released *My Beautiful Land* on the Canyon Records label with fifteen popular songs in this new genre. Recently, Navajo music has seen a new genre: music with newly created Navajo texts and melodies. This genre is well represented by Sharon Burch. "She credits her inspiration as a songwriter to the songs, prayers and chants she recalls from her childhood" (Burch 1989).

Arliene Nofchissey Williams has been called "the Navajo nightingale." Her compositions stem from the Mormon sect of Christianity and express, musically and in words, both her religious perceptions and her Indian heritage. She wrote one of her songs, "Proud Earth," when she was a student at Brigham Young University. Musically, there are such Indian elements as the use of a steady, repetitive drumbeat and vocables, as well as Euro-American elements such as a string orchestra, harmonies, interpretive dynamics, and English text. The use of the voice of the late Chief Dan George, an Indian film star, as narrator adds to the richness of the production. The song has been a "hit" on the Navajo reservation and elsewhere among Indian people. It was produced in Nashville with all the musical technology that the name implies, and a more recent rendition can be heard on Williams (1989).

This song tells the world what the Native Americans feel they have to contribute to world culture from their poetic myths and philosophy of nature. The words reflect the Mormon respect for Native American culture and the Indian closeness to nature. At the same time, the song conveys the aspiration of the Latter Day Saints to unite the Indian people under one God.

The beat of my heart is kept alive in my drum,
And my plight echoes in the canyons, the meadows, the plains,
And my laughter runs free with the deer,
And my tears fall with the rain,
But my soul knows no pain.

I am one with nature,
Mother Earth is at my feet,
And my God is up above me,
And I'll sing the song of my People.

Come with me, take my hand, come alive with my chant (*heya, heya*)
For my life already knows wisdom, balance and beauty.
Let your heart be free from fear (*heya, heya*)
And your joy meet with mine,
For the peace we can find.

We are one with nature,
Mother Earth is at our feet,
And our God is up above us,
And we'll sing the song, the song of the people (*heya, heya*),
And we'll sing the song, the song of the people.

―――――――
"Proud Earth" by Arliene Nofchissey Williams. With permission of Arliene Nofchissey Williams.

The Native American Flute Revival

The Native American flute revival probably began in the 1970s in Oklahoma when "Doc Tate" Nevaquaya made the first commercial recording consisting entirely of music of the Plains courting flute (Smythe 1989:68). But it was a Navajo, R. Carlos Nakai (Figure 2.10), whose moving, improvi-

Figure 2.10
R. Carlos Nakai, Navajo flutist and educator.

John Running

satory compositions, often with synthesizer or orchestral accompaniments, carried the instrument to worldwide popularity and created a large following of imitators, both Indian and non-Indian (McAllester 1994). Nakai's first album appeared in 1982; since then he has made nineteen others, one of them in Germany and another in Japan. *Cycles* (1985) was chosen by the Martha Graham Dance Company to provide the music for their ballet *Nightchant.* Nakai has performed with several symphony orchestras and was awarded the Arizona Governor's Arts Award in 1992 and an honorary doctorate by Northern Arizona University in 1994. In that same year, *Ancestral Voices*, his third collaboration with the guitarist William Eaton, was a Grammy Awards finalist in Best Traditional Folk Music. In all of his work the commentary accompanying the music stresses respect for the environment and a Navajo celebration of tribal connections and harmony with nature.

In the latter part of this chapter, we have explored the music of several generations and several religions in an effort to find clues to the thought of just one Indian tribe. Even so we have barely touched on the complexities of this rich and rapidly changing culture. One of the most powerful messages that reaches the outsider is that Indian traditional culture remains vital in its own ways even while Native American people are adopting new ideas and technology from the Euro-American culture around them. This fact is clearly reflected in the many different kinds of music that coexist on the Navajo reservation and in thousands of Navajo homes in Chicago, Los Angeles, San Francisco, and many other locations away from the reservation.

To varying degrees this picture of Navajo music exemplifies what is happening in other Indian communities around the country. The different Indian cultures have embarked on an adventure in which the larger population around them must inevitably share. Many Indian elements have already become part of the culture that is called "American." Some of these are relatively superficial: an Indian word such as *squash* or *moose,* or a bit of local legend. Other contributions have produced an enormous economic impact, such as the corn and potatoes that feed much of the world. There is now evidence that some of the music and the other Indian arts, and the religious and philosophical ideas that lie beneath them, are becoming accessible to an increasingly sympathetic American public. No culture remains static, and the Indians will continue to contribute to other world cultures, which are themselves in the process of change.

Study Questions

1. How is Native American music diverse and complex?

2. Why is it misleading to consider the vocables in a Yeibichai song meaningless?

3. What is the name of the ceremony that contains the Yeibichai songs? What is the purpose of the ceremony? What are some of its features?

4. Compare the Fenders' recording of "Folsom Prison Blues" with that of Johnny Cash. What are the similarities and differences? How have the Fenders made the song their own?

5. How is the song "Shizhané'é" meant to be humorous? Why is the understatement of the lyrics more effective than a fuller text would be?

6. How do traditional Navajos understand the causes and cures for disease? What is the role of music in curing? How does this compare with your understanding of disease and curing?

7. Summarize the Enemyway ceremony among the Navajo. What is its purpose? What are some of its features?

8. How does the music of the Native American Church differ from traditional Navajo music? What might account for that difference?

9. What are the differences between traditional and new music among the Navajos? What purposes does the new music serve?

Note on Navajo Pronunciation ♫♫♫

'	the accent mark indicates a glottal stop, as in "oh-oh!" (ó-ó)
v	is unvoiced with the breath coming out on either side of the tongue, as in the Welsh ll in Flloyd
aa	indicates a long *a* as in lake. Likewise, other double vowels—**oo** (as in mole), **ee** (as in beet), **ii** (as in bite), **uu** (tube)—indicate a long vowel sound.
á	indicates a nasal *a* as in can. Other vowels with the same accents take a nasal sound.
é	indicates an e at a high pitch. (Navajo has speech tones like Chinese.)
ée	indicates a long e (as in beet) falling from a high to low tone.

Vowels have "continental values."

Glossary

call-and-response A musical form in which one part seems to be linked as a "response" to the previous part. The response part appears to be an "answer" or "comment" on the first or "call" part.

Enemyway ceremony An elaborate curing ritual among the Navajos featuring many songs and war drama.

falsetto A high voice that comes from the head rather than the chest.

field recordings Recordings made with portable gear on location rather than in a recording studio.

flageolet An end-blown wind instrument like the recorder except that two of the holes are in the back and closed with the thumbs, whereas on the recorder one is in the back and is closed with the left thumb.

longhouse Among the Iroquois, a meetinghouse with a stove at each end of the hall and benches along the sides.

Native American Church A religious movement that began in Mexico in the nineteenth century and spread to the United States, particularly the American Southwest. Its music, rituals, and beliefs combine Christian and Native elements.

Ndáá' **songs** War dance songs, the largest body of traditional popular music among the Navajo; the "hit tunes" of traditional Navajo life.

portamento See *slide.*

powwow A traditional Native American ceremonial and spiritual gathering featuring food, singing, and dancing.

slide Sounding all the frequencies between two pitches of an interval in sequence, upward or downward, as in the sound produced by a slide-whistle; synonymous with *portamento.*

tail The last brief section of a song; an Indian term similar to *coda* in Western classical music theory.

tempo Apparent speed of a piece of music; how slow or fast it appears to be going.

tonic In Western music theory, the basic tone, or note, of a melody or a section of a piece; the most important pitch; usually the pitch that occurs most often; often the last tone of a melody, the pitch that the melody seems to be gravitating toward.

vocables Syllables that do not make up words; "nonsense" syllables that may nonetheless have meaning in that they signify or symbolize something.

Resources

References

Burch, Sharon. 1989. *Yazzie Girl.* Phoenix, Ariz.: Canyon Records CR534. Cassette j-card.

Faris, James C. 1990. *The Nightway: A History and a History of Documentation of a Navajo Ceremonial.* Albuquerque: Univ. of New Mexico Press.

Fenton, William. 1942. *Songs from the Iroquois Longhouse.* Washington, D.C.: Smithsonian Institution Publication 369.

———. n.d. *Songs from the Iroquois Longhouse.* Library of Congress AFS L6.

Haile, Berard. 1938. *Origin Legend of the Navajo Enemy Way.* New Haven, Conn.: Yale Univ. Press.

Kluckhohn, Clyde, and Dorothea Leighton. 1938. *The Navajo.* Cambridge, Mass.: Harvard Univ. Press.

McAllester, David P. 1949. *Peyote Music.* New York: Viking Fund Publications in Anthropology, no. 13.

———. 1954. *Enemy Way Music.* Papers of the Peabody Museum of Archaeology and Ethnology, vol. 41, no. 5. Cambridge, Mass.: Harvard Univ. Press.

———. 1994. "The Music of R. Carlos Nakai." In *To the Four Corners: A Festschrift in Honor of Rose Brandel,* edited by Ellen C. Leichtman. Warren, Mich.: Harmonie Park Press.

Nakai, R. Carlos. 1985. *Cycles: Native American Flute Music.* Phoenix, Ariz.: Canyon Records Productions CR614-C. Cassette.

Reichard, Gladys A. 1928. *Social Life of the Navajo Indians.* New York: Columbia Univ. Press.

Smythe, Willie. 1989. "Songs of Indian Territory." *In Songs of Indian Territory: Native American Music Traditions of Oklahoma.* Oklahoma City, Okla.: Center for the American Indian.

Williams, Arliene Nofchissey. 1989. *Encircle . . . in the Arms of His Love.* Composed and performed by Arliene Nofchissey Williams, featuring flutist John Rainer, Jr. Blanding, Utah: Proud Earth Productions PE-90. Cassette.

Witherspoon, Gary. 1977. *Language and Art in the Navajo Universe.* Ann Arbor: Univ. of Michigan Press.

Witmer, Leland C. 1973. "Recent Change in the Musical Culture of the Blood Indians of Alberta, Canada." *Yearbook for Inter-American Musical Research* 9:64–94.

Additional Reading

Bailey, Garrick, and Roberta Glenn Bailey. 1986. *A History of the Navajos: The Reservation Years.* Santa Fe, N. Mex.: School of American Research Press.

Deloria, Vine, Jr. 1969. *Custer Died for Your Sins: An Indian Manifesto.* London: Collier-Macmillan.

Densmore, Frances. 1910. *Chippewa Music.* Washington, D.C.: Bureau of American Ethnology Bulletin 45.

Dyk, Walter. 1966. *Son of Old Man Hat.* Lincoln: Univ. of Nebraska Press.

Goodman, James B. 1986. *The Navajo Atlas: Environments, Resources, People, and the History of the Diné Bikeyah.* Norman: Univ. of Oklahoma Press.

Hadley, Linda. 1986. *Hózhóójí Hané' (Blessingway).* Rough Rock, Ariz.: Rough Rock Demonstration School. [In English and Navajo.]

Kurath, Gertrude P. 1966. *Michigan Indian Festivals.* Ann Arbor, Mich.: Ann Arbor Publishers.

Mitchell, Frank. 2003. *Navajo Blessingway Singer.* 2nd ed. Edited by Charlotte Frisbie and David P. McAllester. Albuquerque: Univ. of New Mexico Press.

Neihardt, John G. 1961. *Black Elk Speaks.* Lincoln: Univ. of Nebraska Press.

Underhill, Ruth M. 1953. *Red Man's America.* Chicago: Univ. of Chicago Press.

Additional Listening

Anilth, Wilson, and Hanson Ashley. 1981. *Navajo Peyote Ceremonial Songs.* Vol. 1. Taos, N. Mex.: Indian House 1541. LP.

Boniface Bonnie Singers. 1968. *Navajo Sway Songs.* Taos, N. Mex.: Indian House 1581. LP.

Boulton, Laura. 1957. *Indian Music of the Southwest.* Washington, D.C.: Smithsonian/Folkways 8850. LP. With 11-page booklet.

———. 1992. *Navajo Songs.* Recorded by Laura Boulton in 1933 and 1940. Annotated by Charlotte Frisbie and David McAllester. Washington, D.C.: Smithsonian/Folkways SF 40403. CD, cassette.

Burch, Sharon. 1989. *Yazzie Girl.* Phoenix, Ariz.: Canyon Records CR534. CD, cassette.

Burton, Bryan. 1993. *Moving within the Circle: Contemporary Native American Music and Dance.* Danbury, Conn.: World Music Press WMP 012. Cassette.

The Chinle Galileans. n.d. *Navajo Country Gospel.* Larry Emerson, Jerry Tom, Roland Dixon, Donnie Tsosie, Lee Begaye, Emerson Luther. Chinle, Ariz.: LPS 9039. LP.

DeMars, James. 1991. *Spirit Horses, Concerto for Native American Flute and Chamber Orchestra.* Composed for and performed by R. Carlos Nakai. Phoenix, Ariz.: Canyon Records Productions CR-7014. CD, cassette.

The Fenders. 1966. *Second Time 'Round.* Thoreau, N. Mex. LP. Patrick Hutchinson made a careful study of "Folsom Prison Blues," noting interesting textual and rhythmic elisions and complications not found in the original Johnny Cash recording. These are similar to alterations noted by Robert Witmer in popular music performed by Blood Indians in Canada (1973:79–83).

Four Corner Yeibichai. 1988. Phoenix, Ariz.: Canyon Records Productions 7152. LP, cassette.

Iroquois Social Dance Songs. 1969. 3 vols. Ohsweken, Ontario, Canada: Iroqrafts QC 727. LP.

Isaacs, Tony. 1968. *Night and Daylight Yeibichai.* Taos, N. Mex.: Indian House IH 1502. LP.

My Beautiful Land and Other Navajo Songs. n.d. Danny Whitefeather Begay, Cindy Yazzi, and Roger McCabe. Phoenix, Ariz.: Canyon Records Productions ARP 6078. LP.

Nakai, R. Carlos. 1985. *Cycles: Native American Flute Music.* Phoenix, Ariz.: Canyon Records Productions CR614-C. CD, cassette.

Rhodes, Willard. 1949. *Music of the Sioux and the Navajo.* Washington, D.C.: Smithsonian/Folkways 4401. LP. With 6-page pamphlet.

Rhodes, Willard, ed. n.d. *Navajo: Folk Music of the United States.* Washington, D.C.: Library of Congress, Division of Music, Archive of American Folk Song AFS L41.

———. n.d. *Puget Sound: Folk Music of the United States.* Washington, D.C.: Library of Congress, Division of Music, Archive of American Folk Song AAFS L34. With 36-page booklet on Northwest Coast culture (Erna Gunther) and music (Willard Rhodes).

Sioux Favorites. n.d. Phoenix, Ariz.: Canyon Records Productions ARP 6059. Cassette.

Smith Family Gospel Singers. 1987. *Touching Jesus.* Vol. 2. Phoenix, Ariz.: Canyon Records 620. Cassette.

Songs from the Navajo Nation. n.d. Recorded by Kay Bennet (Kaibah). Gallup, N. Mex.: K. C. Bennet (producer). LP.

Williams, Arliene Nofchissey. 1989. *Encircle . . . in the Arms of His Love.* Composed and performed by Arliene Nofchissey Williams, featuring flutist John Rainer, Jr. Blanding, Utah: Proud Earth Productions PE-90. Cassette.

———. n.d. *Proud Earth.* Performed by Chief Dan George, Arliene Nofchissey Williams, and Rick Brosseau. Provo, Utah: Salt City Records SC-60. LP.

XIT. 1972. *Plight of the Red Man.* Detroit: Motown Record Corp. R536L. LP. Protest songs in rock style; XIT is an acronym for "Crossing of Indian Tribes," in reference to the pantribal makeup of the group.

Major Sources for Recordings

Canyon Records Productions, 3131 W. Clarendon Ave. Phoenix, Ariz. 85017-4513; (800) 268-1141. This is the main distributor of Native American recordings. It not only stocks the large inventory under its own label but also keeps in print many of the recordings of smaller distributors, some of which might otherwise have gone out of business. It carries recordings of traditional music and also newer genres such as Indian rock, gospel, and country and western.

Indian House, Box 472, Taos, N. Mex. 87571; (505) 776-2953. This company specializes in traditional Indian music and typically devotes an entire recording to one genre such as Taos Round Dance songs or Navajo Yeibichai songs. The abundant examples and the excellent notes make these recordings valuable for scholars as well as other interested listeners.

Library of Congress. Archive of Folk Culture, Motion Picture, Broadcast, and Recorded Sound Division, Library of Congress, Washington, D.C. 20540;

(202) 707-7833. This collection includes the Willard Rhodes recordings of Native American music: excellent recordings and notes from all across the country.

Smithsonian/Folkways. The Folkways Collection, Smithsonian Institution, Office of Folklife and Heritage, Washington, D.C. 20560; (202) 275-1140. The inventory of the Ethnic Folkways Records and Service Corp., formerly of New York City, has been preserved at the Smithsonian Institution and new recordings on a joint label are being produced. Their holdings include many early recordings of Native American music.

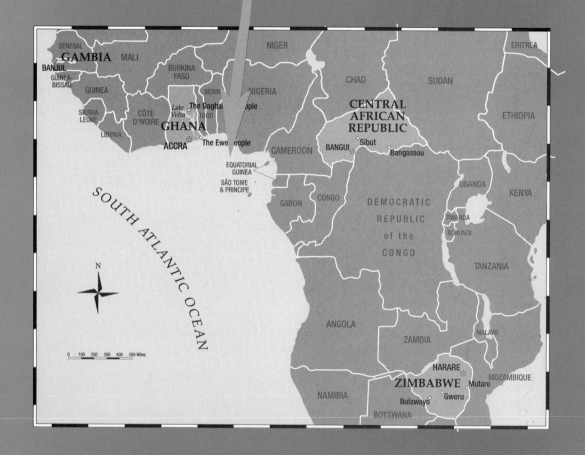

CHAPTER

3

Africa/Ewe, Mande, Dagbamba, Shona, BaAka

David Locke

Consider a misleadingly simple question: Where is Africa's beginning and end? At first you might say that they lie at the borders that mark the continent. But musically, Africa spills over its geographic boundaries. Calling to mind the narrow Strait of Gibraltar, the Suez Canal, the often-crossed Red and Mediterranean Seas, and the vast Atlantic Ocean, we realize that people from Africa have always shaped world history. If we invoke images—Egypt, Ethiopia, the Moors, Swahili civilization, commerce in humans and precious metals—we know that Africa is not separate from Europe, Asia, and America. As pointed out in Chapter 1, music is humanly made sound; it moves with humankind in our explorations, conquests, migrations, and enslavement. This chapter, therefore, refers us not only to the African continent but also to the many other places we can find African music-culture.

Another question: What music is African music? We could be poetic and say, "Where its people are, there is Africa's music—on the continent and in its diaspora." The truth, however, is messier. Music is never pure; music-cultures are always changing and being shaped by many outside influences. From Benin and Luanda to Bahia, Havana, London, and Harlem, music-cultures blend along a subtle continuum. African-influenced music now circulates the planet by means of electronic media. After people learn new things about music, their own music-cultures adjust.

The African continent has two broad zones: (1) the Maghrib, north of the Sahara Desert, and (2) sub-Saharan Africa. North Africa and the Horn of Africa have much in common with the Mediterranean and western Asia; Africa south of the Sahara in many ways is a unique cultural area. Even so, history records significant contacts up and down the Nile, across the Sahara, and along the African coasts. Just as civilizations from the north (Greece, Rome) and east (Arabia, Turkey) have made an indelible impact on northern Africa, the south has influenced the Maghrib as well. Similarly, Africa south of the Sahara has been isolated from the Old World civilizations of Europe

Salient Characteristics of Africa ♪♪♪

- African continent divided into two broad cultural zones: the Maghrib, north of the Sahara Desert, and sub-Saharan Africa in the south.
- Can be viewed symbolically, psychologically, and geographically.
- Defining the term *African* involves numerous factors that make up individual identity.
- More than a thousand different tribes are spread throughout Africa's fifty-three countries.
- Profound effect of African music on music throughout the world.

and Asia. As this chapter will show, the history and cultural geography of sub-Saharan Africa vary tremendously (see Bohannan and Curtin 1995).

Permit an ungrammatical question: When is an African? In everyday circumstances, people in Africa do not usually think of themselves as "African" (Mphahlele 1962). Identity arises from local connections of gender, age, kinship, place, language, religion, and work. Ethnicity comes into play only in the presence of people from a different group. One "becomes" a Serer, so to speak, in the presence of a Wolof, an African when among the French, a white in the company of a black, a yellow, a red (Senghor 1967). Rather than marking essential characteristics of individuals, these terms suggest relationships among people. Although physical appearance and genetic inheritance do not determine culture, the bogus concept of "race" persists, feeding the ignorance that spawns prejudice and the bigotry that fosters injustice (Appiah 1992). Such labels should therefore be marked: USE WITH CARE.

"Africa" serves as a resonant symbol for many people. People of African descent, wherever they are in the world, may regard Africa as the ancestral homeland, the place of empowerment and belonging (Asante 1987). Industrialized citizens of "information societies" may envision Africa as either a pastoral Eden or the impoverished Third World. Historically regarded as a land of "heathens" by Muslims and Christians, Africa is a fount of ancient wisdom for those who practice religions such as *santería* or *vodun.* Famine relief and foreign aid, wilderness safari and Tarzan, savage or sage—Africa is a psychic space, not just a physical place.

The sections that follow introduce five African music-cultures. They show Africa's diversity and some of its widely shared characteristics. Information for two of the sections comes from my own field research; other sections are based on the ethnomusicological scholarship of colleagues— Roderic Knight, Paul Berliner, Michelle Kisliuk, and the late James Koetting. The cooperative effort that underlies this chapter seems fitting, because one vital function of African music is to mold separate individuals into a group.

I n Chapter 1, you first heard the sounds of African postal workers canceling stamps (**CD 1, Track 1**). As promised, we shall revisit this intriguing
recording, this time examining how it reflects some of the general characteristics of African music-culture. To start, recall Koetting's description:

> This is what you are hearing: the two men seated at the table slap a letter
> rhythmically several times to bring it from the file to the position on the
> table where it is to be canceled (this act makes a light-sounding thud). The
> marker is inked one or more times (the lowest, most resonant sound you
> hear) and then stamped on the letter (the high-pitched mechanized sound
> you hear). . . . The rhythm produced is not a simple one-two-three (bring
> forward the letter—ink the marker—stamp the letter). Rather, musical
> sensitivities take over. Several slaps on the letter to bring it down, repeated
> thuds of the marker in the ink pad and multiple cancellations are done for
> rhythmic interest. . . .
>
>   The other sounds you hear have nothing to do with the work itself.
> A third man has a pair of scissors that he clicks—not cutting anything,
> but adding to the rhythm. . . . The fourth worker simply whistles along.
> He and any of the other three workers who care to join him whistle
> popular tunes or church music that fits the rhythm. (Koetting 1992:98-99)

How does this musical event exemplify widely shared characteristics of
African music-culture?

Generalizations about African Music-Culture

Music-Making Events

A compelling feature of this recording is its setting. Canceling stamps can
sound like this? How marvelous! Obviously, the event was not a concert,
and this most definitely is not art for art's sake. Like work music everywhere, this performance undoubtedly lifted the workers' spirits and
enabled them to coordinate their efforts. The music probably helped the
workers maintain a positive attitude toward their job. Music often helps
workers control the mood of the workplace (Jackson 1972). (See "Music of
Work" in Chapter 4.)

   African music often happens in social situations where people's
primary goals are not artistic. Instead, music is for ceremonies (life cycle
rituals, festivals), work (subsistence, child care, domestic chores, wage
labor), or play (games, parties, lovemaking). Music making contributes to
an event's success by focusing attention, communicating information,
encouraging social solidarity, and transforming consciousness.

Expression in Many Media

Just as Africans set music in a social context, they associate it with other
expressive activities (drama, dance, poetry, costuming, sculpture). Indeed,
this example is unusual because it is a wordless instrumental. Although
music making is usually not the exclusive purpose of an event, people do
value its aesthetic qualities (see Chapter 1). Music closely associated with a
life event is also enjoyed at other times for its own sake.

Postal Workers
Canceling Stamps

 CD 1:1

Postal workers canceling stamps at
the University of Accra, Ghana, post
office (2:58). The whistled tune is the
hymn "Bompata," by the Ghanaian
composer W. J. Akyeampong (b. 1900).
Field recording by James Koetting.
Legon, Ghana, 1975.

Musical Style

The whistled tune probably seems familiar to many listeners. It is a hymn called "Bompata," written by the Ghanaian composer W. J. Akyeampong (b. 1900). While the melody has European musical qualities, the percussion exhibits African stylistic features such as polyrhythm, repetition, and improvisation.

History

These observations about genre and style lead to an important point about the history of music in Africa: The music-cultures of Europe, Asia, and the Americas have strongly affected those in Africa. Foreigners—Christians and Muslims, sailors and soldiers, traders and travelers—have brought to Africa their instruments, musical repertories, and ideas. Modern media technologies such as radio and audio recording have only increased the intensity of an old pattern of border crossing. Like people everywhere, Africans have imitated, rejected, transformed, and adapted external influences in a complex process of culture change.

The concert music repertory of Europe has historically attracted few Africans; however, many other outside musical traditions have affected African music making. Throughout Africa, Christianity and Islam have exerted a profound influence on musical style. West Asian civilization has had an effect on African musical instruments such as the plucked lutes, double reeds, and goblet-shaped drums of the Sahel area. Euro-American influence shows up in the electric guitar and drum set, although East Asians manufacture many of these instruments. We hear the American influence of Cuban rumba on pop music from central Africa, and African American spirituals on southern African religious music. From praise singers to pop bands, musical professionalism is an idea about music that developed in Africa by means of the intercultural exchange of ideas.

Participation

On the CD track, the postal workers join simple musical parts together to make remarkably sophisticated and satisfying music. This kind of musical design welcomes social engagement. Others could participate by adding a new phrase to the polyrhythm or cutting a few dance moves. Undoubtedly, Koetting "got down" while picking up his mail! Much African music shares this generous, open-hearted quality that welcomes participation.

Training

We admire the postal workers because their music seems effortlessly beautiful. The genius we sense in this recording lies in the way the workers are musical together, in their sensitivity to a culturally conditioned musical style. Here, a musical education depends on a society-wide process of *enculturation*, that is, the process of learning one's culture gradually during childhood. Babies move on the backs of their dancing mothers, youngsters play children's games and then join adults in worship and mourning, teenagers groove to pop tunes. Raised in this manner, Africans learn a way-of-being in response to music; intuitively, they know how to participate effectively. Genetic and sacred forces may shape musicality, but culture is the indispensable element in musical training.

Beliefs and Values

Often, Africans conceive of music as a necessary and normal part of life. Neither exalted nor denigrated as art, music fuses with other life processes. Traditional songs and musical instruments are not commodities separable from the flux of life. In his book *African Music: A People's Art,* Francis Bebey quotes a musician who was asked to sell his instrument:

> He replied rather dryly that he had come to town to play his drum for the dancing and not to deliver a slave into bondage. He looked upon his instrument as a person, a colleague who spoke the same language and helped him create his music. (1975:120)

Intercultural Misunderstanding

These beliefs and attitudes about music make intercultural understanding a challenge, especially for scientifically minded people from what might be called concert-music-cultures. What a non-African listener assumes is an item of music may be the voice of an ancestor to an African. When he recorded this example, Koetting found himself in this type of cross-cultural conundrum:

> It sounds like music and, of course, it is; but the men performing do not quite think of it that way. The men are working, not putting on a musical show; people pass by the work place paying little attention to the "music" (I used to go often to watch and listen to them, and they gave the impression that they thought I was somewhat odd for doing so). (1992:98)

Toward Participation

I, too, think this recording "sounds like music," but I hesitate to say that "it *is* music," because that would imply that the postal workers share my ideas about music. However, even though they do not "quite" regard this as music, what they are doing sounds great to me. I want to participate. In my music-culture, analysis through close listening can be an effective path toward active involvement, a bridge into the musical style of another culture. I use the tools of musical analysis with caution, however, because music can never be pinned to cardboard like a lifeless butterfly. For many Africans, music is "a living thing ensouled by the spiritual energy that travels through it" (Amoaku 1985:37).

This example gives us a feeling for African music in general. The next example affords a more detailed look at a type of music with profound connections to the history of a specific African ethnic group, the Ewe people.

Counter Number	Commentary
0:00	Fade in during last phrase of the tune.
0:08	Complete rendition of tune; two-part harmony; restrained percussion.
0:44	Another time through the tune; solo whistle.
1:27	Brief interlude before another time through the tune; two-part harmony.
2:04	Another time through the tune; melodic invention in whistling and rhythmic variety in percussive accompaniment.
2:44	Fade out as next repetition begins.

Salient Characteristics of the Ewe and Their Music

- Founded settlements near the mouth of the Volta River.
- Society based on territorial divisions headed by chiefs.
- Unit of social life is the extended family.
- In worldview, religion permeates all aspects of family and community life.
- *Agbekor* (extended music and dance performance) an important cultural and musical event in Ewe life.

Agbekor: Music and Dance of the Ewe People

Drawing on my field research in West Africa during the 1970s, we now consider a type of singing and drumming called *Agbekor* (pronounced ah-*gbeh*-kaw). As we shall hear on **CD 1, Tracks 11 and 12**, *Agbekor*'s music features a percussion ensemble and a chorus of singers. A complex lead drumming part rides on a rich polyrhythmic texture established by an ensemble of bells, rattles, and drums of different sizes. Songs are clear examples of call-and-response. *Agbekor* is a creation of Ewe-speaking people (*eh*-way) who live on the Atlantic coast of western Africa in the nation-states of Ghana and Togo.

The Ewe People

History

Triumph over adversity is an important theme in Ewe oral history. Until they came to their present territory, the Ewe people had lived precariously as a minority within the kingdoms of more populous and powerful peoples such as the Yoruba and the Fon. One prominent story in their oral traditions recounts their exodus in the late 1600s from Agokoli, the tyrannical king of Notsie, a walled city-state located in what is now southern Togo. Intimidating Agokoli's warriors with fierce drumming, the Ewes escaped under cover of darkness. Moving toward the southwest, they founded many settlements along a large lagoon near the mouth of the Volta River.

In these new lands, the Ewe communities grew and multiplied. Eventually the small Ewe settlements expanded into territorial divisions whose inhabitants could all trace male ancestors to the original villages. Family heads or distinguished war leaders became chiefs. Despite bonds of common culture and history, each division zealously cherished its independence. The Ewe people have never supported a hierarchical concentration of power within a large state (compare them with the Mande and Dagbamba kingdoms, discussed later in this chapter).

Ever since those early days, the important unit of Ewe social life has been the extended family. Members of a lineage—that is, people who can trace their genealogy to a common ancestor—share rights and obligations. Lineage elders hold positions of secular and sacred authority. The ever-present spirits of lineage ancestors help their offspring, especially if the living perform the necessary customary rituals.

Religious Philosophy

An Ewe scholar has commented on the sacred worldview of his people:

> A traveler in Anlo is struck by the predominating, all-pervasive influence of religion in the intimate life of the family and community. . . . The sea, the lagoon, the river, streams, animals, birds and reptiles as well as the earth with its natural and artificial protuberances are worshipped as divine or as the abode of divinities. (Fiawo 1959:35, in Locke 1978:32)

The Ewe supreme being, Mawu, is remote from the affairs of humanity. Other divinities, such as Se (seh), interact with things in this world. Se embodies God's attributes of law, order, and harmony; Se is the maker and keeper of human souls; Se is destiny. Many Ewes believe that before a spirit enters the fetus, it tells Se how its life on earth will be and how its body will die. If you ask Ewe musicians the source of their talent, they will most likely identify the ancestor whose spirit they have inherited. Ask why they are so involved in music making, and they will say it is their destiny.

Ancestral spirits are an important force in the lives of Ewe people.

> The Ewe believe that part of a person's soul lives on in the spirit world after his [or her] death and must be cared for by the living. This care is essential, for the ancestors can either provide for and guard the living or punish them. (Nukunya 1969:27, in Locke 1978:35)

Funerals are a significant social institution, because without ritual action by the living, a soul cannot become an ancestral spirit. A funeral is an affirmation of life, a cause for celebration because another ancestor can now watch over the living. Because spirits of ancestors love music and dance, funeral memorial services feature drumming, singing, and dancing. Full of the passions aroused by death, funerals have replaced war as an appropriate occasion for war drumming such as *Agbekor*.

Knowledge of Ewe history and culture helps explain the great energy found in performance pieces like *Agbekor*. Vital energy, life force, strength—these lie at the heart of the Ewe outlook:

> In the traditional . . . Anlo society where the natural resources are relatively meager, where the inexplicable natural environment poses a threat to life and where the people are flanked by warlike tribes and neighbors, we find the clue to their philosophy of life: it is aimed at life. (Fiawo 1959:41, in Locke 1978:36)

Agbekor: History and Contemporary Performance

Legends of Origin

During my field research, I interviewed elders about how *Agbekor* began. Many people said it was inspired by hunters' observations of monkeys in the forest. According to some elders, the monkeys changed into human form, played drums, and danced; others say that the monkeys kept their animal form as they beat with sticks and danced. Significantly, hunters, like warriors, had access to esoteric power.

> In the olden days hunters were the repository of knowledge given to men by God. Hunters had special herbs. . . . Having used such herbs, the hunter could meet and talk with leopards and other animals which eat human beings. . . . As for Agbekor, it was in such a way that they saw it and brought it home. But having seen such a thing, they could not reveal it to others just like that. Hunters have certain customs during which they drum, beat the double bell, and perform such activities that are connected with the worship of things we believe. It was during such a traditional hunting custom that they exhibited the monkey's dance. Spectators who went to the performance decided to turn it into a polished dance. There were hunters among them because once they had revealed the dance in the hunting customary performance they could later repeat it again publicly. But if a hunter saw something and came home to reveal it, he would surely become insane. That was how Agbekor became known as a dance of the monkeys. (Kwaku Denu, quoted in Locke 1978:38-39)

Although many Ewes consider them legend rather than history, stories like this signify the high respect accorded to *Agbekor*. Hunters were spiritually forceful leaders, and the forest was the zone of dangerously potent supernatural forces. We feel this power in a performance of *Agbekor*.

Agbekor as War Drumming

The original occasion for a performance of *Agbekor* was war. Elders explained that their ancestors performed it before combat, as a means to attain the required frame of mind, or after battle, as a means of communicating what had happened.

> They would play the introductory part before they were about to go to war. When the warriors heard the rhythms, they would be completely filled with bravery. They would not think that they might be going, never to

I conducted these interviews with the assistance of a language specialist, Bernard Akpeleasi, who subsequently translated the spoken Ewe into written English.

return, for their minds were filled only with thoughts of fighting. (Elders of the Agbogbome Agbekor Society, quoted in Locke 1978:44)

Yes, it is a war dance. It is a dance that was played when they returned from an expedition. They would exhibit the things that happened during the war, especially the death of an elder or a chief. (Alfred Awunyo, quoted in Locke 1978:43)

If they were fighting, brave acts were done. When they were relaxing after the battle, they would play the drums and during the dance a warrior could display what he had done during the battle for the others to see. (Kpogo Ladzekpo, quoted in Locke 1978:43)

The Meaning of the Name *Agbekor*

I asked whether the name *Agbekor* has meaning. One elder told me this:

> I can say it signifies enjoying life: we make ourselves happy in life. The suffering that our elders underwent was brought out in the dance, and it could be that when they became settled, they gave the dance this name, which shows that the dance expresses the enjoyment of life." (Kwaku Denu, quoted in Locke 1978:47)

Another elder told me that when people played *Agbekor* during times of war, they called it *Atamuga* (ah-*tam*-gah), which means "the great oath." Before going to battle, warriors would gather with their war leaders at shrines that housed spiritually powerful objects. They would swear on a sacred sword an oath to their ancestors to obey their leaders' commands and fight bravely for their community. (Kpogo Ladzekpo, quoted in Locke 1978:45–46)

The word *Agbekor* is a compound of two short words: *agbe* ("life") and *kor* ("clear"). The professional performer Midao Gideon Foli Alorwoyie translates *Agbekor* as "clear life": The battle is over, the danger is past, and our lives are now in the clear (Locke 1978:47). Many people add the prefix *atsia* (plural *atsiawo*), calling the piece *atsiagbekor* (ah-chah-*gbeh*-kaw). The word *atsia* has two meanings: (1) stylish self-display, looking good, or bluffing and (2) a preset figure of music and dance. As presented shortly, the form of the lead drumming and the dance consists of a sequence of *atsiawo*.

Learning

In Ewe music-culture, most music and dance is learned through enculturation. *Agbekor*, on the other hand, requires special training. The eminent African ethnomusicologist J. H. K. Nketia describes learning through slow absorption without formal teaching:

> The very organization of traditional music in social life enables the individual to acquire his musical knowledge in slow stages. . . . The young have to rely largely on their imitative ability and on correction by others when this is volunteered. They must rely on their own eyes, ears and memory. They must acquire their own technique of learning. (Nketia 1964:4)

Gideon Alorwoyie explains how one learns from the performance of an expert:

> All you have to do is know when he is going to play. . . . You have to go and pay attention to what you hear . . . to how the drums are coordinated and to the drum language, to what the responses are to the calls, and so on. You have to use your common sense right there to make sure that you get the patterns clear. Up to today, if you want to be a drummer, you go to the place where people are playing and then pay attention and listen. That's it. (Davis 1994:27)

Because of its complexity *Agbekor* is hard to learn in this informal way. Members of an *Agbekor* group practice in a secluded area for up to a year before they appear in public. Instruction entails demonstration and emulation. With adept dancers in front, the whole group performs together. No one breaks it down and analyzes it. People learn sequences of movement and music not through exercises but in a simulated performance context. (Compare this with the teaching of *karnataka sangeeta,* described in Chapter 6.)

This style of learning depends on gifted students. A precocious youngster may be the reincarnation of an ancestor who was a renowned musician. One village drummer told me of a special drummer's ritual:

> My father was a drummer and he taught me. It was when he was old and could no longer play that he gave me the curved sticks. A ceremony has to be performed before the curved sticks are handed over to you. . . . If the custom is not done the drum language will escape your mind. (Dogbevi Abaglo, quoted in Locke 1978:53)

Gideon Alorwoyie explains the effects of this ritual:

> Once the custom has been made, you can't sleep soundly. The rhythms you want to learn will come into your head while you sleep. . . . The ceremony protects the person in many ways. It protects your hands when you play and protects you from the evil intentions of other people who may envy you. (Locke 1978:54–55)

Performing Organizations

Times have changed since Ewe hunters created *Agbekor.* Britain, Germany, and France administered Ewe territory during a brief colonial period (1880s to the 1950s); now the Ewe people live in the nation-states of Ghana and Togo. Today, relatively few villages have preserved their heritage of *Agbekor.* But the tradition vigorously continues within mutual aid organizations, school and civic youth groups, and theatrical performing companies. Throughout Africa, voluntary mutual aid societies are an important type of performing group (Ladzekpo 1971). Many members are poor and cannot afford funeral expenses. People solve this financial problem by pooling resources. When a member dies, individuals contribute a small amount so the group can give a lump sum of cash to the family. The society's performance of music and dance makes the funeral grand.

Godwin Agbeli

Figure 3.1
The Anya Agbekor Society
(with the author) in performance.

In the mid-1970s I studied *Agbekor* with members of this type of cooperative society, the Anya Agbekor Society of Accra (see Figure 3.1). One of their leaders recounted how the group came into existence:

> The first Anya Agbekor group in Accra was formed by our elder brothers and uncles. They all scattered in the mid-sixties and that group died away. We, the younger ones, decided to revive it in 1970. Three or four people sat down and said, "How can we let this thing just go away? Agbekor originated in our place, among our family, so it is not good to let it go." We felt that it was something we had to do to remember the old family members. (Evans Amenumey, quoted in Locke 1978:63)

I also studied with school groups trained by my teacher Godwin Agbeli. In colonial times, missionaries whipped students for attending traditional performance events. These days, most Ewes value their traditional repertory of music and dance as a cultural resource. Since Ghana achieved statehood in 1957, the national government has held competitions for amateur cultural groups from the country's many ethnic regions. Young people often join groups because rehearsals and performances provide social opportunities. Like many African nations, Ghana sponsors professional performing-arts troupes. With its spectacular, crowd-pleasing music and dance, *Agbekor* is a staple of their repertory.

A Performance

On Sunday, March 6, 1977, in a crowded working-class section of Accra, the Anya Society performed in honor of the late chief patron of the group. The evening before, the group had held a wake during which they drummed *Kpegisu* (Locke 1992). Early Sunday morning they played *Agbekor* briefly to announce the afternoon's performance. People went home to rest and returned to the open lot near the patron's family house by 3:30 in the afternoon for the main event.

The performance area was arranged like a rectangle within a circle. Ten drummers sat at one end, fifteen dancers formed three columns facing the drummers, ten singers stood in a semicircle behind the dancers, and about three hundred onlookers encircled the entire performance area. All drummers and most dancers were male. Most singers were female; several younger women danced with the men. Group elders, bereaved family members, and invited dignitaries sat behind the drummers. With the account book laid out on a table, the group's secretary accepted the members' contributions.

The action began with an introductory section called *adzo* (ah-*dzo*), that is, short sections. Dancers sang songs in free rhythm. After the *adzo*, the main section, *vutsotsoe* (voo-*tsaw*-tso-eh), that is, fast drumming, started. The first sequence of figures honored the ancestors. Following this ritually charged passage, the dancers performed approximately ten more *atsiawo*. The lead drummer spontaneously selected these "styles" from the many drum and dance sequences known to the group. The singers were also busy. Their song leader raised up each song; the chorus received it and answered. One song was repeated five to ten times before another was begun.

After about twenty minutes the *adzokpi* (ah-*dzoh*-kpee) section of the performance began. Group members came forward in pairs or small groups to dance in front of the lead drummer. The dance movement differed for men and women. Friends invited each other to move into the center of the dance space. When everyone had their fill of this more individualistic display, the lead drummer returned to the group styles. Soon, he signaled for a break in the action by playing the special ending figure.

During the break, the group's leaders went to the center of the dance area to pour a libation. Calling on the ancestors to drink, elders ceremonially poured water and liquor onto the earth. An elder explained later:

> We pour libation to call upon the deceased members of the dance [group] to send us their blessings [so we can] play the dance the same way we did when they were alive. How the Christians call Jesus, call God, though Jesus is dead—they do not see him and yet they call him—it is in the same manner that we call upon the members of the dance [group] who are no more so that their blessings come down upon us during the dancing. (Kpogo Ladzekpo, quoted in Locke 1978:82–83)

The performance resumed with *vulolo* (voo-*law*-law), that is, slow drumming, the processional section of *Agbekor*. After about fifteen minutes, they went straight to *vutsotsoe*, the up-tempo section, and then *adzokpi*, the "solos" section. After a brief rest they did another sequence of group figures at slow and fast pace, followed by individual display.

At the peak of the final *adzokpi* section elders, patrons, and invited guests came out onto the dance area. While they danced, singers and dancers knelt on one knee as a mark of respect. After dancing back and

Perhaps because the word *atsia* means "stylishness," many English-speaking Ewe musicians refer to the preformed drum and dance compositions as "styles."

forth in front of the drummers, they returned to their position on the benches in back of the drummers.

By 6:00, with the equatorial sun falling quickly, the performance had ended. As the group members contentedly carried the equipment back to the Anya house, the audience dispersed, talking excitedly about the performance.

Although a performance of *Agbekor* follows a definite pattern, it is not rigidly formalized. A. M. Jones, a pioneering scholar of African music, has commented on the elasticity of African musical performance: "Within the prescribed limits of custom, no one quite knows what is going to happen: It depends quite a lot on the inspiration of the leading performers. These men [and women] are not making music which is crystallized on a music score. They are moved by the spirit of the occasion." (Jones 1959:108)

Songs

Texts

Agbekor songs engage the subject of war. Many songs celebrate the invincibility of Ewe warriors; others urge courage and loyalty; some reflect on death and express grief. Songs memorialize heroes but do not provide detailed historical information. Unlike the freshly composed songs found in contemporary idioms of Ewe traditional music, *Agbekor* songs come from the past. A song's affective power derives, in part, from its association with the ancestors.

Structural Features

In performance, a song leader and a singing group share the text and melody. This call-and-response idea supports a variety of subtly different musical forms. Perhaps because the tonal system of *Agbekor* songs has evolved without being influenced by musical instruments, singers' intonation seems aimed at pitch areas rather than precise pitch points (compare with tuning in South Indian music-culture, Chapter 6). Melodic motion usually conforms to the rise and fall of speech tones, but Ewe speakers easily understand song lyrics even if the melodic contour contradicts the tonal pattern of the spoken language. Songs add another layer to the rhythm of *Agbekor*. On **CD 1, Track 11**, we hear excerpts from my recording of a performance by an *Agbekor* group from the town of Anlo-Afiadenyigba on August 14, 1976.

 CD 1:11

Agbekor (5:32). Traditional music of the Ewe people. Field recording by David Locke. Anlo-Afiadenyigba, Ghana, 1976.

a. Three slow-paced songs (0:00–2:52)
b. One song in free rhythm (3:02–4:20)
c. One fast-paced song (4:27–5:35)

Close Listening
CD 1:11

Agbekor vulolo (slow-paced section)

Counter Number	Commentary
0:00	Fade in on song 1.
0:05	One time through song 1.
0:38	Song leader begins song 1 again, but group raises song 2 so song leader joins them.
0:48	Song 2 sung seven times, each time taking about 10 seconds.
2:01	Song 3.
2:19	Song 3 repeated.
2:38	Fade out during repetition of song 3.

Song 1 announces that people should prepare for the arrival of the *Agbekor* procession.

Leader: ‖: *Emiawo miegbona afeawo me.*
        Afegametowo/viwo, midzra nuawo do.
Group: Repeat lines 1 and 2. :‖
Leader: ‖: *Oo!*
Group: *Midzra nuawo do.*   :‖
All: Repeat lines 1 and 2.
Leader: ‖: We are coming into the homesteads.
            People/Children of the noble homes, get the things ready.
Group: Repeat lines 1 and 2. :‖
Leader: Oh!
Group: Get the things ready.

Song 2, set at sunrise on the day of battle, urges Manyo and his warriors to "be cunning."

Leader: *Agbekoviawo, midze aye.*
Group: *Ada do ee,*
        Kpo nedze ga nu.
        Ada do!
Leader: *Manyo hawo, midze aye ee*
Group: Repeat lines 2–4.
Leader: *Agbekor* group, be cunning.
Group: The day has come.
        Beat the double bell.
        The day has come.
Leader: Manyo's group, be cunning.
Group: Repeat lines 2–4.

Close Listening   CD 1:11

Agbekor adzo (free rhythm interlude)

Counter Number	Commentary
2:50	Silence between recorded selections.
3:02	Song 4.
3:37	Exhortation from lead drum and song leader.
3:41	Song 4 repeated.

Song 3 expresses an important sentiment in *Agbekor* songs: celebrating the singers' power and denigrating the opponent; here, the enemy is a "horn-less dog," that is, an impotent person, and "we" are incomparably great.

Leader: ‖: *Avu matodzo,*
        Dewoe lawuma?
Group: Repeat lines 1 and 2.   :‖
Leader: ‖: *Dewoe?*
Group: *Dewoe lawuma?*
All: *Avu matodzo*
        Dewoe lawuma?
Leader: A hornless dog.
        Are there any greater than we?
Group: Repeat lines 1 and 2.
Leader: Any?
Group: Greater than we
All: Repeat lines 1 and 2.

Song 4 compares the Agbekor group's strength with the power of the ocean and derides the potency of the enemy's weapons.

Leader: ‖: *'Gbekoviwo, xe de ado ahoyo gbe,*
        Be tsawoyo?
Group: *Xe ke lado gbe,*
        Gavi tsawoyo?   :‖
Leader: *Tu nedi!*
Group: *Miahee de alada me.*
Leader: *Hewo nu,*
Group: *Miahee de alada me.*
All: *Be la bada fo soshi*
        Ko de alada me.
        Tu la kaka,
        Mietsoe da de agboawo dzi
        Xe de mado ahoyo gbe ee?

Avusu Kpowoe mado lo na xe
Be xe nedo dika na alado me.
Tsawoyo
Repeat lines 3 and 4.

Leader: ‖: Members of the *Agbekor* group, can a bird cry like the sea, "Tsawoyo?"
Group: Which bird can cry like the sea, "Gavi Tsawoyo?"   :‖
Leader: Fire the gun!
Group: We will turn it aside!
Leader: The tips of knives,
Group: We will brush them aside!
All: A wild animal has found a horsetail switch
And put it at his side.
The gun broke,
We put it on the barricade.
Can a bird cry like the sea?
Avusu Kpo and his people cannot talk in proverbs to the bird.
[unknown]
"Tsawoyo."
Repeat lines 3 and 4.

Song 5 opens with the vivid image of a confrontation between two war gods (*So*). The Fon from Dahomey and the Anlo are about to fight; the beautiful warriors are preparing; will they have the courage to enter the fray?

Leader: ‖: *So kpli So, ne ava va gbedzia*
Tsyo miado.
Group: *Woyawoya*
Ava va gbedzia,
Tsyo miado.   :‖
Leader: *Oo,*
Group: *Fowo do gbea,*
Miayia?
Anlowo do gbe.
Leader: *Oo,*
Group: *Anawo do gbea*
Tsyo miado.
All: Repeat lines 3–5.
Leader: ‖: So and So—if war breaks out on the battlefield
We will have to dress gorgeously.
Group: "Woyowoya"
War breaks out on the battlefield.
We have to dress gorgeously.   :‖
Leader: Oh,
Group: The Fon are out on the battlefield,
Should we go?
The Anlo are out on the battlefield.

Agbekor vutsotsoe (fast-paced section)

Counter Number	Commentary
4:18	Silence between recorded selections.
4:26	Song 5 sung three times, each time taking about 18 seconds.
5:22	Fade out as new song is raised.

Leader: Oh,

Group: The cowards are out on the battlefield.
          Should we go?
          The Anlo are out on the battlefield.
          Repeat lines 3–5.

Music of the Drum Ensemble

We now turn to music of the percussion ensemble for the slow-paced section of *Agbekor*. Instruments in the *Agbekor* ensemble include a double bell (*gankogui*), a gourd rattle, and four single-headed drums (see Figure 3.2). Listen to **CD 1, Track 12**, to hear the bell by itself, followed by each instrument with the bell (*axatse, kaganu, kidi, kloboto,* and *totodzi*), and finally the polyrhythm of all the parts. *Note:* I have chosen not to present the music of the lead drum here. Not only is the material quite complicated, but I believe it best if students approach lead drumming only after a significant period of study, preferably with an Ewe teacher.

CD 1:12

Demonstration: *Agbekor* (3:53). Performed by David Locke. You will hear the bell by itself, followed by each instrument with the bell (*axatse, kaganu, kidi, kloboto,* and *totodzi*), and finally, the polyrhythm of all the parts.

Demonstration: *Agbekor* percussion ensemble

Counter Number	Commentary
0:00	*Gankogui* part played solo; phrase occurs twelve times; each phrase starts on high-pitched tone and ends on low-pitched tone; slight variation during final repetition.
0:34	Duet of *axatse* and *gankogui* parts; starts during second occurrence of bell phrase.
1:07	Duet of *kaganu* and *gankogui* parts; starts during second occurrence of bell phrase.
1:40	Duet of *kidi* and *gankogui* parts; starts during second occurrence of bell phrase.
2:13	Duet of *kloboto* and *gankogui* parts; starts during second occurrence of bell phrase.
2:46	Duet of *totodzi* and *gankogui* parts; starts during second occurrence of bell phrase.
3:19	Full percussion ensemble; starts during second occurrence of bell phrase.

Figure 3.2
Agbekor ensemble. (Drawing by
Emmanuel Agbeli)

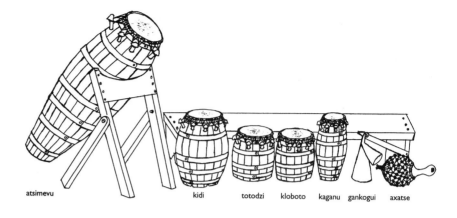

atsimevu   kidi   totodzi   kloboto   kaganu   gankogui   axatse

One by one the phrases are not too difficult, but playing them in an ensemble is surprisingly hard. The challenge is to hear them within a polyphonic texture that seems to change depending on one's point of musical reference. The reward in learning to play these parts is an experience of African musical time.

"Listen to the bell"—that is the continual advice of Ewe teachers. Every act of drumming, singing, and dancing is timed in accordance with the recurring musical phrase played on an iron bell or gong called a *gankogui* (gahng-*koh*-gu-ee). On first impression, the part may seem simple, but when set in the rhythmic context of Ewe drumming, it becomes a musical force of great potency. Repetition is key. As the seven strokes in the phrase repeat over and over (long-short-long-long-long-short-long), participants join together in a circling, spiraling world of time. As the part repeats in polyrhythmic context, the musical ear groups the bell tones into a variety of patterns. Although the sonic phenomena never change, the part appears different. We experience an aural illusion.

The *axatse* (ah-*ha*-tseh) is a dried gourd about the size of a cantaloupe covered with a net strung with seeds. In some *Agbekor* groups its role is to mark four equal units within each bell phrase. (I refer to these units as the "four-feel beats."). In another frequently heard phrase, downward strokes on the player's thigh match the *gankogui* while upward strokes against the palm fill in between bell tones. The rattle phrase is like the flesh on the bones of the bell phrase; it fills in between all bell strokes except the low-pitched one. To me, that longer duration makes the low-pitched bell stroke feel like the end of the phrase. As the only instrument played by many people at once, the *axatse* "section" is vital to the ensemble's energy.

The high pitch and dry timbre of the slender *kaganu* (kah-gahng) drum cuts through the more mellow, midrange sounds of the other drums. Many Ewe teachers advise students to focus on the synchrony between *kaganu* and bell tones 3 and 4. The *kaganu* phrase is quite short—just two notes; it occurs four times over the span of one bell phrase. *Kaganu* marks a ternary structure within each four-feel beat (silence-stroke-stroke). The late Freeman Donkor, one of my first teachers of Ewe music, said that the rhythm of *kaganu* brings out the flavor of the other parts, like salt in a stew.

The *gankogui, axatse,* and *kaganu* parts create a distinctive quality of musical temporal experience (Locke 1988:16–36). The long and short tones in the bell phrase sculpt time into asymmetrical proportions. Symmetrical units also are important: the duration of the bell phrase is a literal measure of time; the tones of *kaganu* mark that measure into four equal ternary units. All four beats are strong, but the moments when bell and beat fall together are specially marked in musical awareness. These stable qualities of musical time provide the solid rhythmic foundation for the shifting offbeats found in the songs and lead drumming.

In descending order of relative pitch, the three other drums in the ensemble are *kidi, kloboto,* and *totodzi* (*kee*-dee, *kloh*-boh-toh, and toh-toh-*dzee*). Each drum adds its own phrase to *Agbekor*'s unique polyphony. There are two ways of striking a drum skin. In bounce strokes the stick bounces off the drum skin, producing an open ringing sound; in press strokes the stick presses into the drum skin, producing a closed muted sound. Bounces contribute the most to the group's music; presses keep each player in a groove.

- The *kidi* part has three bounces and three presses.
- The *kloboto* part's main idea is a brief bounce-press, offbeat-onbeat figure. *Kloboto's* insistent accentuation of offbeat moments can reorient a listener into perceiving them as onbeats, adding to the multidimensional quality of the music.
- The *totodzi* part has two bounce strokes that match bell tones and three press strokes that match four-feel beats 3, 4, and 1.

To get into the drumming, begin by hearing each phrase in duet with the bell. Then, hear ever-larger combinations with other parts. The point is to explore the potency of these phrases, not to create new ones. Stretch your way of hearing, rather than what you are playing. Strive for a cool focus on ensemble relationships, not a hot individual display (Thompson 1973).

Drum Language

Ewe drum phrases often have vernacular texts, usually known only by drummers. Secrecy makes restricted information valuable and powerful. In many parts of Africa "speech must be controlled and contained if silence is to exercise its powers of truth, authenticity, seriousness and healing" (Miller 1990:95).

During my field research, I asked many experts whether they knew drum language for *Agbekor.* Saying he learned them from elders in his hometown of Afiadenyigba, Gideon Alorwoyie shared the following with me. *Agbekor*'s themes of courage and service are apparent. His word-for-word and free translations appear beneath the following Ewe text of *Agbekor* drum language.

Totodzi   *Dzogbe dzi dzi dzi.*
             battlefield/on/on/on
             We will be on the battlefield.

Kloboto	'Gbe dzi ko mado mado mado.
	Battlefield/on/only/I will sleep/I will sleep/I will sleep
	I will die on the battlefield.
Kidi	Kpo afe godzi. Kpo afe godzi.
	Look/home/side-on. Look/home/side-on.
	Look back at home. Look back at home.
Kaganu	Miava yi afia.
	We will come/go/will show.
	We are going to show our bravery.

As we have seen, *Agbekor* is a group effort. Music and dance help cement social feeling among members of an *Agbekor* society. Others types of African music depend more on the virtuosity and special knowledge of individuals. We turn now to an example of such a solo tradition. Information for the next section of the chapter draws primarily on the research of the ethnomusicologist Roderic Knight.

Mande Jaliya: "Lambango"

On **CD 1, Track 13**, we hear the artistry of Mariatu Kuyateh (vocal), her husband, Kekuta Suso (stringed instrument), and Seni Jobateh (speech and percussion) as they perform the piece "Lambango" in praise of three twentieth-century Gambian leaders. You may be drawn toward Kuyateh's wordy solo song and Suso's virtuosity on the *kora* (a twenty-one-string bridge harp). These experts in speech, song, and the playing of instruments are often called *griots* (*gree*-oh). Not only musicians, they are counselors to royalty, entertainers for the public, and guardians of history (see Figure 3.3).

Figure 3.3
Mariatu Kuyateh and Kekuta Suso (with *kora*). Boraba, the Gambia, 1970.

Roderic Knight

Salient Characteristics of the Mande and Their Music ♪♪♪

- Live in the West African savanna.
- *Jalolu* or *griots* (professional musicians) transmit the oral history of the Mande through songs.
- *Jalolu* held secure social position serving wealthy patrons within the Mali empire.
- *Jalolu* musical craft learned through master–apprentice training.
- Vocal solos commonly accompanied by the *kora*, a twenty-one-string bridge harp.

The performers, who call themselves *jalolu* (singular *jali*), are professional "sound artisans" of the Mande ethnic tradition (see Charry 2000). *Jaliya*, that is, what *jalolu* do, has played many important roles in Mande civilization since the thirteenth century, when Sunjata Keita founded the empire of Mali. At its apogee (fourteenth to sixteenth centuries), Mali exerted authority over a vast territory of river and grassland stretching west from the Upper Niger to the Atlantic coast. Age-old patterns of Mande culture remain influential today.

Historical and Social Background

Cultural Crossroads

Distinct civilizations meet in the West African savanna south of the desert and north of the forest—Sudanic African, Tuareg, Berber, Arab, European. The routes of intercultural communication run north and south as well as east and west. For Arabic speakers on trading caravans between the Mediterranean and the Sudan (*Bilad es Sudan*, "Land of the Blacks"), the Sahara was a sand sea. The semiarid Sahel was its southern "coast." East–west travel followed rivers such as the Gambia, the Senegal, and most importantly the Niger, whose seasonal floods fostered an agricultural base for empire.

Mali

A succession of great states arose in this broad cultural crossroads: first Ghana, then Mali, Songhai, Kanem-Bornu, Hausa, Mossi, and others. Mali was fabulously wealthy. It was a centralized, hierarchically organized empire with distinct social classes. Islamic libraries and universities of world renown flourished in great cosmopolitan cities. A class of literati (writing in Arabic) operated the empire's systems of commerce and law. The duty of Mande *jalolu* was to serve this array of wealthy patrons.

> The jali held the only records of genealogy and history and was the only one who knew and could perform the music called for on important occasions. The people who most often employed the services of these people were in a position to provide ample recompense in the form of lodging, cattle, clothing and other manifestations of wealth. For the jali . . . this meant that he was virtually assured of permanent patronage. . . . As one jali has put it, "The jali was king." (Knight 1984:62)

Learning helped determine one's status in such cities as Timbuktu. Some intellectuals became praise singers (*muddah*) who received alms for lauding the Prophet Muhammad (Saad 1983:86). Such refined professionals included erudite *jalolu.* In the Islamic Sudan, the formal exchange of praise for wealth remains a respected institution. In this music-culture, gifts to a *jali* are not commercial payments for products sold but rather are respectful offerings that mark the interdependence of praiser and praised.

Although the political leaders were nominally Muslim, the bulk of the population kept faith with pre-Islamic religion. Some Mande peoples still retain a mythic consciousness that links natural landmarks to the primordial, creative feats of superhuman ancestors (Dieterlen 1957, in Skinner 1973). In addition to serving their elite patrons, the *jalolu* transmit these ancient, secret mysteries to every member of society (Laye 1983).

After 1600, the history of these Sudanic empires is a story of fracture and gradual decline. Forces of change included internal rebellion, invasion by a Moroccan expeditionary force (1591), the Atlantic slave trade (1700s), Islamic jihads (1800s), and finally British and French colonialism (1900s). All the while, in songs like "Lambango," the Mande bards told legends of the empire's founder, Sunjata Keita, and news of more recent heroes.

Kingdoms along the Gambia

At the western edge of the Mande heartland, many small kingdoms formed along the Gambia River. Modeled on the much larger empires of the Upper Niger, each state had its hierarchy of royals, courtiers, warriors, state officials, merchants, clerics, and so on. Prospering through trade with Europe— notably, slaves for manufactured goods—the elite were remarkably cosmopolitan.

> French traders in the eighteenth century reported that the *mansas* of Niumi [kings of a state on the north bank of the Gambia] lived in European-style houses and dressed in elaborate costumes. . . . [One] mansa's daughter, who was said to read and write French, Portuguese and English, had established herself as the chief intermediary between the traders and her father. At one time married to a Portuguese, she lived in a large square European house and held soirees for the commercial community in a style that boasted fine table linen and other imported luxuries. (Quinn 1972:41)

A distinctive music-culture of *jali* with *kora* developed in these kingdoms along the Gambia.

Music-Culture

Social Organization

Where do the *jalolu* fit within the Mande system of social rank and its associated roles? Slavery existed in this African society; even today, descendants of the freeborn (*horon*) are distinguished from persons of slave descent (*jong*), especially in the matter of marriage. Among the freeborn, *nyamalo*— craft specialists including *jalolu*—occupy a separate niche from *sula*—

nonspecialists, including royals, Islamic literates, merchants, and farmers—who are a *jali*'s prospective patrons. Among *nyamalo*, boys inherit their fathers' craft as a lifelong profession; young women marry within their fathers' occupational group (see Knight 1984:60–66).

Duties to Patrons

In former times when kings were rich, *jali* and patron shared a mutually beneficial relationship. Playmates as children, they retained their intimacy as adults.

> Griots woke the king each morning by singing his praises outside his quarters, they accompanied him wherever he traveled, singing and playing behind him and especially when he met another king, they were in attendance singing their patron's praises. From time to time a court griot would entertain the king and members of his court by reciting accounts of the careers of some of the king's forebears, perhaps of some deeds of the king himself. . . . The whole narration glorified the king, often bathing him in the reflected glory of his mighty ancestors. . . . [The griot] would take real pride in [this] history and would want to present it in the best possible light, for he would surely feel able to share in the glory of his patron's family. (Innes 1976:5)

Before our era, the *jali* received the wholehearted respect merited by a learned artist with significant duties in the affairs of state. A *jali*'s performance bridged time and space, bringing the historical and mythic past into the lives of the living.

> When the jali sings the name of a past hero, he views what he is doing as waking him up, bringing him back to life (*Mb'a wulindila*). . . . If in the end the listener can say of the music, *Wo le dunta n na* (It has entered me), then the desired effect will have been achieved." (Knight 1984:73)

This music-culture changed after the Gambia became a British protectorate in 1894. Because the wealth of the royals was much reduced, their patronage alone could not sustain a *jali*. Thus today, *jalolu* must serve a broader clientele by freelancing at social occasions such as weddings and naming ceremonies where people value their knowledge and artistry. Yet even in our cash-oriented, dislocated world, where an African royal may hold a menial job in Europe, the *jalolu* retain warm relations with their patrons and provide a vital link to profound dimensions of Mande culture.

Transmission

A *jali* learns the craft of playing a musical instrument through formal apprenticeship with a single master. During adolescence and young adulthood, fathers send their sons to a relative who enforces a strict training regimen. Some *jalolu* specialize in the *kora;* others play xylophone (*balo*) or a plucked, long-neck lute (*konting, ngoni,* or guitar). Young women, whose primary duty is to sing, participate in a more informal apprenticeship. While they serve their elders, young *jalolu* gradually learn an impressive body of knowledge. *Jalolu* keep elaborate genealogies and stories of their patrons' forebears.

More than dry objective historical accounts, their performances entail rousing artistry designed to elicit the respect and gratitude of an audience.

The *Jali's* Knowledge

A key element in *jaliya* is speech (*kuma*). Songs contain wise sayings about people and situations that are always relevant to the living. Here are some examples (Knight 1984:78–80):

Islamic fatalism:	"Before God created life, he created death."
Moral judgments:	"The talkative kings are plentiful, but men of great deeds are few."
Advice:	"The world is ever-changing. If someone doesn't know your past, don't tell him your present affairs."
Observations:	"Life is nothing without conversation."
On wealth:	"The wealthy inherit the wealth."
On *jaliya*:	"For the person who puts one hundred in my hand, I will give him a hundred-worth praise with my mouth."

Elements of Performance

Kora

The *kora* is an indigenous African instrument with a unique array of parts (Figure 3.4). Scholars of musical instruments (organologists) classify the instrument as a spiked bridge harp: "spiked" because its straight neck passes entirely through the large, skin-covered, half-calabash resonator, "bridge" because the strings pass through notches on the sides of a high bridge, and "harp" because the plane of the strings is perpendicular to the soundboard (see Charry 1994, 2000; DeVale 1989; Knight 1971, 1972).

Figure 3.4
The *kora.*

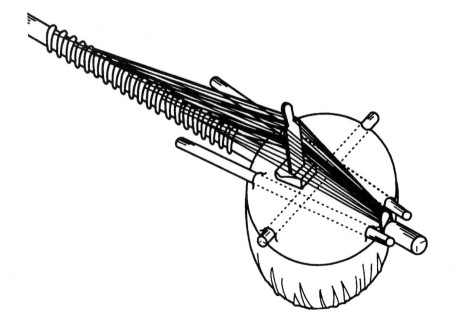

The *kora* has left and right sides, just like the human body. Plucking in left-right alternation, the player takes full advantage of this bilateral symmetry. Sometimes a flat metal rattle attached to the bridge enhances the flavor of the rhythm and timbre. As in "Lambango," pieces may call for *konkon,* an ostinato (repeated phrase) rapped on the resonator. By adjusting the tuning rings along its neck, the *jali* tunes his *kora*'s twenty-one strings in patterns of seven pitches per octave. Just as the tonality of each Javanese *gamelan* is a unique variant of a general standard, the intervals between pitches on a *kora* are not precisely reckoned against an invariant abstract standard.

As in most music-cultures, Mande musicians metaphorically link musical pitch to physical space through words like *high-low* and *ascend-descend.* English speakers and Mande speakers, however, use these terms in opposite ways (Charry 2000:325–27). For instance, *kora* players call the bass strings "high," the treble strings "low." This is because the longer, thicker strings are physically above the shorter, thinner strings when a *jali* holds the instrument. An ascending passage in Western terms "goes down" for the *kora* player.

During performance, when the emphasis is on text, the *kora* player accompanies the singer with *kumbengo,* an instrumental ostinato. Virtuosic instrumental passages (*birimintingo*) provide interludes between vocal sections. On **CD 1, Track 13,** Suso accompanies Kuyateh by playing *kumbengo* with occasional *birimintingo*-like passages.

During apprenticeship, lessons focus on the *kumbengo.* Talented youngsters pick up *birimintingo* riffs as they listen to their master's playing. Interestingly, a master does not teach tuning until an apprentice is ready to leave. "Giving him an actual lesson on how to tune the instrument is regarded as the final key to his independence. This lesson is therefore withheld from him until his master feels he is fully qualified to embark on his own career" (Knight 1984:77).

CD 1:13

"Lambango" (2:56). Mande song. Mariatu Kuyateh. Performed by Mariatu Kuyateh, Kekuta Suso, and Seni Jobateh. Field recording by Roderic Knight. The Gambia, 1970.

Verbal Art

The "Lambango" recording shows that singers can mix several styles of verbal presentation in one performance. At different points in a performance, *jalolu* may tell stories in everyday speech, chant narrative songs associated with specific heroes, sing tunefully, or declaim highly formulaic praises and proverbs. The preferred timbral quality, a forceful chest resonance sung with a tensed throat, evokes the strength of the Mande heroes in sound itself.

The vocalist works with two building blocks of form: *donkilo,* a tune with several phrases of text, and *sataro,* an open-ended, extemporaneous passage of spoken or chanted text. In her performance of "Lambango," Kuyateh begins by ever so briefly singing the tuneful *donkilo;* the rest of the performance is *sataro.* As Jobateh taps the *konkon* part, he interjects comments and praises with stylized speech.

Close Listening   CD 1:13

"Lambango"   *(Texts and translation by Alhaji Papa Susso, and Roderic Knight)*

Counter Number	Commentary
0:00–1:27	Praises for Musa Molo.
0:05–0:10	Spoken announcement, "I am Kekuta Suso, with Seni Jobateh and Mariatu Kuyateh. We are recording here today."
0:13–0:26	Donkilo sung by Kuyateh.
1:17–1:22	*Wo ka mansaya ke, duniya; wolu bee, i jamano banta.* Those people made kingship in this world; all of them, their days are gone.
1:27–2:42	Praises for Dembo Danso.
1:49–1:53	*Wo fanang mu ninsi dimba le ti. A ka a dingolu balundi, aning wandi dingolu balundi.* He was like a mother cow. He could feed his own young and those of others too.
2:22–2:28	*Ntelu keta konoba ti. M be yaarana; sita yoro te n na. I salam aleka.* We [jalis] have become like vultures. We are soaring; we have no place to sit down. My peace be upon you.
2:42–3:00	Praises for Jewunu Kurubali.
2:50–2:53	*Sibo banta. I salam aleka.* The great one is gone. Peace be upon you.

Women (*jali musolu*) set the standard for all singers. As one *jali* told Roderic Knight:

> A *ngara* [superior singer] is a woman who is not afraid of crowds, not afraid of anything, except God. She can stand before a crowd with all eyes upon her and not become confused (*kijo fara*). She can shout (*feten*), literally "split" the air with her voice, but do it with feeling (*wasu*) and sentiment (*balafa*), so that people will sympathize with her. She sticks to her forte (*taburango*) in performing, never jumbling the words together (*faranfansandi*) so that they are unintelligible, but choosing words which contain the essences of her message (*sigirango*), words which all listeners will agree are true (*sahata*). (Nyulo Jebateh, quoted in Knight 1984:74)

A Drummer of Dagbon

CD 1:14

"Nag Biegu" ("Ferocious Wild Bull") (2:04). Traditional Praise Name Dance song of Dagbon. Performed by *lunsi* drummers of the Dagbamba people. Field recording by David Locke. Ghana, 1984.

Musicians have had important functions in the political affairs of many African traditional states. We turn now to the life story of one such person.

On **CD 1, Track 14**, we hear singing and drumming of the Dagbamba people (also known as Dagomba) from the southern savanna of western Africa (Ghana). I recorded the music in 1984. The performers are *lunsi* (*loon*-see; singular *lunga*, pronounced *loong*-ah), members of a hereditary clan of drummers. Like a Mande *jali*, a *lunga* fulfills many vital duties in the life of the Dagbamba—verbal artist, genealogist, counselor to royalty,

> ### Salient Characteristics of Dagbamba and Their Music ♪♪♪
>
> - Live in the southern savanna of western Africa in present day Ghana.
> - Centralized and hierarchical kingdom.
> - *Lunsi* (drummers) are members of a hereditary clan.
> - *Lunsi* each act as speech artist, family historian, royal advisor, cultural specialist, and entertainer.
> - Drummed texts make up choruses of some songs.

cultural expert, entertainer. The *lunsi* tradition developed in Dagbon, the hierarchical, centralized kingdom of the Dagbamba (Chernoff 1979; Djedje 1978; Locke 1990).

The Drums

Lunsi play two kinds of drums—*gung-gong* (goong-*gawng*) and *lunga* (see Figure 3.5). For both types, a shoulder strap holds the drum in position to receive strokes from a curved wooden stick. The *gung-gong* is a cylindrical, carved drum with a snare on each of its two heads. The cedar wood of a *lunga* is carved into an hourglass shape. By squeezing the leather cords strung between its two drumheads, a player can change the tension of the drum skins, which changes the pitch of the drum tones. In the hands of an expert, the drum's sound closely imitates Dagbanli, the spoken language of the Dagbamba. *Lunsi* "talk" and "sing" on their instruments. These musicians are storytellers, chroniclers of the history of their people and their nation.

Figure 3.5
Lunsi in performance.

Patsy Marshall

Counter Number	Commentary
0:00	Call by leading *lunga* drum.
0:08	Chorus by answer *lunga* and *gung-gong* drums.
0:21	Praises by vocalist and leading *lunga* drum.
0:59	Chorus.
1:10	Praises by vocalist and leading *lunga* drum.
1:45	Chorus.
1:55	Fade out during verse.

A Praise Name Dance

"Nag Biegu" (*nah*-oh bee-*ah*-oo) is one of the many Praise Name Dances (*salma*) of Dagbon. Its title means "ferocious wild bull." This *salma* praises Naa Abudu, a king of Dagbon in the 1800s who is remembered for his courage and firm leadership. Scoffing at the challenge of a war leader from a neighboring nation, Naa Abudu said, "You call yourself a wild bull. Let us meet and see who is stronger." As they dance to the drumming, people recall the bravery of the king.

The music has a two-part musical form, reminiscent of an alternation between verse and chorus. In the verse sections, the vocalist and leading *lunga* drummers praise Naa Abudu and allude to events of his chieftaincy; the answering *lunsi* and two *gung-gong* drummers punctuate the verses with booming, single strokes. The drummed chorus phrase works like a "hook" in a pop song, that is, a catchy, memorable phrase.

Life Story: Abubakari Lunna

I first met my teacher from Dagbon, Abubakari Lunna, when in 1975 he was working as a professional with the Ghana Folkloric Company, a government-sponsored performing arts company based in Accra, the capital of Ghana. In 1988 he retired from government service and returned to northern Ghana, where he served his father, Lun-naa Wombie, until his death. Presently, Lunna supports his large family as a drummer, farmer, and teacher. The following excerpt of his life story focuses on his teachers.

"My Education in Drumming"

My father's grandfather's name is Abubakari. It is Abubakari who gave birth to Azima and Alidu; Azima was the father of [my teacher] Ngolba and Alidu was father of Wombie, my father. Their old grandfather's name

Figure 3.6
Studio portrait of Abubakari as a young man.

Courtesy of Abubakari Lunna

is the one I am carrying, Abubakari. My father never called me "son" until he died; he always called me "grandfather." We always played like grandson and grandfather.

When I was a young child, my father was working as a security guard in the South at Bibiani, the gold town. I was living with one of my father's teachers, his uncle Lun-naa Neindoo, the drum chief at Wariboggo, a village near Tolon. When I was six or seven, my mother's father, Tali-naa Alaasani [a sub-chief of Tolon], took me to his senior brother, a chief of Wariboggo at that time. I was going to be his "shared child." In my drumming tradition, when you give your daughter in marriage and luckily she brings forth children, the husband has to give one to the mother's family. So, I was living in the chief's house.

I was with my mother's uncle for four or five years when he enrolled me in school. They took four of us to Tolon, my mother's home. I lived with my mother's father. We started going to the school. Luckily, in several weeks' time my father came from the South. He called my name, but his uncle told him, "Sorry. The boy's grandfather came and took him to be with the chiefs. Now he is in school." My father said, "What?! Is there any teacher above me? I am also a teacher. How can a teacher give his child to another

There are significant differences of ecology, history, and culture between what Abubakari calls "the North" and "the South."

While his father comes from a long line of drummers, Abubakari's mother comes from a royal family.

Figure 3.7
Studio portrait of Lun-naa Wombie,
Abubakari's father.

Courtesy of Lun-naa Wombie

teacher for training in a different language?" Early in the morning, he
walked to Tolon. He held my hand. I was happy because my father had
come to take me [see Figure 3.7].

My father spent one month. When he went to the South, he took me
with him. Unfortunately, at Bibiani my father didn't have time to teach me.
One year when my father came back to Dagbon for the Damba Festival
[an annual celebration of the birth of the Prophet Muhammad], he told my
grandfather, Lun-naa Neindoo, "If I keep Abubakari at Bibiani, it will be
bad. I want to leave him at home. I don't want him to be a southern boy."

I began learning our drumming talks and the singing. Lun-naa Neindoo
started me with *Dakoli Nye Bii Ba*, the beginning of drumming [that is, the
first repertory learned by young *lunsi*]: "God is the Creator. He can create
a tree, He can create grass, He can create a person." You drum all before
you say, "A Creator, God, created our grandfather, Bizung [the first *lunga*]."
The elders have given *Dakoli Nye Bii Ba* to the young ones so that they can
practice in the markets. When they know that you are improving, they start
you with drumming stories and singing stories. On every market day we,
the young drummers, came together and drummed by ourselves.

When the Wariboggo chief made my father *Sampahi-naa,* the drum
chief second to the *Lun-naa* [the highest rank of drum chief], he could not
go back to Bibiani. My father said, "Now, I am going to work with you on

**Just as the royals of Dagbon have
an elaborate hierarchy of chief-
taincies, so the *lunsi* have a
pyramid-like system of titled
positions of authority.**

our drumming history talks." He began with the story of Yendi [seat of the paramount chieftaincy of Dagbon]: how Dagbon started, how we traveled from Nigeria and came to Dagbon, how we became drummers, how it happened that our grandfather Bizung made himself a drummer. If he gave me a story today, tomorrow I did it correctly.

I was with my father for a long time, more than five years. My father was hard. I faced difficulty with my father because of his way of teaching. My father would not beat the drum for you. He would sing and you had to do the same thing on *lunga*. If you couldn't do it, he would continue until you got it before adding another.

[Later] . . . my father sent me to my teaching-father, Ngolba. He had a good voice, a good hand—every part of drumming, he had it. He had the knowledge, too, and people liked him. When he was drumming, he would make people laugh. People would hire him: "We are having a funeral on this day. Come and help us." I traveled with him, carrying his *lunga*. Because of his drumming, Ngolba never sat at home: every day we went for drumming. That was how people got to know me. Any time I was walking, people started calling, "Ngolba, small Ngolba." And with my sweet hand and my quick memory, everyone liked me.

Already I knew something in drumming, so for him to continue with me was not hard. I only had to listen to his story and follow him. When we went to a place and he told stories, I tried to keep it in my mind. When we were resting that night, I asked him, "Oh, my uncle, I heard your talk today. Can you tell me more about it?" There, he would start telling me something. That is how I continued by education with Mba Ngolba. I was very young to be drumming the deep history rhythms with a sweet hand.

My father called Ngolba and advised him, "I am not feeling happy about all the traveling you and Abubakari are doing. Drummers are bad. Somebody might try to spoil your lives. Find something to protect yourself. And protect Abubakari too." Father Ngolba—I can never forget him. Sometimes, when I was sitting at home, he would call me to get something to drink. I couldn't ask him, "Father, what is this?" In Dagbon, you can't ask him—you have to drink it. My Mba Ngolba did it for me several times.

Another reason why I liked my teacher, my Father Ngolba, is that despite his quick temper, he didn't get angry with me. He loved me. He didn't take even one of his ideas and hide it from me. Even if I asked him about something common that many drummers know, the thing left—he didn't hide it. He would tell me, "I have reserved something. If you bring all your knowledge out in public, some people with quick learning can just collect it."

I respected Ngolba like my father. During farming time I got up early in the morning and went straight to the farm. When he came, he met me there already. If it was not farming time, I would go to his door, kneel down, and say good morning to him. I would stay there, not saying anything until at last he would ask me, "Do you want to go some place?" Only then could I go. Teachers can give you laws like your own father. That is our Dagbamba respect to teachers.

Father Ngolba died in the South. When an old drummer dies, we put a *lunga* and a drumstick in the grave. The man who was with Ngolba when he died told me, "Your father said, 'Only bury me with this drumstick—

"Mba" means "father"; for a *lunga* drummer, your teacher becomes your teaching-father.

According to Dagbamba etiquette, children never question the orders of their father.

Figure 3.8
Abubakari holding the frame of Mba Ngolba's *lunga*.

David Locke

don't add my *lunga* to bury me. Give my *lunga* to Abubakari.'" I said thank you for that. We finished the funeral back in Dagbon. The second brother to Ngolba spoke to all their family, "Ngolba told me that if it happens he dies, Abubakari should carry on with his duties. He should take his whole inheritance. And Ngolba had nothing other than his *lunga*." I have his *lunga*; it is in my room now.

Shona Mbira Music

The recording of "Nhemamusasa" (**CD 1, Track 15**) features another uniquely African type of musical instrument. It is known outside Africa as "thumb piano"; speakers of the Shona language call it *mbira* (mmm-*bee*-rah). The "kaleidophonic" sound of its music (Tracey 1970:12) provides us with another insight into the musical potential of African rhythmic structures. Further, the *mbira* tradition shows another way African music can transform a group of separate individuals into a participatory polyphonic community. Information for this section draws primarily on the research of the ethno-musicologist Paul Berliner (1993).

> ### Salient Characterisitcs of the Shona and Their Music
>
> - A Bantu-speaking people who live in present-day Zimbabwe.
> - A decentralized, agricultural society.
> - *Mbira*, a plucked idiophone, is the important instrument in the Shona musical tradition.
> - *Mbira* music connects the Shona with their ancestral spirits.

Cultural Context

History

The Shona, who live in high plateau country between the Zambezi and Limpopo rivers, are among the sixty million Bantu-speaking people who predominate in central and southern Africa. Since about 800 c.e., kingdoms of the Shona and neighboring peoples have ruled large territories; stone fortresses such as the Great Zimbabwe number among Africa's most impressive architectural achievements. These kingdoms participated in a lively Indian Ocean commerce with seafaring powers such as the Arabs, Persians, and Indians (Mallows 1967:97–115). The Portuguese arrived about 1500. Eventually, the large-scale Shona states faded under pressure from other African groups, notably the more militaristic Ndebele in the 1800s. The Shona became a more decentralized, agricultural people.

At the turn of the twentieth century, English-speaking settlers took over the land and imposed their culture and economy on the local Africans. The colonial period in what was then called Rhodesia was brief, but it radically affected most local institutions. As in neighboring South Africa, a systematic policy of land grabbing left Africans materially impoverished. Racist settlers scorned African culture; many local people came to doubt the ways of their ancestors. For two decades after the independence of other contemporary African nation-states in the 1950s and 1960s, white Rhodesians maintained their dominance. Finally, a war of liberation (1966–1979) culminated in majority rule and the birth of the nation-state Zimbabwe in 1980.

Music played a part in the struggle. Popular and traditional songs with hidden meanings helped galvanize mass opinion; spirit mediums were leaders in the war against white privilege (Frye 1976; Lan 1985). After decades of denigration by some Africans who had lost faith in traditional culture, the *mbira* became a positive symbol of cultural identity.

Shona Spirits

From the perspective inherited from the Shona ancestors, four classes of spirits (literally *mweya* or breath) affect the world: spirits of chiefs (*mhondoro*), family members (*mudzimu*), nonrelatives or animals (*mashave*), and witches (*muroyi*) (Lan 1985:31–43). Although they are invisible, ancestral spirits nonetheless have sensory experience, feel emotions, and take action to help and advise their beloved descendants. *Mbira* music helps connect the living with their ancestors.

Humans and spirits communicate by means of possession trances. In possession, a spirit enters the body of a living person, temporarily supplanting his or her spirit. Once embodied in its medium, an ancestral spirit can advise his or her living relatives, telling them things they have done wrong and how to protect themselves and ensure good fortune. Possessions occur at *mapira* (singular *bira*), all-night, family-based, communal rituals. *Mbira* music and dancing are significant elements in these events (Berliner 1993:186–206; Zantzinger n.d.).

The *Mbira*

On our recording of "Nhemamusasa" we hear an instrument that is frequently used at spirit possession ceremonies: the *mbira dzavadzimu* (mmm-*bee*-rah dzah-vah-*dzee*-moo), literally "*mbira* of the ancestors."

Construction

Mbiras of many different styles of construction occur throughout Africa and its diaspora. Most *mbiras* have four features of construction: (1) a set of long, thin keys made of metal or plant material, (2) a soundboard with a bridge that holds the keys, (3) a resonator to shape and amplify the sound of the plucked keys, and (4) jingles that buzz rhythmically when the keys are plucked. Like the *kora,* the instrument matches the bilateral symmetry of the human body; that is, left-side keys are for the left thumb, right-side keys are for the right thumb and index finger (Berliner 1993:8–18).

In performance, musicians place the *mbira* within a large gourd resonator (*deze*) that brings out the instrument's full tone; when playing for personal pleasure or during learning-teaching sessions, the resonator may not be needed (see Figure 3.9).

Bottle cap rattles or snail shells attached to the soundboard and resonator add the important buzzing ingredient to the music. Performances usually include hand clapping, singing, and a driving rhythm played on a pair of gourd rattles called *hosho.*

Tuning (*Chuning*)

Shona musicians refer to the tonal qualities of an *mbira*'s sound with the English word *tuning* or the modified term *chuning.* Artists use *chuning* to refer not only to interval configurations but also to qualities of tone, sound projection, pitch level, and overtones (Berliner 1993:54–72). Musicians debate the affective quality of different chunings and symbolically link the *mbira* keys with features of culture such as family relationships, emotional or physical responses to music, and animal imagery.

The Player and the Instrument

In performance, the instrument faces toward the player. Repeatedly plucking the keys in prescribed patterns, musicians establish cycles of harmony, melody, rhythm, and counterpoint. Each key on the *mbira* emits a fundamental pitch and a cluster of overtones; the resonator shapes, reinforces,

Figure 3.9
Mbira players.

Paul Berliner

prolongs, and amplifies this complex tone. The buzzing bottle caps not only provide rhythm to the music's texture but also add to the instrument's array of tuned and untuned sounds. Tones overlap. The *mbira*'s sound surrounds the player. In this music, the whole is far more than the sum of the parts (Berliner 1993:127–35).

Creative, participatory listening is an essential aspect of this music-culture. Performer and audience must hear coherent melodies in the *mbira*'s numerous tones. Many pieces exploit the creative potential of 3:2 relationships; often one hand is "in three or six" while the other is "in two or four." Hand-clapping phrases provide a good way to join in the performance and experience this polymetric feeling.

For players immersed in the process, the *mbira* takes on a life of its own. Here is how Dumisani Maraire, one of the first teachers of Shona music to non-Africans, explains it:

> When a mbira player plays his instrument . . . he is . . . conversing with a friend. He teaches his friend what to do, and his friend teaches him what to do. To begin with, the mbira player gives the basic pattern to the mbira; he plays it, and the mbira helps him produce the sound. He goes over and over playing the same pattern, happy now that his fingers and the mbira keys are together. So he stops thinking about what to play, and starts to listen to the mbira very carefully. (Maraire 1971:5–6)

"Nhemamusasa"

According to the Shona, ancestral spirits love to hear their favorite *mbira* pieces. Musical performance is an offering that calls them near, thus making possession more likely. Because of its important social use, this repertoire remains stable over many generations. Pieces for *mbira dzavadzimu,* most of which have been played for centuries, are substantial musical works with many fundamental patterns, variations, styles of improvisation, and so

Close Listening   CD 1:15

"Nhemamusasa"

Counter Number	Commentary
0:00	*Kushaura mbira* part by itself.
0:47	*Kutsinhira* and *kushaura mbira* parts in duet.
1:45	*Hosho* (rattle) joins the two *mbiras*.

CD 1:15

"Nhemamusasa" (lit. "cutting branches for shelter"), *kushaura* section (2:36). Traditional Shona. Field recording by Paul Berliner. Zimbabwe, 1971.

forth. These pieces have two interlocking parts: *kushaura,* the main part, and *kutsinhira,* the interwoven second part. Because each part is polyphonic in its own right, the interaction of parts creates a wonderfully multilayered sound. The vocal music, which has three distinct styles—*mahonyera* (vocables), *kudeketera* (poetry), and *huro* (yodeling)—adds depth to the musical texture and richness to the meanings expressed in performance.

On **CD 1, Track 15**, we hear "Nhemamusasa" (*neh*-mah-moo-*sah*-sah), revered by the Shona as one of their oldest and most important pieces. It was played for Chaminuka, a powerful spirit who protects the entire Shona nation. The song title literally means "cutting branches for shelter." One of Berliner's teachers reports that "'Nhemamusasa' is a song for war. When we [the Shona] were marching to war to stop soldiers coming to kill us, we would cut branches and make a place [tent shelter] called a *musasa*" (John Kunaka, quoted in Berliner 1993:42). In 1991 Erica Kundizora Azim, an experienced American student of *mbira,* heard a contemporary interpretation of the song's meaning from a female Shona friend:

Homeless people sit in their shantytowns with nothing to do.
No work.
Trouble is coming.

Evidently the piece evokes profound feelings. For the Shona, sentiments evoked by pieces such as "Nhemamusasa" make them effective for use in rituals of spirit possession. Even for those of us without inside knowledge of Shona cultural history, the musical surface of "Nhemamusasa" sparks powerful feelings.

The BaAka People Singing: "Makala"

Our final example of African music-culture differs dramatically from the traditions of the Ewe, Mande, Dagbamba, and Shona. It brings us full circle to the communal, inclusive spirit of African music so clearly present in the music of the Ghanaian postal workers. Information for this section relies on the field research of Michelle Kisliuk (1991, 1998).

On **CD 1, Track 16**, we hear the singing, hand clapping, and drumming of the BaAka people (*bah*-ka). The immense, ancient, thickly canopied

Salient Characteristics of the BaAka and Their Music

- Live in the forested areas of tropical central Africa.
- One of several distinct ethnic groups who share common characteristics.
- Social unit: small, close-knit group of families and friends.
- Move from place to place in search of food through cooperative hunting and gathering.
- Music reflects the relaxed and spontaneous social structure.

tropical forest exerts a powerful influence on life in central Africa. The BaAka are one of several distinct ethnic groups who share certain physical, historical, cultural, and social features as well as adaptations to the natural world (Turnbull 1983). Here I shall refer to these groups collectively as Forest People. Because of their physical size, non-Africans have called the Forest People "Pygmies." It is an ethnocentric label; their size is a benefit in the forest and plays a minor role in the way they are viewed by their larger African neighbors.

For millennia the Forest People existed in ecological balance with their environment. Sheltered in dome-shaped huts of saplings and leaves, they lived with kin and friends in small, loose-knit groups. Because these hunting bands needed only portable material possessions, they could easily shift their encampments every few months according to the availability of food. They obtained a healthy diet through cooperative hunting and gathering, allowing them ample time for expressive, emotionally satisfying activities such as all-night sings. The social system was informal and flexible: Men and women had roughly equal power and obligations, consensus decisions were negotiated by argument, children were treated gently. Individuals were not coerced by formal laws, distant leaders, or threatening deities. The forest was God, and people were children of the forest (Turnbull 1961:74).

At this point you may be wondering why the preceding paragraph was written in the past tense. During the colonial and postcolonial eras, external forces have confronted the Forest People to a degree unprecedented in their history. They now live within unstable nation-states forged in violent anticolonial wars; multinational timber and mining companies are at work in the forest; scholars and adventurers visit some of them regularly. In short, the Forest People now face great changes.

Let us now look at three images that reflect the conflicting roles that the Forest People play in the world's imagination.

Three Images of the Forest People

Primal Eden

For thousands of years, members of the world's imperial civilizations have found renewal in the music of the Forest People. In 2300 B.C.E. an Egyptian pharaoh wrote to a nobleman of Aswan who had journeyed south to the Upper Nile:

> Come northward to the court immediately; thou shalt bring this dwarf with thee, which thou bringest living, prosperous and healthy from the land of the spirits, for the dances of the god, to rejoice and (gladden) the heart of the king of Upper and Lower Egypt, Neferkere, who lives forever. (Breasted 1906, in Davidson 1991:55)

Today, aided by books and recordings, the Forest People continue to exert a pull on the world's imagination. In particular, the beautiful life of the BaMbuti recounted in Colin Turnbull's *The Forest People* has entranced many. Recordings by Simha Arom have introduced listeners to the intricacy of BaAka vocal polyphony (Arom 1987). For many people, this music-culture evokes cherished values—peace, naturalness, humor, community. In the music of the Forest People we want to hear an innocence lost to our complex, polluted, violent world.

Primitive Savage

Paired with this image of primal utopia is the notion of primitive savagery. According to this view, "Pygmies" represent an early stage of cultural evolution, a primitive way of life associated with the Stone Age. By definition primitives do not know the achievements of "high" civilization—science, mathematics, engineering, philosophy; they have no electricity, no industry, no nations, no armies, no books. If this is the stuff of civilization, then like other native peoples in remote locations on earth, the Forest People must be "primitive."

But calling a human group "primitive" establishes a dangerous inequality. It can justify genocide; enslavement; servitude; colonialism; underdevelopment; land grabbing for lumbering, mining, agriculture, and tourism; and reculturization through evangelism, schooling, wage labor, and military service. From this imperialist perspective, cultures that differ from the "modern" way must change or be eradicated.

Unique Culture in a Global Village

Instead, we can characterize the Forest People with concepts that are less emotionally charged. They are nonliterate and nonindustrial, with a relatively unspecialized division of labor and a cashless barter/subsistence economy; theirs is a homogeneous society with small-scale, decentralized social institutions, egalitarian interpersonal social relations, and relative gender equality. Their God is everywhere in this world, and they exist within the web of nature.

Forest life is not an idyllic paradise, however. Hunters sometimes share meat from the day's hunt only after other members of their group complain about its unfair distribution. People suffer from disease, hunger, violence, and anxiety. For the past four hundred years they have shared the forest with Bantu and Sudanic agriculturalist villagers; more recently, they have adjusted to international forces. Compared to one's own culture, the Forest

Figure 3.10
BaAka in perfomance.

People may seem better in some ways, worse in others. Undoubtedly, their culture is unique.

The next section presents a description of a BaAka song. This will set the stage for seeing how the music-culture of the Forest People functions as a resource in their adaptation to change.

"Makala," a *Mabo* Song

Setting

The performance-studies scholar and ethnomusicologist Michelle Kisliuk recorded "Makala" (*mah*-kah-lah) in December 1988 in the Central African Republic. The setting was a performance event, or *eboka*, of *Mabo* (*mah*-boh), a type of music and dance associated with net hunting (see Figure 3.10). At this performance, novices (*babemou*) and their entourage from one group had walked to a neighboring camp to receive hunting medicine and related dance instruction from experts (*ginda*). Over the course of two days, performers presented *Mabo* for this ritual purpose as well as for the pleasure of learning new songs and dance flourishes. At times a small-scale affair involving only the *Mabo* specialists and their students, the *eboka* sometimes swelled into a much larger social dance attended by a crowd of BaAka and villagers. Kisliuk recorded this song on the evening of the first day (Kisliuk 1998:98ff.).

Music Sound

An *eboka* of *Mabo* consists of sections of singing, drumming, and dancing. Each song has a theme, that is, a text and tune. By simultaneously improvising melodic variations, singers create a rich polyphony. After five to fifteen minutes of play with one song, they begin another. From time to

CD 1:16

"Makala" (name of unknown person) (2:14). Traditional BaAka song. Field recording by Michelle Kisliuk. Central African Republic, 1988.

time, the *eboka* is "spiced up" with an *esime,* a section of rhythmically intensified drumming, dancing, and percussive shouts (Kisliuk 1998:40–41).

Men and women of all ages sing "Makala." Using both chest and head voices, they obtain a great variety of tone colors that range from tense/raspy to relaxed/breathy. One striking feature, yodeling, involves quick shifts between head and chest voices. Musical instruments include drums and hand claps. Two different drum parts are played on the drum skins that cover the ends of carved, cone-shaped logs. Often, Forest People enrich the percussion by rapping with wooden sticks on the drum's body and striking together metal cutlass blades. Forest People also make music with instruments such as flutes, trumpets, and harps, but not in *Mabo.*

As in Native American songs, singers mostly use vocables (see Chapter 2). The sparse text of "Makala" is typically cryptic (Kisliuk 1998:99).

moto monyongo	beautiful person
Makala	name of an unknown deceased person from the Congo, where *Mabo* originated
na lele, oh	I cry [implying a funeral setting in this song]

Turnbull reports that songs of the BaMbuti often mean "We are children of the Forest" or "The Forest is good." In troubled times they sing a longer text: "There is darkness all around us; but if darkness *is,* and the darkness is of the forest, then the darkness must be good" (Turnbull 1961:93).

Music-Culture as an Adaptive Resource

Restoring Balance

The active force of music-making contributes to the Forest People's enduring yet ever-changing way of life. The BaMbuti encode the practical, moral effect of song in their words for conflict and peace: *akami,* noise, and *ekimi,* silence or ordered sound (Turnbull 1983:50–51). Troubles arise when synergy among people and symbiosis with the forest is disrupted. Communal singing "wakes the forest," whose benevolent presence silences the *akami* forces (Turnbull 1961:92). With yodels echoing off the trees, the forest physically becomes one of the musicians.

Enacting Values and Creating Self

The improvised, open-ended polyphonic musical style of "Makala" embodies egalitarian cultural values such as cooperation, negotiation, argument, and personal autonomy. By making social relations tangible, performance helps individuals develop identity within a group.

Autonomy within Community

Most members of a BaAka community acquire music-making skills as they grow up (enculturation). During times of crisis, the group needs the musical participation of every member. For example, in a memorable scene from

Close Listening   CD 1:16

"Makala"

Counter Number	Commentary
0:00	The music takes shape as male singers, drummers, and women gradually join in.
0:13	The theme is sung once.
0:20	Theme is elaborated in rich multipart chorus.
0:53	Prominent high-pitched yodeling.
1:14	Different drumming and prominent countermelody.
1:43	Theme briefly stands out in the recording.
1:50	Hand clapping joins in until recording fades out.

The Forest People, even when others in the hunting group insult and ostracize a man for setting his hunting net in front of the others', he joins the all-night singing and is forgiven (Turnbull 1961:94–108).

Although collective participation in performance is highly valued, individuals may stand out. Kisliuk said that the community knows the composers of individual songs and originators of whole repertories like *Mabo.* Explicit teacher–student transmission does take place between the old and young of one group and among members of groups from different regions. Turnbull wrote of an acclaimed singer/dancer who seemed particularly emotional and prone to time/space transformation during performances: "He was no longer Amabosu; he had some other personality totally different, and distant" (Turnbull 1961:89). BaAka repertory has a varied history and a dynamic future. Music connects the people to their past, while helping them negotiate their present.

Conclusion as Discussion

Contrary to the images of chaos and despair conveyed by international mass media, we have encountered African music-cultures of stability, resourcefulness, and self-respect. Abubakari Lunna's life story reveals the rigor of an African musician's education. The erudition, commitment, suffering, and love are profound. Although he says good drumming is "sweet," clearly it is not frivolous or just fun. We have seen that many Africans value the achievements of their ancestors. The Ewe rigorously study *Agbekor* and recreate it with passionate respect in performance. Classics of the Shona *mbira* repertory inspire modern freedom fighters. Mande songs apply the wisdom of the elders to the problems of today.

African music-cultures are strongly humanistic. The human body inspires the construction and playing technique of musical instruments like the *mbira* and *kora.* The spontaneous performances of postal workers and the ritual ceremonies of Forest People point out an important feature of many African music-cultures: Music serves society. As we have experienced, many kinds of African musics foster group participation.

Although I encourage African-style musicking, musicians who cross cultural borders need sensitivity to limits and contradictions. To me, nothing approaches the power of time-honored repertory performed in context by born-in-the-tradition bearers of culture. The history of an African musical heritage like Mande *jaliya* casts a humbling light onto recent idioms. When non-Africans, especially those of us with white skin, play African music, the legacy of slavery and colonialism affects how an audience receives the performance. How many enthusiasts for African music love its aesthetic surface but regard spirit possession as superstition?

Music is a joyful yet rigorous discipline. The hard work of close listening yields important benefits. The sophistication of African musical traditions promotes an attitude of respect. An understanding of musical structure provides an ear map for appreciative listening and informed performance. The musical examples in this chapter use rhythms based on 3:2, a profound and elemental timing ratio that animates many African traditions.

Writing about music raises big questions that resist simple answers: Can thought be expressed without words? What approach to music yields the best information and explanation? By treating music as an object, does analysis wrongly take music from its authentic cultural setting? How can people know each other through musical activities? Each chapter in this book benefits from this type of questioning. We seek to know how people understand themselves, but we must acknowledge the impact of our own perspective. An active involvement in music not only provides a wonderful way to learn about other people but can change a person's own life as well. From this perspective, ethnomusicology helps create new and original music-cultures.

A cross-cultural encounter can be an active process of self-development rather than an act of cultural tourism. When we seek knowledge of African music-cultures, we can also reevaluate our own. As we try our hands at African music, we encounter fresh sonic styles and experience different ways of doing things with other people. Just as African cultures are always undergoing change, each student's personal world of music is a work in progress.

Study Questions

1. How does African music help people cope with the challenges, responsibilities, opportunities, and problems in their lives?

2. How has the outward and inward flow of people, ideas, and things to and from Africa had an impact on African music, and vice versa?

3. How do general features of African musical style become meaningful in specific cultural situations? For example, how do call-and-response, multipart texture, or Islam-influenced vocal style function in actual social situations?

4. How do the culture, history, and music-culture differ among different regions of Africa or within one region, such as West Africa?

5. How does the *Agbekor* performance reflect the history and culture of the Ewe people?

6. How did Abubakari Lunna learn to play the *lunga?* What does this indicate about the music-culture of the Dagbamba people?

7. How are generalizations about African music-cultures exemplified in each of the five specific examples presented in Chapter 3?

Glossary

Abubakari Lunna A Dagbamba *lunga;* the author's teacher.

adzo (ah-*dzo*) The introductory section of the fast-paced section of an *Agbekor* performance.

adzokpi (ah-*dzoh*-kpee) A section of the fast-paced part of *Agbekor* in which people dance in pairs or small groups.

Agbekor (ah-*gbeh*-kaw) A war dance of the Ewe people; the name means "clear life."

Agokoli The tyrannical king from whom the Ewe fled.

akami Noise, disordered sound, an out-of-balance social condition.

Atamuga (ah-*tam*-gah). "The great oath," another name for *Agbekor*.

atsia (ah-chah) An Ewe word that means (1) stylish self-display, looking good, or bluffing and (2) a preset figure of music and dance. Plural: **atsiawo.**

atsiagbekor (ah-chah-*gbeh*-kaw) Another name for *Agbekor*.

axatse (ah-*ha*-tseh) A dried gourd, about the size of a cantaloupe, covered with a net strung with seeds.

BaAka (*bah*-ka) One of several ethnic groups known to Europeans as Pygmies or Forest People.

babemou Novices.

balo Gambian xylophone.

Bibiani Town in southern Ghana where Lun-naa Wombie worked.

birimintingo Virtuosic instrumental passage played on the *kora.*

Bizung The first Dagbamba *lunga* player and founder of the *lunsi* occupational clan.

call-and-response A musical form in which one part seems to be linked as a "response" to the previous part. The response part appears to be an "answer" or "comment" on the first or "call" part.

Chaminuka A powerful spirit who protects the entire Shona nation.

chuning The tonal qualities of an *mbira*'s sound.

Dagbamba Ethnic group of Abubakari Lunna.

Dagbon Kingdom of the Dagbamba people.

Dakoli Nye Bii Ba The first repertory learned by young *lunsi.*

deze Large gourd resonator for *mbira.*

donkilo A tune with several phrases of text.

drum language The vernacular meaning of a drummed phrase.

eboka A performance event.

ekimi Silence, ordered sound, a harmonious social condition.

esime A section of rhythmically intensified drumming, dancing, and percussive shouts.

Ewe (*eh*-way) Ethnic group that performs *Agbekor*.

gankogui (gahng-*koh*-gu-ee) Double bell.

ginda Experts.

griots (*gree*-oh) European term for Mande experts in speech, song, and the playing of instruments; counselors to royalty, entertainers for the public, and guardians of history.

gung-gong (goong-*gawng*) A cylindrical, carved drum with a snare on each of its two heads.

habobo An Ewe mutual aid society that often is also a music and dance group.

horon Gambian persons of freeborn descent.

hosho A pair of gourd rattles that accompany *mbira.*

huro Style of Shona singing that uses yodeling.

jali musolu Female jali.

jaliya What *jalolu* do.

jalolu Professional "sound artisans" of the Mande ethnic tradition. Singular: **jali.**

jong Gambian persons of slave descent.

kaganu (kah-gahng) Ewe drum.

kidi (*kee*-dee) Ewe drum.

kloboto (*kloh*-boh-toh) Ewe drum.

konkon An ostinato rapped on the resonator of the *kora.*

konting Gambian plucked long-necked lute.

kora A twenty-one-string bridge harp.

kudeketera Style of Shona singing that uses poetry.

kuma Speech.

kumbengo An instrumental ostinato played on the *kora.*

kushaura The main part in a two-part arrangement of *mbira* music.

kutsinhira The interwoven second part in a two-part arrangement of mbira music.

"Lambango" Mande *jaliya* song.

libation A ritual communication to the spirit world involving drinks and speech.

lunga (*loong*-ah) A Dagbamba verbal artist, genealogist, counselor to royalty, cultural expert, entertainer; also, the name of the hourglass-shaped tension drum that he plays. Plural: **lunsi** (*loon*-see).

Lun-naa Wombie Father of Abubakari Lunna.

Mabo (*mah*-boh) A type of music and dance associated with net hunting.

Maghrib Africa north of the Sahara Desert.

mahonyera Style of Shona singing that uses vocables.

"Makala" (*mah*-kah-lah) A *Mabo* song.

mansa King.

mapira All-night, family-based, communal rituals at which spirit possessions occur. Singular: **bira.**

Mawu The Ewe Supreme Being.

Mba Ngolba Abubakari Lunna's second teaching-father.

mbira (mmm-*bee*-rah) Plucked, tuned idiophone ("thumb piano").

mbira dzavadzimu (mmm-*bee*-rah dzah-vah-*dzee*-moo) Literally, "*mbira* of the ancestors."

mudzimu Shona ancestral sprits.

"Nag Biegu" (*nah*-oh bee-*ah*-oo) One of the many Praise Name Dances of Dagbon.

ngara A superior singer.

ngoni Gambian plucked long-necked lute.

"Nhemamusasa" (*neh*-mah-moo-*sah*-sah) One of the oldest and most important Shona *mbira* pieces.

nyamalo Gambian craft specialists, including *jalolu*.

polymeter Simultaneous presence of different structures of music's temporal organization, such as time span and/or beats.

polyphony Multipart music.

primitive A derogatory term placing an ethnic group at an early stage of cultural or technological evolution.

Rhodesia Name of white-ruled state that was renamed Zimbabwe.

Sahel The semi-arid zone known to ancient Arabs as the southern "coast" of the sand sea (Sahara Desert) where the Sudan ("Land of the Blacks") began.

salma Praise Name Dances of Dagbon such as *"Nag Biegu."*

sataro An open-ended, extemporaneous passage of spoken or chanted text.

se (seh) The Ewe concept of fate or destiny.

Shona Ethnic group in Zimbabwe noted for its *mbira* music.

Sub-Saharan Africa Africa south of the Sahara Desert.

sula Gambian nonspecialists, including royals, Islamic literates, merchants, and farmers.

Sunjata Keita Founder of the first Mande empire.

totodzi (toh-toh-*dzee*) Ewe drum.

vulolo (voo-*law*-law) The slow-paced processional section of *Agbekor.*

vutsotsoe (voo-*tsaw*-tso-eh). The fast-paced part of an *Agbekor* performance.

Wariboggo Village where Abubakari Lunna grew up with his mother's father, Talinaa Alaasani.

work music Musical performance that lifts the workers' spirits and enables them to coordinate their efforts and maintain a positive attitude toward their job by setting the mood of the workplace.

Resources

References

Amoaku, W. Komla. 1985. "Toward a Definition of Traditional African Music: A Look at the Ewe of Ghana." pp. 31–40 in *More Than Drumming,* edited by Irene Jackson. Westport, Conn.: Greenwood Press.

Appiah, Anthony. 1992. *In My Father's House.* Cambridge, Mass.: Harvard Univ. Press.

Arom, Simha. 1987. *Centrafrique: Anthologie de la Musique des Pygmees Aka.* Ocora CD559012 13.

Asante, Molefi. 1987. *The Afrocentric Idea.* Philadelphia: Temple Univ. Press.

Bebey, Francis. 1975. *African Music: A People's Art.* Translated by Josephine Bennet. New York: Lawrence Hill.

Berliner, Paul. 1993. *The Soul of Mbira.* Rev. ed. Berkeley: Univ. of California Press.

Bohannan, Paul, and Phillip Curtin. 1995. *Africa and Africans.* 4th ed. Prospect Heights, Ill.: Waveland Press.

Breasted, J. H. 1906. *Ancient Records of Egypt.* Chicago: Univ. of Chicago Press.

Charry, Eric. 1994. "West African Harps." *Journal of the American Musical Instrument Society* 20:5–53.

———. 2000. *Mande Music: Traditional and Modern Music of the Maninka and Mandinka of Western Africa.* Chicago: University of Chicago Press.

Chernoff, John. 1979. *African Rhythm and African Sensibility.* Chicago: Univ. of Chicago Press.

Davidson, Basil. 1991. *African Civilization Revisited: From Antiquity to Modern Times.* Trenton, N.J.: Africa Word Press.

Davis, Art. 1994. "Midawo Gideon Foli Alorwoyie: The Life and Music of a West African Drummer." M.A. thesis, Univ. of Illinois-Urbana-Champaign.

DeVale, Sue Carole. 1989. "African Harps: Construction, Decoration, and Sound." Pp. 53–61 in *Sounding Forms: African Musical Instruments,* edited by Marie-Therese Brincard. New York: American Federation of Arts.

Dieterlen, Germaine. 1957. "The Mande Creation Myth." In *Peoples and Cultures of Africa,* edited by Eliot Skinner. Garden City, N.Y.: Doubleday.

Djedje, Jacqueline. 1978. "The One-String Fiddle in West Africa." Ph.D. diss., Univ. of California–Los Angeles.

Fiawo, D. K. 1959. "The Influence of the Contemporary Social Changes on the Magico-Religious Concepts and Organization of the Southern Ewe-Speaking People of Ghana." Ph.D. diss., Univ. of Edinburgh.

Frye, Peter. 1976. *Spirits of Protest.* Cambridge, England: Cambridge Univ. Press.

Innes, Gordon. 1976. *Kaabu and Fuladu: Historical Narratives of the Gambian Mandinka.* London: School of Oriental and African Studies, Univ. of London.

Jackson, Bruce. 1972. *Wake up Dead Man: Afro-American Worksongs from Texas Prisons.* Cambridge, Mass.: Harvard Univ. Press.

Jones, A. M. 1959. *Studies in African Music.* London: Oxford Univ. Press.

Kisliuk, Michelle. 1991. "Confronting the Quintessential: Singing, Dancing, and Everyday Life among the Biaka Pygmies (Central African Republic)." Ph.D. diss., New York Univ.

———. 1998. *"Seize the Dance!": BaAka Music Life and the Ethnography of Performance.* New York: Oxford University Press.

Knight, Roderic. 1971. "Towards a Notation and Tablature for the Kora." *African Music* 5(1): 23–36.

———. 1972. *Kora Manding: Mandinka Music of the Gambia.* Sound recording and booklet. Tucson, Ariz.: Pachart Ethnodisc er 12102.

———. 1984. "Music in Africa: The Manding Contexts." In Gerard Behague, ed., *Performance Practice.* Westport, Conn.: Greenwood Press.

Koetting, James. 1992. "Africa/Ghana." In *Worlds of Music.* 2nd ed. New York: Schirmer Books.

Kubik, Gerhard. 1962. "The Phenomenon of Inherent Rhythms in East and Central African Instrumental Music." *African Music* 3(1): 33–42.

Ladzekpo, Kobla. 1971. "The Social Mechanics of Good Music: A Description of Dance Clubs among the Anlo Ewe-Speaking People of Ghana." *African Music* 3(1): 33–42.

Lan, David. 1985. *Guns and Rain.* Berkeley: Univ. of California Press.

Laye, Camara. 1983. *The Guardian of the Word.* Translated by James Kirby. New York: Vintage Books.

Locke, David. 1978. "The Music of Atsiagbekor." Ph.D. diss., Wesleyan Univ., Middletown, Conn.

———. 1988. *Drum Gahu.* Tempe, Ariz.: White Cliffs Media.

———. 1990. *Drum Damba.* Tempe, Ariz.: White Cliffs Media.

———. 1992. *Kpegisu: A War Drum of the Ewe.* Tempe, Ariz.: White Cliffs Media.

Mallows, A. J. 1967. *An Introduction to the History of Central Africa.* London: Oxford Univ. Press.

Maraire, Dumisani. 1971. *The Mbira Music of Rhodesia.* Booklet and record. Seattle: Univ. of Washington Press.

Miller, Christopher. 1990. *Theories of Africans.* Chicago: Univ. of Chicago Press.

Mphahlele, Ezekiel. 1962. *The African Image.* London: Faber and Faber.

Nketia, J. H. Kwabena. 1964. *Continuity of Traditional Instruction.* Legon, Ghana: Institute of African Studies.

Nukunya, G. K. 1969. *Kinship and Marriage among the Anlo Ewe.* London: Athlone Press.

Quinn, Charlotte. 1972. *Mandingo Kingdoms of the Senegambia.* Evanston, Ill.: Northwestern Univ. Press.

Saad, Elias. 1983. *Social History of Timbuktu: The Role of Muslim Scholars and Notables.* Cambridge, England: Cambridge Univ. Press.

Senghor, Leopold Sedar. 1967. *The Foundations of "Africanite" or "Negritude" and "Arabite."* Translated by Mercer Cook. Paris: Presence Africaine.

Skinner, Eliot, ed. 1973. *Peoples and Cultures of Africa.* Garden City, N.Y.: Doubleday.

Thompson, Robert F. 1973. "An Aesthetic of the Cool." *African Arts* 7(1): 40–43, 64–67, 89.

Tracey, Andrew. 1970. *How to Play the Mbira (Dza Vadzimu).* Roodepoort, Transvaal: International Library of African Music.

Turnbull, Colin. 1961. *The Forest People.* New York: Simon & Schuster.

———. 1983. *The Mbuti Pygmies: Change and Adaptation.* New York: Holt, Rinehart, & Winston.

Zantzinger, Gei. n.d. "Mbira: Mbira dza Vadzimu: Religion at the Family Level." Film. Available from Univ. Museum, Univ. of Pennsylvania.

Additional Reading

Agawu, Kofi. 1995. *African Music: A Northern Ewe Perspective.* Cambridge Univ. Press.

Arom, Simha. 1991. *African Polyphony and Polyrhythm.* Cambridge, England: Cambridge Univ. Press.

Brincard, Marie-Therese, ed. 1989. *Sounding Forms: African Musical Instruments.* New York: American Federation of Arts.

Collins, John. 1992. *West African Pop Roots.* Philadelphia: Temple Univ. Press.

Eyre, Banning. 2000. *In Griot Time.* Philadelphia: Temple Univ. Press.

Friedson, Steven. 1996. *Dancing Prophets: Musical Experience in Tumbukas Healing.* Univ. of Chicago Press.

Knight, Roderic. 1991. "Music out of Africa: Mande Jaliya in Paris." *The World of Music* 33(1): 52–69.

Locke, David. 1982. "Principles of Offbeat Timing and Cross-Rhythm in Southern Eve Dance Drumming." *Ethnomusicology* 26(2): 217–46.

Nketia, J. H. Kwabena. 1974. *The Music of Africa.* New York: Norton.

Nzewi, Meki. 1991. *Musical Practice and Creativity.* IWALEWA-Haus, Univ. of Bayreuth.

Stone, Ruth. 2000. *Garland Handbook of African Music.* New York: Garland.

Additional Listening

Berliner, Paul. 1995. *Zimbabwe: The Soul of Mbira.* Nonesuch Explorer Series 9 72054-2.

Chernoff, John. 1990. *Master Drummers of Dagbon.* Vol. 2. Rounder CD 5406.

Knight, Roderic. 1972. *Mandinka Kora.* Ocora 70.

Locke, David. n.d. *Drum Gahu: Good-Time Drumming from the Ewe People of Ghana and Togo.* White Cliffs Media WCM 9494.

Lunna, Abubakari. 1996. *Drum Damba featuring Abubakari Lunna, a Master Drummer of Dagbon.* White Cliffs Media WCM 9508.

Viewing

A Performance of Kpegisu by the Wodome-Akatsi Kpegisu Habobo. 1990. Produced by David Locke. Boston: Educational Media Center, Tufts Univ.

Konkombe: Nigerian Music. 1988. Produced and directed by Jeremy Marre. Harcourt Films production. Newton N.J.: Shanachie Records.

Mbira Dza Vadzimu Urban and Rural Ceremonies, with Hakurotwi Mude. 1978. Devault, Pa.: Constant Spring Productions.

Music and Culture of West Africa: The Straus Expedition. Gloria J. Gibson and Daniel B. Reed. Bloomington: Indiana Univ. Press. CD-ROM.

Rhythm of Resistance: The Black Music of South Africa. 1988. Produced by Jeremy Marre. Directed by Chris Austin and Jeremy Marre. Harcourt Films production. Newton, N.J.: Shanachie Records.

The Language You Cry In. 1998. Produced and directed by Alvaro Toepke and Angel Serrano. San Francisco: California Newsreel; Inko Producciones.

Web Resources

- African Music and Drumming Resources on the Web
  http://echarry.web.wesleyan.edu/africother.html
- African Music Encyclopedia
  http://africanmusic.org
- African Music On RootsWorld
  http://www.rootsworld.com/africa/

- AfricaOnline.com—Africa Entertainment
  http://www.africaonline.com/site/africa/entertainment.jsp

- Afropop Worldwide
  http://www.afropop.org

- allAfrica.com: Music: Newsfeed source for news and reports on music
  in Africa
  http://allafrica.com/music/

- BBC—Music/Features—Echoes of Africa
  http://www.bbc.co.uk/aboutmusic/features/africa/

- Cora Connection
  http://www.coraconnection.com/

- Google Directory—Regional > Africa > Arts and Entertainment
  http://directory.google.com/Top/Regional/Africa/Arts_and_Entertainment

- International Library of African Music
  http://ilam.ru.ac.za

- Stern's Music On-line
  http://www.sternsmusic.com/

- Yahoo! Groups: african_music; mailing list established in 1995
  http://groups.yahoo.com/group/african_music/

North America/Black America

Jeff Todd Titon

Music of work, music of worship, music of play: The traditional music of African American people in the United States has a rich and glorious heritage. Neither African nor European, it is fully a black American music, forged in America by Africans and their descendants, changing through the centuries to give voice to changes in their ideas of themselves. Through all the changes, the music has retained its black American identity, with a core of ecstasy and improvisation that transforms the regularity of everyday life into the freedom of expressive artistry. Spirituals, the blues, jazz—to Europeans, these unusual sounds are considered America's greatest (some would say her only) contribution to the international musical world. African American music in the twentieth century transformed popular music in North America—then Europe—and eventually throughout the world.

Music of Worship

The easiest way to get acquainted with a music-culture in the United States is to survey its popular music on the radio. Despite recent consolidations in the media industry, many North American cities have a radio station programming African American music. If possible, listen for a couple of weeks; you will hear mostly contemporary black music, with occasional side trips into older forms and styles. But on Sundays the standard fare is recorded religious music, along with remote broadcasts of worship services from black churches in the city and surrounding suburbs. These live church broadcasts showcase a broad spectrum of black religious music: modern gospel quartets, powerful massed choirs, and soloists whose vocal acrobatics far exceed those of their counterparts in nonreligious music. Some of these broadcasts include congregational singing: camp-meeting choruses, particularly among Pentecostals, and hymns, particularly among Baptists.

Salient Characteristics of African American Music

- Traditional music of African American people engaged in work, worship, or play.
- Unique style—neither African nor European, but fully African American.
- Stylistic core of ecstasy and improvisation.
- Vocal style that can be close to the rhythm and tone of ordinary talk.
- Has transformed popular music throughout the world.

CD 1:17

"Amazing Grace" (2:33). Traditional. Performed by deacon and congregation of the New Bethel Baptist Church. Field recording by Jeff Todd Titon. Detroit, Michigan, 1977.

Listen now to a hymn sung by a black Baptist congregation in Detroit **(CD 1, Track 17).** It is the first verse of the familiar Christian hymn "Amazing Grace," but the performance style is unfamiliar to most people outside the black church. A deacon leads the hymn. He opens it by chanting the first line by himself: "Amazing grace how sweet it sound." The congregation then joins him, and very slowly they repeat the words, sliding the melody around each syllable of the text. Next, the deacon sings the second line by himself: "That saved a wretch like me"; then the congregation joins him to repeat it, slowly and melismatically (that is the sliding effect, with three or more notes per syllable of text). The same procedure finishes the verse.

That one verse is all there is to the performance. The singers do not use hymnbooks; they have memorized the basic tune and the words. Notice that the congregation, singing with the deacon, do not all come in at the same time; some lag behind the others a fraction, singing as they feel it. Not everyone sings exactly the same tune, either. Some decorate the basic tones with more in-between tones than others do. Some improvise their ornamentation as they go along.

The listening chart contains the words. Listen to this track on the CD several times, and try singing along with the congregation. Hesitant at first, you will get better as you learn the song and begin to feel the beauty and power of this performance. Your efforts to sing will increase your understanding of the music as well as your pleasure in the musical experience.

As we saw in Chapter 3, this way of organizing the singing, in which one sings (or plays) a line and another follows, and after that they continue taking turns, is termed *call-and-response*. (The technical musical term is *antiphony*.) When a leader sings a line and then repeats it with the church congregation, it is called *lining out*. Lining out psalms and, later, hymns was a standard practice in colonial America. Call-and-response was, and is, an important feature throughout black African music. Black slaves and freedmen worshipped with whites and picked up lining-out from their example, elaborating the melodies even more. The influence then became mutual. Today lining out remains in a great many black Baptist churches throughout the United States, where the hymn repertory is called "meter hymns," or "Dr. Watts" after the composer of many of the lyrics, Isaac Watts (1674–1748). Among white churches today, lining out survives among Old Regular Baptists in the coal-mining country of the southern Appalachian mountains.

Close Listening

"Amazing Grace"

Counter Number	Commentary	Lyrics
0:00	Leader gives out the first line.	Amazing grace how sweet it sound
0:09	Congregation joins leader to repeat first line, to a very slow and elaborate melody, with much melismata.	Amazing grace how sweet, ah
0:45	Leader gives out the second line.	That saved a wretch like me!
0:49	Congregation joins leader to sing second line.	That saved a wretch like me!
1:14	Leader gives out the third line.	I once was lost but now am found,
1:20	Congregation joins leader to sing third line.	I once was lost but now am found,
1:56	Leader gives out the fourth line.	Was blind but now I see.
2:01	Congregation joins leader to sing fourth line.	Was blind but now I see.

This version of "Amazing Grace" has many characteristics typical of African American music in the United States. The words are sung in English, and they fall into stanzas as most English folk songs do. But the style of the performance is black African. Consider some of the components of a music-culture, as indicated in Chapter 1. Movement: The singers sway freely to the music, dancing it with their bodies. Social organization of the singing group: The leader-chorus, call-and-response is the predominant African group vocal organization. Timbre: The singing tone quality alternates between buttery smooth and raspy coarse. The tune is playful—ebbing and eddying like the ocean tide.

Suppose we enter the black church where I recorded "Amazing Grace" and observe it firsthand. It is a Baptist church with a large sanctuary, seating perhaps fifteen hundred on this warm Sunday morning. Older men are dressed in blue or black vested suits, with black socks and shoes. A few of the younger men are conspicuous in trendy clothes. The women wear dark suits or dresses, and many have on fashionable hats; all of them wear stockings and dress shoes. Choir members wear green robes over their formal attire. To keep a breeze, they swing cardboard fans supplied by the funeral homes that have printed their advertisements on them.

When we hear "Amazing Grace," we have come to the deacons' devotional, an early part of the worship service consisting of old-time congregational hymn singing, scripture reading, and a chanted prayer offered by a deacon while the congregation hums and moans a wordless hymn in the background. The praying deacon improvises his chanted prayer—the words and tune—which begins as speech and then gradually turns into a chant; the congregation punctuates the deacon's phrases with shouts of "Yes," "Now," and so forth. This punctuating is another example of call-and-response.

Figure 4.1

Reverend C. L. Franklin, pastor, chanting ("whooping") as he delivers the sermon's climax. New Bethel Baptist Church, Detroit, Michigan, 1978.

Jeff Todd Titon

The deacons lead the devotional from the altar area, and after the devotional is through, the activity shifts to the pulpit, where announcements are made, offerings are taken up, and responsive reading is led. Interspersed are modern gospel songs, sung by soloists and the high-spirited youth choir, accompanied by piano and organ. The preacher, who has thought about the sermon ahead of time but does not have it written down, begins speaking; after about fifteen minutes he shifts into a musical chant, all the while improvising and carrying on the message. This change from speech to chant (the chant is called "whooping") is accompanied by a change from a playful timbre that alternates between clear and coarse and between light and buzzy, to a continuously hoarse timbre. As they did for the praying deacon, the congregation responds to the preacher's phrases with shouts of "Well," "Yes," and so forth. Sometimes the preacher fits the chant into a regular meter for brief periods, lasting from perhaps ten seconds to a minute.

The late Reverend C. L. Franklin (Figure 4.1) of Detroit spoke to me of the rhythm of his chanted preaching: "It's not something I can beat my foot to. But I can feel it. It's in me." It is also in the members of the congregation who sway back and forth with each phrase. Reverend Franklin's sermons were extraordinarily popular—he toured the nation to preach in the 1950s and 1960s, often with his daughter, Aretha. Recordings of his sermons can often be found in the gospel bins in record stores in black communities.

Eventually the sermon closes and an invitational song follows, led by a soloist from the choir. Three or four people heed the invitation and come forward to join the church. A final offering is taken up, the preacher gives the benediction, and the choir comes down from the choir stand, locks arms in the altar area facing the pulpit, and joins the congregation in singing "Amen."

Altogether, song and chant have taken up at least half the running time of the worship service: the old-style singing of the deacons' devotional, the

Figure 4.2
Religious music quickens the Holy Spirit and sends a woman into trance. Detroit, Michigan, 1977.

Jeff Todd Titon

traditional chant of the prayer and sermon, and the modern gospel songs. The music is literally moving; it activates the Holy Spirit, sending some people into shouts of ecstasy, swoons, shakes, holy dance, and trance (Figure 4.2). If they get so carried away that they are in danger of fainting or injuring themselves, they are restrained by their neighbors until members of the nurses' guild can reach them and administer aid. In this setting, music is an extremely powerful activity—and the church is prepared for its effects.

Much of the music of black Christian worship in the United States is traditional. We have seen that the lining-out tradition dates from colonial America, and many of the hymns sung have the same vintage. The Negro spiritual developed later, born of the camp-meeting revivals in the late eighteenth and early nineteenth centuries. The delivery style of these chanted prayers and sermons is at least as old as the early nineteenth century, and probably older, though of course the deacons and preachers improvise the content. Today the spirituals can be heard in their most traditional form as the "choruses"—one verse repeated several times—in Pentecostal services, while in black Baptist and Methodist services they are featured in carefully arranged, multiversed versions sung by trained choirs in a tradition that hearkens back to the Fisk Jubilee Singers of the late nineteenth century.

Music of Work

A work song, as the name suggests, is a song workers sing to help them carry on. It takes their minds off the monotonous and tiring bending, swinging, hauling, driving, carrying, chopping, poling, loading, digging, pulling, cutting, breaking, and lifting. A work song also paces the work. If the job requires teamwork, work song rhythms coordinate the movements of the workers (Figure 4.3).

Work songs were widely reported among black slaves in the West Indies in the eighteenth century and in the United States in the nineteenth.

Figure 4.3
Workers lining track. Alabama, 1956.

Frederic Ramsey, Jr.

While African American work songs may have been influenced by British work songs (sea chanteys and the like), the widespread, ancient, and continuing African work song tradition is the most probable source.

Work music is hard to find in the United States today. Where people once sang, machines now whine. But in an earlier period, African Americans sang work songs as they farmed and as they built the canals, railroads, and highways that became the transportation networks of the growing nation. This daily music helped make the African American sound what it was then and what it is now. In his autobiography, *My Bondage and My Freedom* (1855), the ex-slave Frederick Douglass wrote,

> Slaves are generally expected to sing as well as to work. A silent slave is not liked by masters or overseers. "Make a noise," "make a noise" and "bear a hand," are the words constantly addressed to the slaves when there is silence amongst them. This may account for the almost constant singing heard in the southern states.

After Emancipation, the singing continued whenever black people were engaged in heavy work: clearing and grading the land, laying railroad track (Figure 4.3), loading barges and poling them along the rivers, building levees against river flooding, felling trees. And the inevitable farm work: digging ditches, cutting timber, building fences, plowing, planting, chopping out weeds, and reaping and loading the harvest.

The words and tunes of these work songs fit the nature of the work. People working by themselves at their own pace sang slow songs without a pronounced beat; the singer hummed tunes or fit in words as desired, passing the time. Not surprisingly, the words of these songs show that the singers wished to be elsewhere. For example, as a farm boy Leonard "Baby Doo" Caston learned to sing "field holler" work songs by copying the practice of older farmhands **(CD 1, Track 18).**

In group labor that required teamwork and a steady pace, people sang songs with a pronounced beat, which coordinated their movements. A

 CD 1:18

Field Holler (0:40). Traditional solo work song. Performed by Leonard "Baby Doo" Caston. Field recording by Jeff Todd Titon. Minneapolis, Minnesota, 1971. (Background noise from the apartment is audible.)

Close Listening

CD 1:18

Field holler (work song)

Counter Number	Commentary	Lyrics
0:00	Caston sings first line, drawing out the length of tones as he wishes.	Hey, one of these mornings, mornings, and it won't be long;
0:10	Second line; like the first and all others in a flexible rhythm without a steady beat. Here, "captain" means boss.	You're gonna look for me, captain, and up the road I'll be gone.
0:17	Caston speaks.	"And this other guy named Curtis used to sing a song, says,"
0:21	Caston sings first line of second verse. Notice the melismata in "-try" of "country."	I'm goin' up the country, baby, and I can't take you.
0:33	Caston sings second line of second verse.	There's nothing up the country that a monkey woman can do.

Additional verses

Hey—captain don't you know my name?
I'm the same old fellow who stole your watch and chain.

I'm going away, baby, to wear you off my mind.
You keep me worried and bothered all the time.

sweet-sounding voice always in tune may be desirable in other situations, but it is not important in the group work song tradition. In some southern prisons black inmates sang work songs well into the twentieth century.

For example, in the song "Rosie" **(CD 1, Track 19)** the meter regulated the axe blows when the workers were felling large trees. You can easily hear the leader's call alternate with the group's response. Feel the timing of the axe blows, coordinated on the beat just before the leader or group begins to sing. Sometimes as many as ten men circled the tree and chopped, five pulling their axes out just before the other five all struck at once. Axes were swinging through the air, back and forth; the work was dangerous and the timing was crucial. Without work songs, the white and Latino inmates chopped two to a tree. With work songs, the black inmates chopped four, six, eight, or ten to a tree. The work went faster and better, and the singing group felt pride and solidarity in its accomplishment. In the words of Bruce Jackson, an experienced collector of prison work songs,

> The songs [may] change the nature of the work by putting the work into the worker's framework rather than the guards'. By incorporating the work with their song, by, in effect, co-opting something they are forced to do anyway, they make it theirs in a way it otherwise is not. (1972:30)

In African American music, whether of work or worship, calls answered by responses signal the social nature of this music. This is not a predictable and predetermined music. Improvisations in lyrics and melodies, as well as

 CD 1:19

"Rosie" (2:46). Traditional work song. Performed by prisoners at Mississippi State Penitentiary. Field recording by Alan Lomax. Parchman, Mississippi, 1947.

Close Listening

"Rosie"—excerpt from first verse with call-and-response

Counter Number	Commentary	Lyrics
0:01	Axes sound, call (leader).	Be my woman, gal, I'll
0:04	Axes sound, response (leader and group).	Be your man.
0:07	Axes sound, call (again).	Be my woman, gal, I'll
0:11	Axes sound, response (again).	Be your man.

Close Listening

"Rosie"

Counter Number	Commentary	Lyrics
0:00	Verse 1	Be my woman, gal, I'll be your man. Be my woman, gal, I'll be your man. Be my woman, gal, I'll be your man. Every Sunday's dollar in your hand. In your hand, lordy, in your hand. Every Sunday's dollar in your hand.
0:39	Verse 2	Stick to the promise, gal, that you made me. Stick to the promise, gal, that you made me. Stick to the promise, gal, that you made me. Wasn't going to marry till I go free. I go free, lordy, I go free. Wasn't going to marry till I go free.
1:17	Verse 3	Well, Rosie, oh lord, gal. Ah, Rosie, oh lord, gal.
1:29	Verse 4	When she walks she reels and rocks behind. When she walks she reels and rocks behind. Ain't that enough to worry a convict's mind? Ain't that enough to worry a convict's mind?
1:53	Repeat verse 3	Well, Rosie, oh lord, gal. Ah, Rosie, oh lord, gal.
2:05	Verse 5	Be my woman, gal, I'll be your man. Be my woman, gal, I'll be your man. Be my woman, gal, I'll be your man. Every Sunday's dollar in your hand.
2:29	Repeat verse 3	Well, Rosie, oh lord, gal. Ah, Rosie, oh lord, gal.

Collected by Alan Lomax; transcribed by Mieczyslaw Kolinksi. From Courlander 1963. Reprinted courtesy of Columbia University Press.

changes in timbre, show the high value African Americans place on innovation, creativity, and play.

Music of Play

As we have seen, black religious songs and work songs in performance involve play. For example, churchgoers admire the beautiful performance of a verbally adept preacher as he plays with the resources of language and gesture, and they clap their approval as a solo gospel singer sustains a climactic pitch or goes through intricately improvised melodic variations with great feeling. Work songs introduce a playful, distancing attitude toward the labor at hand. Like call-and-response, this sort of play with pitch, timbre, and rhythm is a marker of both African and African American musics.

Although religious songs and work songs contain elements of play, their main purpose is worship and work. In contrast, the music of play serves mainly as entertainment, performed mainly for pleasure even when its effect is also serious.

Imagine that we are walking through the black neighborhood outside the church after the service we "attended" earlier in the chapter. We find ourselves surrounded by the music of play. Children skip rope on the side streets, chanting jump rope rhymes and taunts at one another. Teens walk down the street listening to CD players. Deep bass tones boom out through powerful car stereos that throb with the latest hip-hop hits. Jukeboxes can be heard in the bars and barbecue joints that line both sides of the main street. When night falls, some of the bars have live entertainment—a local band that plays rhythm and blues, and in a fancy nightspot a nationally known jazz combo. Downtown in the city auditorium a nationally known artist is scheduled, while in the public gardens a concert of classical music offers the premiere performance of an electronic composition by a black composer who teaches at the city university.

Blues

The rest of this chapter focuses on just one of many African American musics of play: blues. The blues seems a familiar music, but its very familiarity presents problems. Chief among them is the current emphasis on blues as a roots music. If blues is the root, then rock is the fruit—or so the story goes in the blues film and radio program series produced in 2003, which the U.S. Congress declared the "year of the blues." But blues is a music in and of itself. It is wrapped tightly around the history and experiences of African Americans in the United States and deserves to be understood in this light. A second area of confusion about blues arises over the relationship between blues and jazz. Is blues a part of jazz? Did the stream of blues flow into the river of jazz? That common metaphor is not very accurate. Historically, blues and jazz are more like parallel highways with crossroads between them. Blues can be understood as a feeling—"the blues"—and as a specific musical form. Jazz, which engenders complex and varied feelings, is best thought of as a technique, as a way of forming. Jazz musicians applied their technique to the blues form, as to other musical forms.

> ### Salient Characteristics of Blues
>
> - A feeling, as well as a specific musical form.
> - Lyrics that attempt to tell the truth about life and speak for most of the audience (as well as the performer), often dealing with troubled male–female relationships.
> - *Blue notes*—achieved by an instrumentalist or vocalist sliding in between standard pitches.
> - A common form (*aab*)—a series of three-lined stanzas, the first line stated twice followed by the third line.

Muddy Waters (Figure 4.4), Howlin' Wolf, B. B. King, John Lee Hooker, and Buddy Guy (Figure 4.9), all of whom rose to national prominence as blues singers, came from a vital tradition. For decades the blues music-culture—with its singers, country juke joints, barrelhouses, city rent parties, street singing, bar scenes, nightclubs, lounges, recordings, and record industry—was a significant part of the black music-culture in the United States. In the 1960s, when desegregation and the Civil Rights Movement changed African American social and economic conditions, blues faded in popularity among African Americans while it gained a large and appreciative white audience. Nowadays, of course, the blues music-culture incorporates white as well as black musicians, and its audience is worldwide.

Blues and the Truth

The best entry into the blues is through the words of the songs. It is hard to talk at length about words in songs, and harder still to talk about music.

Figure 4.4
Muddy Waters (McKinley Morganfield) relaxes between songs at the Ann Arbor Blues Festival. Ann Arbor, Michigan, 1969.

Jeff Todd Titon

As Charles Seeger, one of the founders of the Society of Ethnomusicology, reminds us, it would be more logical to "music" about music than to talk about it (Seeger 1977:16). And in the blues music-culture, when the setting is informal, that is just what happens when one singer responds to another by singing verses of his or her own. The most common response to blues music is a feeling in the gut, dancing to the beat, nodding assent, a vocalized "that's right, you got it, that's the truth"—not unlike the black Christian's response to a sermon or a gospel song. A good, "deep" blues song leaves you feeling that you have heard the truth in a way that leaves little more to be said. Yet much *can* be said about the words to blues songs. Because the words pass from one singer to another as a coin goes from hand to hand, they become finely honed and proverbial in their expression—in other words, truthful.

We begin by taking an extended look at a single blues performance **(CD 1, Track 20)**, "Poor Boy Blues," by the Lazy Bill Lucas Trio. Bill Lucas (Figure 4.5) is the vocalist; he accompanies himself on electric guitar, and he is joined by two other musicians, one on acoustic guitar and the other on drums. Listen to the recording now, paying particular attention to the lyrics (see listening chart).

 CD 1:20

"Poor Boy Blues" (3:14). Performed by Lazy Bill Lucas Trio. Field recording by Jeff Todd Titon. Minneapolis, Minnesota, 1970.

Close Listening   CD 1:20

"Poor Boy Blues"

Counter Number	Commentary	Lyrics
0:00	Instrumental introduction led by guitar.	
0:13	Lucas sings verse 1. Drums play mostly long-short figures; guitar plays mostly Da-da-da, Da-da-da figures when Lucas is silent between lines.	I'm just a poor boy; people, I can't even write my name. I'm just a poor boy; people, I can't even write my name. Every letter in the alphabet to me they look the same.
0:50	Lucas sings verse 2. Accompaniment as for verse 1.	Mother died when I was a baby; father I never seen. Mother died when I was a baby; father I never seen. When I think how dumb I am, you know it makes me want to scream.
1:26	Lucas sings verse 3. Interplay of the two guitars when Lucas is silent between lines.	Ever since I was the age around eleven or twelve, Ever since I was the age around eleven or twelve, I just been a poor boy; ain't caught nothing but hell.
1:59	Lucas speaks, signaling an instrumental break. "Lay your racket" means "play your instrument."	"Lay your racket, boy, lay your racket."
2:03	Instrumental break the length of one verse. Da-da-da figures mostly throughout on guitar.	"Have mercy."
2:36	Lucas sings verse 4.	When I was a child Santa Claus never left one toy. When I was a child Santa Claus never left one toy. If you have any mercy, please have mercy on poor boy.

Used with permission of William Lucas.

Figure 4.5
Lazy Bill Lucas. Minneapolis, Minnesota,
1968.

Jeff Todd Titon

Response to the Lyrics of "Poor Boy Blues"

I did not choose "Poor Boy Blues" because the words were outstanding;
they are typical. For me, some of it is good, some not; some of it works,
some does not. "I'm just a poor boy; people, I can't even write my name"
produces an automatic response of sympathy for the poor boy, but it is not
a very deep response. I am sorry for the poor boy's illiteracy, but, heck,
everyone has problems. "Every letter in the alphabet to me they look the
same" brings to my mind's eye a picture of a strange alphabet in which all
letters look alike or, rather, in which the differences in their shape have no

meaning. The image is clear, it works, and it involves me. And not only does the image itself succeed, but the delay of the most important word in the line, same, until the end, and the impact of its rhyme with name, convinces me I am hearing the truth. Blues singer Eddie "Son" House told me about how he put his blues stanzas together: "I had enough sense to try to make 'em, rhyme 'em so they'd have hits to 'em with a meaning, some sense to 'em, you know" (Titon 1994:47).

I do not respond to "Mother died when I was a baby"; I resist a statement that sounds sentimental. This is not because I think of myself as some kind of tough guy, but because I want the sentiment to be earned. I much prefer the statement at the close of the line: "father I never seen." The effect is in the contrast between the mother who died and the father who might as well be dead. In the image of the father who has never been seen is the mystery of not knowing one's parents. It is not just missing love; for all we know the poor boy was raised by loving relatives. But a child takes after parents, inherits the biology, so to speak; without knowing your parents you do not fully know yourself. "When I think how dumb I am, you know it makes me want to scream" is a cliché; the rhyme is forced. Okay, scream.

The final stanza takes great risk with sentimentality, calling up Christmas memories, but it succeeds by a matter-of-fact tone: "When I was a child Santa Claus never left one toy" dispels the scene's stickiness. Santa Claus never left a toy for anyone, but a child who believes in Santa can enjoy an innocent world where presents reward good little boys and girls. If he could not believe in Santa, I wonder if he ever had any part of the innocent happiness people seem to need early, and in large doses, if they are going to live creative lives. Or it could have been the other way around: He believed in Santa, but Santa, never bringing him a toy, simply did not believe in him.

The song now leads up to its final line, a plea for mercy. "You" are addressed directly: If you have any mercy, show it to the poor boy. Will you? If you heard this from a blind street singer, would you put some coins in his cup? The song will strike some people as sentimental, calling up an easy emotion that is just as quickly forgotten as it is evoked. T. S. Eliot, in a widely influential argument, said that in a work of literature any powerful emotion must have an "objective correlative"; that is, the work itself must demonstrate that there is good reason for the emotion (Eliot [1920] 1964). Has "Poor Boy Blues" given you good reason for mercy? Have you been told the truth?

Autobiography and the Blues

Considering the effect of "Poor Boy Blues" on an imaginary listener can take us only so far. What do the words mean to someone in the blues music-culture? What do they mean to Lazy Bill Lucas? Does the "I" in the "Poor Boy Blues" represent Lucas? What, in short, is the relationship between the song and the singer?

The blues singer's image as wandering minstrel, blind bard, and untutored genius is idealized; however, according to Samuel Charters, "there is no more romantic figure in popular music than the bluesman, with everything the term involves. And it isn't a false romanticism" (1977:112). The result is that most books on blues are organized biographically. Some writers have gone so far as to derive the facts of a blues singer's life and personality from the lyrics of his or her recorded songs. On the other hand, published life stories of blues singers in their own words are rare (see, for example, Brunoghe 1964; Titon 1974). If we read these first-person life stories properly, we can understand them as far more reliable expressions of the blues singer's individuality than song lyrics are, because the lyrics are often borrowed from tradition. Still, most people just assume that the lyrics of a blues song speak for the singer. Paul Oliver wrote, for example, "One of the characteristics of the blues is that it is highly personalized—blues singers nearly always sing about themselves" (1974:30). If that is true, then "Poor Boy Blues" is most likely a reflection of the life and thoughts of Lazy Bill Lucas. Is it?

I was a close friend of Bill Lucas's for six years, playing guitar in his blues band for two of them. During the course of our friendship, in a project like the one suggested in Chapter 9, I tape-recorded his recollections of his life, edited and excerpted for publication first in *Blues Unlimited* (Titon 1969), a British blues research journal, and later in the accompanying notes to his first American LP (Lucas 1974; Titon 1994). Let us look, then, at parts of Lucas's life history and see if "Poor Boy Blues" speaks for him.

The Life History of Bill Lucas, Blues Singer

I was born in Wynne, Arkansas, on May 29, 1918. I never heard my mother say the exact time I was born: she was so upset at the time I guess she wouldn't remember. I have two sisters and three brothers; I was third from my baby sister, the third youngest.

Ever since I can remember, I had trouble with my eyesight. Doctors tell me it's the nerves. I can see shapes, I can tell colors, and I know light and dark, but it's hard to focus, and no glasses can help me. An operation might cure it, but there's a chance it could leave me completely blind, and I don't want to take that gamble.

My father was a farmer out in the country from Wynne. He was a sharecropper, farming on the halvers. About every two or three years we moved from one farm to another. We owned cattle, we owned pigs. We had about thirteen milk cows, and we had leghorn chickens that gave us bushels of eggs.

There weren't many guitars around, but in 1930 my daddy got me a guitar. I remember so well, just like it was yesterday, he traded a pig for it. Money was scarce down there; we didn't have any money. The boy wanted $7 for it. We didn't have money but we had plenty of pigs. Our neighbors had some boys that played guitar, but they never did take pains and show me how to do it. I would just watch 'em and listen. I learned from sounds. And after they were gone, then I would try to make the guitar sound like I heard them make it sound. I wanted the guitar because I liked the noise and it sounded pretty.

After I got it and come progressing on it, a tune or two here or there, my dad and mama both decided that would be a good way for me to make my living. I knew all the time I wanted to make a career out of it, but after I came progressing on it, well they wanted me to make a career out of it too. But they said I had to be old enough and big enough to take care of it, not to be breaking strings and busting it all up.

My father got me a piano in 1932 for a Christmas present. That was the happiest Christmas I ever had. He didn't trade pigs for that; he paid money for it. Got it at our neighborhood drugstore. It was an upright. It had been a player piano but all the guts had been taken out of it. Well, at the time I knew how to play organ, one of those pump organs; I had played a pump organ we had at home that came about the same time as the guitar. So it didn't take me long to learn how to bang out a few tunes on the piano.

I didn't know what chords I was making. We got a little scale book that would go behind the keyboard of the piano and tell you all the chords. It was a beginner's book, in big letters. I could see that. You know, a beginner's book is in big letters. And I wanted to learn music, but after I got that far, well, the rest of the music books were so small that I couldn't see the print. And that's why I didn't learn to read music.

I did learn to read the alphabet at home. My parents taught me, and so did the other kids. I used to go to school, but it was just to be with the other kids, and sometimes the kids would teach me. I was just apt; I could pick things up. I had a lot of mother-wit.

So I bumped around on the piano until 1936, when we left the country and came to Cape Girardeau, Missouri. I had to leave my piano; we didn't have room for it. I almost cried. That was when I started playing the guitar on street corners.

We lost our mother in 1939. We buried her in Commerce, and we left Commerce after she died. My dad, he went to St. Louis in 1940, still trying to find better living conditions. Later that year he brought me to St. Louis, and that's where I met Big Joe Williams. At that time he wasn't playing in bars or taverns; he was just playing on the street. So he let me join him, and I counted it an honor to be playing with Big Joe Williams because I had heard his blues records while I was still down South. And so we played blues in the street.

But I didn't stay in St. Louis long. My dad and I came to Chicago the day after New Year's in 1941. Sonny Boy Williamson was the first musician I met with up there. We were playing one-nighters in taverns and parties. Sonny Boy would book himself, and I went around with him. There wasn't much money in it; Sonny Boy paid my expenses and a place to stay with his friends. He was known all up around there. We didn't play nothing but the funky blues. He just needed somebody to keep time, back him up on guitar.

I started in my professional career in 1946 when I joined the union. We all joined the union together, me and Willie Mabon and Earl Dranes, two guitars and a piano. We took our first job in 1946 on December 20, in the Tuxedo Lounge, 3119 Indiana, in Chicago. They paid union scale, but scale wasn't much then. The leader didn't get but twelve dollars a night, the side-men ten dollars. We worked from 9 P.M. until 4 A.M. It was a real nice club. We had a two-week engagement there, and I thought it was real good money. But then we were kicked back out on the street.

Little Walter [Walter Jacobs, pioneer of amplified blues harmonica] and I used to play along with Johnny Young at a place called the Purple Cat—

Figure 4.6

Lazy Bill and His Blue Rhythm, studio photo. Chicago, Illinois, 1954. From left to right: Lazy Bill Lucas, James Bannister, "Miss Hi-Fi," and Jo Jo Williams.

Courtesy of Jo Jo Williams

1947. That's where he gave me the name "lazy" at. Little Walter thought I should go up and turn on the amps, but I never did go up and do that thing, so that's why he started calling me "lazy" Bill, and the name stuck.

I switched to playing piano in 1950 because they had more guitar players than piano players. But of course I'd been playing piano all along—just not professionally, that's all.

I had a trio, Lazy Bill and the Blue Rhythm, for about three or four months in 1954 [Figure 4.6]. We were supposed to do four records a year for Chance, but Art Sheridan went out of business and we never heard about it again. We did one record. Well, I didn't keep my group together long. You know it's kind of hard on a small musician to keep a group together in Chicago very long because they run out of work, and when they don't get work to do, they get with other guys. And there were so many musicians in Chicago that some of 'em were underbidding one another. They'd take a job what I was getting twelve dollars for, they'd take it for eight dollars. Work got so far apart. Every time I'd run out of an engagement, it would be a long time before another one came through. And so Mojo and Jo Jo, [harmonica player George "Mojo" Buford and electric guitar and bass player Joseph "Jo Jo" Williams] they had come up here to Minneapolis. They had been working at the Key Club, and they decided they needed a piano player. I wasn't doing anything in Chicago; I was glad to come up here. I had no idea I was going to stay up here, but I ended up here with a houseful of furniture.

©1974 by William Lucas and Jeff Todd Titon. A fuller version accompanies Lucas 1974 and Titon 1994.

Lazy Bill Lucas and "Poor Boy Blues"

Bill Lucas's account of his life ends in Minneapolis in 1964. The following year I began my graduate studies at the University of Minnesota and met him at a university concert. By that time he had two audiences: the black people on the North Side of the city who still liked the blues, and the white people in the university community. The 1960s was the period of the first so-called blues revival (Groom 1971), during which thousands of blues records from the previous four decades were reissued on LPs, dozens of older singers believed dead were "rediscovered" and recorded, and hundreds of younger singers, Bill Lucas among them, found new audiences at university concerts and coffeehouses and festivals. The revival, which attracted a predominantly young, white audience, peaked in the great 1969 and 1970 Ann Arbor (Michigan) Blues Festivals, where the best of three generations of blues singers and blues bands performed for people who had traveled thousands of miles to pitch their tents and attend these three-day events (Figure 4.7). Bill Lucas was one of the featured performers at the 1970 festival. For his performance he received four hundred dollars plus expenses, the most money he ever made for a single job in his musical career.

In the 1960s and 1970s Bill Lucas could not support himself from his musical earnings. A monthly check (for roughly a hundred times the minimum hourly wage) from government welfare for the blind supplemented his income in Minneapolis. Most of Minneapolis's black community preferred soul and disco music to blues, while others liked jazz or classical music. Nor was there sufficient work in front of the university folk music audience for Bill. He sang in clubs, in bars, and at concerts, but the work was unsteady. When I was in his band (1969–1971), our most dependable job was a six-month engagement for two nights each week in the "Grotto Room" of a pizza restaurant close to the university. Classified by the

Jeff Todd Titon

Figure 4.7
Action at the Ann Arbor Blues Festival, 1969, which took place on the same weekend as the legendary rock festival in Woodstock, New York. Big Mama Thornton sings while T-Bone Walker plays guitar.

musicians' union as a low-level operation, it paid the minimum union scale for an evening's work from 9:00 P.M. to 1:00 A.M.: $23 for Bill, $18 for sidemen. On December 11, 1982, Bill Lucas died. A benefit concert to pay his funeral expenses raised nearly two thousand dollars. Today, he is fondly remembered by the Twin Cities blues community, where a weekly blues radio show is named after him.

His life history not only gives facts about his life but also expresses an attitude toward it. We can compare both with the words of "Poor Boy Blues" to see whether the song speaks personally for Bill Lucas. Some of the facts of the poor boy's life correspond, but others do not. I asked him whether the line about all the letters in the alphabet looking the same held any special meaning for him, and he said it did. Unless letters or numbers were printed very large and thick, he could not make them out. But unlike the poor boy in the song who never saw his father, Lucas and his father were very close. His Christmases were happy, and one year he received a piano. What about the attitudes expressed in the song and in the life history? Neither show self-pity. Bill did not have an illustrious career as a blues singer, yet he was proud of his accomplishments. "I just sing the funky blues," he said, "and people either like it or they don't."

"Poor Boy Blues" does not, then, speak directly for Bill Lucas's personal experience. Yet it speaks for tens of thousands of people who have been forced by circumstances into hard times. In their broad cultural reach, the words of blues songs tell the truth.

Learning the Blues

"Poor Boy Blues" was composed and recorded by "St. Louis" Jimmy Oden in 1942. Lucas learned the song from the record. In the African American music-culture almost all blues singers learn songs by imitation, whether in person or from records. In his life history, Lucas tells how he listened to neighbors play guitar and how he tried to make it sound like they did. After he developed a rudimentary playing technique, he could fit accompaniments behind new songs that he learned from others or made up himself.

Unquestionably the best way to come to know a song is to make it your own by performing it. Listen once again to "Poor Boy Blues" with the listening chart close by, and concentrate now on the instrumental accompaniment. When Lucas is not singing, the accompanying guitarists usually give each beat three equal parts, with an accent on the first: Da-da-da, Da-da-da, Da-da-da, Da-da-da, and so on. The drummer usually ties the second of the three parts to the first part, giving a long-short rhythmic figure: Daaa-da, Daaa-da, and so on. This rhythm is a common way of dividing the beat in slow blues songs.

Next listen to the rhythm of Lucas's vocal, and try to feel both rhythms, vocal and accompaniment, at the same time. You might find this difficult. The reason is that Lucas seldom starts his tones squarely on the beat. He sings with a great deal of syncopation, that is, with delayed attacks or anticipations of the beat. Lucas is not having a hard time finding the beat; on the contrary, he is playing around with it.

In Chapter 3 we saw that two-against-three polymeter characterizes black African music. Here we see a deep connection between African and African American music in terms of rhythmic complexity and polymeter. But our example from the blues does not reflect continuous polymeter, as in Africa. Rather, blues music (and jazz, and reggae) shifts into and out of polymeter, playfully teasing the boundary. When these shifts occur rapidly, the boundary between single meter and polymeter breaks down. The result is a new sense of time: the graceful forward propulsion we hear as "swing" that makes us feel like moving our whole body in response.

The Blues Scale

Lucas sings "Poor Boy Blues" in a musical scale I have elsewhere called the blues scale (Titon 1971). This scale is found in field hollers, work songs, lined-out hymns, blues, jazz, spirituals, gospel tunes, soul, disco, hip-hop, and other black American music. An original African American invention, the blues scale also is the most important scale in rock music. It differs significantly from the usual Western scales, such as the major scale illustrated in Chapter 1 ("Joy to the World"). The blues scale can be thought of as another example of African American "playing," this time playing with the pitch of a few of the tones in the major scale. Sing "Joy to the World" again now, pausing on "to" and "Lord":

Joy to the world, the Lord has come.
8 7 6   5   4   3   2   1

For convenience, we shall number each of these tones as above. Each number corresponds to what is called a "degree" of the scale. The tones that you paused on, 7 and 3, are the main "blue notes," the ones that the blues singer most often plays with—sometimes sounding them right on pitch, sometimes a little below, sometimes sliding around them about the distance between the tones given off by a white and black key next to each other on the piano. To hear a singer use the blues scale, listen again to Baby Doo Caston's field holler **(CD 1, Track 18).** The first time he sings "morn-ings," notice how he slides down from the initial pitch of "-ings" to a blue note below, while holding the same syllable. The starting pitch of "-ings" is like "Joy" (8) in "Joy to the World," but the ending pitch is a little below "to" (7) yet not quite down to "the" (6). For an even more dramatic example, listen to Baby Doo sing "morn-ings" the second time (right after the first). Here he slides from the initial pitch on "morn" (4) down through several pitches, going through the blue note around "Lord" (3) in the major scale of "Joy to the World," until he reaches the final pitch (1) on "-ings," comparable to "come" in the Christmas carol. Now listen again to "Poor Boy Blues" and see if you can hear the blue notes.

Composing the Blues

Besides learning blues songs from other singers and from records, blues singers make up their own songs. Sometimes they think out a song in advance; sometimes they improvise it during performance. Often a performance embodies both planning and improvisation. The blues song's first composition unit is the line. If you sing the blues most of your life, blues lines will run through your mind like proverbs, which many indeed are: for instance, "You never miss your water till your well runs dry." A male singer might rhyme it with a line like "Never miss your woman till she say good-bye." (A female singer's rhyme: "Never miss your good man till he say good-bye.") The singer has just composed his stanza:

You never miss your water till your well runs dry,
No, you never miss your water till your well runs dry,
I never missed my baby till she said good-bye.

If the blues singer plans the stanzas in advance, he or she memorizes them, sometimes writing them down. As we have seen, the stanzas may or may not speak directly for the personal experience of the singer. St. Louis Jimmy, the author of "Poor Boy Blues," said this about another of his songs, "Goin' Down Slow":

> My blues came mostly from women. . . . "Goin' Down Slow" started from a girl, in St. Louis—it wasn't me—I've never been sick a day in my life, but I seen her in the condition she was in—pregnant, tryin' to lose a kid, see. And she looked like she was goin' down slow. And I made that remark to my sister and it came in my mind and I started to writin' it. . . . I looked at other people's troubles and I writes from that, and I writes from my own troubles. (Oliver 1965:101–2)

Songs that blues singers memorize usually stick to one idea or event. A memorized song, Lucas's "Poor Boy Blues" has four stanzas on the circumstances leading to the poor boy's cry for mercy. In contrast, the words in a spontaneously improvised song seldom show the unity of time, circumstances, or feeling evident in a memorized song. After all, unless you have had lots of practice, it is hard enough to improvise rhymed stanzas, let alone keep to a single subject. So an improvising singer usually mixes in some memorized, traditional stanzas along with stanzas he or she puts together on the spot.

A Blues Song in the Making

Today a few blues songs are improvised in performance, but most are memorized beforehand. The influence of recordings is so overpowering that singers seldom change lyrics when learning other people's songs, and like rock bands trying to "cover" hit records, they copy the instruments, too.

In 1954 Art Sheridan, the owner of Chicago-based Chance Records, asked Lazy Bill Lucas to make a record. During the early 1950s Lucas had played piano as a sideman on several of Homesick James Williamson's

Close Listening   CD 1:21

"She Got Me Walkin'"

Counter Number	Commentary	Lyrics
0:00	Instrumental introduction.	
0:14	Lucas sings verse 1. Interplay among all accompanying instruments. Instrumental response to the vocal "calls" (instruments respond when Lucas pauses between phrases and lines).	My baby got me walkin' all up and down the street. My baby got me walkin' all up and down the street. She left me for another man 'cause she wanted to be free.
0:56	Lucas sings quatrain starting verse 2.	My baby told me one day, And I laughed and thought it was a joke; She said I'm going to leave you, You don't move me no more.
1:09	Refrain, verse 2.	She got me walkin' all up and down the street; She left me for another man 'cause she wanted to be free.
1:35	Lucas speaks, signaling an instrumental break.	"Play it for me, boy."
1:37	Instrumental break.	
2:17	Quatrain starting verse 3. "Snook" is James "Snooky" Prior.	I don't want to see Snook, Not even Homesick James; The way my baby left me, I really believe he's to blame.
2:30	Refrain, then verse 3.	She got me walkin' all up and down the street; She left me for another man 'cause she wanted to be free.

Words and music by William Lucas. Used by permission.

recordings, and he was a member of the Blues Rockers, a group with the minor recording hits "Calling All Cows" and "Johnny Mae." For his own session as leader, Lucas was billed as "Lazy Bill and His Blue Rhythm." He chose an original song, "She Got Me Walkin'" **(CD 1, Track 21).** Lucas composed the lyrics in advance and memorized them for the recording session, which took place in Chicago on October 28, 1953. Accompanying Bill's vocal and piano were Louis Myers on electric guitar and Elga Edmonds on drums.

The first thing you may notice in "She Got Me Walkin'" is that the stanza form differs from that of "Poor Boy Blues." In that song Lucas sang a line, then more or less repeated it, and closed the stanza with a rhyming punch line. Most blues stanzas fall into this three-line pattern, particularly traditional stanzas. But some, like verses 2 and 3 of "She Got Me Walkin'," fall into a different line pattern consisting of a *quatrain* (four lines rhymed abcb) and a rhymed two-line *refrain* that follows to close out each verse or stanza. You can easily hear the contrast between the three-line stanza and the quatrain-refrain stanza. The quatrain-refrain stanza became popular after World War II. It usually offers vignettes in the quatrain as instances to

CD 1:21

"She Got Me Walkin'" (3:00). William "Lazy Bill" Lucas. Performed by Lazy Bill and His Blue Rhythm: Lazy Bill Lucas, piano and vocal; Louis Myers, guitar; Elga Edmonds, drums. Words and music by William Lucas. Chance 100 78-rpm record. Chicago, Illinois, 1954.

prove the truth of the repeated refrain. Because any stanza form is by nature preset, it acts as a mold into which the improvising singer pours his or her words.

Lucas told me that he thought getting the names of some of his musician friends into "She Got Me Walkin'" would make the song more interesting and popular. "Snook" was the harmonica player Snooky Pryor. James Williamson had recorded under the name "Homesick James" and was well-known to the people who frequented the Chicago bars and clubs to hear blues. When I asked Lucas whether the lyrics were based on a true story, he replied "More or less." The "she" of the song turns out to be none other than Johnny Mae, whom Bill had sung about for the Blues Rockers a few months earlier. Johnny Mae was Homesick James's girlfriend.

As Lucas's lyrics and autobiography show, during the years following World War II blues musicians in Chicago formed a social as well as a musical community. They kept each other company, played on each other's recordings, substituted for one another at various club dates, and both competed with and supported one another in the music business and social world. These relationships persisted for years. For example, Muddy Waters and Howlin' Wolf were rivals. Even as late as 1970, at the Ann Arbor Blues Festival, this rivalry was evident. Waters was scheduled to come onstage after Wolf's set, but Wolf prolonged the set well beyond the agreed-on ending time in a bid to steal time from Waters.

The life histories and social ties of blues singers have clearly influenced their music. Our discussion to this point has focused on the lives and songs of blues musicians. The next section relates blues songs to the lives of their listeners.

Social Context and the Meaning of the Blues

Although the "feelingful" aspects of blues are embodied in such musical aspects as the singer's delivery and in the way the musicians "play around" with the blues scale and rhythmic syncopation, the most direct expression of blues feeling comes from the lyrics. Most blues lyrics are about lovers, and they fall into a pattern arising from black American life. The blues grew and developed when most African Americans lived as sharecroppers on Southern cotton farms, from late in the nineteenth century until just before World War II, when farm mechanization began to displace the black workers, and factory work at high wages in the Northern cities attracted them. Down home, young men and women did not marry early; they were needed on the farm. If a young woman became pregnant, she had her baby and brought the child into the household with her parents. She did not lose status in the community, and later she often married the father of her child. When a woman did marry young, her partner usually was middle-aged and needed a woman to work and care for his children from a prior marriage. It was good to have plenty of children; when they came of age to work, more hands could go into the cotton and corn fields. Adoption was common; when families broke up, children were farmed out among relatives.

Sociologists and anthropologists, some of them black (such as Charles Johnson), studied this sharecropping culture in the 1920s and 1930s. They found that when partners separated it was because one could not live with the other's laziness, violence, or adultery. A woman was reported as saying her current lover was "nice all right, but I ain't thinking about marrying. Soon as you marry a man he starts mistreating you, and I ain't going to be mistreated no more" (Johnson [1934] 1966:83). Blues songs reflected these attitudes; mistreatment was the most common subject. Once this subject was established, people began to expect that blues songs would be about love and mistreatment. After World War II the sharecropping culture was less important; the action now took place in the cities where most black people had gone: Atlanta, New York, Washington, Detroit, Memphis, St. Louis, Chicago, Dallas, Houston, Los Angeles, Oakland. But black family patterns persisted among the lower classes in the urban ghettos, and so did the blues.

Blues lyrics about mistreatment fall into a pattern. The singer casts himself or herself in the role of mistreated victim, introduces an antagonist (usually a mistreating lover), provides incidents that detail the circumstances of the mistreatment, and draws up a bill of indictment. Then, with the listener's tacit approval, the victim becomes the judge, and the drama turns on the verdict: Will he or she accept the mistreatment, try to reform the mistreater, or leave? Resigned acceptance and attempted reform resolve a minority of blues songs. Most often the victim, declaring independence, steps out of the victim's role with an ironic parting shot and leaves.

Blues music helps lovers understand each other. Because the themes are traditional and shared by the community, blues songs also give listeners community approval for separation in response to mistreatment. The listener who recognizes his or her situation in the lyrics of a blues song receives a nice definition of that situation and a possible response to it. At a Saturday night party, or at home alone, a mistreated lover finds consolation in the blues (Figure 4.8). Of course, mistreatment is not the only theme in

Figure 4.8
Dancing at a juke joint. Alabama, 1957.

Frederic Ramsey, Jr.

Figure 4.9
Buddy Guy at the Ann Arbor Blues Festival, 1970.

Jeff Todd Titon

blues lyrics. They portray virtually all kinds of relationships among partners. And the theme of mistreatment extends from lovers to bosses.

The Blues Yesterday

In this chapter we have approached blues as an African American music. But today more people recognize the name of the British blues singer-guitarist Eric Clapton than the names Muddy Waters (Figure 4.4) and Buddy Guy (Figure 4.9). About thirty-five years ago blues entered mainstream U.S. culture, and in our mass-mediated global village today blues is an attractive commodity. You can hear blues played in Prague, Dar es Salaam, and Tokyo by citizens of Czechoslovakia, Tanzania, and Japan. Nowadays blues is regarded as a universal phenomenon, accessible to all.

It is true that African Americans invented blues, and it is also true that early on people outside the black communities were attracted to it. The African American composer W. C. Handy popularized blues in the 1910s with songs such as "St. Louis Blues," but white singers such as Sophie Tucker recorded blues songs before African American singers did. African American blues queens such as Bessie Smith made blues the most popular African American music in the 1920s, and it attracted a small white audience as well as a large black one. The 1920s also brought the first recordings of downhome blues: Blind Blake, the greatest ragtime guitarist; Charley Patton, a songster regarded as the father of Mississippi Delta blues; and a host of others brought the music out of the local juke joints and house parties and onto recordings that were circulated back into the black communities. Jimmie Rodgers, the first star of country music, whose brief

Figure 4.10
Pee Wee Crayton in performance at the Ann Arbor Blues Festival, 1969.

recording career lasted from 1927 through 1933, sang many blues songs, particularly his "blue yodels." Rodgers, a white Mississippian, learned many of his songs and much of his relaxed singing style from black railroad men. Blues has been an important component within country music ever since. African American rhythms, jazz instrumental breaks, and the blues scale were critical in the formation of bluegrass, which ironically is usually regarded as an Anglo-American musical tradition (see Cantwell 1984). Further, the banjo—the quintessential bluegrass instrument—is derived from an African instrument.

Blues has always been a popular form within jazz and remains so today. In the 1930s and 1940s, blues "shouters" such as Jimmy Rushing with Count Basie's orchestra bridged the line between blues and jazz. African American rhythm and blues of the 1940s followed in the tradition of these blues shouters, such as Wynonie Harris, Tiny Bradshaw, and Joe Turner, along with crooners such as Charles Brown. In the meantime an urban blues sound arose featuring singers with small bands led by electric guitar. Aaron "T-Bone" Walker invented it in the 1940s, Riley "B. B." (Blues Boy) King made it immensely popular in the 1950s, and it gained strength on the West Coast through singer-guitarists such as Pee Wee Crayton (Figure 4.10). Rock and roll in the 1950s began as a white cover of black rhythm and blues, but by the early 1960s black Americans competed well in that arena, and singers like Ray Charles and Motown groups like Diana Ross and the Supremes became immensely popular. Ray Charles's biggest hit, "What'd I Say," was a blues song; blues such as "Maybelline" were among Chuck Berry's best-selling recordings; it even became possible for downhome singers such as Jimmy Reed, whose "Big Boss Man" climbed high on the pop charts, to cross over into the white music charts.

Blues was crucial in British rock during the 1960s. Groups such as the Rolling Stones (whose name came from one of Muddy Waters' songs, and whose early albums featured copies of Chicago blues standards) participated in the British blues revival. Dozens of British blues bands could be found in such cities as London and Liverpool, and talented instrumentalists such as John Mayall and Eric Clapton arose from this ferment in the 1960s. An American blues revival in the same decade gave the white musicians Paul Butterfield and Charlie Musselwhite a start, and a new phenomenon appeared: bands whose personnel included a mixture of black and white musicians. Muddy Waters, for example, featured the white harmonica player Paul Oscher and in the 1970s had a white guitarist, Bob Margolin, in his band. Lazy Bill Lucas, the leader of the band I played in during the 1960s, led an integrated band. At the 1970 Ann Arbor Blues Festival, Luther Allison and Johnny Winter sang and played a set together (Figure 1.3).

Since the late 1960s many white American rock bands have covered black blues hits from the 1950s and 1960s. The screaming guitar lines of heavy metal music are an interpretation (some would say a misinterpretation) of the blues lead-guitar styles of B. B. King, Albert King, Freddy King, Elmore James, and others. Most rock fans do not realize the debt that rock owes to blues and the African American community. But in the 1960s most of black America saw blues as old-fashioned. Outside of strongholds in the Mississippi Delta and Chicago, blues accounted for a small proportion of jukebox records and received little radio airplay. Black intellectuals dismissed blues as a music of resignation, unfit for the contemporary climate of civil rights and black power. Soul music was much more attractive. Yet during this same decade many blues singers revived their careers, finding a new audience. The blues revival of the 1960s brought commercially recorded blues music and black musicians before a largely white public in North America and Europe. Buddy Guy, very popular today, was equally active, but overshadowed, in the 1960s revival (see Figure 4.9). Magic Sam, B. B. King, Muddy Waters, and Howlin' Wolf represented variety in the modern electric blues sound then, while singers who had made recordings before World War II performed on the folk music circuit, sounding much as they had decades before: Roosevelt Sykes, Mississippi John Hurt, Son House, Skip James, John Lee Hooker, Lightnin' Hopkins, Big Joe Williams, and Jessie Mae Hemphill (Figure 4.11), to name a few.

The Blues Today

A second blues revival began in the 1980s with the Blues Brothers' appearances on *Saturday Night Live,* their film, and the founding of the House of Blues clubs in major U.S. cities in the early 1990s. Buddy Guy and John Lee Hooker revived their careers, Robert Cray and Stevie Ray Vaughn began theirs, and Rory Block, Bonnie Raitt, Bobby Rush, Gatemouth Brown, and Koko Taylor came to the attention of a new audience. Although the African American audience preferred hip-hop, there was no shortage of

Jeff Todd Titon

Figure 4.11
Jessie Mae Hemphill at the National Downhome Blues Festival, Atlanta, Georgia, 1990.

black blues singers and musicians. The U.S. Congress declared 2003 the "Year of the Blues"; and blues is back on the scene once more.

For an example of contemporary blues we turn to a masterpiece by an older singer, Otis Rush (Figure 4.12). "Ain't Enough Comin' In" **(CD 1, Track 22)** was voted the outstanding blues recording of the year 1994 by the readers of *Living Blues* magazine. "Ain't Enough Comin' In," which Rush wrote and arranged, is as outstanding a performance of contemporary urban blues as can be heard today. The song starts with an authoritative drumbeat, and immediately the electric bass sets a heavy rhythmic riff that repeats until the end of the song. In its rhythmic constancy the bass provides something akin to the bell pattern in *Agbekor* (see Chapter 3) that anchors the entire performance. The drummer plays simply but forcefully and unerringly, marking the beat 1–2–3–4, with the accent on 3. A rock drummer would be busier than this—and a lot less relentless. The electric bass is louder than the drums, which has been characteristic of black popular music since the 1970s.

Listeners who can recognize the difference between major and minor chords will realize that unlike most blues "Ain't Enough Comin' In" is based on minor chords. The first chorus is instrumental. Rush plays the

 CD 1:22
"Ain't Enough Comin' In" (5:41). Otis Rush. Performed by Otis Rush on *Otis Rush: Ain't Enough Comin' In*. Mercury CD 314518769-2, 1994.

Figure 4.12
Otis Rush performing at the Ann Arbor Blues Festival 1969. Note that he plays left-handed.

Jeff Todd Titon

electric guitar lead above a riffing rhythm section that includes a trumpet and saxophone as well as an organ. The direct, spare playing here sets a somber mood for his powerful vocals that follow. The song features a bridge section ("Now when it's all over . . .") that departs from the usual verse patterns, but otherwise the song has a typical blues structure. After the vocals, Rush takes the tune twice through with a guitar solo, and this is followed by two choruses in which a saxophone leads, taking some of Rush's ideas and developing them. The bridge returns, followed by two more verses, and Rush takes it out with one more instrumental chorus. Hear how the sound of the guitar vibrates at the beginning of the last chorus. This is a tremolo, and Rush is known for getting this effect by pushing his fingers from side to side on the strings (a hand tremolo) rather than using the tremolo bar attached to the electric guitar.

Rush's vocal style is striking. Like many blues singers he hoarsens his voice at times to show great emotion, but he also makes his voice tremble at times, an effect that mirrors his guitar tremolo (and vice versa). Blues writers have called Rush's voice "tortured" with a "frightening intensity" and a "harrowing poetic terror" (Rowe 1979:176) and "tense and oppressive" (Herzhaft 1992:300). There is no denying that Rush has a full, powerful voice. Its vehemence and falling melodic curve may remind you of the Navajo Yeibichai singers (Chapter 2).

Rush's lyrics are clever and subtle. In the beginning of his career he relied on the professional songwriter Willie Dixon, but after his first hit

Close Listening

"Ain't Enough Comin' In"

Counter Number	Commentary	Lyrics
0:01	Instrumental introduction.	
0:09	Rush's guitar takes the lead and is accompanied by the band for one verse.	
0:35	Rush sings first verse, with band accompanying.	Oh, I ain't got enough comin' in to take care of what's got to go out. It ain't enough love or money comin' in, baby, to take care of what's got to go out. Like a bird I got my wing clipped, my friends; I've got to start all over again.
1:02	Rush sings second verse.	If the sun ever shine on me again, Oh lord if the sun ever shine on me again. Like a bird I got my wing clipped, my friends; I've got to start all over again.
1:28	Bridge section (third verse)—different melodic and harmonic structure.	Now when it's all over and said and done, money talks and the fool gets none. The tough get tough and the tough get goin'; come on baby let me hold you in my arms.
1:46	Rush sings fourth verse while band continues to back him up as in the second verse.	It ain't got enough comin' in to take care of what's got to go out. Ain't enough love or money comin' in, baby, to take care of what's got to go out. My friends, I got my wings clipped; I've got to start all over again.
2:12	Rush takes the lead on the electric guitar for an entire verse, accompanied by the band.	
2:38	Rush continues to play an instrumental lead for another verse. Listen to how he "bends" the pitch of some notes by pushing the string to the side.	
3:05	Tenor saxophone lead for a verse; notice the deliberately raspy, buzzy tone.	
3:31	Tenor sax lead for another verse.	
3:57	Rush repeats bridge (third verse).	When it's all over and said and done, money talks and the fool gets none. The tough get tough and the tough get goin'; come on baby let me hold you in my arms.
4:16	Rush sings sixth verse.	Ain't got enough comin' in to take care of what's got to go out. It ain't enough love or money comin' in, baby, to take care of what's got to go out. Like a bird I got my wings clipped, my friends; I've got to start all over again.
4:40	Rush sings seventh verse.	If you don't put nothin' in you can't get nothin' out; You don't put nothin' in, baby, you can't get nothin' out; Like a bird I got my wings clipped, my friends; I've got to start all over again.
5:07	Rush plays instrumental lead guitar to ending fade out. Notice the vibrating guitar (hand tremolo).	

songs he decided that he could "write one better than that" (Forte 1991:159). When I hear the first line, I think "ain't enough comin' in" refers to money; but in the second line Rush lets me know that I should think of the parallel between love and money: The singer feels that he's giving too much and not getting enough of either in return.

Who is Otis Rush? Is he the latest singer-guitarist to capitalize on the blues revival? Not at all: Otis Rush has been a blues legend since the 1950s, well-known to musicians and serious blues aficionados if not to the general listening public. Stevie Ray Vaughn named his band Double Trouble in honor of Rush's finest song from that decade. Led Zeppelin covered Rush's "I Can't Quit You Baby," with guitarist Jimmy Page lifting Rush's instrumental break note-for-note (Forte 1991:156). Rush's guitar playing turned Eric Clapton into a disciple. When Rush met Clapton in England in 1986 he called Clapton a "great guitar player" and modestly went on, "Everybody plays like somebody. It's good to know that somebody's listening. To me, I'm just a guitar player. I'm not trying to influence nobody, I'm just trying to play, and play well. And hopefully I can sell some records" (Forte 1991:161).

Otis Rush was born in Philadelphia, Mississippi, in 1934 and began playing at age ten. Left-handed, he plays the guitar upside down, with the bass strings closer to the ground; this accounts for some of his special sound (see Figure 4.12). For example, to "bend" a note on the treble strings, Rush pulls the string down, whereas a right-handed guitarist must push the string up (harder to do). Like Bill Lucas, he first sang country music, not blues. It was not until the late 1940s, when he came to Chicago and began visiting the blues clubs, that he decided to sing and play the blues.

Although B. B. King, T-Bone Walker, and Magic Sam were among the musicians who influenced him most strongly, Rush developed his own version of modern blues guitar. His style is subtle, spare, cool—the instrumental equivalent of caressing a lover. There is nothing egotistical about it, no showing off. He likes to make his guitar talk and sing; that is, he phrases his lead guitar playing the way a singer delivers a song, with feeling. His use of silence is brilliant. "Well, I can play fast stuff, but I try to take my time and make you feel what I'm doin'," he told Jas Obrecht. "You can play a bunch of notes so fast, but then you turn around, and somebody out there listening says, 'What did he play?' Sound good, but can't remember nothin'. Take your time and play. Measure it out enough where they got time to hear what you're doing" (2000:243). Like a fine aged wine at its peak, at its best his music has great presence, neither understated nor flashy: substantial, direct, powerful, and commanding respect.

Rush takes risks onstage and in recordings. Often he would rather try something new than stick with the same old thing. "I can make that guitar say what you sayin' right now," Rush told Obrecht. "I can say The Lord's Prayer on my guitar and you'll say, 'That's every word of it.' Just like you talkin' there? I can make my guitar say just what you said. . . . I can sing with my guitar, just like I sing with my voice" (2000:243). Rush's guitar isn't merely imitating his vocals. It replies to them and extends them, in another example of the African call-and-response aesthetic. The album from which

"Ain't Enough Comin' In" is taken represented a long overdue turning point in Rush's career. He is, today, one of the very best of the older generation of blues singer-guitarists, a generation whose music was formed prior to the blues revival of the 1960s.

A Few Final Words

Mass-mediated popular music, presented outside community settings in concerts, recordings, radio, and television, forms communities of listeners and would-be performers who may otherwise have little in common. As we have seen, until the 1960s the blues music-culture was based in African American communities; today it embraces people from all over the world. Blues is but one of many local and regional musics that have become immensely popular outside their area of origin; reggae is another, and hip-hop yet another.

Now, in the twenty-first century, we are in the midst of a new blues revival as Americans honor blues as roots music and new generations (both black and white) discover the music for the first time. Acoustic blues has also made a comeback among African American performers. In the 1960s blues revival, the only notable young African American acoustic blues guitarist was Taj Mahal. Today young African American singers such as Keb' Mo', Corey Harris, and Alvin Youngblood Hart are carving out successful careers as acoustic blues singer-guitarists. Yet marketing blues as a roots music has its drawbacks. Claiming that blues is important chiefly because it shaped and influenced what came after it implies that blues is a music of the past, not the present. We can only wonder what its future may be.

Today's most active blues music-cultures are in the Mississippi Delta and in Chicago, a city with a history of great hospitality to the blues. Dozens of blues clubs can also be found in such cities as Houston; St. Louis; Memphis; Clarksdale, Mississippi; Oakland; San Francisco; and Detroit. Whereas in the past these clubs and bars were expressions of the local black communities, today's clubs cater to a tourist audience. Well-known blues singers such as B. B. King and Buddy Guy tour nationally and, sponsored by the U.S. Department of State, as goodwill ambassadors abroad. The radio, television, and film productions for 2003, the "Year of the Blues," brought blues back into the mainstream of American culture, where it had not been since the *Blues Brothers* film. How long it will remain there is anyone's guess.

Study Questions

1. What is the difference between the three-line blues stanza and the quatrain-refrain stanza? Illustrate with an example of each.

2. How do blues singers "compose" their songs? What sources do they draw on? How important is originality?

3. What are the functions of work songs? What do field hollers have in common with blues?

4. What are the advantages and disadvantages of marketing blues as a roots music?

5. Why is the history of blues important? Why does it matter that the music was invented and nurtured by African Americans?

6. Compare the version of "Amazing Grace" on the CD with another version you may be familiar with. How does each version achieve its effects?

7. What is the blues scale? How does it differ from the standard do-re-mi scale? Why is the blues scale important?

8. How did African American music change the sound of popular music in the United States and then the world in the twentieth century?

9. Do blues singers sing mostly about themselves, or do they represent many people?

10. How are the African American approaches to rhythm in music similar to the African approaches described in Chapter 3? How are they different?

11. What is a musical revival? Why did blues undergo revivals in the 1960s and later, beginning in the 1980s?

12. What is the role of tradition in African American music?

Glossary

acoustic guitar The original form of the guitar, without any electronic amplification.

Ann Arbor Blues Festival The first major festival in the United States devoted entirely to blues; it began in 1969 and attracted more than ten thousand fans annually for the first few years. Attendance fell off drastically in the early 1970s as the blues revival waned.

autobiography Speaking, singing, or writing about one's own life. (In biography, the subject is understood to be someone else's life.)

blues revival The period between about 1959 and 1971 when blues gained a large audience among young white people in Europe and North America.

blues scale A scale (see Chapter 1) found in blues, jazz, gospel, soul, and just about every kind of African American music. Singers and musicians play around with the third and seventh scale degree, moving the pitch microtonally between the major and minor interval.

call-and-response A musical form in which one part seems to be linked as a "response" to the previous part. The response part appears to be an "answer" or "comment" on the first or "call" part.

Chicago blues Although Chicago has been an important blues city ever since the 1920s, "Chicago blues" refers to a sound of blues that arose among former Mississippi musicians living in Chicago just after World War II. Pioneers of this sound were Muddy Waters, Little Walter, and Howlin' Wolf.

Civil Rights Movement Broadly, the African American struggle for equality under the law and for social justice; more narrowly it refers to the gathering momentum and force of this nonviolent struggle in the 1950s and 1960s, particularly as it centered on the 1954 *Brown v. Board of Education* case that ended school desegregation, and the career and achievements of the Reverend Martin Luther King, Jr.

Delta blues Downhome blues (see glossary definition) from the Mississippi River Delta, often regarded as the deepest or most profound downhome blues. Pioneers included Charley Patton, Son House, and Robert Johnson.

Dr. Watts African American name for the kind of hymn that is lined out. The name comes from a reference to the author Isaac Watts, who wrote the words to many of the hymns in this repertoire.

> ## Salient Characteristics of Japanese Traditional Music ♪♪♪
>
> - A diversity of scale tuning systems with pentatonic scales at the root.
> - A broad range of timbres with sounds of both definite and indefinite pitch.
> - Monophonic and heterophonic textures (homophonic textures in Western-influenced music).
> - Both metrical and "beatless."

"transposes" the melody to start on a higher pitch, but the pitch relationships in the melody remain the same—everything goes up the same amount because of the equal temperament on the piano. Before Bach, though, Western music was based not on the equal-tempered scale but on the Pythagorian scale, so-called after the musical writings of the Greek Pythagoras. This scale, based on the pitches from strings that vibrate in small ratios (1:2, 2:3, 3:4, etc.), does not produce equal temperament, though it comes close.

Japanese scales are diverse. Like the Chinese, in their traditional music the Japanese recognize a Pythagorian rather than an equal-tempered scale. The exact pitch intervals between notes differ in traditional music according to genre, school, the piece performed, and the individual performer (Koizumi 1974:73). No single set of pitches is used by all musicians. For example, the scale used in *gagaku* (orchestra music derived from T'ang China) differs from that used in music for the *koto* (a thirteen-string zither). The *gagaku* modal system is linked to Chinese systems, while the *koto* system developed several centuries later in Japan.

Considering this diversity in scale systems, it is not surprising that music historians have developed a wide range of theories to describe the way they work. Older scholars have claimed that two pentatonic (five-tone) scales, the *in* and *yo*, form the basis of traditional Japanese music. Today it seems more accurate to interpret Japanese music on the basis of tones located a fourth scale degree apart (to hear this interval, sing the do-re-mi scale from "do" to "fa"; then produce the interval by singing "do" and then "fa": do-re-mi-fa, do-fa) and whatever important notes appear between them (Koizumi 1974:76). In fact, much melodic movement tends to emphasize this interval of the fourth (for example, in "Hakusen no," **CD 1, Track 24**).

Timbre

The Japanese aesthetic sense favors the use of a broad range of sounds and tone qualities in their music. In particular, "unpitched" sounds are commonly heard in the middle of instrumental melodies. When we hear a sound wave with a stable frequency, it is easy for us to distinguish pitch. But if the frequency varies too quickly, we do not hear a pitch. A cymbal, for example, is unpitched compared with an oboe. In Japanese music, examples of unpitched sound include the breathy sound made on the *shakuhachi* bamboo flute or the hard twang produced when the plectrum strikes the *shamisen* lute. Just as Japanese poetry is full of appreciation for unpitched sounds of nature such as water flowing or trees whispering in the wind, Japanese music recreates such sounds for the enjoyment of their listeners. (Unpitched sound can be heard in **CD 1, Track 23**, "Tsuru no sugomori.")

Melody/Harmony

The diversity of Japanese melodies makes generalization difficult—the melodies of folk songs differ greatly in rhythm, pitch, and structure from those of *shakuhachi* music, for example. Japanese melodies often contain short bits that are repeated, in part or in their entirety, throughout a piece. (Hear, for example, **CD 1, Track 24**, "Hakusen no," in which segments of phrases are repeated and varied.) Complete repetition of phrases sometimes occurs at the beginning and end of a piece, such as in the *shamisen* accompaniment to "Hakusen no," thereby lending an air of finality to the conclusion.

In the *shakuhachi* piece **(CD 1, Track 23)** the pitch movement in the melody strikes the non-Japanese listener as extremely slow; in fact, the changes in timbre and loudness, rather than rapid changes in pitch, give the melody its life. In contrast to this, much vocal music contains elaborate ornamentation, as heard in **CD 1, Tracks 24 and 25.**

Only Western-influenced Japanese music uses Western harmony. Most common when two or more instruments (or voice and instrument) play together is a heterophonic texture, in which both or all parts play basically the same melody but in slightly different versions.

Rhythm

One distinctive characteristic of Japanese music lies in the flexibility of pulse in many pieces. In Western music, pulses almost always occur at regular time intervals (forming "beats") and are arranged most commonly in groups of two, three, four, or six (creating a "meter"). Music can also have irregular intervals between the pulses, however, and this is sometimes called "beatless" or "flexible" or "free" rhythm. Those accustomed to Western music may have difficulty at first listening to music that lacks a steady beat, because it seems hard to follow without the firm rhythmic structure they expect. Because of its freedom and flexibility, however, this music conveys a powerful expression of feeling. Such beatless rhythm is found in many kinds of Japanese music, from folk song to music of the *shakuhachi*.

Even when a steady beat is present, there can be a sense of flexibility to it. When there is a sense of beat in Japanese music, those beats usually occur in groups of two, four, or eight.

Japanese music uses a wide variety of tempos, from very slow to very fast. Often, in music associated with the theater, the tempo accelerates as excitement and drama build in the play.

Musical Form

The most common musical form in Japanese music is called *jo-ha-kyū* and is based mainly on rhythmic rather than melodic changes. *Jo* means "introduction" and is the slow beginning section: *ha* is literally "breaking apart," and here the tempo builds; finally, *kyū,* or "rushing," finds the tempo reaching its peak, only to slow before the piece ends. As a loose form, this tripartite structure applies in some cases to entire pieces as well as to sections of those pieces and individual phrases.

In the following sections, several different kinds of Japanese music will be explained, illustrating some of the colorful diversity of musical life in that country today. The history of each instrument or musical genre provides a fascinating look into the rich, vibrant life of traditional Japanese cities and villages during the times of the *samurai,* wandering Buddhist priests, and *geisha.*

The *shakuhachi* flute is linked to the social turbulence of early Tokugawa times, as well as to Zen philosophy and aesthetics. A *shakuhachi* piece provides an example of free rhythm, one of the most important characteristics of Japanese music. The *geisha* and O-Yo, a female composer of the late Tokugawa period, were important in the development of the short *kouta* songs. These songs, sung to the accompaniment of the *shamisen,* exemplify heterophonic texture in Japanese music.

These kinds of music are generally labeled "art" or "classical" music. Compared with "folk" music, art music has stricter guild systems, more regulation over skill level, and more professionalism. The terms *art* and *folk* are imported from the West, however, and the dividing line between the two categories has become blurred today as folk musicians become more professionalized and form their own guild systems.

Later in the chapter we shall look at folk songs from northern Japan, described in its contemporary contexts to show how traditional music is faring in modern Japan. Finally, we shall explore present-day Japanese popular music, which shows musical features of both East and West, and the world of *karaoke* singing, in which live singing and technology are mixed in a unique way.

The Shakuhachi (Bamboo Flute)

Considering its range of tones from soft and ethereal to rough and violent, the *shakuhachi* (Figure 5.1) appears surprisingly simple in construction. This flute is made of a length of bamboo from the bottom part of a bamboo stalk, including part of the root. The name *shakuhachi* derives from the length of the standard instrument. *Shaku* signifies a traditional unit of measure (equivalent to about 30 centimeters) and *hachi* stands for 8, together meaning 1.8 *shaku,* or about 54 centimeters. The standard *shakuhachi* has four holes in the front of the instrument and one in the back for the thumb of the left hand.

The *shakuhachi*'s versatility in pitch and tone production is due to its construction. Held vertically, the flute has a mouthpiece at the top that is cut obliquely on the side away from the player. By partially covering the

Figure 5.1
Kawase Junsuke playing the *shakuhachi.*

Linda Fujie

finger holes and changing the angle of the lips to the mouthpiece, a player can produce a wide variety of pitches and tone qualities. Not only does the *shakuhachi* easily produce microtones—that is, quarter-tones and pitches "between the cracks" of the piano—but it also generates tones ranging from "pure" (with few overtones) to quite breathy, sounding almost like white noise.

Solo *shakuhachi* performance flourished during the Tokugawa period (1600–1867). This was a golden age in Japanese cultural life. It was a time of peace, during which the *shōgun* living in Tokyo ruled over a united country, while the Kyoto emperor held only nominal power. After centuries of violent struggles between different factions of aristocrats and military leaders, Japan welcomed peace and prospered under it.

During this period, a group of priests called *komusō* (literally "emptiness monks") wandered the countryside, playing the *shakuhachi*. The *honkyoku*, or main solo repertoire for the instrument, derives from the pieces played by the *komusō*. All of these pieces, the most spiritual and meditative of the present-day *shakuhachi* repertoire, have a free rhythm; that is, they lack a regular beat.

Komusō were organized into the Fuke sect of Buddhism, which propagated a Zen basis for *shakuhachi* playing. Zen Buddhism, a philosophy that has spread throughout much of Asia and the world in various forms, is based on the idea that intellect is not needed in the pursuit of truth. We can search to know *about* things, but we do not really *know* them. To know them, we must throw away our notions of scientific investigation and logical reasoning and instead rely on a heightened awareness and intuition about life.

Various means for reaching that state of heightened awareness of enlightenment (*satori* in Japanese) have been proposed. These include pondering *kōan*, or paradoxical riddles (the most famous is "What is the sound of one hand clapping?") and the practice of *zazen*, sitting in silent meditation. In the Fuke sect, playing the *shakuhachi* also was regarded as a means of reaching enlightenment. For this reason, the *shakuhachi* was not called a musical instrument by its performers but a *hōki*, or "spiritual tool." The spiritual approach to the playing of the instrument is called *suizen*, or "blowing Zen."

According to *suizen*, the goal of *shakuhachi* coincides with the goal of Zen: to reach enlightenment, proceeding into unlimited "knowing." How this is done is not formulated precisely (as it cannot be, from the Zen perspective), but one common notion is called *ichōon jōbutsu*, or "enlightenment in a single note." According to this theory, one could reach enlightenment suddenly when blowing a single tone.

Breathing is crucial in *shakuhachi* playing and its connection with Zen. Exhaling is heard in the dynamic level and tone quality of a pitch; at the same time, it carries with it the possibility of instant spiritual enlightenment. Thus, each moment of "performance," whether the intake of breath or its slow release, whether the subtle, delicate shading of a tone or the explosion of air through the instrument, can be interpreted in the context of a larger spiritual life.

The breathing pattern is crucial in playing the *shakuhachi.* Each phrase takes one full breath, with dramatic shifts in dynamic level according to how quickly the air is expelled. The typical phrase in *shakuhachi honkyoku* music follows the natural breathing pattern, the sound growing fainter toward the end of the phrase as the air in the lungs runs out. When this dynamic pattern is broken by a gradual or sudden increase in volume, it makes a pronounced impression on the listener.

The performer of the *shakuhachi* piece in **CD 1, Track 23**, Kawase Junsuke (Japanese names are given in the Japanese order: family name followed by given name) is one of the best known *shakuhachi* musicians in Japan and the head of a stylistic school of playing (Figure 5.1). This piece, a part of the *honkyoku* repertory of the Kinko style of performance, is called "Tsuru no sugomori," or "Nesting Cranes." The version recorded here is performed in the *kabuki* theater and therefore is accompanied by *shamisen* (Figure 5.2). The music describes a winter scene during which cranes make their nests. The fast trills in the *shakuhachi* imitate the bird's fluttering wings. "Tsuru no sugomori" is performed in one of the most famous *kabuki*

CD 1:23

"Tsuru no sugomori" ("Nesting Cranes") (3:40). Performed by Kawase Junsuke, *shakuhachi* (flute), and Kawase Hakuse, *shamisen* (lute). Field recording by Linda Fujie. Tokyo, Japan, 1989.

Counter Number	Commentary	Phrase Number
0:00	The *shamisen* enters. The *shakuhachi* enters on a low tone and ascends.	1
0:12	Tone growing from quiet to loud to quiet. (We will use the symbols < | > to indicate this technique.)	2
0:21	< | > within two tones	3
0:27	One tone < | > with *trill* (rapid alterations between two tones, usually next to each other).	4
0:36	Short tone then < | > as in phrase 2.	5
0:45	Slightly faster trill on ascending tones that imitate a bird's fluttering wings. Phrase 1 repeats with some modification.	6
0:52	Ascending tones ending in trill.	7
0:56	At end of phrase < | > with trill, the player lowers the tone—a technique called *meri*.	8

Phrases 9–13 repeat phrases 1–5

Counter Number	Commentary	Phrase Number
1:05	Phrase 1 repeats with some modification. At the end of the phrase the player raises the tone—a technique called *kari*.	9
1:11	Short tone then < | > on one tone (as in phrases 2 and 5).	10
1:18	Trill (as in phrase 3).	11
1:25	Trill on same note growing softer.	12
1:34	Short tone, then < | > on one tone (as in phrases 2, 5, and 10).	13
1:43	Vibrato at the end of the phrase.	14
1:47	Short tone then < | > on one tone (as in phrases 2, 5, 10, and 13).	15
1:54	Trill as in phrases 3 and 11 < | >.	16
2:01	Phrase 1 repeats with some modification. *Meri.*	17
2:08	One held tone with higher short tones.	18
2:17	Builds to climax of song.	19
2:22	High short tones signal the climax of the song.	20
2:30	Fast trill, to slow trill, to even tone. *Meri* then *kari*.	21
2:32	The *shakuhachi* gradually decends; < | > at the end of the phrase. Phrase 1 repeats with some modification in phrase 24.	22–24

Counter Number	Commentary	Phrase Number
2:54	The *shamisen* stops playing at 2:47 and the *shakuhachi* finishes the song. Short tone then < | > on one tone (as in phrases 2, 5, 10, 13, and 15). *Meri.*	25
3:00	Short tone then < | > (as in phrases 2, 5, 10, 13, and 15). Repeat and quicken.	26
3:10	Short tone then < | > on one tone (as in phrases 2, 5, 10, 13, 15, and 25).	27
3:18	*Meri.*	28
3:23	Trill (as in phrases 3, 11, and 16).	29
3:30	Short tone then < | > on one tone (as in phrases 2, 5, 10, 13, 15, 25, and 27).	30

plays, *Kanadehon chushingura,* or *Treasury of Local Retainers,* during a scene when parting lovers suddenly notice the scene outdoors.

The first time one listens to this piece, it is best just to sit back and relax, appreciating the overall mood. After listening to this piece a few times, you may sense that certain phrases are repeated; in fact, this short piece has many repetitions of melodic material. Each phrase ends with a breath and phrase 1 is heard (with some modifications) in phrases 6, 9, 17, and 24. Phrases 1–5 are repeated in phrases 9–13, and most of the other phrases are variations on previous melodic material. There is also a clear climax to the piece, created by changes in pitch and dynamics.

One of the most obvious characteristics of this piece is that almost every phrase increases or decreases in volume; in many cases the musician increases the volume on one long note and decreases it on the next one. This careful breath control must be learned and practiced over years to prevent running out of breath too soon and to maintain constant control over tone quality.

Knowing some of the techniques used to play *shakuhachi* will help explain how some of the tones in this performance are produced. Sometimes the player flattens or sharpens a pitch by changing the angle of the lips to the mouthpiece. This is called *meri* when the pitch is lowered, producing a soft tone, and *kari* when the pitch is raised. (Occasionally the pitch is lowered and again raised.)

The musician changes pitch also through finger techniques, depending on the effect desired. A finger can slowly open or close a hole, quickly tap a hole (creating an accent), or cover only a portion of a hole. These techniques are necessary because tonguing is not used to separate notes in *shakuhachi* playing.

Different techniques of breathing into the flute also create interesting effects such as *muraiki,* an explosion of breath into the instrument. In addition, *shakuhachi* players use flutter tonguing, finger tremolos, and vibrato—all of which can be heard in the first few phrases of "Tsuru no sugomori."

One common technique of producing vibrato is to shake the head, either from side to side or up and down, while blowing into the instrument.

"Tsuru no sugomori" shows both a variety of timbres within one piece and flexibility of pulse, basic characteristics of Japanese music. Some notes have a thin sound, while others have rich, full tone. Some notes sound "purer" to our ears; others are breathier. The *shakuhachi* player expresses the music through such changes in timbre. With the exception perhaps of contemporary music, this variety of tone quality is rarely found within a single piece written for a Western wind instrument. In terms of Japanese musical aesthetics, however, this contrast of timbres is important to the texture and expression of the piece.

The lack of a regular pulse means that learning a piece requires a good ear and an excellent sense of timing on the part of the student. Most forms of musical notation convey the duration of notes easily if the music has a steady pulse. But without such a pulse, the original time values are difficult to communicate in a written score. Perhaps this is one reason that musical notation never developed into an important teaching tool in most forms of traditional Japanese music. Because Japanese musicians could not rely on scores to teach them the rhythm of a piece, they used them more as a device to help them remember how the piece should sound. First, of course, performers must acquire this memory by listening to their teacher (and perhaps other students) many times.

The idea of *ma* (literally "space" or "interval") is linked to both rhythm and to the Zen background of *shakuhachi* playing. *Ma* refers to the overall timing of a piece—not just the pauses and rests, but also the relationship between sound and silence on which all music is fundamentally based. It embraces the idea that sound enhances silence and silence enhances sound. This emphasis on silence conforms with Zen ideas concerning the importance of emptiness and space. The player who is aware of *ma* begins his or her notes with an instinctive care for the length and quality of the silences before and after. This concept applies particularly to music with a beatless rhythm, because the sounds and silences fall at irregular points and the player is quite active in creating those moments.

Performers often link the concept of *ma* to the quality of a musical performance. Musicians speak of "good *ma*" or "bad *ma*," referring to the quality of the sounds and silences and their proportion to one another. When this proportion is deemed appropriate—a subjective judgment that is learned only from years of experience—then the performance has been successful.

Though the Fuke sect priests have long disappeared from the roads of Japan, many players keep the *shakuhachi* tradition alive today, both in Japan and abroad. Because of the instrument's versatility of pitch and timbre, composers and performers like to use it in various contemporary genres, such as jazz, fusion, and New Age music. At the same time, the meditative, spiritual nature of the *honkyoku* is continually reaffirmed through performances given by several active *shakuhachi* master players.

Figure 5.2
Geisha performing at a party. The woman on the right holds a *shamisen*.

The Kouta (Short Song) and Shamisen (Lute)

Another well-loved Japanese traditional instrument is the *shamisen,* a three-string long-necked lute (see Figure 5.2). In contrast to the *shakuhachi,* which has associations with austere spirituality and meditation, the *shamisen* is often used to convey an outpouring of emotion and drama. For this reason it is considered an excellent instrument for the theater, expressing highly dramatic situations in the *bunraku* puppet theater to great effect. It is also used in another major theatrical form, *kabuki,* and sometimes to accompany folk song, as in **CD 1, Track 25**. In a more intimate setting, the *shamisen* also accompanies short, evocative songs called *kouta* (literally, "short song").

The present-day *shamisen* is a descendent of a long line of related instruments stretching back to the *sanshin* of Okinawa, the *san-hsien* of China, and perhaps further back to the Middle East or Central Asia. While the Okinawan *sanshin* is covered with snakeskin, on the Japanese mainland the instrument is traditionally covered with cat skin or sometimes dog skin. (As these are now expensive, however, plastic is commonly found on *shamisen* used for practice.) There are different kinds of *shamisen,* varying in shape, weight, material, and overall size; the type used depends on the musical genre played.

The body of the *shamisen* is made of a wooden box roughly square in shape, covered on both sides with skin or plastic. A long piece of wood, forming the unfretted neck, is inserted into this box. Pegs at the top of the neck hold the three strings, each string of a different thickness. In some kinds of music, a large plectrum is used for striking and plucking the instrument. Sometimes in *kouta,* however, the bare fingers or fingernails pluck the strings, producing a lighter, less percussive sound.

A rather unusual sound in the *shamisen* confirms the importance of unpitched sounds in Japanese music. This is a special buzz or hum called *sawari* (literally, "touch"), which is purposefully added to the instrument when it is made. The lowest string does not rest on the upper bridge but resonates against a special cavity made near the top of the instrument's neck. This string sets a noise in motion, to which the other strings can contribute in sympathetic vibration. The result is a pitchless buzzing sound that is essential to the tonal flavor of the *shamisen*. Japanese instrument makers intentionally build these timbres into their instruments. Buzzing is also deliberately built into many African instruments, such as the *axatse* (Chapter 3).

The *kouta* is a song form that evokes many images and allusions in a short time (generally, one to three minutes). *Kouta* as we know it today dates from the mid-nineteenth century, though the same name was used to describe another kind of song in earlier centuries (Kurada 1982:894–95).

The development of the present-day *kouta* is closely linked to the participation of women in Japanese traditional music. One of the earliest composers of *kouta* was O-Yo (1840–1901). The daughter of the head master of *kiyomoto* (a style of *shamisen* music used in *kabuki*), O-Yo was an excellent musician. As a woman, she was not allowed to take over her father's position after his death; instead she married a man who then inherited his title. But O-Yo took up most of his duties.

O-Yo was not allowed to play the *shamisen* on the *kabuki* stage because only men appeared there. She was nevertheless an active performer at private parties in teahouses and restaurants. For such private gatherings she probably composed *kouta* such as "Saru wa uki," thought to be the first *kouta* ever composed (Kikkawa 1981:350). Although women were banned from participating in many of the elite forms of musical performance in Japan, they played a key role in teaching that music to generations of male performers. O-Yo herself was an important transmitter of the *kiyomoto* tradition of her father, teaching it to many people from all parts of Japan.

O-Yo's musical world and her involvement with both an older form of music (*kiyomoto*) and a new form (*kouta*) can best be understood in the context of the *iemoto* guild system. This system, active also in O-Yo's time, is a powerful influence on the traditional arts—music, dance, flower arranging, the tea ceremony, and many other artistic areas. The guild is the transmitter of knowledge and the legitimizer of teachers and performers in each art form.

In music, several different guilds may be involved with one type of music (for example, music for the *shakuhachi* or for the *nō* theater), but each guild will have its own slightly different performance style and repertoire. By illustration, one who wishes to become a *shakuhachi* performer must decide which style he or she wants to learn, then become affiliated with the guild that follows that style. Often this affiliation lasts as long as the individual performs on the *shakuhachi*.

Guilds not only transmit knowledge; they also control quality. Each guild sets the standards for teachers and pupils. If an individual works diligently, he or she may be given a license to teach and an artistic name from the guild. The *iemoto* system thus provides a structure through which the arts have been taught, performed, and preserved for hundreds of years in Japan. It has contributed positively to maintaining the artistic level in traditional Japanese music. Its strict regulation of performance standards has preserved musical traditions that could otherwise have changed drastically or even died out through the years.

According to the rules of this system, new composition in many genres of music was discouraged or even forbidden. This conservatism is linked to a reverence for tradition in the arts that is still prevalent among Japanese musicians today. Many believe that the "classic" body of music has been handed down with painstaking precision for decades or centuries through the toil of countless musicians. The composition of a new piece of music by an individual was for years considered "arrogant self-expression." If a new piece were composed and proved to have merit, it had to be ascribed to the leader of the guild, who in turn might attribute it to an earlier *iemoto* leader. This reluctance to accept new compositions meant that if they were written, they often had no official recognition. For this reason, when someone like O-Yo composed new music, it was in a new genre such as *kouta*. Because there was no *iemoto* associated yet with that kind of music, the restrictions that would otherwise apply toward composition did not exist.

By the end of the Tokugawa period, the *kouta* was linked to the *geisha* of the city of Edo (which became known as Tokyo in 1868) and the life of the teahouses. For many people today, the lively, intense world of Edo during the Tokugawa period epitomizes the Japanese spirit. Though the official Japanese capital was Kyoto, where the emperor resided, Edo was the actual seat of government where the *shōgun* held state in his castle. It was also the most populous city in Japan as well as one of the largest in the world. The influx of people from all over the country, crowded into tenements and wildly pursuing wealth, pleasure, or both, spurred the coining of the phrase *"Edo wa tenka no hakidamari"* ("Edo is the nation's rubbish heap").

The streets teemed with *chōnin*, townspeople who were members of either the merchant or the artisan classes. With the expansion of the economy during the peaceful Tokugawa period, some *chōnin* became wealthy and powerful. They patronized the theaters, teahouses, and brothels, making their increasingly sophisticated mark on the aesthetics of the drama, music, and dance of the period: a sense of style that combines wit, sensuousness, and restraint. The Edo pursuit of momentary pleasure represents the epitome of the *ukiyo,* or "floating world."

The *kouta,* as sung by the *geisha* of such licensed quarters as the Yoshiwara area of Edo, reflects their world of beauty and style. The songs' lyrics often convey romantic or erotic themes, but such references are subtle. Puns, double-entendres and poetic devices appear frequently in *kouta* lyrics, and sometimes even a Japanese will miss their suggestive undertones.

In the *kouta* example found in **CD 1, Track 24**, "Hakusen no" ("A White Fan"), both the image of a white fan and the beauty of nature are used as metaphors for romantic commitment. This particular song shows little of the whimsical side of *kouta;* it is considered suitable for performance at wedding banquets or private parties. At the wedding banquet, this song would be sung to the honored couple.

Though declining in numbers, *geisha* are still trained in Japan to entertain at such occasions. The traditional musical instrument of the *geisha* is the *shamisen,* which is used often to accompany vocal music such as the *kouta*. This recording was made by a *geisha* in the 1960s who lived near the former Yoshiwara quarter of Tokyo.

Traditional Japanese poetry arranges lines according to their syllabic content, favoring lines with five and seven syllables. The lyrics of "Hakusen no" (see the listening guide) contain alternating lines of five and seven syllables. (Extended vowels and the letter *n* at the end of a syllable count as separate syllables.) A poetic device known as *kakekotoba,* or "pivot word," is found on the sixth line: the word *kagayaku* ("shimmering") can be interpreted as both referring to the silver node of the fan (the pin holding the fan together at the bottom) and to the pine tree boughs, "shimmering" in the shadows. Such pivot words are often found in Japanese poetry and are made possible by the flexibility of Japanese grammar.

Several auspicious symbols appear in the text. The pine tree carries symbolic meaning for the Japanese as a tree of special beauty and longevity. A clear pond, "undisturbed by waves or wind," also presents a peaceful, auspicious image of the future life of a couple. The words *sue hirogari* literally refer to the unfolding of a fan, but can also mean to enjoy increasing prosperity as time goes on.

CD 1:24

"Hakusen no" ("A White Fan") (3:22). Performed by Shitaya Kotsuru for Nippon Columbia WK-170.

Listen now to the recording, **CD 1, Track 24**, and follow along with the listening guide. Besides the *shamisen,* you also hear an accompanying ensemble made up of the *kotsuzumi* and *otsuzumi* drums and the *nōkan* flute. These instruments, typical of the *nō* theater, were added to the commercial recording of this song; *geisha* also sing "Hakusen no" with the *shamisen* alone. Finally, you will hear the calls, known as *kakegoe,* which help to cue the ensemble as well as add to the atmosphere of the song.

A heterophonic relationship (see Chapter 1) between two or more parts is typical of Japanese ensemble music. In "Hakusen no" such a heterophony characterizes the voice and *shamisen*. Rather than sounding simultaneously on the same beat, the two parts tend to weave in and out; sometimes the voice precedes the *shamisen* in presenting the melody and sometimes the *shamisen* plays the notes first. The result of this constant staggering and shifting is a duet in which the melody is shared and enhanced by both voice and instrument. An example of this heterophony can be found in the third line, as the *shamisen* anticipates several of the sung notes. Listening carefully to the entire song, try to find other such examples. Are there also times when the voice anticipates what the *shamisen* will play?

One of the most interesting aspects of the vocal part is the flexibility of beat, which contrasts to the even beat of the *shamisen*. Hear, for example,

Close Listening   CD 1:24

"Hakusen no" ("A White Fan")

Counter Number	Commentary	Lyric and translation	
Introduction			
0:00	*Shamisen* enters and plays an introduction to the vocal part.		
Phrase A			
0:18	Vocalist enters. As the phrase ends, the *shamisen* anticipates several of the sung tones in the next phrase.	*Hakusen no*	A white fan
Phrase B			
0:33	New phrase: B.	*sue hirogari no*	spreading out
Phrase C			
0:50	New phrase: C.	*sue kakete*	lasting forever
0:59	Phrase B repeats.	*kataki chigiri no*	the firm pledges
1:13	Phrase A repeats.	*gin kaname*	like the silver node of the fan
1:22	Phrase B repeats.	*kagayaku kage ni*	shimmering in the shadows
Phrase D			
1:37	New phrase: D.	*matsu ga e no*	the boughs of pine trees
Phrase E			
1:49	New phrase: E.	*ha-iro mo masaru*	the splendid leafy color of
	Phrase B repeats.	*fukamidori*	a deep green
2:04	Phrase E repeats. Notice the flexibility of the rhythm between the *shamisen* and the voice (heterophony).	*tachiyoru niwa no*	the clearness of the pond
2:11	Phrase E repeats.	*ike sumite*	in the garden approached
2:18	Phrase B repeats.	*nami kaze tatanu*	undisturbed by waves of wind
2:33	Phrase C repeats.	*mizu no omo*	the surface of the water.
2:43	Phrase B repeats.	*urayamashii de*	What an enviable life,
2:49	Phrase B repeats.	*wa nai ka na*	don't you think?
Introduction repeats			
3:05	The *shamisen* repeats the tune of the introduction to finish the *kouta*.		

how the rhythm of the vocal and *shamisen* parts fit together in the line beginning "*tachiyoru . . .*"; just as the listener thinks a predictable pattern has been established, the rhythm shifts. The sophistication of this kind of rhythmic contrast has appealed for centuries to the Japanese ear. Together, melodic and rhythmic variety in Japanese ensemble music creates a complex, often exciting musical texture.

The vocal melody contains several thematic phrases that repeat in slightly varied forms. For example, the seven different "B" phrases have in common long, repeated notes followed by a descent in pitch, highly ornamented. These repetitions vary from exact to significantly modified.

The *shamisen* part opens and closes the song with the same rhythmically emphasized theme, and it occasionally plays a short solo phrase between lines of text. Sometimes small motifs are repeated. Hearing this song, the listener is drawn into the refined yet playful atmosphere of the Tokugawa teahouses.

Folk Song

The next music that we shall examine, folk song, traditionally belonged to the farming class or the poorer merchants in the cities. But people from many levels of society, in Tokugawa times as now, know this music. Folk music is still found in many everyday locations: in the streets, in the fields, and at social occasions of both the city and the countryside.

In traditional Japan, people sang folk songs, or *minyō,* while they planted the rice in spring, threw their nets into the sea, wove cloth, and pounded grain. Folk songs accompanied many daily activities—to relieve boredom, to provide a steady beat for some activity, as encouragement for a group working at some task, as individual expression, or as a combination of these.

While the everyday uses of folk song have not entirely disappeared from Japan, fewer contemporary Japanese are finding them relevant to their lives. Still, based on a recent survey of musical preferences, *minyō* is one of the most popular forms of music in Japan today (NHK Hō sō 1982:68). The continuing popularity of folk songs is tied to their identification with the countryside and a sometimes romanticized vision of rural life on the part of city dwellers. Folk songs evoke a past thought to be simpler and more natural, and this appeals to many Japanese today.

In addition to an association with rural life, many Japanese folk songs connect to a specific region of the country. This is the case in "Nikata-bushi," in **CD 1, Track 25,** from the region of Akita, in northwestern Japan. With the growth of industry in the years after World War II, many Japanese left the rural areas to find work in the cities, and today people from a particular region—or their descendants—gather in many of these urban areas and sing folk songs as reminders of the villages from which they came.

Japanese not only listen to folk songs but usually learn to sing a few as well, either from family and friends or in elementary school. Often they sing them at parties, when they are called on to sing a favorite song. Real enthusiasts take lessons with a good singer and attend folk song clubs or

Figure 5.3
Folksinger of Akita. On the right is Asano Sanae, who sings "Nikata-bushi" (CD 1, Track 25). A fellow apprentice, Asano Yoshie, stands on the left. Folklife Festival of the Smithsonian Institution, Washington, D.C., 1986.

Linda Fujie

other gatherings where they can perform in front of other enthusiasts. Amateur folk song contests have become a regular feature on Japanese television, presenting folk singers from around the country. In these contests, singers give their renditions of folk songs, which are then evaluated by a board of "experts," who might tell the singer that his or her vibrato is too broad or hand gestures too dramatic for that particular song.

Folk song preservation societies have sprung up around the country (Groemer 1994). These societies are formed by amateurs who aim to "preserve" local songs and performance styles. The activities of these clubs help foster pride and a sense of identity among the dwellers of a village or a neighborhood within a city (Hughes 1981, 1990–1991).

Folk song performance has become more professional and standardized in recent years owing to televised *minyō* and the changing tastes of the public. Training to sing folk song at a professional level demands years of study. In recent years, folk song has developed its own *iemoto*-like system, modeled after that found in traditional art music. For example, Asano Sanae (Figure 5.3) has been a pupil of the *shamisen* player Asano Umewaka for several years. In the manner of the *iemoto* system, she received her artistic name from him, including her teacher's last name. As a teenager, she moved from Osaka to Akita to become his apprentice, and she now participates regularly in concerts and competitions. Her teacher, in his seventies at the time of this recording, grew up in the Akita area and spent most of his life as a farmer, while slowly gaining a local and then a national reputation as a fine player of the Tsugaru *shamisen,* a type of *shamisen* used for virtuoso accompaniment of folk song. His former students live throughout Japan and teach his style of *shamisen* playing and singing.

Listening to "Nikata-bushi" **(CD 1, Track 25)**, we hear first the sound of the *shamisen* but with a stronger tone than we heard in the *kouta* example.

 CD 1:25

"Nikata-bushi" ("Song of Nikata") (5:04). Performed by Asano Sanae, vocal; Asano Umewaka, *shamisen* (lute). Field recording by Karl Signell. Washington, D.C., 1986.

Close Listening   CD 1:25

"Nikata-bushi" ("The Song of Nikata")

Counter Number	Commentary	Lyrics and Translation	
0:00	*Shamisen* player tunes by playing open strings.		
0:21	*Shamisen* plays rapidly, an interlude before verse 1.		
Verse 1			
1:34	*Shamisen* supplies a steady pulse in contrast to the vocalist's flexible rhythm. Vocalist ornaments the melody in a highly melismatic fashion (see Chapter 4).	*Nikata tera-machi no hana baasama hana mo urazu ni abura uru*	The temple town Nikata a woman selling flowers she doesn't sell them but enjoys herself instead.
Interlude			
2:54	*Shamisen* player retunes strings		
3:02	*Shamisen* repeats the fast patterns of the introduction.		
Verse 2			
3:42	Vocalist sings second verse with similar ornamentation.	*Takai o-yama no goten no sakura eda wa nana eda yae ni saku.*	On a high mountain a cherry blossom tree at a mansion has seven branches and blossoms abundantly.
5:02	End.		

This *shamisen* is indeed different in construction, with a larger body, longer neck, and thicker skin. The first notes sound on the open strings, allowing the player to tune the instrument before beginning the piece. (You can hear the pitch change slightly as the player adjusts the strings.) The same "tuning" occurs later, in the instrumental interlude between verses.

The song text is composed of two verses, each set in the syllabic pattern typical of folk song: 7–7–7–5. The text of each verse is set to almost identical music, even down to the ornamentation used. Similarly, the patterns heard in the *shamisen* part between the two verses almost repeat the patterns played in the introduction.

As in the *kouta* example, the instrument plays a more or less steady pulse while the voice has a flexible rhythm. Notice the held tones and elaborate ornamentation in the vocal part. The perfect fourth (do-fa) and perfect fifth (do-so) are important intervals in this and many Japanese folk songs. Just before the voice enters with each verse, the *shamisen* player makes an exclamation that sounds like "huh!" This is another example of *kakegoe*, as first heard in the *kouta* selection.

Asano Sanae's elderly teacher might be considered a "true," old-fashioned folksinger and *shamisen* player in this Tsugaru style, having learned it from childhood in his native area. On the other hand, his student has studied purposefully to become a professional folksinger. Her performance reflects this training in many ways, as in her ornamentation, precision, clarity of voice, and general presentation. Her singing of *minyō* interests us, however, because Japanese increasingly value these qualities today in a *minyō* singer.

Popular Music

For many centuries, traditional Japanese music genres were conveyed from performer to audience without electronic media. At a single performance the audience was relatively small, and success depended on establishing a rapport with that audience. Today, music performances regularly appear on radio, television, and other media. Millions of people unseen to the musicians may hear a single recorded performance.

In addition to changing the ways traditional music is played and perceived, mass media and technology have also stimulated the growth of a new kind of music in Japan, which we shall call "popular music"—that is, music that was created in the studio, not with the idea of an intimate performance in front of a live audience, but with transmission through radio, television, and recordings primarily in mind. Since 1907, when the first commercial music recording was released in Japan, the composition, performance, and appreciation of music has changed dramatically. Music recorded specifically for commercial release in Japan, with the aim of appealing to the mass audience, exhibits several characteristics, including a set time limit, a steady beat and stanza form, and themes that have broad appeal.

This "Top 40" mentality was novel to the Japanese. In their previous experience it was common for many kinds of music dating from different eras in Japanese history to survive side by side as vital elements of the country's musical life. Now, through the association of songs with a specific point in time, generations have begun to identify with "their" songs, with the result that music can be used as an age marker.

Through the mass media, music performed by "others" (particularly professionals) became more available to more people than ever before. Today, scarcely a home in Japan does not have a radio, television set, stereo, or computer; many have all four. As people listen to the same recordings and to the same performance of a song, they are united by a common musical experience; they also develop certain expectations as to what music should sound like. Of course, a similar process has occurred worldwide as popular music has penetrated all corners of the globe. In Japan, the spread of music through records, tapes, and compact discs has advanced rapidly.

Historical Background

The types of popular music found in today's Japan developed as the modern Japanese state emerged. Interestingly the current music scene has become exceedingly diverse in a country known in the past for its high degree of cultural sameness. The rise of this contemporary varied music-

> ### Salient Characteristics of Japanese Popular Music ♪♪♪
>
> - Performance within a set time limit (generally three to five minutes).
> - A focus on themes that appeal to a broad public (though regional or specialty audiences are also sometimes targeted).
> - Stanza form and a steady beat, making the music more accessible to the Japanese who have become more accustomed to Western music.
> - Performers' attempts in live performance to reproduce the recorded version of the music so as to fulfill audience expectations.
> - Dramatic rise and fall in popularity over time.

culture and specifically "Japanese" popular music can be traced to the latter half of the nineteenth century. At this time, wide-ranging reforms were introduced to Japanese society to enable the country to deal with Western powers. The government introduced a constitutional monarchy and made many structural changes in the society to allow a mercantile and industrial economy to flourish.

After their long era of isolation, the Japanese felt it necessary to "modernize" life around them, which for a while meant adopting Western models. Leaders rapidly installed a system of compulsory education and decided that Japan also needed compulsory singing in its schools. In the late 1870s Izawa Shuji, a Japanese school principal who had studied in Massachusetts, and Luther Whiting Mason, an American who was the director of music for the Boston primary schools, developed a plan for music instruction in Japanese public schools.

In the following years *shōka* songs were introduced to meet the goal of teaching songs that blended Japanese and Western elements. The newly composed songs used melodies based on a traditional Japanese scale within the structure of a stanza form and a regular meter. Other songs introduced in the schools contained Western melodies such as "Auld Lang Syne" and "Swanee River" set with Japanese texts. Through songs like these, both *shōka* and Western songs, the Japanese masses were introduced to Western musical structure, scale, and rhythm.

In the 1880s a new kind of song became popular. Called *enka*, it represented a blend of Western and Japanese music. At first, *enka* lyrics were topical, expressing attitudes toward contemporary social and political movements. But these deeply political songs were transformed through the decades to become comic and finally, after World War II, sentimental songs full of nostalgia and longing. In any case their influence on the development of Japanese popular song as a whole is unmistakable.

One might imagine that the older generation would be the one most likely to appreciate such nostalgic expressions of sadness. Indeed, to many younger people who grew up with rock music, *enka* sounds too old-fashioned and sentimental. By the mid-1970s the audiences for *enka* were growing older, and the genre did not seem to hold much appeal for younger listeners. But then a new phenomenon called *karaoke* appeared on the scene, reinvigorating the *enka* and bringing it to a new, younger audience.

Popular Music Today

Karaoke, or "Empty Orchestra"

Karaoke (ka-ra-oh-kay) originated and became popular in Japan decades before it was exported to North America and Europe. In *karaoke*, anyone with the proper equipment can sing his or her favorite songs to a full orchestral accompaniment. A typical setup includes a CD player, a recording of the musical accompaniment to a favorite song, speakers, and an amplifier with a microphone for the singer. In Japan, *enka* were, and continue to be, the songs of choice for most *karaoke* users. Other kinds of music found on *karaoke* tapes include Japanese folk and contemporary "pop" songs, as well as Western popular songs. A *karaoke* singer may sing the lyrics of these songs either from memory or by consulting a book containing the lyrics to hundreds of songs.

In Japan a large variety of *karaoke* machines are produced, ranging in price from about $200 to $5,000 but averaging about $2,000. The more expensive models are used in restaurants, bars, wedding halls, and special *karaoke* singing centers. At these places, customers or guests sing songs of their choice from a wide selection available on tape, singing either alone or in couples. Models priced in the middle range are often installed in smaller bars as well as on touring buses and trains so that Japanese traveling in groups can sing to each other on long trips. The inexpensive models are designed for home use, so that users can practice for these public performances. There are even battery-powered models for outdoor use.

The *karaoke* technology available to the consumer was developed to support and enhance his or her voice as much as possible. One can adjust the volume of the vocal part in relation to the instrumental background, and even switch on an echo device when desired (to add a kind of "singing-in-the-shower" effect). Today's equipment is digitized, permitting singers to change the key of the original accompaniment tape to one in their own singing range. Even the musical accompaniment is designed to be helpful to the singer; the orchestra stays in the background to avoid stealing the show from the singer, but one instrument reinforces the melodic line, in case the singer becomes lost.

Karaoke equipment has reinforced the traditional Japanese custom of group singing. Japanese feel that singing helps to establish a relaxed atmosphere and feeling of closeness with others. Social groups—based on professional, school, familial, or community relationships—are important in Japanese life, and the Japanese put much effort into harmonious relationships within these groups. For example, to improve relations among company employees, management organizes special activities such as group tours to spas and drinking parties. On these occasions, *karaoke* is used to break down the social barriers created by the company hierarchy. For this purpose, mere conversation, even when mixed with drinking, does not suffice, because it is based on knowledge and wit. *Karaoke* is a different kind of socializing, through which the most sentimental, nostalgic ideas can be expressed— and are even encouraged—when sung through the *karaoke* machine.

Karaoke singing also reinforces group harmony through the expectation that each member of a group will participate by singing in front of the group. Even if someone feels embarrassed and wants to refuse, he or she usually gives in and sings at least one song in order to maintain the spirit of group harmony.

In recent years, *karaoke* has become immensely popular around the world; one can find "*karaoke* bars" in South America, Europe, and the United States, for example. However, public *karaoke* singing in these continents does not influence and control group social dynamics to the same degree as in Japan and other Asian countries.

Karaoke technology works also as an outlet for stress. For instance, the echo feature gives singers a sense of removal from their everyday identity. One Japanese living in the United States stated, "It's great to hear your own voice, resounding throughout the room. You feel all your tension disappear." Some businessmen in Japan enjoy going to *karaoke* bars after work for just that purpose: to relieve the accumulated stress from a day of work by belting down a few drinks and belting out a few songs. One survey shows that *karaoke* is most popular among male, white-collar workers between the ages of twenty and forty-nine; the same survey also found that, within any age group, those who enjoyed *karaoke* the most were "those who like to sing" and "those who like to drink" (NHK Hō sō 1982:24–25).

Japanese businessmen living abroad find *karaoke* bars in which they can spend their after-hours time. In New York City, for example, where several Japanese businessmen work, a fierce competition has broken out among the many *karaoke* bars to install the latest technological developments. One such development involves the DVD player, which shows a series of scenes on large, high-definition TV screens, to accompany each song. Besides adding visual stimulation, this apparatus also allows singers to look up at their listeners and at the screen instead of having their heads buried in the lyric book.

Enka Songs

While the content of the music is quite different, there is an interesting similarity in the way *enka* songs (as sung over *karaoke* machines) and traditional music are learned. Both involve aural skills—listening carefully to an "original" version (of the recording in the case of *enka*, and of the teacher in traditional music) and imitating it as skillfully as possible. These days, some notation can also be involved. Real *karaoke* enthusiasts can even study with a teacher for pointers or technique but, for the most part, singers become familiar with the melody and interpretation of a song by listening to a recorded professional version many times.

At the highest skill level, though, *karaoke* performances are expected to be more than exact imitations of an original performance. For example, some expensive *karaoke* machines can automatically score a performer on a scale of 1 to 100. One enthusiast told me that in his experience "exact" reproduction of a song in its original interpretation might bring a score of

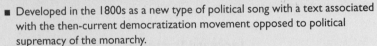

Salient Characteristics of Enka Songs

- Developed in the 1800s as a new type of political song with a text associated with the then-current democratization movement opposed to political supremacy of the monarchy.
- By the early twentieth century, lyrics influenced by then-popular vaudeville (popular comic theater).
- Have become sentimental songs merging elements of traditional Japanese and Western music.
- The song of choice for most *karaoke* performers.

98 or 99, but not 100. For the highest score, an element of "personal expressiveness" is necessary, while at the same time one must completely reproduce the original version. In the traditional music genres described earlier, we have seen this same standardization of music performance among the lower-ranking performers, with expectations for more personal creativity at the highest level.

Enka composers have adapted their songs to the tastes of the younger generation. Background accompaniment ranges from the earlier simple guitar accompaniment to sophisticated orchestral arrangements and heavier, rock-type beats. More "upbeat" *enka* have been issued, with faster tempos and more optimistic lyrics, though these are still in the minority. Finally, vocal ornamentation, so emphasized in earlier *enka*, is toned down in the newer versions because the youth are more accustomed to hearing Western-style vocalization.

The *enka* song found on **CD 2, Track 1** ("Naite Nagasaki," or "Crying Nagasaki") is typical of the more old-fashioned variety of *enka* meant for a middle-aged audience. Recorded in 1988 by a *geisha*, the mournfully romantic theme of the song, its orchestral background, and its vocal style appeal to people who visit a bar with a *karaoke* machine after a long day at work and want to indulge in a little emotionalism. The text describes a woman alone in her room as she contemplates the departure of her lover.

Several images brought out in the song are common to many *enka* songs. The setting of the port town of Nagasaki conjures up romantic associations and particularly the sadness of lovers parting. The scenes of drowning oneself in sake, crying in the windy night, and—on top of all that—rain are also found in hundreds of other *enka* songs. For such themes, the Japanese prefer to use a minor scale. At times, the melody too emphasizes the sad mood, for example in the setting of the words "Naite, naite . . . ," as though the singer were sobbing.

The form of the song is also typical of *enka*—a simple verse with a refrain. It opens and closes with instrumental sections, which also recur between verses. As soon as the voice enters, the background accompaniment becomes minimal, consisting mainly of a bass guitar playing a bass line and other orchestral and electronic instruments filling in the harmony. This accompaniment begins to expand towards the end of the stanza as the

CD 2:1

"Naite Nagasaki" ("Crying Nagasaki") (3:33). Performed by Kanda Fukumaru for Nippon Columbia AH-210.

Close Listening   CD 2:1

"Naite Nagasaki" ("Crying Nagasaki")

Counter Number	Commentary	Lyrics and Translation	
0:00	**Orchestral introduction**		
	Verse 1		
0:22	Vocalist begins. Background accompaniment becomes minimal, with bass guitar playing a bass line and other orchestral and electronic instruments filling in the harmony. Accompaniment by orchestra swells as the verse continues and emotion builds Western arrangement timbre of the electronic keyboard imitates a shamisen muted trumpet sound prominent	*Saka no mukō ni yogisha ga mieru. Anata noseteku nobori no ressha. Okuritai kedo okureba tsurai. Heya no mado kara te o furu watashi.*	On the other side of the hill I can see the night train. Taking you away, the northbound train. I want to send you off but if I do it will be painful. From the window of my room I wave good-bye to you.
Refrain			
0:55	Vocalist inflects singing with sobs.	*Naite naite naite Nagasaki Ame ni narisō, ne..*	Crying, crying, crying, Nagasaki, It looks like rain, doesn't it?
0:58	Choral group enters as if to add emotional emphasis.		
Interlude			
1:10	Full orchestra.		
Verse 2			
1:21	Vocalist sings second verse (same melody as first verse). More vocal ornamentation. Inflects the last part of the verse with sobs.	*Wakarenakereba naranaihito to shitte inagara moyashita inochi sugaritsukitai Maruyamadōri jitto koraete aruita watashi*	That you were someone with whom I'd have to part— although I knew this, a burning fate, wanting to cling to you, along the Maruyamadōri with steady endurance, I walked:
Refrain			
1:54	Vocalist and choral group repeat refrain.	*Naite naite naite Nagasaki Ame ni narisō, ne.*	Crying, crying, crying, Nagasaki, It looks like rain, doesn't it?
Interlude			
2:08	Full orchestra plays phrases from the melody.		

Counter Number	Commentary	Lyrics and Translation	
Verse 3			
2:30	Vocalist sings third verse (same melody as previous verses).	*Minato yokaze fukikomu kabe ni furete setsunai anata no heyagi. Nigai o-sake o abiteru watashi.*	The night wind from the port blows against the wall making flutter your robe hanging there. I drown myself in bitter sake.
Refrain			
3:03	Vocalist and choral group as before.	*Naite naite naite Nagasaki Ame ni narisō, ne.*	Crying, crying, crying, Nagasaki, It looks like rain, doesn't it?
Interlude/Ending			
3:17–3:34	Orchestra completes the song.		

vocal part reaches the climax at "*Naite, naite . . .*" In their harmony, *enka* tend to sound like most Western popular music. "Naite Nagasaki" contains complicated orchestration, background singers, and other elements showing the influence of Western popular music. However, the occasional use of vocal ornamentation reflects Japanese taste in vocal quality.

The large Japanese music industry produces many other kinds of popular music in addition to *enka*. Some are strongly influenced by Western genres, and some show connections to Japanese musical traditions. The term *kayōkyoku* describes Japanese popular song as a whole, and particularly the songs (including *enka*) that mix Western and Japanese musical elements.

This combination is usually a blend of Japanese melodies made from pentatonic scales with Western harmonic progressions and metrical organization. Since the mid-1970s, however, many of the contemporary songs have been written in Western scales, especially major modes, conforming to the imported music listened to by Japanese youth.

In Japan today, popular music includes easy listening, rock, punk, and other musics based on Western models although sometimes deviating from them in interesting ways. In addition, Japanese identify four other types of popular song. *Gunka* (literally, "military songs") are concerned with war. *Fōku songu* ("folk songs") refer to what people in North America call the products of singer-songwriters (such as Bob Dylan), while the lyrics, sung in Japanese by their composers, usually refer to Japanese social or political issues. *Nyū myūshiku* ("new music") developed out of *fōku songu,* but here the lyrics convey an introverted, personal point of view, and the melody is more important than a strong beat. Finally, *pops* is a young teenage music, in which the recording industry plays a major role in developing the teenage singers' musical skills and their images of youth and innocence. Television exposure is critical, and *pops* singers' careers rise and fall rapidly. The

> ### Salient Characteristics of *Taiko* ♪♫
>
> - Meaning "drum" and representing all the various kinds of drums played in Japan.
> - A national symbol of Japan's musical tradition, *taiko* drumming ensembles tour globally.
> - Most *taiko* drumming ensembles are an invention of the post–World War II era.
> - Popularity derived partly from their emphasis on *samurai* values: discipline, hard physical and mental training, group coordination, and perfectionism.

music sounds Western and, to add a touch of sophistication, often includes a few words of English.

Taiko (Drum Ensemble)

Today, *taiko* drumming ensembles are a national symbol of Japan's musical tradition, on par with the *koto* and *shakuhachi*. But unlike *koto* and *shakuhachi*, with their long and complex histories, most of the *taiko* drumming ensembles are an invention of the post–World War II era. Before that, percussion ensembles and music centering on percussion instruments were more the exception than the rule. Drums were usually played individually or in instrumental ensembles at Shinto and Buddhist festivals. At these occasions, only simple rhythms were played to mark the rhythm of a dance or the melody of the *shamisen* or the *yokobue* transverse bamboo flute.

Since the 1970s groups of *taiko* drummers, playing various sizes of Japanese traditional drums and other instruments in a staged presentation, have toured throughout the world and enjoyed great success in many festivals and concert halls outside of Japan. Why are they so popular? Probably in part because they emphasize *samurai* values: discipline, hard physical and mental training, group coordination, and perfectionism. *Taiko* groups show how conflicting musical values are resolved when local groups take the international stage. What is considered locally important loses out before an international audience in favor of a more stereotypical "national" image.

The word *taiko* means "drum" and stands for all the various kinds of drums played in Japan, from the small, double-sided *shimedaiko* to the huge, 3-meter-wide drums used in some folk festivals. The current-day *taiko* ensemble can be defined as a musical group centering on different Japanese drums; in Japanese they are called *kumidaiko* or *taiko guruupu*. During the late 1950s, traditional folk drums inspired some Tokyo musicians to form drumming groups that went far beyond the musical traditions that had inspired them. Eye-catching postures and movements— sometimes related to the martial arts and other forms of strength building— were developed for executing the newly created compositions. Widely publicized appearances at the Tokyo Olympics in 1964 and the Osaka World Exposition of 1970 suddenly put *taiko* groups in the limelight, drawing large audiences as well as many prospective students.

Copyright © 2000, Max Peter Baumann

Figure 5.4
Taiko group Yuukyuu-kai from Nagaoka, performing at street festival. Bamberg, Germany, August 29, 2000.

World tours by professional groups have multiplied the number of *taiko* fans internationally, and amateur *taiko* groups have sprung up throughout the world. In particular, the North American continent has become a second home to *taiko* ensembles: There are now approximately 150 *taiko* groups in the United States and Canada, 47 of these in California alone. In Japan, there are said to be about 1,500 *taiko* groups active at present. Interested amateurs have formed groups throughout Japan, where both children and adults learn *taiko* in their local community centers and perform for neighborhood festivals. *Taiko* drumming is even being used as a form of therapy for handicapped people. Here we shall focus on two professional groups and how they present themselves on the stage, particularly for an international audience. First, listen to *taiko* drumming on **CD 1, Track 26** (see also Figure 5.4).

 CD 1:26

Festival Drumming (1:19). *Taiko* Ensemble Yuukyuu-kai from Nagaoka, Japan, led by M. Kobayashi (Kaicho-san) and Takano Katsuhiro. Field recording by Max Peter Baumann. Bamberg, Germany, August 28, 2000.

Ondekoza and Kodô: Representatives of the New *Taiko* Group

The groups Ondekoza (meaning "devil drum group") and Kodô (literally, "beat of the children") are two of the most successful groups among the professional *taiko* ensembles. Ondekoza was founded in 1970, when the student movement in the cities and universities was at its height. A musician named Den Tagayasu offered a summer course on music on the isolated island of Sado in the Sea of Japan (Waycott 1996:125). About forty young students gathered at Sado that year, and they became the nucleus of Ondekoza. During that summer and the following years, Den developed the musical as well as social concept that was to form the basis of the groups Ondekoza and Kodô and go on to influence countless other groups.

In this ensemble, the *taiko* drum became the center of an experiment for young urban Japanese, many of whom were disillusioned with the competitive, materialistic world of postwar Japan and were searching for some deeper meaning for their lives. In order to learn Den's drum technique, students had to embrace discipline, hard work, and group harmony. The drum itself became a spiritual tool through which these traits could be developed, strengthened, and brought to new heights. In fact, the physical qualities of the *taiko* drum itself inspired this group's mental and spiritual direction.

To make the large barrel drum resound in an impressive way, great strength and stamina are needed. To this end, the group members arose every morning at 4:00 A.M. in order to run 10 kilometers before breakfast. Top physical condition was necessary not only for hitting the drums, but also for carrying out the strenuous movement choreographies that were developed. These movements contributed to the musical performance by providing a coordinating framework for playing the complicated drum strokes. Above all, though, *taiko* choreographies provided visual stimulation and exciting entertainment for the audience. To carry out the movements, drill-like precision was necessary, which itself demanded individual mental concentration and intricate group coordination. Such concentration and coordination were promoted through exercises and activities that filled up the member's daily schedules from morning to night.

The drummers lived in an isolated commune within the rough but beautiful natural setting of Sado Island. At the beginning, Den also had the idealistic idea of developing a close relationship with the local population in Sado, but the islanders found the young urban outsiders a bit strange and they kept their distance. In all, one can see in hindsight that Den and his followers wanted to create a kind of utopia around the drum and drum playing, a utopia based on traditional values and on the nature of large drums—but *taiko* was not based on any specific folk music tradition. Ondekoza represented an alternative lifestyle in a rural setting far from the rat race of Tokyo, a setting where the *taiko* drum and its music were the center of everyone's thoughts and ambitions.

A couple of years after Ondekoza was formed, several members became disillusioned with Den as a leader. They formed their own group, which they named Kodô (Asano Taiko Shiryokan:1996). They did not, however, object to the modest, disciplined way of life that had been developed on Sado by Den. Kodô members still live on Sado Island (as do Ondekoza members), at least when they are not touring through North America or Europe. Both Kodô and Ondekoza are well-known for their physical training and feats of endurance. Their members have frequently participated in the Boston Marathon, wearing their traditional costumes and drumming the *taiko* afterward. In 1990 Ondekoza played a concert in Carnegie Hall in New York that began a U.S. tour, ending back at that concert hall three years later for a farewell performance. During those three years, the group members ran from one concert to the next, giving 355 concerts along the way and covering over 9,000 miles. In total, they wore out 121 pairs of shoes. A sign of the ascetic standards by which they live is that each member spent on average only $2 per day on food (Ondekoza 1985).

Taiko groups are best experienced live. Anyone who has seen the elaborate and vigorous coordinated movements of these groups as they attack the drums can only be disappointed by a sound recording. It is not only the important visual stimulus that is lacking; the strong vibrations from the deep tones of many assembled drums flow through the audiences' bodies, making them a physical part of the performance.

In both the Ondekoza and Kodô groups, the drummers are taught to be well-rounded musicians using one or more additional instruments, according to their individual abilities. Professional musicians of various Japanese traditional instruments and schools are invited to teach these at Sado. Over time these instruments have been incorporated into *taiko* pieces; they are also used in intermission pieces to be played in between the loud, exciting drum selections. In either case, the programs concentrate on instruments used in the folk music tradition, probably because that tradition shapes the atmosphere of these performances as a whole.

As Ondekoza first began to invite teachers to Sado and then to play in public, their conduct insulted many traditional musicians of both folk and art music. These *taiko* musicians had sidestepped the traditional system, which involves years of learning from a particular teacher in a particular style. Mixing different instruments and their strictly separated schools of playing into newly composed pieces also threatened the traditional music world as many professionals knew it. They became even more angry when they realized that Ondekoza and Kodô were being celebrated both at home and abroad as "traditional Japanese folk music." Today such conflicts have lessened, mostly because in Japan the traditional borderlines between musical genres have weakened significantly in recent years. Like other professional *taiko* groups, Ondekoza now often perform fusion experiments with jazz, classical, and pop musicians.

On the domestic and international stages, these two groups and others like them emphasize traditional ties to Japanese folk culture, but these ties are exaggerated. *Taiko* groups create the aura of a centuries-old historical tradition and present themselves as bearers of this tradition, both in their outward appearance and in program notes written for their audiences. They refer, for example, to the long history of the *taiko* drum in general in Japan and its role in traditional festivals throughout the country. One documentary video contains the statement, "The beating of drums is an ancient ritual in Japan, its lineage buried in the mists of pre-historic Asia, when men sought spiritual understanding through legendary healing powers of specially endowed leaders called shamans" (Kodô 1983). But they fail to mention that their specific kind of ensemble and the way they play dates from the 1970s.

Other parts of their performances that underline their imagined ties to Japanese antiquity include their costumes (which are based on festival clothing of urban laborers and of farmers) and their overall stage presence. We sense in their formal, almost aloof, onstage attitude a presence and behavior different from everyday Western ways of living. Groups such as Ondekoza and Kodô propagate a philosophy of single-minded discipline, physical conditioning, and even spiritual living through the *taiko* drum, a philosophy that transmits well and fascinates audience members in Japan and abroad.

At the same time, Western-influenced elements linked to more effective stage presentation have also established themselves in *taiko* performances. Though their usual attitude onstage is formal, we also see flashes of emotion, such as pleasure, amusement or pain, crossing their faces. The Western audience reacts quite favorably to this contrast between the formal and the emotional. *Taiko* groups thus play around with Western concepts of "the folk." "The folk" of Japan seem to be "different" (perhaps related somehow to a "samurai ethic"), but at the same time, they briefly reveal their human and emotional side. They thoroughly revel in their music and enjoy sharing that music with outsiders.

In reality, folk drum playing in Japan is traditionally associated with Shinto and Buddhist festivals, where music is performed as an offering to the gods and therefore is taken quite seriously by the performers. When I learned festival music in Tokyo, I was told to avoid all traces of a smile when I performed, and other groups that showed any kind of emotion while playing were ridiculed. The conservative musicians I learned from also ridiculed groups that inserted an excessive amount of *kakegoe,* the calls like *"so-re"* that punctuate beats and also add to the excited, enthusiastic atmosphere. Some traditional musicians also mock an important element of *taiko* performances that always impresses their audiences: the groups' astounding precision and coordination. In the Japanese musical tradition, when musicians strike a beat, exact ensemble precision is often considered undesirable. But the newer *taiko* groups aim for such precision because their coordinated movements demand it. Finally, joking through gestures rather than words (ideal for cross-cultural entertainment) also plays an important role in Ondekoza performances (e.g., Ondekoza 1992). Such humorous interludes would be unimaginable in traditional Japanese music, other than in a strictly comical stage show. Another modern element in *taiko* shows is the inclusion of women and foreign faces (non-Asians) in their groups (Figure 5.5). This sign of openness appeals particularly to Western audiences, which thereby see a connection between the *taiko* as Japanese tradition and the international community. It also strengthens audiences' idealistic conception of a "folk" culture—the ideas of inclusivity and openness that pave the way toward the creation of a community of humankind.

Relationships between the local, the national, and the international are complex in *taiko* group performances. *Taiko* groups provide program notes for their concerts that indicate local origins for their "traditional" pieces (for example, they say that the piece comes from a certain festival of a particular village). In reality, they have usually taken only a rhythmic pattern from that local drum tradition and developed from that a longer piece of music and visual entertainment. The professional group members also come from different parts of Japan (if not also from abroad), so that a specific local identity cannot be established through the musicians, in spite

Figure 5.5
Nagaoka *taiko* group performs with volunteers from a German audience. Bamberg, Germany, August 29, 2000.

of the fact that local identity is a key marker of traditional folk music in Japan. On the other hand, their national identity as a "Japanese" group is strong both in Japan and on the international stage. This identity comes across as a "folk" identity different from the culture of the upper classes.

When *taiko* groups present themselves on the international stage, what do they do to achieve such an effective performance that pleases the audience aesthetically and emotionally? In this achievement, have they somehow betrayed their "tradition"? In the case of *taiko* groups, to speak of a "traditional" setting versus one that is not traditional is meaningless, because we have seen that their "tradition" is a flexible, modern one. Festival organizers who invite such groups to play abroad depend on the background information provided by the musicians themselves. They then instruct audiences through program notes and stage announcements based on this information—that is, information that stresses their ties to localities and to national tradition. Whether such descriptions reveal the whole story behind these groups probably matters little to the public, which is impressed above all with what they see onstage: astounding skill and precision, physical endurance and strength, and a single-mindedness of purpose that highly impresses and entertains them. *Taiko* performances support the audience's positive images of Japan and enhance their admiration for Japanese culture. Yet, as we have seen, their admiration is built on the audience's own ideas of what "folk" means (or should mean) and on misunderstood history.

In summary, while professional *taiko* groups have come to represent traditional Japanese folk music both at home and abroad, in order to succeed they have altered traditional musical values and processes. The lack of detailed knowledge about Japanese folk traditions, both abroad and increasingly in Japan, has promoted this dilemma. Still, the traditional Japanese cultural values of hard, disciplined work and coordination of that work within a group structure are carried on by *taiko* groups. In the end, *taiko* drumming groups present a highly successful reinterpretation of Japanese folk music. Unlike traditional folk music, its context is already the stage.

The liner notes to one of their recordings summarizes well the ways in which Ondekoza hope to appeal to their audiences:

> Half-naked men shining in sweat, who strike huge barrel drums with their muscular arms using drumsticks like table legs, allow us to experience on this record another Japan that obviously does not match the usual imagine of tender geishas in the middle of a teahouse idyll. Those who until now have always associated Japan with the sound of the koto or of kabuki will now become acquainted, with Ondekoza, with a new facet of Japanese music: from an earthy, wild drum ecstasy that revels in fantastic rolls and syncopations to disciplined crescendi that develop over long passages in "monotone" slow motion. . . . We feel the inner pulse of the musicians, their stoic introspection that seems in accord with the sound of the drums. (Ondekoza 1985)

Final Words

We have reviewed a small sample of the wide variety of music heard in Japan today. This sample contains many examples of the mixture of native with foreign elements in the evolution of new musical forms. The *shakuhachi* was developed from an instrument of Chinese origin that entered Japan around the eighth century. The Zen philosophy that underlay the instrument's use in meditation also originated in China. The prototype of the *shamisen*, used to play *kouta* and to accompany traditional folk song, can be traced to Okinawa, China, and beyond. Finally, popular music as a whole is based in form, rhythmic and harmonic structure, and instrumental accompaniment on Western music; only the melodic component and the lyric content in some cases reflect Japanese traditions.

Of course, one can question the concept itself of "tradition" or the "traditional culture" of a nation or people, especially in terms of "purity" of origin. What culture in the world has not borrowed cultural elements from another, with the roots of that borrowing going so far back that few think of the idea or custom as borrowed? *Taiko* is a deliberately invented tradition, of recent origin, which revives certain real—and legendary—aspects of ancient Japanese music and culture.

We find, in examining the Japanese music-culture, the expression of some aspects of the varied Japanese character. For instance, popular nonsense songs find their roots in a certain outlandish sense of humor that the Japanese sometimes indulge in. (Anyone who has watched Japanese television for any length of time, particularly game shows, can attest to this.) On a more sober note, the idea of emptying one's soul and reaching a state of selflessness as preparation for the performance of *shakuhachi* reflects the strong underlying influence of Zen thought in Japanese culture. This influence touches many other areas of Japanese daily life, in regard to not just mental preparation for a future task, but also self-control and self-discipline. *Taiko* exemplifies this training, along with mental and physical strength, endurance, focus, and precise coordination of individual activities within a group. Finally, the indulgence in pathos and extreme emotional anguish, as expressed in *enka* songs, reveals another side of the Japanese character. Listening to Japanese music and learning about its connections to past and present society, we become aware of the richness of Japanese life.

Study Questions

1. What are the general characteristics of Japanese traditional music?
2. How does flexibility characterize rhythm in Japanese traditional music?
3. How do Zen Buddhist ideas influence music for *shakuhachi*? What is *ma*?
4. What is a "pitchless" sound? Give some examples.
5. Who was O-Yo and why is she important in the history of Japanese music?
6. How do the lyrics in "Hakusen no" differ from ordinary language and show poetic qualities? Compare the poetic achievement of "Hakusen no" with that of "Naite Nagasaki." Which do you like better, and why?
7. What is the *iemoto* system? Beyond music, what does the *iemoto* system tell us about Japanese approaches to life?
8. Discuss Japanese folk song. Why is it popular today?
9. *Karaoke* and *taiko* are both firmly rooted in Japanese culture; what is their appeal to peoples other than Japanese?
10. Is *taiko* an invented tradition?

Glossary

Edo The name of the city of Tokyo before 1868.

enka Popular songs introduced beginning in the 1880s that blended Western and Japanese music. At first political, eventually they became comical, and after World War II romantic and nostalgic. *Enka* is the most popular song genre for *karaoke*.

finger tremolo A playing technique used by wind and brass instrumentalists in which a finger moves rapidly back and forth to cover and uncover a finger hole.

flexible rhythm Music with irregular pulse patterns; music without a steady beat.

flutter tonguing A playing technique used by wind instrumentalists. The tongue flutters back and forth to cover and uncover the blow hole.

folk song See *minyō; taiko*.

gagaku Ancient orchestral music for the court, from China, that accompanies a highly stylized dance.

heterophony See *heterophonic texture* in glossary, Chapter 1.

honkyoku The main solo repertoire for *shakuhachi*.

iemoto A guild or musical "school" with its own performance style and repertoire.

jo-ha-kyū Typical form for tempo (speed) in Japanese traditional music: a three part structure. *Jo* = introduction, usually slow; *ha* = breaking apart, or faster; *kyū* = rushing to the end, but the tempo slows just before the piece is over.

karaoke (ka-ra-oh-kay) Literally, "empty orchestra," or musical accompaniment that is furnished on CD so that an amateur singer can have an orchestra to sing with.

kari A technique in which a *shakuhachi* player raises the pitch of a sound by changing the angle of the lips to the mouthpiece.

komusō Monks who wandered the countryside during the Tokugawa period, begging and playing the *shakuhachi.*

koto Traditional Japanese plucked string instrument with movable frets on the sounding board.

kouta Japanese composed song form, dating from the nineteenth century and related to women singers. The themes are romantic and the lyrics are poetic.

ma A Japanese concept involving the relationship among time, sounds, and silence in a piece of music.

meri A technique in which a *shakuhachi* player lowers the pitch and volume of a sound by changing the angle of the lips to the mouthpiece.

minyō Folk song traditionally associated with the rural or farming class of Japanese, accompanying daily activities, and originally passed along by observation and imitation rather than notation or formal instruction. A revival of *minyō*, among city dwellers, with tendencies toward *iemoto*-like professionalization, is evident in Japan today.

popular music Studio-recorded, mass-media disseminated, modern music meant to appeal to the general public.

sawari A buzzing or humming sound that is purposely built in to the structure of the *shamisen.*

shakuhachi Traditional end-blown bamboo Japanese flute with five holes, 54 centimeters long, associated with Zen Buddhism.

shamisen Traditional Japanese three-string, long-necked, plucked lute.

shōka Songs introduced late in the nineteenth century to teach Japanese the characteristics of Western music.

taiko **drumming** A choreographed performance involving several drummers, different size Japanese drums, and eye-catching movements related to the martial arts. *Taiko* drumming may be considered a representation and reinterpretation of traditional Japanese folk music.

Tokugawa period 1600–1867, a period of peace and prosperity, prior to any extensive contact with the West.

Resources

References

Asano Taiko Shiryokan. 1996. *Taikorojii* (Taikology Biannual), no. 14. "Kodô Narrates." [Special Issue: general historical information on *taiko* groups and instruments]

Groemer, Gerald. 1994. "Fifteen Years of Folk Song Collection in Japan: Reports and Recordings of the 'Emergency Folk Song Survey.'" *Asian Folklore Studies* 53 (2): 199–225.

Hughes, David. 1981. "Japanese Folk Song Preservation Societies: Their History and Nature." In *International Symposium on the Conservation and Restoration of*

Cultural Property, edited by the Organizing Committee of ISCRCP. Tokyo: Tokyo National Research Institute of Cultural Properties.

———. 1990–1991. "Japanese 'New Folk Songs,' Old and New." *Asian Music* 22 (1): 1–49.

Kikkawa Eishi. 1981. *Nihon ongaku no rekishi* [The History of Japanese Music]. Osaka: Sōgensha.

Koizumi Fumio. 1974. *Nihon no ongaku* [Japanese Music]. Tokyo: National Theater of Japan.

Kurada Yoshihiro. 1982. "Kouta." In *Ongaku daijiten* [Encyclopedia Musica], edited by Shitanaka Kunihiko. Tokyo: Heibonsha.

NHK Hō sō Seron Chō sajo, eds. 1982. *Gendaijin to ongaku* [Contemporary People and Music]. Tokyo: Nippon Hō sō Shuppan Kyō kai.

Ondekoza. 1985. *Ondekoza: Devils on Drums.* Recording with commentary. Nektar Records 680.008.

———. 1992. *Za Ondekoza: Live in Atlanta.* Tokyo: S-Two Corporation. VHS video.

Waycott, Angus. 1996. *Sado. Japan's Island in Exile.* Berkeley, CA: Stone Bridge Press.

Additional Reading

Adachi, Barbara. 1985. *Backstage at Bunraku: A Behind-the-Scenes Look at Japan's Traditional Puppet Theater.* New York: Weatherhill.

Adriaansz, Willem. 1973. *The Kumiuta and Danmono Traditions of Japanese Koto Music.* Berkeley: Univ. of California Press.

Asano Kaori. 1996. *Taiko o utsu!* (Beating the *Taiko*). Tokyo: Bakushusha.

Asano Taiko Shiryokan. 1996. *Taikorojii* (Taikology Biannual), no. 14. "Kodô Narrates." [Special Issue: general historical information on *taiko* groups and instruments]

———. 1998. *Taikorojii* (Taikology Biannual), no. 16. "From the Culture of North Americans of Japanese Descent to a Universal Art." [Special Issue: overview of *taiko* activities in North America and interviews with performers]

Blasdel, Christopher Yohmei. 1988. *The Shakuhachi: A Manual for Learning.* Tokyo: Ongaku no Tomo Sha.

Crihfield, Liza. 1979. *Kouta: "Little Songs" of the Geisha World.* Rutland, Vt.: Charles E. Tuttle.

Dalby, Liza Crihfield. 1983. *Geisha.* Berkeley: Univ. of California Press.

Fujie, Linda. 1986. "The Process of Oral Transmission in Japanese Performing Arts: The Teaching of *Matsuri-bayashi* in Tokyo." In *The Oral and the Literate in Music,* edited by Yoshihiko Tokumaru and Osamu Yamaguti. Tokyo: Academia Music.

Groemer, Gerald. 1994. "Fifteen Years of Folk Song Collection in Japan: Reports and Recordings of the 'Emergency Folk Song Survey.'" *Asian Folklore Studies* 53 (2): 199–225.

Gutzwiller, Andreas, and Gerald Bennett. 1991. "The World of a Single Sound: Basic Structure of the Music of the Japanese Flute Shakuhachi." *Musica Asiatica* 6:36–59.

Herd, Judith Ann. 1984. "Play It Again, Isamu!" *Mainichi Daily News,* 9 July 1984, p. 9.

Hughes, David. 1990–1991. "Japanese 'New Folk Songs,' Old and New." *Asian Music* 22 (1): 1–49.

Kishibe Shigeo. 1984. *The Traditional Music of Japan.* Tokyo: Ongaku no Tomo Sha.

Malm, William. 1959. *Japanese Music and Musical Instruments.* Rutland, Vt.: Charles E. Tuttle.

———. 1971. *Modern Music of Meiji Japan.* In *Tradition and Modernization in Japanese Culture,* edited by Donald H. Shirley. Princeton, N.J.: Princeton Univ. Press.

Mitsui Toru. 1984. "Japan in Japan: Notes on an Aspect of the Popular Music Record Industry in Japan." *Popular Music* 3:107–20.

Okada Maki. 1991. "Musical Characteristics of *Enka*." *Popular Music* 10 (3): 283–303.

Waycott, Angus. 1996. *Sado. Japan's Island in Exile.* Berkeley, CA: Stone Bridge Press.

Wong, Deborah. 2000. "Taiko and the Asian/American Body: Drums, Rising Sun, and the Question of Gender." *The World of Music* 42 (3): 67–78.

Additional Listening

"Music of Japanese People." CD Series. King Record Co. (2-12-13 Ottowa, Bunkyo-ku, Tokyo 112).

  Vol. 1: *Harmony of Japanese Music.* KICH 2021.

  Vol. 2: *Japanese Dance Music.* KICH 2022.

  Vol. 3: *Japanese Work Songs.* KICH 2023.

  Vol. 4: *Jam Session of Tsugaru-Shamisen.* KICH 2024.

  Vol. 5: *Music of Okinawa.* KICH 2025.

  Vol. 6: *Music of Yaeyama and Miyako.* KICH 2026.

  Vol. 7: *Music of Amami.* KICH 2027.

  Vol. 8: *Music of Japanese Festivals.* KICH 2028.

  Vol. 9: *Soundscape of Japan.* KICH 2029.

  Vol. 10: *A Collection of Unique Musical Instruments.* KICH 2030.

"Nihon no dentô ongaku" [Japanese Traditional Music]. CD Series. King Record Co. (2-12-13 Ottowa, Bunkyo-ku, Tokyo 112).

  Vol. 1: *Gagaku.* KICH 2001.

  Vol. 2: *Nôgaku.* KICH 2002.

  Vol. 3: *Kabuki.* KICH 2003.

  Vol. 4: *Biwa.* KICH 2004.

  Vol. 5: *Shakuhachi.* KICH 2005.

  Vol. 6: *Sô.* KICH 2006.

  Vol. 7: *Sankyoku.* KICH 2007.

  Vol. 8: *Shamisen. I.* KICH 2008.

Vol. 9: *Shamisen. II.* KICH 2009.

Vol. 10: *Percussion.* KICH 2010.

Viewing

Kodô. 1983. *Kodô: Heartbeat Drummers of Japan.* Lyme, Conn.: Rhapsody Films.

Gojinjo Daiko. 2000. *Gojinjo Daiko.* HMC-0102. DVD.

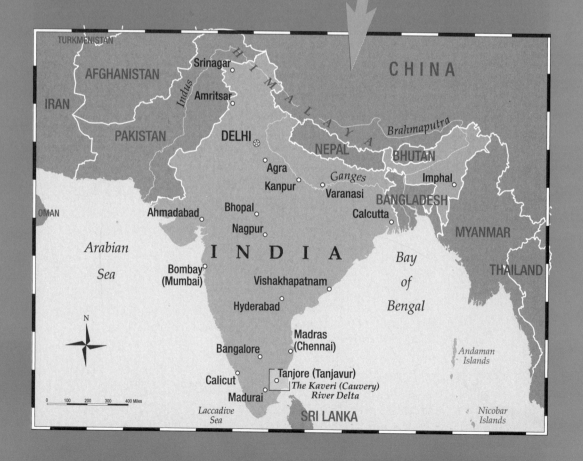

CHAPTER

 6

India/South India

David B. Reck

pproaching the vibrant city of Chennai in southern India from
the air, we would first of all notice in the east the tropical sea,
the rich blue-green of the Bay of Bengal spreading out to the
horizon. Along the coastline is a white ribbon of sand. Facing the ocean
and on broad avenues stretching inland are huge whitewashed government
buildings designed by the British, the orientalist spires and domes of the
University of Madras and High Court, and finally modern glass and
concrete hotels and office buildings.

The colonial British named their provincial capital "Madras," but it had
always been called simply Chennai—"the city"—in Tamil, the language of
the region and the state of Tamil Nadu. The climate, similar to that of
coastal Central America, is described jokingly by local citizens as having
three seasons: " hot, hotter, and hottest!" In truth, November through
January—the season of festivals of music and dance—can be quite pleasant
with a sea breeze in the evenings and the temperatures dipping into the
seventies at night.

In the old days Chennai was a leisurely and genteel city. Most houses
and buildings were one and two stories, with only the temple *gopurams*—
the ornately carved towers—projecting up overhead (see Figure 6.1).
Coconut palm, banyan, neem, jacaranda, ashok, and other trees shaded
houses and streets, while an array of tropical plants filled every yard and
garden. Classical Indian music and *bhajans* (*bhuh*-juhns) (religious songs)
echoed from radios, temples, and outdoor concert halls. Each morning the
day might begin in the cool hours as early as 4:30 or 5:30 A.M. And each
night the town would shut down by 10:00 P.M. to the perfume of incense
and flowering jasmine, and the songs of nightingales.

In Chennai today, with an estimated population of between five and
seven million, modern buildings—apartment high-rises, hotels, shopping
centers, offices, and corporate headquarters—increasingly jut upward from
the sea of green foliage. The streets are clogged with the chaotic traffic of
cars, buses, trucks, vans, auto rickshaws, motorcycles, mopeds, bicycles, and

pedestrians moving in a cacophony of horns beneath a carbon monoxide haze. There is even an appropriately named Hotel Traffic Jam.

Overhead each day dozens of domestic Indian and international flights approach the busy airport. A host of local television stations vie with international channels such as the BBC, ESPN, Nickelodeon, MTV, or Hong Kong's Star Channel. Sari-clad models posing as homemakers plug instant soup, shampoo, or dishwashing detergent. Shop windows display refrigerators, air conditioners, TV sets, VCRs, automobiles, kitchen appliances, furniture, shoes, silks, and ready-made clothing. Modern hospitals equipped with the latest medical technology and with some of the best doctors in the world are found throughout the city. Massive factories and mills produce fabric, steel, automobiles and trucks, polymers, motorcycles, electronic goods, and railway locomotives. Computers and software are everywhere as, here and throughout the planet, India establishes itself as the place where excellent technical schools train a generation whose expertise and innovation feed the global high-tech industry.

In the flash and color and familiarity of the modern world it is easy to forget that South Asia—India, Pakistan, Bangladesh, Nepal, Sri Lanka and several smaller countries—is home to one of the world's most ancient civilizations.

The region's continuous history goes back thousands of years—past independence in 1947, beyond more than three centuries of British colonialism, past the great forts and tombs of the Moguls (around 1400–1700 C.E.), through the courts of countless kingdoms and illustrious emperors such as the Buddhist Asoka (third century B.C.E.), past the ancient well-planned Indus Valley cities of Mohenjo-Daro and Harappa (roughly 2500–1700 B.C.E.), and disappearing into prehistoric collective myth and legend.

The basic philosophies and beliefs of Hinduism still flourish. The gods are alive and well, venerated in temples, homes, ceremonies, and religious festivals. Islam also flourishes among India's 120 million Muslims. India, in fact, has the second largest Muslim population in the world (behind Indonesia). The orderings of caste—a social clan into which one is born—still play a role in status, professions, politics and marriage, and household customs. Many musicians belong to castes associated with music in the south: Brahmin, Devadasi, Pillai, or others.

Down the block from the air-conditioned supermarket, the video store, or the modern pharmacy, we can still find the crowded shops of the bazaar:

Figure 6.1
A towering seventeenth-century *gopuram* at the entrance to the Hindu temple at Rameswaram is typical of those soaring over every city and town in South India.

spices and grains piled high in pyramids in wicker baskets, exotic perfumes in dozens of colors and fragrances, finely woven rugs, and exquisite hand-loomed silks and cotton fabrics spread out like a rainbow. On every street corner a woman sits with a basket of fragrant flowers woven into strands for the hair or garlands for the Gods. In towns and villages the skilled craftsmen for which India is famous follow the trades of their forefathers: carving in stone or sandalwood, weaving in cotton or silk, making intricate jewelry, hammering out fine metalwork in brass or copper, painting, carving, engraving, or making musical instruments. In homes and restaurants a seemingly infinite variety of traditional deliciously spiced dishes in regional styles continue to make South Asia a paradise of fine cooking. Somehow, magically, these ancient traditions persist in a radically changing world—the new and old, the traditional and the innovative, thriving in a unique coexistence.

Everywhere, jarring juxtapositions confront the visitor. A farmer in a loincloth plows behind bullocks in a field next to an airport runway as a

Boeing 787 roars by. A mud and thatch hut sits in the shadow of luxury high-rise apartments. A nuclear power station, its machinery garlanded with flowers, is dedicated at an hour set by astrologers to three-thousand-year-old Hindu chants. A traditional classical music performance takes place around the corner from a trendy coffee shop blasting out the latest American pop hits.

Jawaharlal Nehru, independent India's first prime minister, liked to describe his culture as a *palimpsest,* a manuscript parchment written on again and again in which everything written before is never fully erased. Everything written earlier is somehow still there, visible and readable, blurred perhaps, but never fully replaced or forgotten. The new is constantly added on, but the old, the traditional continues. The multifaceted and complex nature of Indian civilization is one characteristic that makes it so rich in comparison with the increasingly monolithic nature of much of rest of the modern world.

Culture, History, Politics

The facts about India are staggering. Over one billion people—one of every five people on earth—live in an area about a third the size of the United States (say, from the east coast to the Mississippi River). There are fifteen major languages, almost as many alphabets, and dozens of regional dialects. India's continuous history, as noted earlier, stretches back five thousand years and beyond, making the history of relatively new countries such as the United States or Canada seem like mere blips on the cosmic screen.

Owing perhaps to its geography—a diamond shape with a triangular peninsula cut off from neighboring lands by jungles, deserts, and the towering Himalayas with peaks of 29,000 feet, South Asia has developed forms of culture and lifeways distinctly its own. Even so, its size and the variety of its terrain and people account for great regional differences. The largest such difference is between the people of the North, who speak Hindi or related languages such as Bengali or Punjabi, and the Dravidian-speaking peoples of the South, a division that parallels the two main styles of Indian classical music: the northern Hindusthani (hin-du-*stah*-nee) style and the southern Carnatic (kahr-*nah*-tik) tradition.

Despite the geographic barriers, numerous influences have come into India over the centuries. The Indus Valley Civilization has curious connections (perhaps through trade) with Babylon and other ancient cities in the fertile crescent of present-day Iraq. From the third millennium B.C.E., early non-archaeological evidence suggests the immigration of a people from central Asia whose language is related to those of Europe in the Indo-European language family. (Thus the English words for father and mother can be tied both to Latin [*pater* and *mater*] and Sanskrit [*pitr* and *matr*]). Calling themselves Aryans, these immigrants settled on the broad plains of Northern India and Pakistan and created the rich heritage of the four Vedas, the oldest religious books in the world.

The most important later outside influences came from Islamic conquests beginning in the twelfth century C.E. and peaking with the great Mogul emperors of the sixteenth and seventeenth centuries. During this time Persian and Arabic architects, painters, poets, and musicians migrated to the subcontinent to be influenced, in turn, by indigenous styles of the arts. The resulting synthesis of Indian aesthetics with Islamic imports from western Asia can be seen in the ethereal beauty of the Taj Mahal or heard today in the soaring musical improvisations of *sitar* (sih-*tahr*) and *tabla* (*tab*-blah).

In making India "the Crown Jewel of the Empire," the English in the eighteenth through early twentieth centuries brought railways, central authoritarian rule, British law, bureaucracy, universities, Western literature, English language, the movies, and, involuntarily, the ideals of democracy and freedom. They also imported European instruments such as the violin, harmonium, guitar, and clarinet, which talented local musicians readily adapted to Indian musical style. European influences continue today in music. Globalization and instant communication allow Indian musicians to become familiar with Bach, Vivaldi, Beethoven, the Beatles, or the latest rap or pop stars. The saxophone, electric guitar, mandolin, and electronic keyboard have all been adapted to Indian styles and are accepted and enjoyed.

Again and again, foreign cultural ideas and technology have migrated into India over the centuries. Once on the subcontinent—and this is important—they have been absorbed, assimilated, digested, played with creatively, and combined with indigenous cultural elements, emerging eventually in a new and undeniably Indian synthesis. For example, the India *raga* (pronounced *rah*-gah) system of complex scales, intonations, and phrases is uniquely Indian while still clearly related to the classical musical systems of Iran, Turkey, the Arabian peninsula, and North Africa. The *sitar, tabla, shahnai* (shuh-*nai*), *santoor* (sahn-*toor*), and other distinctly "Indian" musical instruments have cousins in Afghanistan, Morocco, and even China, Russia, and Japan.

In South Asia the arts have always been highly valued, and they have flourished from the earliest times. The palaces, temples, forts, monuments, cities, and tombs built by great kings and dynasties remain among the wonders of world architecture. Indian sculpture in stone, wood, and bronze and Indian painting (such as book-sized miniatures or the ancient murals at the caves of Ajanta and Ellora) rank among the greatest masterpieces of world art. Indian artisans to this day support an export trade of fine handicrafts admired worldwide. Traditional literature is dominated by the two Sanskrit epics—the Ramayana and the Mahabharata—written from oral sources sometime between 400 B.C.E. and 400 C.E. (In South India's Carnatic music, many song texts refer to events and characters in these epics.) India has produced thousands of major authors, poets, and playwrights ranging from the court poet Kalidasa (who lived in the fourth and fifth centuries) to contemporary authors such as Salman Rushdie or R. K. Narayan, both of whom write in English. Recently a host of extraordinary filmmakers have appeared. Perhaps the best known is Satyajit Ray, whose works from *The Apu Trilogy* to *Charulata* (described by some scholars as "the perfect film") have gained him recognition as one of a handful of masters of contemporary art cinema.

Indian civilization has also seen great religious development—and religion and the arts, especially music and dance, have always been inseparable. The four Vedas (believed to have crystallized as early as 1200 B.C.E.) and the later Upanishads (or "Forest Books") contain religious and abstract philosophical thought that has fascinated Western thinkers such as Emerson and Thoreau and scientists such as Robert Oppenheimer. The Puranas (beginning in the first century C.E.) are filled with the myths of the gods and goddesses of popular Hinduism. These stories and adventures occur as themes not only in sermons and storytelling but also in music and dance, in popular movies and television serials—even in comic books. The ancient physical and mental discipline of yoga is now practiced all over the world. And in recent times, saintly men such as Mahatma Gandhi (1869–1948) have preached the nonviolence combined with social activism adapted by Martin Luther King Jr. in the U.S. Civil Rights Movement and by many others in confronting the violence and injustices of the world.

Unfortunately, when one reads about India in American or European newspapers it is usually not about the region's remarkable history and cultural accomplishments but rather about some disaster or another. True, the problems of modern South Asia are immense. A virtual state of war exists between India and Pakistan. Both are nuclear powers. Successive governments have attacked but not completely solved problems of overpopulation, terrorism, poverty, corruption, intolerance, and an agriculture dependent on unpredictable monsoon rains. Yet the political system, however chaotic it may appear to an outsider, is based on British parliamentary rule. India is the earth's largest democracy, and its elections are run far more efficiently and accurately than those in the United States. Rapid change is occurring in the face of age-old traditions. A growing and prosperous middle class exhibits world-class competence and brilliance, particularly in the sciences, technology, and business—but also in the arts. In the palimpsest that is South Asia, we find a constant interplay between the ancient and the modern. The old, the traditional, seems able to persist through all the changes of time and history. This coexistence of the old and the new is part of our amazement and fascination with India—and perhaps also its greatest strength.

Many Musics

If we were to stroll through one of the residential neighborhoods of Chennai, we might come into contact with many types of musical sound. In a typical day in the morning come the vendors each pushing a cart of wares—the vegetable man or woman, the pots and pans salesman, the waste newspaper collector, the coconut man (who will climb your tree for a fee), the ice cream man, the sweets and candy vendors, and so on. Like different types of birds, each has a distinctive (and musical) call recognized by the local homemakers.

Figure 6.2
An itinerant minstrel pipes classical music on his double-reed *nagasvaram*, minus the usual accompaniment of the *tavil* (*tah*-vil) drum.

As the day wears on, a mendicant may appear chanting a sacred song and playing a small gong or the sacred conch shell trumpet called a *shanku* (*shan*-ku). Once in a great while a snake charmer may walk the street with a python draped around his shoulders or a bag of defanged cobras. Unforgettable is the distinctive nasal whine of his snake charming music on the *punji* (*pun*-jee)—a double-reed instrument with two pipes (melody and drone) similar in its technology to a miniature bagpipe, with a gourd replacing the bag. Or a wandering hereditary minstrel may go door to door singing her songs for an offering of rice and a few coins. The musician might accompany herself on the *kudam* (*koo*-dam), played like the washtub bass by increasing and decreasing the tension of the single string stretched between the pot and a board under her right foot. Finally, we may hear a minstrel playing the double-reed *nagasvaram* (*nah*-guh-svah-rum) on the street (Figure 6.2). Clearly, here we have entered the rich realm of Indian folk music.

On TV, over the radio, or blasting from the neighborhood snack shops, we hear mostly Indian popular music, also called "cine songs" because almost all popular music originates in movies in Hindi, Tamil, or other regional languages. The Indian film industry is the largest in the world. Virtually all movies have songs that periodically interrupt the plot with MTV-like visuals in exotic settings or elaborate song-and-dance production numbers. The actors and actresses always lip-sync the words, which are actually sung by "playback singers," who along with the "music director" (composer/arranger) and lyricist are the true stars and superstars of India's pop music scene.

Pop Music

Cine music is to some ears a curious and sometimes bizarre blend of East and West. Choppy and hyperactive melodies often in "oriental" scales are belted out by nasal singers over Latin rhythms and an eclectic accompaniment that may include keyboard, guitar, strings, brass, saxophone, xylophone, bongos, a Western drum set, *sitar, tabla,* or bamboo flute. It is an anything goes, "if it sounds good use it" approach to music. The "anything" today might include harmony and counterpoint (that is, chords and simultaneous melodies; see Chapter 1), rap, rock and roll, European symphonic music, and jazz. Although the lyrics, like those of pop music everywhere in the world, tend to focus on the eternal emotions and complications of love and romance, Indian pop music also can be comical, or else deal with religious, ethical, or deeply philosophical themes.

A good place to start is to watch videos (extracted from movies) of several contemporary songs by the great A. R. Rahman. (See the list of DVD Tamil movies at the end of this chapter; your instructor may have these on reserve.) In "Kannalane" ("O Eyes, Look Truly," Song 2 from the film *Bombay*), an eloquent and lilting love song is backed mainly by traditional Indian instruments as dancers swirl in brightly colored skirts in a palatial setting, that of a Moslem wedding. "Sutram Boomi," (Song 2 from *Dumm Dumm Dumm*) and "Azhegama Raatchasiye" ("O Beautiful Demoness," Song 3 from *Mudalvan*) emphasize folk music and instruments in their sound and are set appropriately in agricultural and rural village festival locales. "Desinhu Raja" ("King Desinghu," Song 3 from *Dumm Dumm Dumm*) transforms the hero and heroine into the king and queen of ancient Tanjore. The elaborate production number is filmed in the spectacular temples and palaces of that city. American rock Indian style along with English phrases appear in "Shakalaka Baby" (Song 1 from *Mudalvan*) and "Urvasi Urvasi! Take It Easy" (Song 1 from *Kadalan*) as hip college students dance their heads off. Tamil rap interspersed with a folk tune hilariously interrupts a classical dance scene in "Petta Rap" ("Neigh-borhood Rap," Song 3 from *Kadalan*).

Older Indian pop music as heard in films from the '40s, '50s, and '60s may approach the semiclassical or even classical in style and instrumenta-tion, as in the classic film *Thillana Mohanambal* (1968), about the romance between a famous dancer and a *nagasvaram* virtuoso. Recent songs show greater and more sophisticated use of Western elements (such as harmony, counterpoint, or orchestration) and a more lyrical, crooning use of the human voice. In fact, the timbres, forms, and instrumentation of Indian pop music continue to evolve in extremely varied and creative ways, especially when compared with the relatively static makeup of Western ensembles such as rock and jazz bands or symphony orchestras, or the rigid industry-controlled formulas for most American pop songs. The more one listens to Indian pop music, the more one can appreciate its unique qualities, enjoy the beauty of its lyrics and themes, and gain a better understanding of why this is the favorite music of almost a billion people, old and young, rich and poor, educated and uneducated. Perhaps someday the great contemporary Indian songwriters such as A. R. Rahman and Ilaiyaraja will gain the recognition that they deserve on the world scene.

Religious Music

Religious music is another important category of music in India. Among the dozens of other devotional traditions of South Asia—folk, pop, or classical, primarily Hindu but also Moslem or Christian—is that of the *bhajan*. A *bhajan* is a song, devotional in nature and relatively simple technically, that is sung primarily as an offering to God. *Bhajans* might be sung by a soloist with a backup of violins, flutes, harmonium, and drums (or any combination thereof), with additional rhythmic support coming from small ringing bell-cymbals, clackers, or hand claps. *Bhajans* might also be sung in a congregational call-and-response manner with a leader singing out verses or improvising, while the group responds with either a repetition or a refrain.

The ensemble of *periya melam* (*peh*-ri-yah *may*-luhm) ("large band") consisting of two or more *nagasvaram* double-reed pipes, *tavil* drums, and *sruti*-box drone is associated with temple worship, religious processions, weddings, and other auspicious occasions, such as the opening of a music festival or a new store. The music that the *nagasvaram* plays is largely that of South Indian classical music, which itself includes song texts almost entirely religious in nature.

The classical music of South India is called *karnataka sangeeta*, (pronounced kar-*nah*-tuh-kah sahn-*gee*-tah with a hard "g") or in English simply Carnatic music. It is named after the Carnatic plateau, which dominates the middle of the inland south. The roots of this music lie in the distant past, in the courts and palaces of rajas and maharajas, in the great ancient kingdoms of the Cholas, the Cheras, and the Pallavas, and in the stately temple complexes built between the twelfth and eighteenth centuries—such as those at Madurai, Chidambaram, Srirangam, Thiruvanamalai, Rameswaram, and Tanjore—which number among the wonders of world architecture (Figure 6.1).

Carnatic music shares many of its early theoretical sources with the north. The Natya Sastra by Bharata, an extensive and detailed treatise on theater, dance, and music, dates from between the second century B.C.E.

India's Classical Music

and the fifth century C.E. Through the centuries many more important scholarly books on music have been written in Sanskrit and regional languages, perhaps the most noteworthy being the medieval Sangeeta Ratnakara (c. 1210–1247) by the scholar Sarangadeva.

Sculpture in the ancient temples and palaces as well as murals and miniature paintings give us vivid visual images of the instruments, orchestras, dance styles, and the where and how of musical performance through several thousand years. Although the stone and painted images are silent, they bear a striking resemblance to what is seen in performance today. In addition, many written descriptions of musical performance appear in the epics—the Mahabharata and Ramayana—as well as in stories and religious and mythological works. But the actual sound and practice of India's classical music traditions has been lost up to the twentieth century and the advent of sound recording, movies, and television.

Any oral tradition, such as that of Indian classical music, lives primarily in the hands, voices, memory, and creative imagination of individual human beings (Figures 6.3 and 6.4). In this tradition, the music can never be frozen in time, either by being written down (in words or notation) or by being preserved as a visual entity (as in a painting or photograph). The music, in a sense, lives uniquely in each performance—in the unique rendition of a

Figure 6.3

N. Govindarajan gives a lesson on the clay *ghatam* to a student. Music is transmitted orally, with notation used only as a memory aid.

Figure 6.4
Professor Sudharani Raghupathy (seated in chair) gives a *bharata natyam* (bha-ruh-tah *naw*-tyam) dance lesson to Priya Murle. Seated on the floor are the vocalist Krishnaveni Sundarajan (left); Aruna Subbiah (third from left), who is articulating dance rhythms (*nattuvangam*); and composer and *mridangist* (drummer) K. S. R. Aniruddha (fourth from left).

song on a particular day, at a particular hour, and in the ephemeral spontaneity and creativity of improvisation. Today videos and CDs can preserve a particular performance, but whether this fixity, this documentation, will change the essentially oral nature of Indian music and the liquid way musicians approach their tradition remains to be seen.

From around the thirteenth century, scholars began to notice a difference between the classical Hindusthani style of the North and the Carnatic style of the South. Both use the idea of the *raga* (melodic mode) and *tala* (metric cycle), but the specifics of the *raga*s and *tala*s vary. In general the northern style and its instruments—such as the *sitar* and *tabla*—have been more greatly influenced by Persian and other elements of pan-Islamic culture. In Hindusthani music expansive improvisations move gradually (over an hour or more) from near immobility to sections of great speed and virtuosity.

In contrast, the Carnatic music of the more conservative South is built around an immense repertoire of precomposed Hindu devotional songs. The musical texture in the South is more busy and active, notes are incessantly ornamented, and improvisations fall within clearly defined and relatively brief sections. (Listen to a performance of Hindusthani classical instrumental music on reserve. Compare it with the South Indian performance described later in this text.)

Carnatic music began to take its present shape in the "golden age" of the late eighteenth and early nineteenth centuries, when composers created thousands of exquisite songs. Three great saint-composer-poets dominate this period: Syama Sastry (1762–1827), Tyagaraja (1767–1847), and Muttuswamy Dikshitar (1776–1836). Like singer-songwriters today, these composers wrote both the melodies and the lyrics to their songs.

A clever proverb describes the trademark of each. Dikshitar's songs are like a coconut: The "hard shell" of his intellectual music structures and scholarly song texts must be broken to get to the sweetness inside. Sastry's music is like a banana: The fruit is not so difficult to get to, but one must still peel off the bitter "skin" of tricky rhythm before enjoying the flavor. But Tyagaraja's songs are like mangoes: the "sweet fruit" of both poetry and music are immediately accessible. It is no wonder, then, that Tyagaraja's songs dominate the repertoire today, cherished by musicians and audiences alike.

The Sound World

India's classical music is marked by strong and unmistakable characteristics, an environment of sound that—like the spices of curries or the brilliantly colored silk saris worn by South Asian women—signals at once which place on the planet this music is from. Let us imagine attending a performance of this music. First, we notice the incessant, unchanging sound of a drone of several pitches (tonal center and fifth), often with a nasal buzz created acoustically through the generation of a rich mixture of overtones. (We may be familiar with drones in the music of bagpipes or certain American banjo and fiddle styles.) Against this unchanging background a single melody, perhaps echoed by another voice or instrument, begins to develop. The melody differs greatly from those of Western classical or popular music: Its lines tend to be sinuous, complex, and asymmetrical (in contrast with the symmetrical regularity and relative simplicity of most folk and pop music). Indian melodies are also marked by subtle bends and slides and intense ornamentation, an embroidery of fast notes in sharp contrast to the "plain" notes of most Western music (see Figure 6.5). The notes of Indian scales may also zigzag through intervals unfamiliar to Western ears, in intonation slightly higher or lower in pitch than those of the piano keyboard. (We are familiar with a similar approach to intonation by African American singers and instrumentalists in genres such as gospel, blues, and jazz.)

Returning to the sound world of South India, we might then notice that improvisation plays a key role in performance in Indian music. The musician on the stage is inventing music on the spot, although certain key phrases recur again and again with subtle variation and certain rules and procedures of the tradition are being followed, much as soccer players create their plays and display their skills within the rules of the game.

An interesting timbre or "tone color" strikes us. (Recall from Chapter 1 that timbre is the "sound of a sound," what we hear that enables us to distinguish, for example, between a guitar, a trumpet, or a piano. Though based on acoustic principles, timbre is often described with words such as *mellow, rich,* or *icy*.) The Indian sound world distinctly prefers a "nasal" timbre, whether in the human voice or in musical instruments. (Listen to recordings of Indian singing and compare them with opera or with Frank Sinatra's crooning.) Even adopted European instruments such as the clarinet or violin are played in India in a manner to increase their "nasalness."

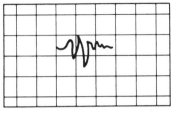

A "note" in Indian music

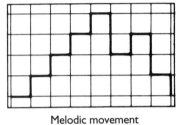

A note on the piano

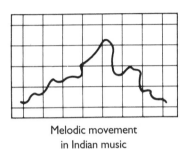

Melodic movement
in Indian music

Melodic movement
on the piano

Figure 6.5

Notes and melodic movement in Indian music, compared with piano. A "note"—called a *svara* (*svah*-rah)—in Carnatic music is quite different from the fixed, stable note as it is represented in Western classical musical notation. A *svara* can be a tiny constellation of ornamented pitches. Further, movement from one *svara* to the next may be in a sliding, gliding movement rather than in the stepwise movement between Western notes.

Music paper or notation is nowhere to be seen: The performers are clearly working by ear in an oral tradition. (Recall that an oral tradition is one in which learning and performance skills are picked up and put together by ear without the intermediary of the written page. Most jazz and rock performers work within oral traditions, at least in part. So do good stand-up comedians. See Chapter 1.) There is no conductor, but each performer has a comfortable and well-defined role to play.

When the drum comes in, we are immediately struck by the energy and complexity of the drummer's rhythms, played with the fingers and hands. One head of the drum is carefully tuned to the tonal center heard in the drone. We can sense a strong beat, but the metrical units seem to be much longer and more complicated than the meters—such as four beats to a measure, or three beats to a measure—that dominate our pop, classical, jazz, and other European and American genres of music.

As the performance progresses, careful listening might reveal the presence of a song with its recurring phrases, themes, and variations, and if the melodic soloist is a singer we can hear syllables of a song text interspersed in the melody. Those of us who understand Indian languages (or have a helpful aficionado sitting nearby to explain), will soon learn that the song texts are usually religious—devotional or philosophical—though beautiful love lyrics also are found.

Concerts usually begin between 5:30 to 6:30 in the evening except at music festival time in December through January, when they take place almost continuously from around 8:30 in the morning until as late as midnight. Each program is sponsored by a *sabha* (*sah*-bhah), a cultural club that brings to its members and the general public music, dance, plays, lectures, and even an occasional movie. The large and prestigious *sabhas* have their own buildings, often large shedlike structures with overhead fans and open sides to catch the evening breeze. Other *sabhas* may use an auditorium, lecture hall, or temple. The audience may sit in rattan chairs or, rarely today, on large striped rugs or mats spread on the floor. The musicians sit cross-legged on a rug on a raised platform or stage, and they are sure to have cronies or fellow musicians sitting in close proximity to offer reactions and encouragement through stylized motions like head wobbling or hand movements, enthusiastic verbal comments, or tongue clicking (which does not mean "Oh, oh, too bad!" as in U.S. culture but rather "Wonderful! Beautiful! Fantastic!").

Concerts are relaxed and informal, compared with classical music concerts in the West. Members of the audience may count time with their hands, periodically chat with friends, or occasionally get up in the middle of a concert to buy snacks or a soft drink at the refreshment stand. Usually there are no printed programs. Mature musicians may not even fully plan their program in advance, and a knowledgeable audience is familiar with the repertoire of songs, *ragas* (melodic modes), and *talas* (time cycles), much in the way that rock fans will be familiar with the songs of their favorite band. A concert today lasts between two and three hours without an intermission, although in the past concerts could go on for four hours or more.

The Ensemble: Musical Texture

In a concert each musician and instrument has a role to play. These roles, which create the musical texture, might be described as functional layers. (Recall that musical texture is the way in which the fabric of music is woven together. For example, in a rock band there might be a singer doing the vocals, a bass guitarist playing bass lines, one or two guitars strumming chords and/or providing melodic licks, and a drummer. See Chapter 1.) In Indian music the layers of the texture are (1) the background drone, (2) the melody, and (3) the rhythm/percussion. One or more musicians may play within each layer (see Figure 6.6).

The Melodic Layer

The principal melodic soloist dominates the ensemble. (In duet concerts two musicians would share this central role.) A backup musician may support the principal melodic soloist. Principal solo melodic instruments today include the violin, the bamboo flute, the plucked *veena* (*vee*-nah) (Figure 6.10), the clarinet, and rarely the *jalatarangam* (juh-luh-tuh-*rahn*-gum) (Chinese porcelain bowls tuned by filling them with water and struck with thin sticks).

The next important role within this layer is the melodic accompanist. In South India today this is usually a violinist, partly because the violin is always used to accompany a vocalist, and most concerts feature voice. The melodic accompanist plays three important roles: He or she must (1) play along on all the songs (following the notes of the soloist instantaneously) and (2) echo and support or respond to the soloist's improvisations, eventually working up to alternating improvisations and a grand climax.

Figure 6.6
An ensemble in concert. The principal artist, bamboo flutist N. Ramani, sits in the center on the stage of a *sabha* under portraits of great composers. T. K. Murthy, assisted by a student, plays *mridangam* on the left. A *tambura* (behind the flutist) provides the *sruti* drone; violin accompanist S. D. Sridhar sits on the right.

The *Sruti* Layer

The drone, or *sruti* (*shroo*-tee), layer includes one or more specialized instruments. The *tambura* (tahm-*boo*-rah) is a four-stringed plucked instrument tuned to the tonal center and fifth. Its buzzing timbre is created by inserting a small length of thread under each playing string on the flat but slightly rounded top of the bridge. By placing the thread at exactly the right node a rich blend of overtones is picked up on each string—it is this sound which is perhaps the most recognizable "Indian" sound of all. The tuned reed *sruti*-box can also be used. Played with a bellows, it gives a continuous reed-organ-like sound. Today most musicians use small synthesizers that can digitally duplicate the sound of either instrument. Plugged in or running on batteries, they can be tuned to any pitch and eliminate the need for additional musicians.

The Percussion Layer

Finally, there is the bedrock of the ensemble, the percussion. The double-headed barrel-shaped *mridangam* (mrih-*dun*-gum) drum is the principal accompanying percussion instrument in Carnatic music. The right drumhead is tuned to the tonal center of the melodic soloist. Played with the palms and fingers of both hands, the *mridangam* is capable of producing up to fifteen distinct sounds on its multilayered drumheads. It is often the only accompanying rhythm instrument. When other subordinate percussion instruments are added in this functioning layer, their players must follow the signals of the *mridangam* player who as "percussion boss" tells them when to play together or singly, or when to drop out. The other percussion instruments used in classical music performance (listed in the order of importance and frequency of use) are the *ghatam* (*guh*-tum), a large clay pot with a ringing, metallic sound (see Figure 6.3); the *kanjira* (kahn-*jih*-rah), a

Figure 6.7
Layers of the musical texture with added instruments.

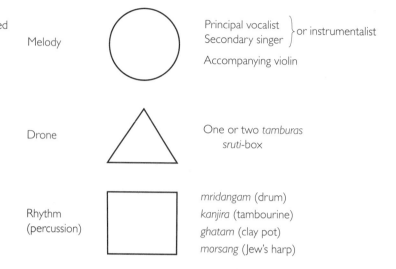

Melody — Principal vocalist / Secondary singer } or instrumentalist
Accompanying violin

Drone — One or two *tamburas* / *sruti*-box

Rhythm (percussion) — *mridangam* (drum) / *kanjira* (tambourine) / *ghatam* (clay pot) / *morsang* (Jew's harp)

tambourine with a snakeskin head and jangles made of coins; and the *morsang* (mor-sung), a Jew's harp that plays the same rhythms as the other percussion instruments.

In a vocal ensemble, the principal singer sits in front. The ensemble might include a backup singer playing a *sruti*-box, a *tambura* player, an accompanist on violin (always), and a *mridangam* player. In our recorded performance (**CD 2, Track 2**) note that there are only two performers. Ranganayaki Rajagopalan plays the *veena* (the melodic layer and the drone) and Raja Rao plays the *mridangam* (the percussion layer). An electronic *sruti*-box, out of sight and plugged into the wall, supplies a drone background.

Now that we have looked at the makeup of a South Indian ensemble, we shall explore two concepts that are central to an understanding of India's classical music. These are *raga*, the melodic system, and *tala*, the time cycles and rhythmic system.

Raga: The Melodic System

The ancient texts define a *raga* as "that which colors the mind." In fact, in Sanskrit the primary meaning of the word is "coloring, dyeing, tingeing." This connection with generating feelings and emotions in human beings—with "coloring" the mind and the heart—is important because a *raga* really has no equivalent in the West. *Raga* is an expressive entity with a "musical personality" all its own. This musical personality is, in part, technical—a collection of notes, a scale, intonation, ornaments, resting or "pillar tones," and so on. Most of all it includes a portfolio of characteristic musical gestures and phrases—bits and pieces of melody—that give it a distinct and recognizable identity. Each *raga* has its rules about the way a musician may move from one note to another and about *gamakas* (gah-muh-kahs)—particular ways of ornamenting certain notes with slides, slithering fast notes, and oscillations. While a few of the facts about a particular *raga* and how it is to be played or sung can be verbalized or written down—its scale, for example—

the concept is too much a part of the oral tradition and therefore too elusive to be understood only in terms of facts. One gets to know a *raga* gradually—by hearing one's guru or other master musicians play it, and by performing it oneself over many months and years. It is said that getting to know a *raga* is like getting to know a close friend: One slowly learns to recognize the face, the expressions, the way of walking, voice, clothes style, and eventually the inner personality with all its quirks, puzzles, and delights.

Traditional texts associate particular *raga*s with certain human emotions (the ten *rasas* (*ruh*-sahs)—literally, "flavors"—of love, sadness, heroism, anger, fear, disgust, wonder, laughter, religious devotion, peacefulness), colors, animals, deities, a season of the year, a time of day (late at night or early morning, for example), or with certain magical properties such as causing rain, calming the mind, creating warmth, or healing the body. Some *raga*s are said to be auspicious; others dark and complex and mysterious; and still others happy or simple. Although South Indian musicians do not focus much on these associations, they are aware of the expressive force of *raga*s and their capability to touch deep emotions in the human heart.

The notes of a *raga* move against the blank screen of the drone, the *sruti*. The notes of a *raga* (even when highly ornamented) constantly move in flux—in various degrees of dissonance and consonance—against this unchanging background of tonal center and perfect fifth.

The *Melakarta* System

In Carnatic music all *raga*s relate to a *melakarta* (*may*-luh-*kahr*-tah), one of seventy-two basic "parent" or "generative" scales. (A *scale* is sequence of tones arranged in ascending and descending order. See Chapter 1.) Each *melakarta* scale has seven tones. Except for the first and fifth, (the fixed notes heard in the drone *sruti*), each of the remaining tones occur in variants of two or three pitches. In the European and American traditions, the seven steps of a scale are called do, re, mi, fa, sol, la, ti (see Chapter 1). Similarly, the seven steps of an Indian scale are called *sa, ri, ga, ma, pa, da, ni. Sa* and *pa*, the drone notes, are fixed (unchanging). *Ri, ga, ma, da,* and *ni* mutate to form a particular scale. Figure 6.8 illustrates the seventy-two tracks by which *melakarta* scales are formed.* A few of the scales might sound familiar to your ear. Others might seem uncommon, "oriental," or "exotic," though to the Indian listener they are part of the normal language of music.

---

*For the student unfamiliar with Western music notation, read the *melakarta* chart (Figure 6.8) by following various tracks. Each horizontal line of the graph represents a fret on the guitar, or an adjacent note on a keyboard (counting both white and black notes). On the guitar, *sa* is the open string.

1. If you chose 1st fret *ri* then you have three options for *ga:* 2nd fret, 3rd fret, or 4th fret.
2. If you chose 2nd fret *ri* then you have two options for *ga:* 3rd fret or 4th fret.
3. If you chose 3rd fret *ri* then you have one option for *ga:* 4th fret.

From any *ga* you have two options for *ma:* 5th fret or 6th fret.

Repeat the process from the fixed note *pa*, 7th fret. When you reach the 12th fret you are at high *sa* and your *melakarta* scale is complete.

Figure 6.8
The *melakarta* system (tracks
read from left to right).

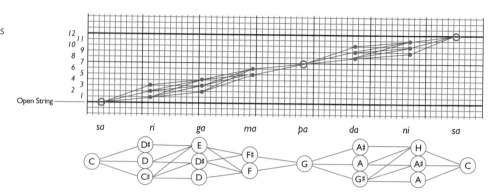

To transform a basic *melakarta* scale into a *raga*, however, requires the addition of a group of specifics that give the *raga* a "musical personality," a recognizable identity. Natai *raga,* for example, may skip certain tones of the *melakarta* scale when the melody ascends. When the melody descends it skips other notes and puts a vibrating ornament (*gamaka*) on *ri*, the "life note"—the strongest characteristic tone—of Natai *raga.*

Finally, a whole range of other characteristics gives a *raga* identity: emphasized tones, resting notes, vibrations and slides, ornaments, subtle intonation, and—most important—a catalogue of bits and pieces of melody, melodic chunks which the musician modifies and arranges and interprets. Thus each of the seventy-two basic *melakarta* scales may have dozens of "children," *raga*s with different characteristics and personalities. Number 36, Chalanata, is the "mother" *melakarta* scale of the "child" Natai *raga.*

In India's classical music there are hundreds of such *raga*s in common use in the tradition. (You will notice that they are named in the performances on CDs and in concerts.) Some of these *raga*s are quite popular, while others may rarely be heard. Some are considered "major," of great scope for improvisation and depth of expressive potential, while others may be viewed as less important, pleasant perhaps but "light." Some are old, going back hundreds of years, but others are newly invented. As you begin to listen seriously and in depth to Indian classical music, you will discover the infinite variety of *raga*s, as well as the expressive use that musicians make of them, shaping them into beautiful melodic compositions or spinning them out in improvisations. *Raga*s are the heart and soul of Indian music.

Tala: The Time Cycle

Tala, the organization of time in music, is part of a conceptual spectrum in Indian thought that moves from a fraction of a second—as the ancient texts picturesquely put it: the time it takes a pin to puncture a lotus petal—to the great *yugas,* or "ages," which like geological time periods span millions of years. The musician regards time initially as a beat, or regular pulse. On the larger level beats are grouped into regularly recurring metric cycles. These cycles are called *talas.* In theoretical texts there are hundreds of *talas,* but in Carnatic music today only the following four *talas* are found in common

Figure 6.9
Umayalpuram Mali practices *mridangam* at home. The many images of deities in the background form a virtual shrine indicative of the sacredness of music.

practice: *adi tala* (*aah*-dee *tah*-lah) (8 beats), *rupaka tala* (*roo*-puh-kah *tah*-lah) (3 beats), *khanda chapu tala* (*khahn*-da *chah*-pu *tah*-lah) (5 beats), *misra chapu tala* (*mish*-ruh *chah*-pu *tah*-lah) (7 beats). Except for *khanda chapu tala* and *misra chapu tala,* which are generally performed at a brisk tempo, all *talas* may be performed at fast, medium, or slow tempo. In slow tempo there are two pulses per beat, as in 1 and 2 and 3 and so on. The *tala* cycles differ from the common time signatures or meters in Western music (see Chapter 1) in that the accents occur in uneven groupings (4 + 2 + 2, or 3 + 2 + 2, or 1 + 2, and so on).

The Drummer's Art

In performance in South India the *mridangam* drummer and other percussionists play in an improvisatory style based on hundreds of rhythmic patterns and drum strokes that they have learned, invented, absorbed, and stored in their brains and hands. In the heat of performance the percussionist may use precomposed patterns, arranging them in predictable or unpredictable groupings. Or he may create entirely new patterns spontaneously, but within the limits and grammar of his rhythmic language (Figure 6.9).

The drummer's art centers on drum strokes—distinctive individual tones produced on different parts of the drumhead by different finger combinations or parts of the hands. These strokes, individually and as part of rhythmic patterns, can be expressed in *sollukattu* (sol-lu-*kaht*-tu), spoken syllables that duplicate both drum strokes and rhythmic patterns.

The drummer's art is complex. At first he must accompany the *kritis* (*krih*-tees) and other song forms of the Carnatic music tradition. He must know each song, picking up the flow and feeling, shaping his accompaniment to the internal rhythms of the song.

The drummer emerges from the background during long-held notes in the melody, or at cadences—endings of sections in a performance—marking endings with a formulaic threefold repetition called a *mora* (*moh*-rah). When the melodic soloist is improvising within the *tala* cycles, the alert drummer is quick to recognize and respond to patterns, to echo them, or to ornament them rhythmically. The South Indian percussionist, however, does not merely "play off the top of his head." Through years of training, study, and listening, his brain in a sense has been programmed with hundreds of rhythmic building blocks, formulas, and possibilities for larger combinations. He is also calculating constantly, like a master mathematician, how his formulas and patterns of asymmetrical lengths will fit into the *tala* cycles to come out right at the end.

At one point in the concert after the main piece played by the soloist, the drummer—and his associates, if any—will play a *tani avartanam*, (*tah*-nee a-*vahr*-tuh-nahm) a rhythmic solo. For those interested in rhythm this is the high point of the concert.

Although we have only touched the surface of the drummer's art, we can begin to appreciate a system as complicated as any on earth, a counterbalance to the melodic beauties of the *raga* system. As an old Sanskrit verse says: "[In music] *raga* is the mother, *tala* is the father."

A Carnatic Music Performance

A concert in South India is marked by a string of compositions, each in a *raga* and *tala*, optionally extended by the forms of improvisation to be described shortly. Each section of a concert will thus have a composition, usually a *kriti* as its centerpiece. (An exception is the mostly improvised form called *ragam, tanam, pallavi*, which has a single phrase of melody and lyrics as its centerpiece. See later discussion.)

We shall listen to a *kriti* performance on **CD 2, Track 2,** played on the seven-string plucked *veena* by Ms. Ranganayaki Rajagopalan accompanied by Srimushnam V. Raja Rao on the *mridangam*. Before examining the performance itself in detail, however, we must meet the musicians.

Ms. Ranganayaki (Figure 6.10), who is now more than seventy years old, was in 1936 a very unruly child. Her parents had "loaned her out" to a childless uncle and his wife in the prosperous southern town of Karaikudi. The uncle was a friend of a great *veena* virtuoso, Karaikudi Sambasiva Iyer, who lived in the town and who was supported by the wealthy merchants and financiers belonging to the Chettiyar caste of the South.

As the story goes, one day Ranganayaki's uncle appeared with his four-year-old niece at the great musician's house. As the elders were talking about music, to illustrate a point Sambasiva sang a tone. To his surprise

Figure 6.10
Ranganayaki Rajagopalan with the *veena* she has played since she was a small girl. She is the principal performer on "Sarasiruha" (CD 2, Track 2).

the young girl, playing nearby, sang the same tone. Sambasiva sang another note. The child duplicated that note. Recognizing the child's rare talent, the great musician took in the four-year-old Ranganayaki as a member of his household, into a traditional musical apprenticeship known as the *gurukula* (gu-ru-*koo*-lah) system.

The discipline was extremely rigorous, with lessons beginning at 6:00 in the morning and continuing throughout each day, as the master teacher taught her and the other youngsters living in his household. Mistakes or laziness were met with strokes from a bamboo rod, but effort and accomplishments were rewarded with kind words and gestures. Ranganayaki describes her life during that period as "not a normal childhood. I had no friends or anything. It was *asura sadhakam* ('devil's practice')" (Personal communication, 2000). But her musical genius gradually developed. By age twelve she was regularly accompanying her guru on the concert stage and giving solo recitals as well. The close relationship continued after her marriage at the age of fifteen and until her guru's death in 1958.

Over the years Ms. Ranganayaki has enjoyed a distinguished career. Reviews have characterized her as "dedicated to her tradition and unmoved by playing to the crowd," and "one of the great *veena* virtuosi of the twentieth century" ("Ranganayaki Rajagopalan" 1971:3). With her phenomenal memory she is considered to be a rare repository of the compositions of her tradition, while her skills at improvisation are unmatched. She has toured Europe and the United States and was regularly featured in national broadcasts of All India Radio. In 2000 she received one of India's highest artistic awards, the National Award for Music, from the Sangeet Natak Akademi. Speaking of the *veena* tradition of which she is the greatest living exponent, she says, "Words cannot describe it. One can only feel it while listening to it. It is just like saying that sugar is sweet. You can only really understand the sweetness by tasting it" (Personal communication, 2000).

Before we go further, a note on women and music is in order. Women have always played an important role in Indian music. Two of the greatest saint-composers—the medieval Rajasthani princess Mirabai and, in the South, Andal—were women. In the contemporary scene many of the most prominent musicians are women, particularly as singers but also on instruments such as the violin, *veena*, and flute. On the other hand, women do not generally play single- or double-reed instruments such as the *nagasvaram* or the clarinet, nor do they commonly play percussion instruments, though there are notable exceptions such as Sukanya Ramgopal (*ghatam*) and Kaleeshabi Mahaboob Subhani (*nagasvaram*) who performs with her husband.

Another musician contributing to our CD selection, Srimushnam V. Raja Rao, is one of the great contemporary performers on the *mridangam*. Known as "a musician's musician," he has accompanied many of the leading singers and instrumentalists of Carnatic music both in India and abroad in Europe, the United States, and Asia. He takes particular pride in his ability to accompany the soft tones of the *veena* with a light but precise touch of fingers and hands on the drumheads. He accompanied Ranganayaki on her first European tour in the 1980s.

Ranganayaki's instrument, the *veena*, has three drone strings and four playing strings. The chromatically placed brass frets are set in black wax, which is scalloped to allow room for the fingers to bend the strings in ornamentation. A set of complex fingerings, slides, and pulled multipitched ornaments (*gamakas*) enable the musician to interpret the character of each *raga* and its subtle intonation.

Raja Rao's instrument, the *mridangam*, has a barrel-shaped body carved from jackwood. Both of its heads are made from multiple layers of leather, the outer layers cut with a circular hole in the middle exposing the lowest drumhead. The lower (untuned) left-hand head has a blob of damp wheat paste applied to its center to give it a booming sound. The center of the right-hand head (which is tuned) has a hard metallic black spot made of many polished layers of rice paste, iron filings, and other ingredients. Acoustically the sophisticated technology of the *mridangam*'s drumheads (like that of the North Indian *tabla*) makes possible a variety of different sounds. The use of the fingers as miniature drumsticks allows the drummer to play passages of incredible speed and virtuosity.

The performance begins with two improvised sections—*alapana* (*aah*-*laa*-pah-*nah*) and *tanam* (*tah*-nahm)—for *veena* alone. *Alapana* (in free time, with "breath rhythms" and no regular pulse) and *tanam* (marked with strong, energetic, and irregular rhythms) must precede a *kriti* and introduce the listener to the *raga*, the melodic mode, in which the *kriti* is set. The beginning of the *kriti* "Sarasiruha" in Natai *raga, adi tala*, is marked by the entrance of the drum. A lively improvised *kalpana svara* section for *veena* with drum accompaniment follows, with a brief drum solo, the *tani avartanam*, at the end.

We shall now discuss more fully the five sections of the performance built around the *kriti* "Sarasiruha." Check the close listening chart for the timings of each section.

Close Listening   CD 2:2

"Sarasiruha"

Counter Number	Commentary
Alapana (improvised)	
0:00	_Veena_ alone. Free rhythm (no regularly recurring beat). Introduces the melodic mode of the Natai _raga_. Begins slowly among the lower-pitched melodic material of the _raga_, then moves faster and explores the higher pitches and phrases.
2:05–3:15	Peak of _alapana_. Reaches highest note; soon thereafter begins descent toward conclusion.
Tanam (improvised)	
3:18	_Veena_ plays alone. Irregular beat. Rhythmic exposition of the _raga_. Listen for _raga_ phrases that begin on low pitches, then move to the middle then high range.
7:48–8:18	_Veena_ switches back to _alapana_ style for descent and close of _tanam_.
Kriti (composed song)—"Sarasiruha"	
8:25	8-beat _adi Tala_ cycles begin with song. Drum (_mridangam_) enters.
13:31	Repeated variants of musical phrase—"Saraswati" invocation—where the name of the goddess appears in the song text, after which the song finishes.
Kalpana svaras 1 (short—one _tala_ cycle or less, improvised)	
14:45	Lively, improvised section. Begins with four short _svara_ improvisations of less than 1 _tala_ cycle each returning to theme (_idam_).
Kalpana svaras 2 (extended, improvised)	
15:10	Three extended _svara_ improvisations of 6½, 7½, and 10½ _tala_ cycles respectively, each returning to theme (_idam_).
17:48	_Kalpana svaras_ end.
Tani avartanam (drum solo)	
18:00	Improvised exploration of rhythmic structures by the _mridangam_ alone as _adi tala_ cycles continue.
21:30	Listen for the _korvai_, a formulaic rhythmic pattern repeated three times that signals the end of the drum solo.
Kriti return and close	
22:04–22:22	_Veena_ joins back in with the _kriti_'s first bit of melody and an improvised close.

Alapana

The first section of the performance **(CD 2, Track 2)** is an _alapana_, a free-flowing exposition and exploration of the _raga_—its facets and phrases, its _gamaka_ ornamentation, its pushes and pulls of intonation, as well as its mood and character. An _alapana_ is nonmetrical, that is, it has no regular beat or recurring _tala_ cycles. Instead, its phrases evolve in flowing prose-like "breath rhythms," phrases that eventually come to rest on important "pillar tones," or resting notes.

An _alapana_ has a general plan set both by the tradition as a whole and by the improvisational habits of the musician. In general, the phrases of an _alapana_ begin slowly and gradually increase in speed and complexity as they move higher and higher in the range of the voice or instrument. After a peak there is a descent back to the lower register with an ending on the

 CD 2:2

"Sarasiruha" (22:27). _Kriti_ in Natai _raga, adi tala,_ by Pulaiyur Doraisamy Ayyar. Performed on _veena_ by Ms. Ranganayaki Rajagopalan, accompanied by Srimushnam V. Raja Rao on the _mridangam_. Recorded for author by recording engineer Rahul K. Raveendran. Chennai, India, 2001.

tonal center (*sa*). The voice or—as in this case—melodic instrument performs *alapanas* against the drone background. The overall shape of the *alapana* begins in the mid to lower range, climbs gradually to higher and higher notes, and then descends to its conclusion.

The *raga* of the *alapana* is derived from that of the *kriti*, the composition, which it precedes. In our performance the *raga* is Natai, an ancient and powerful *raga* associated with the great god Shiva in the form of Nataraja ("the King of Dance"). The dance of Shiva—sculpted often in South Indian bronzes—is said to shake the universe with its power and fury.

Tanam

Tanam is a highly rhythmic exposition of the *raga.* It is usually played or sung only once in a concert and takes place after the *alapana* and before the *kriti.* On the *veena* the musician plucks the playing and drone strings in asymmetrical improvised patterns while simultaneously working through the various notes and phrases of the *raga*. Although there are no *tala* cycles (or drum) in *tanam,* there is a strong sense of beat—but the illusory beats constantly change and shift. Just as in *alapana* the overall shape of a *tanam* follows the range of the instrument from low to high in graduated steps and back down again. The Karaikudi style is famous for its *tanam.*

The *Kriti* "Sarasiruha"

All compositions in Carnatic music are songs, melodies with words, set in a specific *raga* and *tala.* In performance one or more musicians sing and/or play the songs against a drone with an improvised rhythmic accompaniment by the percussionist(s). Because India's music is an oral tradition—unlike the West where composers notate music on a page—there is no fixed, authentic "original." As a song is passed down from guru to disciple on its journey in time from the composer to the present, many variant versions appear. Yet the composition remains recognizably itself—the main turns of phrase and the song text remain despite the variations in detail.

The *kriti* (composition) is the major song form of Carnatic music performance. (The word *kriti* is linguistically related to the same pre-Greek root *kr* as the English word "creation.") A brief *kriti* might be as short as five or six minutes; a long *kriti* could last for fifteen minutes or more. Most *kritis* are in three parts with the opening verse repeated after the subsequent verses as a kind of refrain.

The melody and lyrics of "Sarasiruha" are by the nineteenth-century composer Pulaiyur Doraisamy Ayyar. The *kriti* is addressed to the goddess of music and learning, Saraswati (Figure 6.11). A free translation of its text follows:

O Mother who loves the lotus seat,
Ever delighting in the music of *veena,*
Ever joyful, and ever merciful to me.

Figure 6.11
Saraswati, Goddess of Music and Learning.

Save me who have taken refuge in you!
O You with feet as tender as sprouts,
You charm the hearts of poets.
You dwell in the lotus.
You of the jeweled bracelets.

O Mother who loves the lotus seat,
Ever delighting in the music of *veena,*
Ever joyful, and ever merciful to me.

Lotus-eyed Mother who is gracious to the lowly who seek your mercy,
Mother with a face as lovely as the autumn moon,
Pure Lady! O Saraswati, chaste, ever fond of learning.
Lady with breasts like ceremonial vessels,
Complete Being, who holds a book in her hand which bestows all dominion.

O Mother who loves the lotus seat,
Ever delighting in the music of *veena,*
Ever joyful, and ever merciful to me.

———————
Free translation by Indira Viswanathan Peterson.

Although the words of the song are not audible in an instrumental
performance, the musicians and knowledgeable members of the audience
know the song text well. The importance of this knowledge can be seen in
the performance of "Sarasiruha." At the place in the *charanam* where the
name of the goddess Saraswati appears in the song text (about 14:33–15:10),
the musical phrase is repeated several times, as if an invocation, before
Ms. Ranganayaki moves forward to the completion of the *kriti.*

Kalpana Svaras

Kalpana literally means "imagined," and *svaras* are the "notes" of the scale of the *raga* being performed. *Kalpana svaras* occur as an improvised "interruption" either in the latter part of the *kriti* rendition or after the *kriti* has been completed. Identifying this section in a vocal performance is easy, because the performer sings the names of the notes of the *raga* scale—*sa, ri, ga, ma, pa, da,* and *ni*—instead of a verbal song text. In an instrumental performance, the musicians articulate or pluck each note.

Each individual *kalpana svara* always returns to a phrase from the *kriti*, a familiar island in a sea of improvisation. This phrase, its beginning note, and the place where it begins in the *tala* cycle are important, because ultimately each turn of the *kalpana svaras* will lead back to it. Indeed it is called the *idam* (*ih*-dum), the "place." In Ranganayaki's performance the *idam* is the opening phrase of the *kriti*.

At first the improvised *svaras* will be short, perhaps only filling the last part of one *tala* cycle before returning to the phrase of the *idam*. As time goes on the *svara* improvisations will grow in length and complexity, extending through more and more cycles of the *tala* as the performer's imagination runs free. A final extended improvisation will bring the *kalpana svara* section to a climax before its return to the *idam* and the song.

The Drum Solo: *Tani Avartanam*

In a concert after what is called the "main item"—either the *kriti* with the most extended improvisations or the form called *ragam, tanam, pallavi* (*rah*-gam, *tah*-nam, *pahl*-luh-vee)—the *mridangam* player (and other percussionists, if any) come to the foreground with an extended solo. In a full concert this solo will extend for ten to fifteen minutes or more. In our performance, Raja Rao's solo is concise. As noted earlier, the drum solo gives the percussionist the chance to display the full range of his skills and rhythmic imagination. In each section of the solo the drummer will explore a certain range of patterns and architectural ideas. Finally the solo will end on an extended *korvai*, a cadential pattern repeated three times. This pattern leads back to an entrance of the *idam* by the melodic soloist and the conclusion of the *kriti* performance in an improvised flourish.

One form of improvisation not used in our performance, *niraval* (*nih*-ruh-vahl), is a set of improvisations based on a phrase from the *kriti* and its song text. Always preceding the *kalpana svara* section, this form of improvisation is particularly beautiful in a vocal concert, as the repeating words of a phrase of the song are covered in an expanding web of melismatic notes and ornamental phrases.

On another occasion, at another performance, the musician might decide—using the same *kriti* as a centerpiece—to shape the performance in a different way. The *kriti* might be performed alone, for example, after a perfunctory *alapana* of a few phrases. Or the *tanam* and drum solo might be omitted. While the shape of the *kriti* will remain basically the same, the nature of the improvisations might vary as the musician draws on the procedures, ideas, and performance habits stored in his or her memory and on the interpretation of a particular *raga* on a particular day. This fluidity of performance sparked by the creative instincts of the South Indian musician is one of the delights of the Carnatic music tradition.

Indian Music and the West

As noted earlier, India's culture has long assimilated outside influences and made them its own. The presence of the violin, the saxophone, the guitar, and the mandolin in Carnatic music, and the all-inclusive nature of South India's cine and pop music industry are obvious examples. As the globalization of music through television, movies, CDs, and cassettes continues, mutual influences between India and the West are bound to increase. For example, since the 1970s, South Indian musicians have seen the connections between jazz improvisation and India's classical music traditions. From that awareness the genre known as fusion was born, an interface between East and West that continues to excite a younger generation of musicians and listeners. The violinists L. Shankar and L. Subramanian have worked extensively with American and European jazz and rock musicians over the past twenty years, as has the extraordinary *tabla* player Zakir Hussain.

In the late twentieth and early twenty-first centuries an increasing number of South Asians have been working, studying, and living abroad. Cohesive communities of transplanted Indians, many trained in music, now appear in almost every major city or university town on earth. Cultural clubs and temples support the study and presentation of concerts of classical Indian music and dance. The children of first-generation immigrants often find themselves in a bicultural world where the "Indianness" of their home and family must be balanced against the pervasive mainstream culture of their adopted country. Various Indo-pop styles, such as "bhangra" in Great Britain or "tassa-beat soca" in Trinidad, have also evolved. Here the drones, scales, and sometimes the instruments and languages of Indian music fuse with the beat and electric sound of mainstream rock and pop styles.

Indian music has infiltrated the West since the late 1950s. The *sitar* virtuoso Ravi Shankar was a seminal figure. Having spent years in Paris as a boy with the dance troupe of his brother, Uday Shankar, he has been able to move with ease in the elite worlds of Western classical and pop music. By the late 1960s his concerts with the master *tabla* virtuoso Alla Rakha at venues as varied as the Edinburgh Music Festival and the Monterey Pop Festival eventually gave him superstar status in Europe and the United States, as well as in India.

Over the years Ravi Shankar has released many collaborative recordings. These include the *West Meets East* dialogues with famous Western musicians—among them the classical violinist Yehudi Menuhin, the flute virtuoso Jean-Pierre Rampal, and the jazz musician Paul Horn. In the album *East Greets East* (1978) he performed with traditional Japanese musicians. His *Shankar Family and Friends*, an early 1970s recording made in San Francisco with several dozen Indian and Western musicians (including one listed enigmatically as "Harris Georgeson"), includes some fascinating music.

In the mid-1960s Ravi Shankar acquired the most illustrious of his students, George Harrison of the Beatles. Harrison's interest in Indian classical music and religious philosophy resulted in a series of finely crafted Indian-based songs ranging from "Love You To" to "The Inner Light" (recorded in Bombay) and the post-Beatles "My Sweet Lord." Many of John Lennon's songs of the mid-sixties also had Indian influences, although, as in the beautiful song "Rain," the synthesis is often more opaque. In the musical texture of "Tomorrow Never Knows," Lennon included drones, exotic riffs, and Indian instruments floating in a complex hallucinogenic collage of backward tapes and sound effects (described by one critic as "a herd of elephants gone mad!"). All of this backs the otherworldly dream state of the lyrics themselves, which were inspired by the Tibetan Book of the Dead as interpreted by the LSD guru Timothy Leary.

In "Love You To," from the Beatles 1966 album *Revolver,* the sitar begins with a brief introduction of the notes of a *raga*-like scale in unmeasured time—a hint of an *alapana*. A background drone of *tambura* and bass guitar continues throughout. The *tabla* drumbeat enters, establishing a driving metrical pulse of *tala*-like cycles. Harrison's vocal line is sung in flat tones and ends with a descending melisma of distinct Indian vocal sound. In the second section of the song the repetitive riffs alternating between *sitar* and voice reflect the "question and answer" interplay of Indian musicians in performance. Then there is an instrumental break with the *sitar* and *tabla* improvising first in cycles of seven beats, then in five, and finally in three, all of which leads to a final rendition of chorus and verse. A fast instrumental postlude corresponds to the ending climactic sections of a North Indian performance. All of this in a three-minute song!

Indo-pop music has continued to flourish in Great Britain, where large immigrant communities from the former colonies continue to generate new genres and sounds. The filmmaker Vivek Bald in his documentary *Mutiny: Asians Storm British Music* has surveyed the Indo-Brit scene in the late twentieth century. Singer and composer Sheila Chandra, born in 1965, has treated diverse influences from East and West with intelligence and sensitivity. A former child television star, in the 1980s she joined Steve Coe and Martin Smith to form an innovative East/West fusion band, Monsoon. In her more recent work, such as the albums *Silk* (1991) and *Weaving My Ancestor's Voices* (1992), Chandra has focused on the unique qualities of her voice—often set against electronic and acoustic drones—and explored the synthesis of world vocal traditions from the British Isles, Spain, North Africa, and India.

As Indian classical and popular musicians continue to absorb the varied musics of the world around them, and as world musical traditions continue to be instantaneously accessible, perhaps the ancient traditions of classical Indian music north and south, Hindusthani and Carnatic, will continue to find echoes, reflections, interpretations, and responses in the music of the West.

Study Questions

1. How do you think history, geography, and society influence music in India?
2. How does the context of India's music contrast with the musical scene (as you perceive it) in the United States, Canada, or your native country?
3. What does "acculturation" mean in the context of present day Indian music?
4. South Indian music uses songs mixed with improvisational sections. Can you think of a similar approach in Western music culture? What are the similarities and differences between the two?
5. What are the characteristics of Indian pop/cinema music and performance? How do these differ from pop music in the West?
6. What are some of the social layers of genres of Indian music?
7. What is the role of religion in South India's classical music?
8. What is a *raga,* as a concept as well as a musical blueprint for performance?
9. Why is the relationship between *sruti* (drone notes) important in Carnatic Music? In your opinion, is there a similar relationship in bagpipe music or Appalachian fiddling?
10. What are the functioning layers and relationships between musicians in a South Indian classical music ensemble?
11. In exploring the seventy-two *melakarta* scales, which do you find attractive and interesting? Why?
12. What are the four kinds of improvisation used in Carnatic music? Describe their characteristics.
13. In the context of the fusion music you have heard in this class (Ravi Shankar, Sheila Chandra, the Beatles, and so on), what are the pros and cons of fusion versus strict adherence to tradition?

Glossary

adi tala (*aah*-dee *tah*-lah) An 8-beat *tala* cycle subdivided 4 + 2 + 2.

alapana (*aah-laa*-pah-nah) Improvised introduction to a *raga* in free time.

bhajan (*bhuh*-juhn) A simple religious song, often for group singing.

bharata natyam (*bha*-ruh-tah *naw*-tyam) A South Indian classical dance style.

Carnatic music (kahr-*nah*-tik) South India's classical music style.

gamaka (*gah*-muh-kah) Slides, oscillations, grace notes, and other ornamentation of a tone.

ghatam (*guh*-tum) A large clay pot played with fingers and hands.

guru A teacher who passes on knowledge to his or her disciples.

gurukula system (gu-ru-*koo*-luh) A tradition in which young students live in the house of their teacher for many years to learn music, a craft, or ritual.

Hindusthani music (hin-du-*stah*-nee) North India's classical music style.

jalatarangam (juh-luh-tuh-*rahn*-gum) Instrument made from a semicircle of porcelain bowls tuned by different levels of water and struck with two thin sticks.

harmonium A portable reed organ the size of a small trunk with bellows and Western keyboard.

idam (*ih*-dum) The "place," a pitch and point in the *tala* cycle to which *kalpana svara* improvisations return to.

kanjira (kahn-*jih*-rah) A tambourine of wood and lizard skin, with jangles.

karnataka sangeeta (kahr-*nah*-tuh-kah sahn-*gee*-tah with a hard "g") South India's classical music style.

khanda chapu tala (*khahn*-da *chah*-pu *tah*-lah) A 5-beat *tala* cycle subdivided 2 + 3.

kriti (*krih*-tee). The principle song form of South Indian classical music.

kudam (*koo*-dam) Folk instrument with a single plucked gut string emerging from a clay pot resonator and tied to a wood board. Tension of the string determines pitch.

melakarta system (*may*-luh-*kahr*-tah) A system of seventy-two basic seven-note "mother" scales for classifying *raga*s.

misra chapu tala (*mish*-ruh *chah*-pu *tah*-lah) A *tala* cycle of 7 beats subdivided 3 + 2 + 2.

mora (*moh*-rah) A rhythmic pattern repeated three times to signify a cadence (end of a section).

morsang (*mor*-sung) An Indian type of Jew's harp.

mridangam (mrih-*dun*-gum) Principal South Indian drum, which is barrel-shaped, two-headed, and played with fingers and palms.

nagasvaram (*nah*-guh-svah-rum) Double-reed pipe about 2 to 3 feet in length.

niraval (*nih*-ruh-vahl) Form of improvisation built on variations on a phrase from a song.

periya melam (*peh*-ri-yah *may*-luhm) Instrumental ensemble built around the *nagasvaram* double-reed pipe.

punji (*pun*-jee) Double- or single-reed wind instrument with two pipes (one a drone), played by snake charmers.

raga (*rah*-gah) A musical entity characterized by distinctive elements (scale, ornaments, and so on) that provides the raw material for melodic composition and improvisation.

ragam, tanam, pallavi (*rah*-gam, *tah*-nahm, *pahl*-luh-vee) Extensive improvisational form based on a single phrase of melody and text, done as the main piece in a concert.

rasa (*ruh*-sah) An emotion generated by a work of art. Traditionally there are nine or ten.

rupaka tala (*roo*-puh-kah *tah*-lah) A *tala* cycle of 3 beats subdivided 1 + 2.

sabha (*sah*-bhah) Cultural organization that sponsors concerts, dance recitals, and plays.

santoor, or santur (sahn-*toor*) Trapezoidal hammer dulcimer, instrument of Kashmir.

shahnai (shuh-*nai*) Double-reed conical oboe, instrument of North India.

shanku (*shan*-ku) Conch shell trumpet, blown on auspicious occasions in court and temple.

sitar (sih-*tahr*) Plucked twenty-two–string classical instrument of North India.

sruti (*shroo*-tee) The tonal center chosen by a performer.

sruti-box A drone instrument comprised of a small wooden box with tuned reeds (like a reed organ), with air provided by a hand bellows.

sollukattu (sol-lu-*kaht*-tu) Spoken drumming patterns.

svara (*svah*-rah) A note. The seven notes (*svaras*) of a scale are *sa, ri, ga, ma, pa, da, ni.*

tabla (*tab*-blah) Principal North Indian drum comprising a set of two small drums (one of metal and pot shaped, the other of wood and cylindrical) played with fingers and palms.

tala (*tah*-lah) A recurring time cycle. Can be counted with fingers and hands.

tambura (tahm-*boo*-rah) A four-string long-necked plucked lute tuned to provide the *sruti* (drone).

tanam (*tah*-nahm) A rhythmic melodic improvisation, in a *raga* but without *tala.*

tani avartanam (*tah*-nee a-*vahr*-tuh-nahm) A drum or percussion solo in a concert.

tavil (*tah*-vil) Cylindrical double-headed drum played with fingers and a drumstick.

veena (*vee*-nah) A seven-string plucked instrument with chromatic frets set in black wax.

Resources

References

Beatles, the. 1966. *Revolver*. Parlophone CDP 7 464412. CD.

Chandra, Sheila. 1991. *Silk*. Shanachie 64035. CD.

———. 1992. *Weaving My Ancestor's Voices*. Caroline CAROL 2322-2. CD.

"Ranganayaki Rajagopalan: A Living Tradition." 1971. Felicitation brochure. Chennai, India: West Mambalam Fine Arts Sabha.

Shankar, Ravi. 1974. *Shankar Family and Friends*. Dark Horse SP 22002. [out of print]

———. 1978. *East Greets East*. Deutsche Grammophon 2531-381.

———. n.d. *West Meets East* (with Yehudi Menuhin) I–III. Angel S-36418, S-36026, SQ-37200.

DVD Tamil Movies

The viewing of recommended Tamil movies on DVD is essential for understanding the pop music sections of this chapter. All DVDs have song tracks listed separately on their menus. Make sure to ask for movies with English subtitles. The recommended Tamil movies are *Bombay, Dumm Dumm Dumm, Kadalan, Mudalvan,* and *Thillana Mohanambal*. To order via the Internet in the United States (at below $20 each), go to http://www.AnyTamil.com. To order in the United Kingdom, go to United Kingdom, http://www.ayngaran.com (email: sales@ayngaran.com).

Additional Reading and Viewing

Brown, Robert E. 1971. "India's Music." Pp. 192–329 in *Readings in Ethnomusicology*, edited by David P. McAllester. New York: Johnson Reprint.

Kumar, Kanthimathi, and Jean Stackhouse. 1988. *Classical Music of South India: Karnatic Tradition in Western Notation*. Stuyvesant, N.Y.: Pendragon Press. Beginning lessons and simple songs with free translations of song texts.

Lakshmi, C. S. 2000. *The Singer and the Song*. New Delhi: Kali for Women. Interviews with women musicians.

Mohan, Anuradha. 1994. "Ilaiyaraja: Composer as Phenomenon in Tamil Film Culture." M.A. thesis, Wesleyan Univ.

Nelson, David. 1989. *Madras Music Videos*. Available from D. Nelson, 340 Westhampton Road, Northampton, MA 01060. Videotapes of concert performances of South Indian music.

Reck, David. 1985. "Beatles Orientalis: Influences from Asia in a Popular Song Tradition." *Asian Music* 16(1): 83–149.

Shankar, Ravi. 1968. *My Music, My Life*. New York: Simon & Schuster.

Viswanathan, T., and Matthew Harp Allen. 2004. *Music in South India*. New York: Oxford Univ. Press.

Wade, Bonnie. 1988. *Music of India: The Classical Traditions*. Riverdale, Md.: Riverdale.

Additional Listening: Carnatic Music

An Anthology of South Indian Classical Music. Ocora 5900001/2/3/4. Four CDs.

Gopinath, Kadri. *A Tribute to Adolphe Sax*. Oriental 230/231. [saxophone]

Iyer, Semmangudi Srinivasa. *The Doyen of Carnatic Music*. Oriental CD-163 and 164. Set of two CDs. [vocal]

———. *Sangita Kalanidhi*. Oriental CD-186. [vocal]

Jayaraman, Lalgudi J. *Violin Virtuoso: Lalgudi J. Jayaraman*. Oriental AAMS-125.

Krishnan, T. N. *Melodious Strings of the Indian Violin*. Oriental CD-296.

Mahalingam, T. R. ("Mali"). *Divine Sounds of the Bamboo Flute.* Oriental 183/184. Two CDs.

Moulana, Sheik Chinna. *Nadhasvaram.* Wergo SM-1507. [*nagasvaram*]

Music for Bharata Natyam. Oriental 176. [South Indian dance music]

Narayanaswamy, K. V. *Guru Padam.* Koel 063. [vocal]

Padmanabhan, Rajeswari. *Surabi.* SonicSoul Acoustics. [*veena*; no number; released in 1998]

Ramani, N. *Lotus Signatures.* MOW CDT-141. [flute]

Ranganayaki Rajagopalan. Makar 029. [*veena*]

Sankaran, Trichy. *The Language of Rhythm.* MOW 150. [mridangam]

Subbulakshmi, M. S. *M. S. Subbulakshmi Live at Carnegie Hall.* EMI India 147808/809. Two CDs. [vocal]

———. *M. S. Subbulakshmi Radio Recitals.* EMI India CDNF 147764/65. Two CDs. [vocal]

Viswanathan, T. *Classical Flute of South India.* JVC VIGG-5453.

Additional Listening: Hindusthani Music

(Compiled by Peter Row, New England Conservatory of Music)

Ajoy Chakrabarty, Vocal, Raga Bageshri—Malkauns (Vol 2). Ajoy Chakrabarty (*khyal*) with Samar Saha (*tabla*) and Sultan Khan (*sarangi*): *raga*s Bageshri and Malkauns. Navras Records: NRCD 0011.

Buddhadev Das Gupta—Nayak ki Kanra. Buddhadev Das Gupta (*sarod*) with Anand Gopal Bandopadhyay (*tabla*): *raga* Nayak ki Kanra. Raga Records: RAGA 210.

Chant Dhrupad—Nasir Zahiruddin Dagar et Nasir Faiyazuddin Dagar. Nasir Zahiruddin Dagar and Nasir Faiyazuddin Dagar (*dhrupad*) with Laxmi Narain Pawar (*pakhawaj*): *raga*s Bageshri and Bhatiyar. Ethnic: B 6159.

Gathering Rain Clouds. Vishwa Mohan Bhatt (*mohan vina*) with Sikhvinder Singh Namdhari (*tabla*): *raga*s Miya ki Malhar and Gavati. Water Lily Acoustics: WLA-ES-22-CD.

Great Masters of the Rudra-Veena. Ustad Zia Mohiuddin Dagar (*rudra veena*) with Manik Munde (*pakhawaj* drum): *raga*s Pancham Kosh and Malkauns. Auvidis: A 6131.

Lakshmi Shankar: The Hours and the Seasons. Lakshmi Shankar (*khyal* and *bhajan*) with Sadanand Naimpalli (*tabla*): *raga*s Ahir Bhairav, Dhani, Khafi, and Bhajans in *raga*s Megh and Bhairavi. Ocora: C 581615.

Lalita. Ustad Imrat Khan (*surbahar*): rag Lalit (*alap, jor,* and *jhala*). Water Lily Acoustics: ASIN B000002VYH.

Padmabhushan Nikhil Banerjee—Sitar Recital. Nikhil Banerjee (*sitar*) with Kanai Dutt (*tabla*) and Swapan Choudhury (*tabla*): *raga*s Komal Rishabh Asavari, Jaunpuri, Mand, and Dhun (Baul folk song). EMI: CDNF 150043.

Rag Kaunsi Kanhra. Hariprasad Chaurasia (flute) with Sabir Khan (*tabla*): rag Kaunsi Kanhra. Nimbus Records: NI 5182.

Ravi Shankar in Celebration—Classical Sitar. Ravi Shankar (*sitar*) with Chatur Lal (*tabla*), Kumar Bose (*tabla*), Anoushka Shankar (*sitar*), Zakir Hussain (*tabla*), Alla Rakha (*tabla*) and Kanai Dutt (*tabla*): *raga*s Charu Keshi, Bhatiyar, Adarini, Marwa, and Dhun Kafi. Angel: 7243 5 55578-2.

Sitar Recital Selection, Shahid Parvez. Shahid Parvez (*sitar*) with Bikram Ghosh (*tabla*): *raga*s Bilaskhani Todi, Desh, and Bhatiali Dhun. Sagarika: Cat No. S-500-01-4.

Ustad Ali Akbar Khan, Pandit Nikhil Banerjee: Rag Manj Khammaj, Rag Misra Mand. Ali Akbar Khan (*sarod*) and Nikhil Banerjee (*sitar*) with Mahapurush Misra (*tabla*): *ragas* Manj Khammaj and Misra Mand. Alam Madina Music Productions: AMMP CD 9405.

Ustad Ali Akbar Khan, Signature Series: Vol. 1: *Three Ragas.* Ali Akbar Khan (*sarod*) with Mahapurush Misra (tabla): *ragas* Chandranandan, Gauri Manjari, and Jogiya Kalingra. Alam Madina Music Productions: AMMP CD 9001.

Ustad Amjad Ali Khan [Compilation]. Amjad Ali Khan (*sarod*) with Samta Prasad, Chandra Mohan, and Shafaat Ahmed Khan (*tabla*): *ragas* Sughrai Kanada, Bihag, and Tilak Kamod. Gramophone Company of India: CDNF 150209.

Ustad Vilayat Khan—Sitar. Vilayat Khan (*sitar*) with Akram Khan (*tabla*): *raga* Jaijaivanti. India Archive Music: CD 1010.

Veena Sahasrabuddhe, A Morning Raga: Bhoopal Todi. Veena Sahasrabuddhe (*khyal*) with Sanjay Deshpande (*tabla*): *raga* Bhoopal Todi. Navras Records: NRCD 0031.

Other Recordings

Ilaiyaraja. *How to Name It.* Oriental Records ORI/AAMS CD-115. CD.

McLaughlin, John. *Best of Mahavishnu.* Columbia PCT-36394.

———. *Shakti.* Columbia Jazz Contemporary Masters CK-46868. CD.

Shankar, Ravi. *Concerto for Sitar and Orchestra.* Angel SPD 36806.

———. *Ragamala: Concerto for Sitar and Orchestra No. 2.* Angel DS 37935.

Major Sources for Recordings

Music of the World (MOW label). P.O. Box 3620, Chapel Hill, NC 27515; (888) 264-6689; http://www.rootsworld.com/rw/motw/indexx2.html.

Oriental Records. P.O. Box 387, Williston Park, NY 11596; http://www.oriental records.com.

Raag Music. Los Angeles, Calif.; (310) 479-5225; http://www.webcom.com/raag/ ca-v-art.html.

SonicSoul Acoustics. 15183 Dane Lane, Portland, OR 97229; (503) 531-0270; kartha1@aol.com.

Web Resources

- Carnatic.com
  http://www.carnatic.com
- Carnatica: Ultimate Unison of Tradition and Technology
  http://carnatica.com
- Carnatic Music: Supplementary Recording List
  http://www.medieval.org/music/world/carnatic/cblsup.html
- *Mutiny:* A Documentary by Vivek Bald
  http://www.mutinysounds.com/film
- Sampurna
  http://www.euronet.nl/users/l_pesch/
- Sangeetham
  http://sangeetham.com

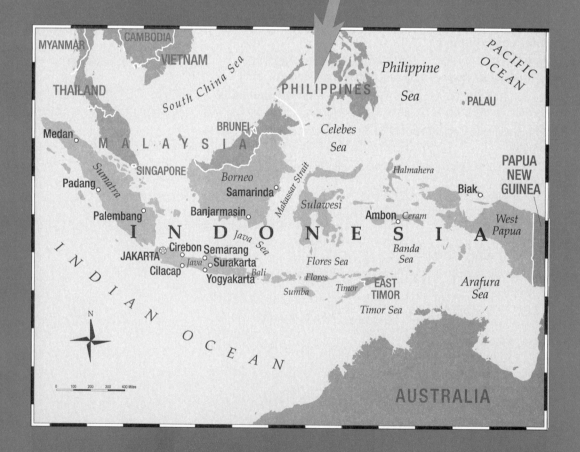

Asia/Indonesia

R. Anderson Sutton

$\mathcal{I}$ndonesia is a country justly proud of its great cultural diversity. Nowhere is this diversity more evident than in the stunning variety of musical and related performing arts found throughout its several thousand populated islands. Known formerly as the Dutch East Indies, Indonesia is one of many modern nations whose boundaries were formed during the centuries of European colonial domination, placing peoples with contrasting languages, arts, systems of belief, and conceptions of the world under a single rule. The adoption of a national language in the early twentieth century was a crucial step in building the unity necessary to win a revolution against the Dutch (1945–1949). More recently, a pan-Indonesian popular culture has been contributing to an increased sense of national unity, particularly among the younger generation. Nevertheless, though we can identify some general cultural traits, including musical ones, shared by many peoples of Indonesia, it is still problematic to speak of an "Indonesian" culture, or an "Indonesian" style of music. Regional diversity is still very much in evidence, contributing to the economic and political turmoil that has kept Indonesia in the news in the past few years.

Most Indonesians' first language is not the national language (Indonesian) but one of the more than two hundred separate languages found throughout this vast archipelago. And though many Indonesians are familiar with the sounds of Indonesian pop music and such Western stars as Britney Spears and Justin Timberlake, they also know, to a greater or lesser extent, their own regional musical traditions. Many kinds of music exist side by side in Indonesia, in a complex pluralism that reflects both the diversity of the native population and the receptiveness of that population to centuries of outside influence. Indonesia is, then, a country that can truly be said to be home to worlds of music.

What sort of impressions might you first have of this country? You would probably arrive in the nation's capital, Jakarta (jah-*kar*-tah), a teeming metropolis of about ten million people—some very wealthy, most rather poor. Jakarta is near the western end of the north coast of Java (*jah*-vah),

> **Salient Characteristics of Indonesia**
>
> - Fourth largest national population in the world.
> - Island nation of diverse regional cultures (including languages and music traditions).
> - National culture is emerging, but regional cultures still predominate.
> - Former Dutch colony.
> - Predominantly Muslim, but with significant Hindu and Christian minorities.
> - Largest ethnic group is Javanese.

Indonesia's most heavily populated (but not largest) island. The mix of Indonesia's many cultures is nowhere more fully realized than in this special city. Many kinds of music are heard here. Western-style night clubs and discos do a lively business until the early hours of the morning. Javanese *gamelan* (percussion ensemble; pronounced *gah*-muh-lahn) music accompanies nightly performances of dance-dramas from central Java. You might also run across Jakarta's own small percussion ensembles, or perhaps a troupe from Bali, Sumatra (soo-*mah*-trah), or any of the many other islands performing traditional music and dance at the Jakarta Arts Center. You will almost certainly hear the call to prayer from one of Jakarta's many mosques. Indonesia's population, the fourth largest in the world, is predominantly Muslim, but with significant Hindu and Christian minorities and a diversity of approaches to religious belief and practice. You can get a sense of Indonesia's many cultures by roaming this complex city, but much of what you encounter there has strong roots in the various regions from which it has been derived.

Central Java

Java is an island of just less than 50,000 square miles—very nearly the size of New York State and slightly smaller than Nepal. With just over 100 million people, it is one of the most densely populated regions in the world. (Indonesia's total population is about 212 million.) Most of the central and eastern two thirds of the island is inhabited by Indonesia's largest ethnic group, the Javanese, 70 million people who share a common language and other cultural traits, including music, though some local differences persist. In the western third of the island live the Sundanese, whose language and arts are distinct from those of the Javanese. Despite its dense population, Java remains mostly a farming society, with wet-rice agriculture as the predominant source of livelihood. While most Javanese profess to be Muslim, a rather small percentage follows orthodox practice. More adhere to a blend of Islam with Hinduism and Buddhism (introduced in Java over one thousand years ago) and with what most scholars believe to be a still earlier layer of belief in benevolent and mischievous spirits and in ancestor veneration. From Jakarta a twelve-hour ride on bus or train through shimmering wet-rice fields, set in the plains between gracefully sloping volcanic mountains, leads to Yogyakarta (jog-jah-*kar*-tah; often abbreviated to "Yogya," pronounced *jog*-jah), one of two court cities in the cultural heartland of central Java. The other, less than fifty miles to the northeast, is Surakarta (soo-rah-*kar*-tah; usually known as "Solo" [*soh*-loh]). Most Javanese point to these two cities as the cultural centers where traditional *gamelan* music and related performing arts have flourished in their most elaborate and refined forms. These courtly developments contrast with the rougher styles associated with the villages and outlying districts.

Yogya is a sprawling city with a population of close to 500,000. It has few buildings taller than four stories. Away from the several major streets lined with stores flashing neon signs and blaring popular music, Yogya is in many ways like a dense collection of villages. Yet at its center is one of Java's two major royal courts, official home of the tenth sultan, His Highness Hamengku Buwånå X (hah-*muhng*-koo bu-*waw*-naw). Unlike any Western palace or court, this one is a complex of small buildings and open pavilions, appropriate for the warm, tropical climate. Its design is not merely for comfort, however. The court is endowed with mystical significance as an earthly symbol of the macrocosmos, the ordered universe, with orientation to the cardinal directions. And the ruler, whose residence is located at the very center of the court, is imbued with divine powers, like the Hindu-Javanese kings of many centuries ago.

In many of these pavilions the court *gamelan* ensembles are kept. Some date back many centuries and are used only for rare ritual occasions; others were built or augmented more recently and are used more frequently. Most of these, like other treasured heirlooms belonging to the court, are believed to contain special powers and are shown respect and given offerings. Also kept in the court are numerous sets of finely carved and painted shadow puppets, made of water buffalo hide and used in all-night performances of highly sophisticated and entertaining shadow plays. Classical Javanese dance, with *gamelan* accompaniment, is rehearsed regularly and performed for special palace functions.

Though the court is still regarded as a cultural center, it is far less active now than it was prior to World War II (during which the Japanese occupied Indonesia). Much activity in the traditional Javanese arts is to be found outside the court, sponsored by private individuals and also by such modern institutions as the national radio station and public schools and colleges. In the rural villages, which long served as a source and inspiration for the more refined courtly arts, a variety of musical and related performing arts continue to play a vital role in Javanese life.

Gamelan

The word *gamelan* refers to a set of instruments unified by their tuning and often by their decorative carving and painting (see Figure 7.1). Most *gamelans* consist of several kinds of metal slab instruments (similar in some ways to the Western vibraphone) and tuned knobbed gongs. The word *gong* itself is one of the very few English words derived from Indonesian languages. (Two others are *ketchup* and *amok*.) In English, *gong* may refer to any variety of

Figure 7.1
The *gamelan* Kyai Kanyut Mèsem (*kyah*-ee *kah*-nyoot *me*-suhm) ("The Venerable Tempted-to-Smile") in the Mangkunegaran palace, Surakarta, Central Java.

Arthur Durkee, Earth Visions Photographics

percussion instrument whose sound-producing vibrations are concentrated in the center of the instrument, rather than the edge like a bell. In Javanese, it refers specifically to the larger hanging knobbed gongs in *gamelan* ensembles and is part of a family of words relating to largeness, greatness, and grandeur— *agung* (great, kingly), *ageng* (large), and *gunung* (mountain). In addition to gongs and other metal instruments, a *gamelan* ensemble normally has at least one drum and may have other kinds of instruments: winds, strings, and wooden percussion instruments (xylophones).

Some ancient ceremonial *gamelans* have only a few knobbed gongs and one or two drums. The kind of *gamelan* most often used in central Java today is a large set, comprising instruments ranging from deep booming gongs three feet in diameter to sets of high-pitched tuned gongs (gong-chimes) and slab (or key) instruments, with three drums, several bamboo flutes, zithers, xylophones, and a two-string fiddle.

Instruments in the present-day *gamelan* are tuned to one of two scale systems: *sléndro* (*slayn*-dro), a five-tone system made up of nearly equidistant intervals, normally notated with the numerals 1, 2, 3, 5, and 6 (no 4); and *pélog* (*pay*-log), a seven-tone system made up of large and small intervals, normally notated 1, 2, 3, 4, 5, 6, and 7. Some *gamelans* are entirely *sléndro*, others entirely *pélog*, but many are actually double ensembles, combining a full set of instruments for each system. The scale systems are incompatible and only in a few rare cases are they played simultaneously. Neither of these scale systems can be played on a Western piano, and neither is entirely standardized, as I shall explain.

The instrumentation of a full *sléndro-pélog gamelan* varies slightly but usually includes all or most of the instruments illustrated in Figure 7.2.

Salient Characteristics of Javanese Music ♪♪♫

- Emphasis on percussion instruments (metal slab and knobbed gong, drums).
- Bronze preferred for metal percussion instruments.
- Use of two scales (five-tone *sléndro* and seven-tone *pélog*) that differ from the Western scale.
- *Gamelan* ensemble music that is either "loud playing" or "soft playing."
- Stratified texture (main melody, punctuation, multiple variations, and drum pattern).
- Cyclic repetition of phrases.
- Use of different-sized gong instruments to "punctuate" phrases.
- Binary orientation in length of phrases and subdivision of main beats.
- Ensemble directed aurally primarily by a drummer, not visually by a conductor.
- Often accompanies dance, dance-drama, and shadow puppetry.
- Flexibility in elaboration of main melody, tempo, dynamics, and number of repetitions.

Among these many instruments, it will be useful in listening to the Javanese examples on the CD to know the following:

- The *saron* (*sah*-ron) and *slenthem* (*sluhn*-tuhm), instruments with six of seven keys, which play the main melody (referred to as slab instruments)

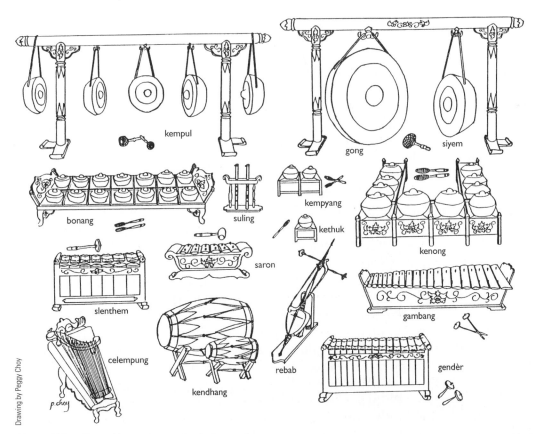

Drawing by Peggy Choy

Figure 7.2   Central Javanese *gamelan* instruments.

Figure 7.3

Gamelan musicians in the Kraton Kasunanan (royal palace) in Surakarta, Central Java. In foreground, *bonang* (gong-chime, left) and *slenthem* (instrument with seven metal slabs, right).

Arthur Durkee, Earth Visions Photographics

- The *gong* and *siyem* (*see*-yuhm) the two largest hanging gongs, which mark the end of major phrases of the main melody
- The *kenong* (kuh-*nong*), large kettles, resting horizontally, which divide the major phrases evenly (playing simultaneously with the *gong* or *siyem* at the end of major phrases, and subdividing evenly in between: usually two or four times per major phrase)
- The *kempul* (kuhm-*pool*), smaller hanging gongs, which evenly subdivide phrases
- The *kethuk* (kuh-*took* [as in English t*oo*k]), a small kettle, resting horizontally, which subdivides secondary phrases (between *kenong* beats)
- *Bonang* (*bo*-nahng), middle and high-register gong-chimes with 10 to 14 kettles, which embellish the main melody (see Figure 7.3)

Most of the other instruments perform elaborations and variations of the main melody to create a rich and subtle texture.

The *gamelan* instruments are normally complemented by singers: a small male chorus and female soloists. Java also supports a highly developed tradition of unaccompanied vocal music called *tembang* (tuhm-*bahng*), which serves as a major vehicle for Javanese poetry. In fact, the word *tembang* is best translated into English as "sung poetry." Although Javanese have recorded their *tembang* in several writing systems for over one thousand years, these are normally neither read silently nor read aloud in a speaking voice, but sung. Even important letters between members of the nobility were, until this century, composed as *tembang* and delivered as song. Though the postal system has eliminated this practice, vocal music, whether with *gamelan* or unaccompanied, enjoys great popularity in Java today.

The relation between vocal and instrumental orientations in *gamelan* music is reflected in the two major groupings of instruments in the present-day Javanese *gamelan:* "loud-playing" and "soft-playing." History suggests that these two groupings were once separate ensembles and were combined as recently as the sixteenth or early seventeenth centuries. Loud-playing ensembles were associated with festivals, processions, and other noisy outdoor events and were strictly instrumental. Soft-playing ensembles were intended for more intimate gatherings, often indoors, and involved singing. Even today, performance style distinguishes these two groupings. In loud-playing style, only the drums and louder metal instruments (gongs and slab instruments) are used. In soft-playing style, these instruments, or most of them, are played softly, and the voices, strings, flutes, and softer percussion instruments are featured.

Gamelan Construction

Bronze is the preferred metal for *gamelan* manufacture, owing both to its durability and to its rich, sweet sound quality. Brass and iron are also used, especially in rural areas. They are considerably cheaper than bronze and easier to tune, but less sonorous. Bronze *gamelan* instruments are forged (some cast in their basic shapes and then forged) in a long and difficult process. Though the metal worker in many societies occupies a low status, in Java he has traditionally been held in high regard. The act of forging bronze instruments not only requires great skill but also is imbued with mystical significance. Working with metals, transforming molten copper and tin (the metals that make bronze alloy) into sound-producing instruments, is believed to make one especially vulnerable to dangerous forces in the spirit world. For this reason the smiths make ritual preparation and may actually assume mythical identities during the forging process. The chief smith is ritually transformed into Panji, a powerful Javanese mythical hero, and the smith's assistants become Panji's family and servants (Becker 1988; Kunst 1973:138).

The largest gongs may require a full month of labor and a truckload of coal for the forge that heats the metal. Only after appropriate meditation, prayer, fasting, and preparation of offerings does a smith undertake to make a large gong. The molten bronze is pounded, reheated, pounded, reheated, and gradually shaped into a large knobbed gong that may measure three feet or more in diameter. A false hit at any stage can crack the gong, and the process must begin all over.

Gamelan Identity

A *gamelan*, particularly a bronze set with one or two fine large gongs, is often held in great respect, given a proper name, and given offerings on Thursday evening (the beginning of the Muslim holy day). Though *gamelan* makers have recently begun to duplicate precise tuning and decorative designs, generally each *gamelan* is a unique set, whose instruments would both look and sound out of place in another ensemble. Formerly, attempting even to copy the tuning and design of palace *gamelan* instruments was forbidden, as these were reserved for the ruler and were directly associated with his power.

The variability in tuning from one *gamelan* to another is certainly not the result of a casual sense of pitch among Javanese musicians and *gamelan* makers. On the contrary, great care is taken in the making and in the occasional retuning of *gamelan* sets to arrive at a pleasing tuning—one that is seen to fit the particular physical condition of the instruments and the tastes of the individual owner. I spent one month with a tuner, his two assistants, and an expert musician as they gradually reached consensus on an agreeable tuning and then altered the tuning of the many bronze gong and metal slab instruments through a long process of hammering and filing—all by hand. Bronze has the curious property of changing tuning—rather markedly during the first few years after forging, and more subtly over a period of twenty to thirty years, until it is finally "settled." It might seem that the lack of a standard tuning would cause musical chaos, but the actual latitude is small.

Gamelan Performance Contexts

Despite the changes wrought by modern institutions (formal musical instruction in schools and dissemination through the mass media) in the contexts of music making and the ways music is understood, Javanese music is more closely interrelated with other performing arts and more intimately bound to other aspects of life than are the arts in the West. "Concerts" of *gamelan* music simply do not occur, at least not in anything like the circumstances of a Western classical music concert. Instead, Javanese may have *gamelan* musicians perform at a wedding or other family ceremony, or simply hold an informal gathering to listen to *gamelan* music—better understood as social events that involve *gamelan* music than as "concerts." Normally a family or individual sponsors such an event and invites neighbors and relatives, while others are welcome to look on and listen (Figure 7.4). The invited guests are served food and are expected to socialize freely through the duration of the event. No one expects the guests to be quiet during the

Figure 7.4
Musicians playing the *gamelan* Kyai Kanyut Mèsem. Mangkunegaran palace, Surakarta, Central Java.

Arthur Durkee, Earth Visions Photographics

Figure 7.5
Dancers at Pujokusuman in Yogyarkarta perform a *srimpi* (*sreem*-pee), a female court dance.

performance of pieces or to pay rapt attention to them the way an audience does at a Western classical music concert. Rather, the music, carefully played though it may be, is seen to contribute to the festiveness of the larger social event, helping to make it lively in a positive way. Connoisseurs among the guests will ask for a favorite piece and may pay close attention to the way the ensemble or a particular singer or instrumentalist performs, but not to the exclusion of friendly interaction with the hosts and other guests. While the music is intended to entertain those present (without dance or drama), it also serves a ritual function, helping to maintain balance at important transitional points in the life of a person or community.

More often, *gamelan* music is performed as accompaniment for dance or theater—a refined female ensemble dance (see Figures 7.5, 7.6), a flirtatious female solo dance; a vigorous, martial lance dance; or an evening of drama based on Javanese legendary history, for example. A list of traditional

Figure 7.6

Dancers at Pakualaman Palace in Yogyakarta perform a *bedhåyå* (buh-*daw*-yaw), a female court dance (here with innovative costumes).

Arthur Durkee, Earth Visions Photographics

genres currently performed in central Java with *gamelan* accompaniment would be long. Some are presented primarily in commercial settings, with an audience buying tickets. Others are more often part of a ritual ceremony.

The genre held in the highest esteem by most Javanese, and nearly always reserved for ritual ceremony, is the shadow puppet theatre, called *wayang kulit* (*wah*-yang *koo*-lit), which dates back a thousand years. Beginning with an overture played on the *gamelan* during the early evening, shadow puppet performances normally last until dawn. With a screen stretched before him, a lamp overhead, and puppets to both sides, one master puppeteer operates all the puppets, performs all the narration and dialogue, sings mood songs, and directs the musicians for a period of about eight hours, with no intermission. (Note that almost all Javanese puppeteers are male.)

The musicians do not play constantly throughout the evening, but they must be ever ready to respond to a signal from the puppeteer. He leads the musicians and accents the action of the drama through a variety of percussion patterns that he plays by hitting against the wooden puppet chest to his left and by clanging metal plates suspended from the rim of the chest. If he is holding puppets in both hands, he uses his foot to sound these signals. He must be highly skilled as a manipulator, director, singer, and storyteller.

What the puppeteer delivers is not a fixed play written by a known playwright, but rather his own rendition of a basic story—usually closely related to versions performed by other puppeteers, but never exactly the same. It might be a well-known episode from the Ramayana or Mahabharata, epics of Indian origin that have been adapted and transformed in many parts of Southeast Asia and have been known in Java for a thousand years. The music is drawn from a large repertory of pieces, none specific to a single play and many of which are played in other contexts as well.

A good musician knows many hundreds of pieces, but the pieces, like the shadow plays, are generally not uniform. Many regional and individual variants exist for some pieces. More important, the very conception of what constitutes a "*gamelan* piece" or "*gamelan* composition" (in Javanese: *gendhing* [guhn-*deeng*]) differs from the Western notion of a musical piece, particularly as that notion has developed in the Western art music or "classical" tradition.

Gamelan Music: A Javanese *Gendhing* in Performance

We can best begin to understand what a Javanese *gendhing* is by considering one in some detail—how it is conceived and how it is realized in performance. Listen to *Bubaran* "Kembang Pacar" (boo-*bah*-rahn kuhm-*bahng* pah-char) **(CD 2, Track 3).** To enable you to hear and understand the individual layers of the music, I had my advanced students of Javanese *gamelan* at the University of Wisconsin–Madison perform this special version, which begins with only the main melody played by itself (all four major phrases), with successive layers added, one by one. The timed listening guide gives the order in which these instrumental layers are added, and the counter number for each. Once all the layers are in place, the ensemble plays the entire piece as it would be heard in Java, including the gradual slowing down to end. This *gendhing* consists of four major phrases of melody (we can refer to them as A, B, C, and D). In this demonstration version, all four are first played alone, with no punctuation, drum, or elaboration. As the *gendhing* repeats, one layer of punctuation, drum pattern, or elaboration is

CD 2:3

Demonstration of *Bubaran* "Kembang Pacar" (3:38). *Balungan* melody played alone, followed by the addition of other instruments one by one. Performed by University of Wisconsin–Madison Javanese *gamelan* ensemble, directed by R. Anderson Sutton. Recorded at the University of Wisconsin–Madison, December 2000.

Close Listening   CD 2:3

Bubaran "Kembang Pacar"

Counter Number	Commentary
Main melody—Phrases A through D	
0:02	*Saron* and *slenthem* play major phrase A, 1st statement, 16 beats. (metal slab instruments)
0:17	Major phrase B, 1st statement, 16 beats.
0:32	Major phrase C, 1st statement, 16 beats.
0:46	Major phrase D, 1st statement, 16 beats.
1:00	*Gong* enters, marking end of major phrase D. (Large hanging gong; marks the ends of all major phrases)
Major phrase A, 2nd statement	
1:04	*Kenong* enters, playing on every 4th beat. (Large kettle, horizontally mounted; subdivides the major phrase)

(continued)

Counter Number	Commentary

Major phrase B, 2nd statement

| 1:20 | *Kempul* enters, playing on the 6th, 10th, and 14th beats. (Medium hanging gongs; subdivides the major phrase) |

Major phrase C, 2nd statement

| 1:30 | *Kethuk* enters, playing on the 1st and 3rd beat of every group of 4 (every other beat throughout). Small kettle; subdivides the *kenong* phrase) |

Major phrase D, 2nd statement

| 1:43 | *Kendhang* (kuhn-*dahng*) enters, playing rhythmic patterns that fill the length of each major phrase (16 beats). (Set of large and small barrel drums; directs tempo and dynamics) |

Major phrase A, 3rd statement

| 1:56 | *Saron peking* enters, echoing each tone of the main melody. (Smallest, highest pitched *saron*, metal slab instrument; doubles main melody except at slower tempos, when it usually varies the melody) |

Major phrase B, 3rd statement

| 2:09 | *Bonang barung* enters, playing variations and embellishments. (Larger, lower-pitched gong-chime; elaborates the main melody and subdivides its beats) |

Major phrase C, 3rd statement

| 2:21 | *Bonang panerus* enters, playing variations and embellishments twice as fast as the *bonang barung* earlier. (Smaller, higher-pitched gong-chime; elaborates the main melody) |

Major phrase D, 3rd statement

| 2:34 | Full instrumentation. |
| 2:38 | Drummer speeds up tempo nearing the end of major phrase D. |

Major phrase A, 4th statement

| 2:45 | Full instrumentation. |

Major phrase B, 4th statement

| 2:56 | Full instrumentation. |

Major phrase C, 4th statement

| 3:06 | Full instrumentation. |

Major phrase D, 4th statement

| 3:17 | Full instrumentation. Drummer signals slowing of tempo to end the piece. |

added in each successive major phrase (marked by the *gong*), as shown in the listening guide.

Once all the instruments have entered, the ensemble finishes out the third full statement of the *gendhing* and continues through a fourth statement (A, B, C, and D) slowing to end.

You will note that it is an example of loud-playing style throughout. And it is in the *pélog* scale system with small and large intervals. It uses the *pélog bem* (*pay*-log buhm) scale—tones 1, 2, 3, 5, and 6, with an occasional 4, but no 7. But what about its structure: How are the sounds organized in this piece?

The structure of this *gendhing,* like most of the Javanese repertory, is based on principles of balance, divisions and subdivisions, and cycles that repeat. The major phrases in a *gendhing* are marked off by the sound of either the large *gong* or the slightly smaller gong *siyem*. For most *gendhings*, these phrases are of regular length as measured in beats of the main melody, the part usually played on the *slenthem* and the *saron* family (slab instruments)—almost always some factor of two: 8 beats, 16 beats, 32 beats, 64 beats, 128 beats, 256 beats. (In the genre of pieces that serve as the staple for accompanying dramatic action, as we shall see, the major phrases are of irregular length and the regular unit is marked instead by the medium hanging gongs known as *kempul.*) A major phrase is usually subdivided into two or four shorter phrases by the *kenong,* and these are further subdivided by *kempul* and *kethuk* (small kettle).

The result is a pattern of interlocking percussion that repeats until a sound signal from the drummer or one of the lead melodic instruments directs the performers to end or to proceed to a different piece. Whereas in Western music composers provide explicit directions for performers to repeat a section, in Javanese *gamelan* performance repetition is assumed. As we speak of "phrases" in describing music, Javanese liken the major phrase to a sentence and conceive of the subdividing parts as "punctuation." For *Bubaran* "Kembang Pacar," the pattern of punctuation, shown in Figure 7.7 (the first major phrase), is repeated throughout, with each major phrase. Today many Javanese musicians refer to notation to learn or to recall particular pieces, but they do not generally read from notation in performance. Further, what is notated is usually only the main melody; parts played on other instruments are recreated in relation to the main melody and are open to some degree of personal interpretation.

The main melody phrase (Figure 7.7) is the first of the four that comprise the piece and consists of 16 even beats. The pattern of punctuation (*kethuk*, rest, *kethuk*, *kenong*, *kethuk*, *kempul*, *kethuk*, *kenong*, *kethuk*, *kempul*, *kethuk*, *kenong*, *kethuk*, *kempul*, *kethuk*, and finally *kenong* and *gong* simultaneously) is played for each major phrase, continuously throughout the piece (Figure 7.7).

The time distribution of the beats is even, but the degree of stress or weight is not (even though no beat is played more loudly than any other on any single instrument). The strongest beat is the one coinciding with the largest and deepest sounding punctuator, the *gong* (G), and the *kenong* (N)—

Figure 7.7

Interlocking punctuation pattern in *Bubaran* "Kembang Pacar." The notation system used here is the cipher (number) system now widely used throughout Java, and reads from left to right. Note the vertical alignment of the numerals, letters, and dots. Each numeral represents a tone in the scale. Dots indicate a beat on which the player does not play—a rest—or, more correctly, the sustaining of the previous tone. An extra space or two is often given after groups of four beats as a means of demarcating a "measure"— though in Java the stress is on the *last* beat, not the first.

The main melody phrase given here is the first of the four that comprise the piece and consists of 16 even beats: tone 3, tone 6, tone 3, tone 5, tone 3, tone 6, and so on until tone 2 at the end of the phrase, at which point the performers would go directly to the second main melody phrase (not shown here).

Each punctuation instrument's part appears on a separate line, and at the bottom all appear in one line, making it easier to see how they interlock with one another.

Main Melody, 1st major phrase, played by the *saron* and *slenthem*																
	3	6	3	5	3	6	3	5	3	6	3	5	6	5	3	2
Punctuation Parts																
kethuk (small kettle):	t	.	t	.	t	.	t	.	t	.	t	.	t	.	t	.
kempul (medium gongs):	.	.	.	.	.	P	.	.	.	P	.	.	.	P	.	.
kenong (large kettles):	.	.	.	N	.	.	.	N	.	.	.	N	.	.	.	N
Large *Gong* (or *siyem*):	.	.	.	.	.	.	.	.	.	.	.	.	.	.	.	G
Punctuation pattern (composite):	t	.	t	N	t	P	t	N	t	P	t	N	t	P	t	NG

at the end of the major phrase. Javanese would count this as one, *two*, three, *FOUR*, and so on, with the strongest beat being the sixteenth. This is the only beat where two punctuating instruments (*gong* and *kenong*) coincide. It is this "coincidence" that gives a sense of repose, a release of the rhythmic tension that builds through the course of the major phrase.

Although in the West one may dismiss events as "mere coincidence," in Java the simultaneous occurrence of several events, the alignment of days of the week and dates (like our Friday the 13th), can be profoundly meaningful. It is not uncommon to determine a suitable day for a wedding, or for moving house, based on the coincidence of a certain day in the seven-day week with a certain day in the Javanese five-day market week, and this in turn within a certain Javanese month (in the lunar calendar rather than the solar calendar used in the West). And the simultaneous occurrence of what to Westerners would seem to be unrelated (and therefore meaningless) events—such as the sounding of a certain bird while a person is carrying out a particular activity—can be interpreted in Java as an important omen.

This deep-seated view of the workings of the natural world is reflected in the structure of *gamelan* music, where coincidence is central to the coherence of the music. The sounding of the *gong* with the *kenong* marks the musical instant of greatest weight and is the only point at which a *gendhing* may end. Yet other lesser points of coincidence also carry weight. If we consider the piece from the perspective of the main melody, it is at the coincidence of the main melody with the *kenong* strokes that the next strongest stress is felt. And in pieces with longer major phrases (32, 64, or 128 beats, for example), where there are many more beats in the main melody and therefore many of them do not coincide with any punctuating gong, each *kenong* stroke and even each *kethuk* (t) stroke may be an instance of emphasis and temporary repose.

The ethnomusicologist Judith Becker has argued convincingly that the cyclic structure of Javanese *gendhings* reflects the persistence of Hindu-Buddhist conceptions of time introduced to Java during the first millennium C.E. and not wholly eliminated by the subsequent adoption of Islam. (For an elaboration of this theory, see Hoffman 1978, Becker 1979, and especially Becker 1981.)

The punctuation pattern and its relation to the main melody are indicated in the first word of the full name of a *gendhing*. In fact, the way Javanese refer to *gendhings* normally includes their formal structure (in this case *bubaran*)—16 main melody beats per major phrase, with 4 *kenong* beats per major phrase, the name of a particular melody (in this case "Kembang Pacar"—a kind of red flower), the scale system (*pélog*), and the modal category (*pathet nem*).

The drummer in the Javanese *gamelan* acts as a conductor, controlling the tempo and the dynamics (the relative levels of loudness and softness). He or she need not be visible to other musicians, because the "conducting" is accomplished purely through sound signals. He or she does not stand in front of the ensemble but sits unobtrusively in the midst of it. The whole *gendhing* can be repeated as many times as the drummer desires, or as is appropriate to the context in which it is performed. Pieces in *bubaran* form usually are played at the end of performances—*bubar* means "to disperse." The guests or audience are expected to leave during the playing of the piece; thus the number of repetitions may depend on the length of time it takes those in attendance to leave.

Already we have a fairly good understanding of the structure of this piece as performed. Let us focus our attention now on the part played by the drummer, using the smallest and largest drums in combination. Throughout the piece he plays a pattern specific not to this particular piece, but, like the punctuating pattern, generic to the *bubaran* form. That is, the drumming, as well as the punctuation pattern, for any of the forty or so other pieces in this form would be the same: an introductory pattern, several variant patterns for the main phrases, and a special contrasting pattern reserved only for the playing of the final major phrase and that, together with the slowing of tempo, acts to signal the ending. The patterns are made up of a vocabulary of drum strokes, each with a name that imitates the actual drum sound (*dung, tak, dang, ket*, and so forth). It is the drummer who first begins to play faster, thereby signaling the ensemble to speed up a few phrases before they are to end. To end, other musicians all know they need to slow down during the final major phrase, but the precise rate is determined by the drummer. The playing of a special drum pattern used only for the final major phrase confirms to all the musicians that it is time to end.

We have seen how the punctuating gong parts and the drumming fit with the main melody in *Bubaran* "Kembang Pacar." We can now turn to the elaborating melodic instruments—here the gong-chimes (*bonangs*)—which normally play at a faster rate, providing variations based on the main melody. I mentioned earlier that the only part normally notated is the main melody. The embellishing parts are derived through processes generally understood by practicing musicians. Ideally all musicians can play all the parts. In reality this is true only in the best professional groups, but most musicians have at least a passive knowledge of all the instruments and know how to respond to various signals and subtler nuances.

The two *bonangs* here perform in a style called "walking," usually alternating left and right hands in sounding combinations of tones derived from the main melody. The players have not learned particular *bonang* parts or sets of variations, note for note, for this one piece. Rather, they have thoroughly internalized a vocabulary of traditional patterns known to fit with certain phrases of the main melody. Both *bonangs* embellish or elaborate on the main melody, with the *bonang panerus* (*bo*-nahng *pa*-nuh-roos)—the smaller, higher-pitched *bonang*—playing at twice the rate of the larger *bonang barung* (*bo*-nahng *ba*-roong). Yet it is not simply a matter of mechanical replication throughout, for alternate tones can be substituted (for example, 6 5 3 5 instead of 6 5 6 5) and other choices can be made. Still, we can understand why the Javanese often refer to the main melody with a word that translates as "outline" or "skeleton," for it provides just that for the elaborating instruments and, in soft-playing style, for the voices as well. The degree to which the main melody actually sounds like an outline depends on its tempo and the resulting levels at which it is subdivided by the elaborating instruments.

Iråmå Level

In this performance of *Bubaran* "Kembang Pacar," the *bonang barung* plays at twice the density of the main melody, subdividing it by two. This ratio defines one of five possible levels of main-melody subdivision, known as the *iråmå* (ee-*raw*-maw) level. If the tempo had slowed sufficiently, this *bonang* would double its ratio with the main melody, subdividing each beat by four. The anthropologist Ward Keeler aptly likens the process to a car shifting gears, in this case down-shifting as it goes up a steep grade (Keeler 1987:225). And the *bonang panerus*, in order to maintain its two-to-one relationship with the larger *bonang*, would double as well, resulting in an eight-to-one ratio with the main melody. At the slowest main-melody tempo in some *gendhings*, the larger *bonang* would have a ratio of 16 beats to one main melody beat, and the smaller *bonang*, along with several of the soft-playing instruments, would play a full 32 beats for each beat of the main melody!

Gamelan Music and Shadow Puppetry

Wayang kulit, or Javanese shadow puppetry, is Java's consummate perform- ing art form, originating over 1000 years ago and still widely performed today (Figure 7.8). With the exception of a few recent experiments and shortened versions for tourists and television broadcast, Javanese shadow puppetry performances begin around 8:00 or 9:00 P.M. and last until dawn. And while they are usually entertaining, with virtuosic displays of puppet manipulation and humorous interludes, shadow puppet performances are almost always given as part of a family or community ritual (celebrating a wedding, a bountiful harvest, or the opening of a new office or business, for example). During the entire eight hours or so, one master puppeteer sits on one side of a stretched white screen, operating flat leather puppets whose shadows are cast on the screen by a lamp (now usually electric, but formerly oil). Originally, the audience likely sat on the opposite side of the screen, watching only the shadows, but nowadays many audience members prefer to watch from the puppeteer's side, rather than the shadow side.

Arthur Durkee, Earth Visions Photographics

Figure 7.8
Puppeteer Ki Gondo Darman (kee *gon*-do *dar*-mahn) performing *wayang kulit* at the ASKI Performing Arts Academy in Surakarta.

A full array of *gamelan* musicians sit behind the puppeteer, providing musical accompaniment throughout the long night. The musicians respond to the musical demands of the puppeteer, who directs and signals them through verbal cues and a system of percussive signals he gives both by knocking a wooden beater against the wooden puppet chest positioned to his immediate left and by clanging metal plaques that hang from the side of the puppet chest. Thus, the puppeteer is master performer—not only operating the puppets, but also providing dialogue (in a great variety of voices), narrating, singing mood songs, and directing the *gamelan* musicians.

Now let us consider some of the music most closely associated with shadow puppet performance. The piece we have studied is seldom played for dance or dramatic accompaniment. The musical staples of the shadow puppet repertory are pieces with dense punctuation patterns and main phrases of varying length—pieces that generate a level of excitement, partly because of the dense gong punctuation. For each *pathet* (*pah*-tuht) (mode) there are at least three of these staple pieces: one that is relatively calm, another that is somewhat excited, and a third that is very excited. The punctuation is densest in the very excited pieces and less so in the calm pieces. Which piece is to be played is determined by the puppeteer, who must be just as thoroughly at home with the *gamelan* music as he is with the many hundreds of characters and stories that make up this tradition.

We are going to listen to a short version of one of the "somewhat excited" pieces, *Playon* "Lasem" (*plah*-yon *lah*-suhm) *sléndro pathet nem* **(CD 2, Track 4).** Depending on the mood the puppeteer wishes to establish, the piece can be played in loud-playing or in soft-playing style, or switched at any point. (The calmest of the three kinds of dramatic *gendhing* is usually in soft-playing style; the most excited is always performed in loud-playing style.) Also, the length of the piece can be radically tailored to suit the needs

 CD 2:4

Playon "Lasem," *sléndro pathet nem* (1:18). Central Javanese *gamelan* music for shadow puppetry. Performed by *gamelan* group of Ki Suparman. Field recording by R. Anderson Sutton. Yogyakarta, Java, Indonesia, 1974.

of the dramatic moment. Sometimes it may go on, through repetition of a central section, for five or ten minutes. The version we shall hear takes a little over a minute, beginning to repeat only when the puppeteer signals the playing of a special ending phrase. All the musicians must know one or two of these ending phrases for each main phrase tone and be ready to tag the appropriate one on to any main phrase, if the signal comes.

Close Listening   CD 2:4

Playon "Lasem"

Time	Commentary	Phrase in Main Melody
Introduction		
0:00	Puppeteer knocks on puppet chest to signal musicians to play.	
0:03	Full *gamelan* ensemble begins to play in soft-playing style, including female singer (*pesindhèn*).	Phrase A, 10 beats of the main melody.
0:11	Puppeteer clangs loudly on metal plaques. *Gamelan* speeds up and switches to loud-playing style. Female singer and soft instruments drop out.	Phrase B, 12 beats.
0:18	Brief shouts by the puppeteer as rival characters engage in fight.	Phrase C, 12 beats.
0:24	Continued clanging on metal plaques accompanies the fight.	Phrase D, 12 beats.
Central section (repeatable)		
0:31	Drumming and clanging on metal plaques accentuate fight action.	Phrase E, 16 beats of the main melody.
0:38	Lively accompaniment continues.	Phrase F, 8 beats.
0:41	More loud shouts by puppeteer.	Phrase G, 16 beats.
0:50	Lively action and accompaniment continue. Drumming is especially active here.	Phrase H, 8 beats.
0:53	Lively action and accompaniment continue	Phrase I, 12 beats.
1:00	Lively action and accompaniment continue.	Phrase J, 8 beats.
Repeat		
1:04	Section repeat begins; lively action.	Phrase E, 16 beats of the main melody.
1:10	Puppeteer performs pattern of knocks that signal *gamelan* musicians to move to ending phrase (K).	Two beats before the end of Phrase E.
Coda		
1:12	Puppeteer's signal knocks continue, confirming his intention to end the piece.	Phrase K, 6 beats of the main melody.
1:15	Performance of *Playon* "Lasem" ends; puppeteer continues knocking on puppet chest to set mood, and he begins to speak.	

Note that here the frequency of "coincidence" between punctuators is very high: Every 2nd beat the *kenong* (large kettle) sounds together either with the *kempul* (medium hanging gong) or, at the end of each main phrase, with the *gong*. To Javanese, this makes for exciting music, appropriate for scenes charged with emotion, even for fights. Quick rapping on the puppet chest signals the musicians to play. The drummer, playing the middle-sized drum, and sometimes the *kenong* player as well, enter just before the rest of the ensemble.

During the course of the all-night performance at which I recorded this example, the puppeteer (Ki Suparman [kee soo-*par*-mahn]) signaled this piece to be played eighteen times—all within the *pathet nem* section of the night, which lasted from about 9:00 P.M. until about 1:30 A.M. During the following sections, similar pieces, but in different modes (*pathet*) would be played: about 1:30 A.M. to about 3:30 A.M. *pathet sångå*; about 3:30 A.M. to about 5:00 A.M. (dawn), *pathet manyurå*.

The rendition you hear **(CD 2, Track 4)** begins in soft style but speeds up and gets loud at the end of the first phrase. It then proceeds through the entire *gendhing,* begins to repeat (from phrase E), and ends, on signal, after the first phrase of this repeatable section. Throughout most of the selection, you can hear the puppeteer adding to the excitement by clanging several metal plaques, which hang from the puppet chest positioned to his immediate left. While he operates puppets with his hands, he activates the metal plaques with the toes of his right foot! At several points in the selection, we also hear the puppeteer's shouts, as he gives voice to the puppet characters, who are engaged in a fierce fight.

This *gendhing* and others like it have potential for a great variety of renditions, through changes in tempo, instrumentation, and ending points. This is the essence of shadow puppet music—a very well known *gendhing,* played over and over, but uniquely tailored each time to fit precisely with the dramatic intentions of the puppeteer and kept fresh by the inventiveness of the instrumentalists and singers, who constantly add subtle variations.

Bali

Lying just east of Java, separated by a narrow strait, is the island of Bali (*bah*-lee), whose unique culture and spectacular natural beauty have fascinated scholars, artists, and tourists from around the world. It is also a place where almost everyone takes part in some activity we would call artistic: music, dance, carving, painting. And while the Balinese demonstrate abilities that often strike the Westerner as spectacular, they maintain that such activities are a normal part of life. The exquisite masked dancer by night may well be a rice farmer by day, and the player of lightning-fast interlocking musical passages accompanying him may manage a small eating stall.

Most of the several million people inhabiting this small island adhere not to Islam, Indonesia's majority religion, but to a blend of Hinduism and Buddhism resembling the religion that flourished in Java prior to the spread of Islam (fifteenth to sixteenth centuries C.E.). Though it would be a mistake

Salient Characteristics of Balinese Music

- Emphasis on percussion instruments, slab and knobbed gongs, and drums (as in Java).
- Use of two scales (*sléndro* and *pélog*) different from Western scale (as in Java).
- Use of different-sized gong instruments to "punctuate" phrases (as in Java).
- Often accompanies dance, dance-drama, and shadow puppetry (as in Java).
- Ensemble directed by melodic instrument player, with drummers (usually two of them).
- Almost all *gamelan* music strictly instrumental; variety of different ensembles.
- Shimmery effect from tuning one instrument of a pair slightly higher than the other.
- Emphasis on interlocking (often very fast) melodic and rhythmic patterns.
- Abrupt shifts in tempo and dynamics (volume level).
- Variety of textures, often stratified.
- Cyclic repetition of phrases in some sections; but free, non-repeating phrasing in others.
- Flexible in some aspects; but in many pieces, melodic patterns, tempo, dynamics, and number of repetitions all determined by composer, before performance.

to believe that what exists in Bali today represents a living museum of Javanese Hindu-Buddhist culture, the Balinese and Javanese share elements of a common cultural heritage. As in Java, we find percussion ensembles known as *gamelan* (or *gambelan*), with metal slab instruments and knobbed gong instruments that look and sound very similar to those of the Javanese *gamelan*. Some of the names are the same (*gendèr, gong, gambang, saron, suling, rebab*) or similar (*kempur, kemong*). (See glossary for pronunciations.) Most ensembles employ some version of the *pélog* scale system (some with all seven tones, others with five or six). The accompaniment for Balinese shadow puppetry, as in Java, employs the *sléndro* scale system, although the instruments used consist only of a quartet of *gendèrs* (guhn-*dehr;* instruments with metal slabs suspended by string over individually tuned resonators) augmented by a few other instruments for Ramayana stories.

Many Balinese pieces employ punctuating patterns similar in principle to those of Java. The Balinese play *gamelan* for ritual observances, as in Java, though usually at temple festivals, or in procession to or from them, rather than at someone's residence. Nevertheless the music of these two neighboring cultures is not the same. One fundamental difference is that the Balinese maintain a variety of ensembles, each with its distinct instrumentation and associated with certain occasions and functions. There is no single large ensemble that one can simply call the Balinese *gamelan*. Still, the style of music one hears performed by most ensembles in Bali (1) is strictly instrumental, (2) is characterized by changes in tempo and loudness (often abrupt), and (3) requires a dazzling technique by many of the musicians, who play fast interlocking rhythms, often consisting of asymmetrical groupings of two or three very fast beats. People often comment that Balinese music is exciting and dynamic compared with other Indonesian music, exploiting contrasts in the manner of Western art music.

Figure 7.9
The *gamelan gong kebyar* of Bali.

Listeners also comment on the shimmering quality of the many varieties of bronze ensembles. This quality is obtained by tuning instruments in pairs, with one instrument intentionally tuned slightly higher in pitch than its partner. When sounded together, they produce very fast vibrations. In the West, piano tuners rely on these same vibrations, called "beats," to "temper" the tuning, though on a piano the intervals are made intentionally "out of tune," rather than having identical strings sounding the same tone. Of course, the intentionally "out-of-tune" pairs of metallophones are perceived to be "in tune" (that is, culturally correct) in Bali, just as the piano is in our culture.

The most popular ensemble in Bali today is the *gamelan gong kebyar* (Figure 7.9), which developed during the early twentieth century, along with the virtuosic dance it often accompanies (also called *kebyar* [kuh-*byar*]— literally "flash," "dazzle"). *Kebyar* music is indeed flashy, requiring not only great virtuosity of the players but also a consummate sense of ensemble— the ability of many to play as one. Listen to "Kosalia Arini" (ko-*sal*-yah a-*ree*-nee) **(CD 2, Track 5),** a piece composed by the prolific Balinese composer and skilled drummer Wayan Beratha (*wah*-yan buh-*rah*-tuh) in 1969 for a *gamelan* festival. This piece demonstrates features typical of *gamelan gong kebyar,* many of which contrast markedly with Javanese *gamelan* music, as well as with older styles of Balinese music. These include episodic structure—the piece is clearly divided into sections with contrasting instrumentation, rhythm, and texture. Portions of the piece involve cyclic repetition, but the overall design is neither cyclic nor rigidly binary as in Javanese *gamelan* pieces.

Michael Tenzer, a U.S. scholar, composer, and performer of Balinese *gamelan gong kebyar,* has provided a detailed analysis of this piece (Tenzer 2000:367; 381–83), from which my much briefer commentary derives. Most

 CD 2:5

"Kosalia Arini" (10:40). By Wayan Beratha. *Gamelan gong kebyar.* Performed by STSI (Sekolah Tinggi Seni Indonesia) *gamelan* musicians, directed by Nyoman Windha and Pande Gde Mustika. Recorded by Michael Tenzer and Ketut Gde Asnawa, with Yong Sagita. STSI campus, Denpasar, Bali, August, 1998.

Close Listening

CD 2:5

"Kosalia Arini"

Counter Number	Commentary	Tonal Center
Noncyclic section		
0:00	*Genders* (metal slab instruments) at different pitch registers play fragments of asymmetrical phrases. Mostly soft dynamic level. Occasional louder and flashy full-ensemble fragments (*kebyar* interruptions).	C#
0:46	Partial *kebyar* interruption.	
1:43	Full *kebyar* interruption.	
2:16	Flute solo, with low-register *gendèr*. Very soft.	D
Transition		
2:41	Higher-pitched *genders* enter, marking transition to next section. Mostly soft.	D
Cyclic section		
2:49	*Genders* play 4-beat phrases; highly repetitive; alternates between soft and medium dynamic level.	D
***Kebyar* interruption**		
4:39	Full ensemble. Sudden, loud flash.	D
4:41	Short passage featuring the *reyong* (ray-yong) (kettle gong-chime played by four musicians).	D
Cyclic section		
4:53	Drum variations (by two drummers) open second cyclic section. Loud and fast, then softer.	D
5:13	*Gendèr* and *reyong* alternate. Mostly soft, fast tempo. Section stops abruptly, with no *gong*.	E
Transition		
7:22	*Genders* play transition to third cyclic section.	E
Cyclic section		
7:34	*Genders* now play in 8-beat phrases. Mostly loud, full instrumentation, alternating with some soft passages.	C#
Coda		
10:30	12-beat coda, full ensemble.	C#

basic are the contrasts between what Tenzer calls "stable" (cyclic) and "active" (noncyclic) sections.

The piece proceeds through four main sections. As you listen to the piece, follow the listening guide, noting changes (often abrupt) in tempo, instrumentation, dynamics (soft and loud), and register (high pitch or low pitch). Each section is identified not only by characteristic rhythm and texture but also by tonal center.

Though repetitive in some sections, the whole piece is much more like a fantasia or an exuberant study in contrasts (especially in dynamics and in rhythm) than even the most dramatic renditions of Javanese pieces.

Rarer today, though making something of a comeback in modified form after its near extinction eighty years ago with the decline of the Balinese courts, is the *gamelan semar pegulingan* (suh-*mar* puh-*goo*-leeng-ahn). The name has been rendered in English as "*gamelan* of the love god." It was formerly played for the king's pleasure within the court during the late afternoon and evening and with slight modification became the favored ensemble to accompany the famous *lègong* (*leh*-gong) (an intricate dance performed by three young girls). It is a rather delicate-sounding ensemble, yet unmistakably Balinese. It is this ensemble that the late composer and scholar of Balinese music Colin McPhee heard by chance on early recordings and that enticed him to travel in 1931 to Bali, where he stayed to study Balinese music for nearly ten years. (This and other varieties of Balinese *gamelan* may be heard on the CDs listed at the end of this chapter.) Even in the older and quieter Balinese *gamelan* ensemble styles, one can hear the shimmering metallic filigree, the asymmetrical rhythms, and the changes in tempo so important to Balinese music, as we heard in "Kosalia Arini."

Popular Music

Most of the music Indonesians would identify as "popular" is, like most popular music anywhere in the world, characterized by the use of at least some Western instruments and Western harmony (Hatch 1989). It is disseminated through the mass media, performed by recognized stars, and is essentially a "commercial" genre. Without going into the interesting history of Western-influenced music in Indonesia, which has primarily been in the popular vein, I would like to introduce one variety of contemporary popular music and consider one key representative musical group. The forces of globalization have intensified since the 1980s, inundating the Indonesian marketplace with the commercial cultural products of the West, including various forms of American pop, rock, and jazz. Our final musical example represents one response to this process. By a group called Krakatau (kra-ka-*ta*-oo) named after the famous volcanic island lying just west of Java, it involves a careful synthesis of Indonesian (in this case, Sundanese, i.e., West Javanese) *gamelan,* and fusion jazz.

Krakatau was founded in the late 1980s by Dwiki Dharmawan (*Dwee*-kee Dar-*ma*-wan), a jazz keyboardist whose skill in imitating the styles of Joe Zawinul (Weather Report) and Chick Corea won him an award from the Yamaha Music Company of Japan in 1985. The early recordings of Krakatau present original fusion jazz tunes with complex harmonies and rhythms. They included jazz songs, some in English, sung by an Indonesian (Javanese-Sundanese) female singer, Trie Utami (tree oo-*tah*-mee), whose imitations of African American jazz vocal styles are polished and sophisticated. Yet beginning around 1993–1994, members of the group, particularly Dwiki and Trie, decided that they were tired of only trying to imitate the music they admired from the West. Because the core membership had all spent much of their youth in West Java (Sunda [*soon*-dah]), they decided to incorporate Sundanese musical elements into their music, adding local experts on *saron bonang, rebab* (ruh-*bab*) (two-string fiddle), and drum.

They set out with the intention of creating a hybrid variety of music, mixing Western and indigenous Indonesian musical instruments and elements, not exactly a new idea, except in the way they went about it. Experiments in such combinations have been taking place in Indonesia for centuries. Special challenges are posed by the fact that many Indonesian instruments and songs use tunings and scales, such as *sléndro* and *pélog,* that are not compatible with those in the West. In the nineteenth century, brass band instruments were played with *pélog gamelan* instruments in the courts of Central Java, representing a symbolic fusion of Javanese and Dutch power. And in the early twentieth century, Javanese composers began to write pieces combining Javanese singing with Western instruments. In the 1990s, Indonesia saw a sudden growth in experimental combinations of pop/rock instruments and certain indigenous Indonesian ones. The musician often acknowledged as the inspiration for this trend is Guruh Sukarno Putra (*goo*-rooh soo-*kar*-no *poo*-tra), who produced a landmark album (commercial cassette, *Guruh Gipsy*) in 1976 involving piano, synthesizers, and rock instruments playing along with Balinese *gendèrs* and drums, incorporating Central Javanese vocal styles and West Javanese scales and melodies. Guruh is the youngest living son of the founding father of the Republic of Indonesia, President Sukarno. His music has sometimes been referred to as "heavy pop" (Hatch 1989), but where Guruh drew on various regional Indonesian styles, the members of Krakatau have attempted to focus on their own region, Sunda.

In 1994 they released an album (cassette) entitled *Mystical Mist,* with some pieces sounding more like jazz fusion and others sounding more Sundanese. In their most recent release, an album entitled *Magical Match* (CD and cassette), however, the blend is more even throughout. One of the ingenious ideas they have employed is the tuning of their Western instruments to the scales of Sundanese traditional music. Dwiki programmed into his keyboard a complex alteration of pitches and worked out special fingerings so that when he strikes the right combination of black and white keys on his keyboard, he can produce the tones of *sléndro;* with a different combination, the tones of *pélog;* and with others, tones that make up still other scales typical of Sundanese traditional music. The bass player uses an electric bass with no frets (the horizontal metal strips found on guitars that facilitate production of the Western scale). With skillful placement of his fingers, he can play bass patterns in *sléndro* and other non-Western scales. Some of the items on this album are vocal, with Trie Utami singing not like a jazz singer, but instead with the distinctive sound quality (timbre) of a Sundanese female singer (*pesindhèn* [puh-*seen*-dehn]). The example on the **CD 2, Track 6,** however, is purely instrumental, illustrating most clearly the skill of the musicians in creating a piece that tries to be not just Sundanese and not just Western, but to achieve a "magical match" between the two.

CD 2:6

"Shufflendang-Shufflending" (excerpt) (2:10). Ethno-jazz fusion, Sundanese. Performed by Krakatau: Dwiki Dharmawan, keyboard; Pra Budidharma, fretless bass; Budhy Haryono, Western drum set ("traps"); joined by Yoyon Darsono, *rebab* and flute; Adhe Rudiana, *kendang;* Elfik Zulfiqar and Tudi Rahayu, *saron;* Zainal Arifin, *bonang. Magical Match.* Kita Music. 2000.

Close Listening   CD 2:6

"Shufflendang-Shufflending"

Counter Number	Commentary
0:00	Western instruments open piece with a repeating short musical phrase.
0:15	Hints of a *pélog* scale (small and large intervals between tones).
0:42	Abruptly, *sarons* (metal slab instruments) play in *sléndro* scale (near equidistant tones).
0:50	*Sarons* play in *pélog* scale.
0:59	*Sarons* return to play in *sléndro* scale.
1:09	Switch to *rebab* (two-string fiddle) playing in *pélog* scale.
1:35	Back to fusion jazz style, as in beginning, although not exact repetition. Similar rotation of scales continues through excerpt.

Listen to **CD 2, Track 6,** an excerpt from a piece entitled "Shufflendang-Shufflending" (shuf-luhn-*dahng* shuf-luhn-*deeng*). Even the title is a mix of the English word *shuffle* (a type of African American ecstatic song/dance combination performed in worship, also known as ring-shout) and the Sundanese words for drum (*kendang*) and *gamelan* musical piece (*gending*). One of the musicians, Adhe Rudiana, teaches traditional music at the Indonesian College of Performing Arts in Bandung (*ban*-doong), West Java; three of the other musicians—Yoyon Darsono (on *rebab*) and Elfik Zulfiqar and Tudi Rahayu (on *saron*)—are recent graduates of this institution.

The piece begins with a repeated figure (what musicologists call an ostinato) on Western instruments in fusion jazz style, but with hints of *pélog*. Shortly, we hear *sarons* (metal slab instruments) playing in *sléndro*, then in *pélog*, then back to *sléndro*, followed by a *rebab* (fiddle) in *pélog*, and then back to jazz. This kind of rotation continues, although not in exact repetition, throughout the excerpt (and, in fact, throughout the whole piece).

Although listeners can enjoy the sounds and the rhythm without knowing their origins, the meaning this music has for Krakatau members, and for their fans in Indonesia, is its ability at once to "Sundanize" jazz or pop music and to "jazz" or "modernize" Sundanese music. Its ambiguity provides a bridge between the seemingly incompatible worlds of local Indonesian traditional culture and Western modern culture. Dwiki and other members of the group, whom I got to know in August 2000, did not have a clear sense of what to call their music. We talked about "New Age," "world music," and "ethno-pop." They clearly hope that this music will reach beyond Indonesia to attract listeners from around the world, not only to their own music, but also to the rich treasury of Indonesia's traditional music.

Conclusion

Throughout this chapter we have experienced some of the great diversity within Indonesia's music. We have listened to four examples that contrast with one another, yet share certain similarities that make them "Indonesian." Of course, we must be careful about drawing broad conclusions about an entire country's music from just four examples. After all, what four examples could you think of from your own country that could fairly represent the diversity of music heard there?

All of these examples, even the fusion example by Krakatau, have involved some form of Indonesian percussion ensemble (*gamelan*). There are many kinds of popular music in Indonesia that use the national or local languages but otherwise sound close to Western pop music, with squealing electric guitars, pounding electric bass and bass drum, keyboard synthesizers, harmony, and so forth. And there are indigenous traditions featuring solo voice, chorus, or instruments that sound very different from any of the examples we have covered. Nevertheless, some of the features we have heard are indeed characteristic of Indonesia and much of Southeast Asia as well. These include (1) the use of knobbed gong instruments; (2) the use of other percussion instruments (mostly metal slab instruments); (3) the stratified layering of main melody, punctuation, melodic elaboration, and drum pattern; (4) the flexibility in performance (particularly in accompanying drama); and (5) the binary (2, 4, 8, 16, etc.) orientation in phrasing and subdivision of the beat. All four of our examples have emphasized the dense, filled-in, constantly "busy" approach to musical sound that we would also hear in many other kinds of music from this vast and diverse island nation, but not in East Asian countries, such as Japan, for example.

At the dawn of the twenty-first century, it is difficult to predict the future for Indonesia's various musical activities. In June 1999 Indonesia experienced its first free elections in more than forty years, with a staggering forty-eight political parties vying for seats in the people's consultative assembly (a new diversity based more on political philosophy and religion than on regional or ethnic identity). This new openness has already begun to affect Indonesian music by engendering an outpouring of political songs on commercial cassettes and videodiscs (VCDs), a sharp increase in the number of amateur street singers accompanying their urgent and impassioned songs with guitars and shouts of "Reformasi!" ("Reformation!"). Yet at the same time, musicians young and old continue to play traditional and innovative *gamelan* music in Java and Bali, and pop musicians work out new approaches to music making, responding to the social world that inevitably shapes all musical activity.

Study Questions

1. What material or materials are used in constructing a *gamelan*?
2. How do Javanese and Western musical scales differ from one another?
3. What is a *gendhing*?
4. How are loud-playing and soft-playing styles distinguished from one another?
5. What instruments mark the "punctuation" in a Javanese *gendhing*?

Note on Pronunciation ♪♪♪

Pronunciation for Indonesian (national language), Javanese, Balinese, and Sundanese (regional languages) is quite consistent with spelling. Consonant sounds are close to or identical to consonants in English or European languages, with a few exceptions:

c	is pronounced "ch"
d	is pronounced with the tongue touching the back of the front teeth ("dental d")
dh	is pronounced with the tongue touching the roof of the mouth ("retroflex d")
t	is pronounced with the tongue touching the back of the front teeth ("dental t")
th	is pronounced with the tongue touching the roof of the moth ("retroflex t")
r	is rolled, as in Spanish.

Vowels are mostly as in Spanish, with two pronunciations of **a** (from Java and Bali) and several pronunciations of **e** (from Java, Bali, and Indonesia).

a	as in B*a*ch, or f*a*ther
å	as in b*ou*ght, or l*aw*, in open final (and sometimes penultimate) syllables in Javanese
é	as in p*ay*
è	as in b*e*t
i	as in b*ee*t
o	as in b*o*ne
u	as in b*oo*t or as in t*oo*k

The second-to-last syllable often receives a slight accent; for example, Bali is pronounced *bah*-lee, rather than bah-*lee*). However, several exceptions occur, and some words may be accented differently depending on regional dialect. In those cases, the accents shown here each represent one possible correct pronunciation.

6. What instruments play the main melody?

7. What do the other instruments do in the performance of a *gendhing*?

8. What is meant by *iråmå* level and how is it different from tempo?

9. Who directs the musicians in a Javanese shadow puppetry performance, and by what means?

10. What is unusual about the *gendhing*s that are the core musical pieces for accompanying shadow puppetry, such as *Playon* "Lasem"?

11. How do the *gamelan* musicians know when and where to end a *gendhing* when accompanying shadow puppetry?

12. Where is Bali, in relation to Java? How does it compare in size and population?

13. What gives Balinese *gamelan* music its shimmering quality?

14. How do Balinese attain such lightning-fast speed in playing melodic and rhythmic patterns?

15. What are some of the challenges of creating "fusion" music that combines Indonesian and Western instruments?

16. What aspects of traditional *gamelan* music (as seen in the examples from Java) do not seem compatible with fusion music such as Krakatau's "Shufflendang-Shufflending"?

17. In what senses is Indonesia diverse and how does the diversity relate to Indonesia's history?

18. What are some of the ways in which Javanese *gamelan* contrasts with a Western classical orchestra?

19. Can you describe a Javanese shadow puppetry (*wayang kulit*) performance? Think about social context, performance personnel, items used (for the puppetry and for the music), physical layout, length of performance, type(s) of music, and other features.

20. What features of the Balinese *gamelan gong kebyar* music, as exemplified by "Kosalia Arini," contrast most markedly with the two Javanese *gamelan* examples (*Bubaran* "Kembang Pacar" and *Playon* "Lasem")?

21. In what ways is Krakatau's music a response to globalization? How does it differ from mainstream Indonesian popular music?

Glossary

Bali (*bah*-lee) Island just east of Java.

Bandung (*ban*-doong) Large city in West Java.

barung (*ba*-roong) Indicates middle or lower register *bonang, gendèr,* or *saron* (Java).

bedhåyå (buh-*daw*-yaw) Refined court dance by seven or nine female dancers (Java).

bem (buhm) Name for first tone in *pélog* scale; also name of scale that uses that tone (Java).

bonang (*bo*-nahng) Gong-chime, with ten, twelve, or fourteen kettles arranged in two rows (Java).

bubaran (boo-*bah*-ran) Formal structure, 16 beats per *gong,* 4 beats per *kenong;* usually used for dispersal of the audience after a performance (Java).

celempung (chuh-*luhm*-poong) Zither, usually with twenty-four to twenty-six strings in double courses (Java).

Dwiki Dharmawan (*Dwee*-kee Dar-*ma*-wan) Leader of ethno-jazz fusion group Krakatau; keyboardist, arranger, and composer (Indonesia; West Java).

gambang (*gahm*-bahng) Xylophone, with seventeen to twenty-two wooden keys (Java).

gamelan (*gah*-muh-lahn) Word for ensemble of instruments, predominantly percussion (central, eastern, and western Java; Bali; and southern Kalimantan and Malaysia).

gendèr (guhn-*dehr*) Instrument with ten to fourteen metal slabs, suspended over tube resonators (Java and Bali).

gendhing (guhn-*deeng*) Musical piece for *gamelan,* with regular beat and punctuation (Java, sometimes used in Bali also).

gong (gong) Largest variety of hanging knobbed gong (Java and Bali).

Guruh Sukarno Putra (*goo*-rooh soo-*kar*-no *poo*-tra) Musician who combined Western pop and *gamelan* styles; youngest son of Indonesia's first president.

Hamengku Buwånå (hah-*muhng*-koo bu-*waw*-naw) The sultan of Yogyakarta, central Java.

iråmå (ee-*raw*-maw) Level of subdivision of main melody beat by elaborating instruments (Java).

Jakarta (jah-*kar*-tah) Indonesia's national capital city.

Java (*jah*-vah) Indonesia's most densely populated island, home to Javanese, Sundanese, and Madurese.

Jogjakarta/Jogja Alternate spellings for Yogyakarta and Yogya (see Yogyakarta).

kebyar (kuh-*byar*) Lit., "flash," "burst forth." Type of *gamelan* (and dance) created in twentieth-century Bali.

kembang pacar (kuhm-*bahng pah*-char) A type of red flower; title of a *gamelan* piece (Java).

kempul (kuhm-*pool*) Smaller hanging knobbed gong (Java).

kempyang (kuhm-*pyahng*) Pair of small kettle gongs, horizontally mounted (Java).

kendhang (kuhn-*dahng*) Double-headed, barrel-shaped drum (Java); similar term used in West Java and Bali (*kendang*).

kenong (kuh-*nong*) Large kettle gong, horizontally mounted (Java).

kethuk (kuh-*took* [as in English t*oo*k]) Small kettle gong, horizontally mounted (Java).

Ki Gondo Darman (kee *gon*-do *dar*-mahn) Well-known shadow puppeteer, Surakarta style (Java).

Ki Suparman (kee soo-*par*-mahn) Well-known shadow puppeteer, Yogyakarta style (Java).

"Kosalia Arini" (ko-*sal*-yah a-*ree*-nee) Title of a Balinese *gamelan* (*gong kebyar*) piece.

Krakatau (kra-ka-*ta*-oo) Name of ethno-jazz fusion group; also name of volcanic island located between Java and Sumatra.

Kyai Kanyut Mèsem (*kyah*-ee *kah*-nyoot *me*-suhm) Lit., "the venerable tempted-to-smile"; name of *gamelan* at Mangkunegaran palace, Surakarta (Java).

lègong (*leh*-gong) Refined dance-drama, formerly of courts, performed by girls (Bali).

Mahabharata (ma-hah-bah-*rah*-tah) One of two major Indian epics widely known in Java and Bali; centers on conflict between rival sets of cousins, culminating in major war.

nem (nuhm) Lit., "six"; name of mode/*pathet* (Java).

panerus (*pa*-nuh-roos) Indicates highest register *saron, bonang,* or *gendèr.*

pathet (*pah*-tuht) Musical mode; also major section of shadow play (Java).

pélog (*pay*-log) Seven-tone scale, of small and large intervals (Java and Bali).

pesindhèn (puh-*seen*-den) Female singer (Java).

Playon **"Lasem"** (*plah*-yon *lah*-suhm) Title of *gamelan* piece played in first major section of shadow play, Yogyakarta style (Java).

Ramayana (rah-mah-*yah*-nah) One of two major Indian epics widely known in Java and Bali; centers on story of Prince Rama.

rebab (ruh-*bab*) Two-string fiddle (Java; also found in Bali and elsewhere).

reyong (*ray*-yong) Gong-chime, usually with twelve kettles arranged in a single row and played by four musicians (Bali).

saron (*sah*-ron) Instrument with six or seven metal slabs, resting on trough resonator (Java, also Bali).

semar pegulingan (suh-*mar* puh-*goo*-leeng-ahn) Delicate sounding *gamelan* ensemble of Bali.

"Shufflendang-Shufflending" (shuf-luhn-*dahng* shuf-luhn-*deeng*) Title of piece by Krakatau.

siyem (*see*-yuhm) Middle-sized hanging knobbed gong.

sléndro (*slayn*-dro) F-tone scale, with nearly equidistant intervals (Java and Bali).

slenthem (*sluhn*-tuhm) Instrument with six or seven metal slabs, suspended over tube resonators (Java).

Solo (*soh*-loh) Short name for Surakarta.

srimpi (*sreem*-pee) Refined court dance, usually by four female dancers (Java).

suling (*soo*-leeng) End-blown bamboo flute (Java and Bali).

Sumatra (soo-*mah*-trah) Large Indonesian island, west of Java.

Sunda (*soon*-dah) West Java (western third of the island of Java).

Surakarta (soo-rah-*kar*-tah; also pronounced soo-raw-*kar*-taw) One of two famous court cities in central Java.

tembang (tuhm-*bahng*) Sung poetry (Java).

Trie Utami (tree oo-*tah*-mee) Name of female singer, member of Krakatau.

Wayan Beratha (*wah*-yan buh-*rah*-tuh) Name of Balinese composer.

wayang kulit (*wah*-yang *koo*-lit) Shadow puppetry, using flat leather puppets made of water-buffalo hide (Java and Bali).

Yogya (*jog*-jah) Short name for Yogyakarta.

Yogyakarta (jog-jah-*kar*-tah; also pronounced yog-yaw-*kar*-taw) One of two famous court cities in central Java.

Resources

References

Becker, Judith. 1979. "Time and Tune in Java." Pp. 197–210 in *The Imagination of Reality: Essays in Southeast Asian Coherence Systems,* edited by A. L. Becker and Aram A. Yengoyan. Norwood, N.J.: Ablex.

———. 1981. "Hindu-Buddhist Time in Javanese Gamelan Music." In *The Study of Time,* vol. 4, edited by J. F. Fraser. New York: Springer-Verlag.

———. 1988. "Earth, Fire, *Sakti,* and the Javanese Gamelan." *Ethnomusicology* 32 (3): 385–91.

Guruh Gipsy. 1976. PT Dela Rahita, Jakarta.

Hatch, Martin. 1989. "Popular Music in Indonesia (1983)." Pp. 47–67 in *World Music, Politics and Social Change,* edited by Simon Frith. Manchester, England: Univ. Press.

Hoffman, Stanley B. 1978. "Epistemology and Music: A Javanese Example." *Ethnomusicology* 22 (1): 69–88.

Keeler, Ward. 1987. *Javanese Shadow Plays, Javanese Selves.* Princeton, N.J.: Princeton Univ. Press.

Krakatau. 1994. *Mystical Mist.* Krakatau Production, Aquarius AQM16-4 P9603.

Krakatau. 2000. *Magical Match.* Kita Musik, HP Record HPCD-0099.

Kunst, Jaap. 1973. *Music in Java: Its History, Its Theory, and Its Technique.* 2 vols. 3rd rev. ed. by Ernst Heins. The Hague: Martinus Nijhoff.

Tenzer, Michael. 2000. *Gamelan Gong Kebyar: The Art of Twentieth-Century Balinese Music.* Chicago: University of Chicago Press.

Additional Reading

Becker, Judith. 1980. *Traditional Music in Modern Java: Gamelan in a Changing Society.* Honolulu: Univ. Press of Hawaii.

Becker, Judith, and Alan Feinstein, eds. 1984, 1987, and 1988. *Karawitan: Source Readings in Javanese Gamelan and Vocal Music.* 3 vols. Ann Arbor: Univ. of Michigan Center for South and Southeast Asian Studies.

Brinner, Ben. 1995. *Knowing Music, Making Music.* Chicago: Univ. of Chicago Press.

Hood, Mantle. 1954. *The Nuclear Theme as a Determinant of Patet in Javanese Music.* Groningen, Netherlands: J. B. Wolters.

Hood, Mantle, and Hardja Susilo. 1967. *Music of the Venerable Dark Cloud: Introduction, Commentary, and Analysis.* Los Angeles: Univ. of California Press.

Lindsay, Jennifer. 1992. *Javanese Gamelan: Traditional Orchestra of Indonesia,* 2nd ed. New York: Oxford Univ. Press.

Manuel, Peter. 1988. *Popular Musics of the Non-Western World: An Introductory Survey.* New York: Oxford Univ. Press. See especially pages 205–20.

McPhee, Colin. 1966. *Music in Bali.* New Haven, Conn.: Yale Univ. Press.

Sumarsam. 1995. *Gamelan: Cultural Interaction and Musical Development in Central Java.* Chicago: Univ. of Chicago Press.

Sutton, R. Anderson. 1991. *Traditions of Gamelan Music in Java: Musical Pluralism and Regional Identity.* Cambridge: Cambridge Univ. Press.

———. 2002. *Calling Back the Spirit: Music, Dance, and Cultural Politics in Lowland South Sulawesi.* New York: Oxford Univ. Press.

Tenzer, Michael. 1991. *Balinese Music.* Berkeley, Calif.: Periplus.

Additional Listening

Java

Bedhaya Duradasih, Court of Music of Kraton Surakarta II. King Record KICC 5193.

Chamber Music of Central Java. King Record KICC 5152.

Court Music of Kraton Surakarta. King Music KICC 5151.

The Gamelan of Cirebon. World Music Library KICC 5130.

Java: "Langen Mandra Wanara," Opéra de Danuredjo VII. Musiques traditionelles vivantes III. Ocora 558 507/9.

Java: Palais Royal de Yogyakarta, Volume 4: La musique de concert. Ocora (Radio France) C 560087.

Javanese Court Gamelan. Elektra/Nonesuch Explorer Series 972044-2.

Klenengan Session of Solonese Gamelan I. King Record KICC 5185.

Langendriyan, Music of Mangkunegaran Solo II. King Record KICC 5194.

Music from the Outskirts of Jakarta: Gambang Kromong. Smithsonian Folkways SF 40057.

The Music of K. R. T. Wasitodiningrat. CMP Records CD 3007.

Music of Mangkunegaran Solo I. King Record KICC 5184.

Sangkala. Icon 5501 (Distributed by Elektra/Asylum).

Shadow Music of Java. Rounder CD 5060.

Songs before Dawn: Gandrung Banyuwangi. Smithsonian Folkways SF 40055.

The Sultan's Pleasure: Javanese Gamelan and Vocal Music from the Palace of Yogyakarta. Music of the World CDT-116.

Bali

Bali: Gamelan and Kecak. Elektra Nonesuch Explorer Series CD 979204-4.

Gamelan Gong Kebyar, Bali. Elektra Nonesuch CD 79280-2.

Gamelan Music of Bali. Lyrichord LYRCD–7179.

Golden Rain: Gong Kebyar of Gunung Sari, Bali. Elektra Nonesuch CD 79219-2.

Kecak from Bali. Kecak Ganda Sari. Bridge BCD 9019.

Music of Bali: Gamelan Semar Pegulingan from the Village of Ketewel. Lyrichord LYRCD 7408.

Music of the Gamelan Gong Kebyar, Bali. Vital Records 401-2. 2 discs.

Indonesia

Music of Indonesia series, recorded by Philip Yampolsky. 20 CDs, each with extensive descriptive booklet. Smithsonian Folkways SF 40055 through SFW 40447.

Viewing

The JVC Video Anthology of World Music and Dance. 1990. Video recording. Edited by Fujii Tomoaki, with assistant editors Omori Yasuhiro and Sakurai Tetsuo, in collaboration with the National Museum of Ethnology (Osaka). Produced by Ichikawa Katsumori. Directed by Nakagawa Kunihiko and Ichihashi Yuji. Victor Company of Japan, Ltd., in collaboration with Smithsonian Folkways Recordings. Distributed by Rounder Records, Cambridge, Mass. 02140. 30 videocassettes plus guide.

- Volume 9 contains footage of Javanese shadow puppetry (poor quality), along with studio footage of Balinese *kecak* ("monkey chant") and Sundanese music (recorded in Japan).

- Volume 10 contains a variety of Balinese examples, recorded in Bali, mostly employing a *gamelan semar pegulingan* (even for contexts in which this ensemble is not appropriate).

Bali

Bali Beyond the Postcard. 1991. 16mm film and VHS video recording. Produced and directed by Nancy Dine, Peggy Stern, and David Dawkins. Distributed by Filmakers Library, New York, and by "Outside in July," 59 Barrow Street, New York, N.Y. 10014. *Gamelan* and dance in four generations of a Balinese family.

Releasing the Spirits: A Village Cremation in Bali. 1991 [1981]. VHS video recording. Directed by Patsy Asch, Linda Connor, et al. Distributed by Documentary Educational Resources, Watertown, Mass. Cremation rituals in a central Balinese village.

Java

Traditional Dances of Indonesia, Dances of Jogjakarta, Central Java: Langen Mandra Wanara. 1990. Video recording from 16mm film made in 1975. Directed and produced by William Heick. Distributed by University of California Extension Media Center, 2176 Shattuck Ave., Berkeley, Calif. 94704. Dance-opera presenting an episode from the Ramayana.

Traditional Dances of Indonesia, Dances of Surakarta, Central Java: Srimpi Anglir Mendung. 1990. Video recording from 16mm film made in 1976. Directed and produced by William Heick. Distributed by University of California Extension

Media Center, 2176 Shattuck Ave., Berkeley, Calif. 94704. Refined female court dance. (Ten additional video recordings from the same distributor present additional dances from Java, as well as dances from Bali and West Sumatra.)

Web Resources

- American Gamelan Institute: http://www.gamelan.org
  Home page with links to archived materials, musical examples, and other information pertaining to traditional and contemporary *gamelan* music, Javanese, Balinese, Sundanese, and experimental/international.

- Central Javanese Gamelan: http://www.medieval.org/music/world/java.html
  Introductory essay, followed by descriptions of some Central Javanese *gamelan* CDs.

- Dewa 19: http://dewa19.net
  In Indonesian; official Web site of rock group Dewa 19, led by Ahmad Dhani.

- Gamelan Hawaii: http://www.cba.hawaii.edu/remus/gamelan/home.htm
  University of Hawaii *gamelan* Web site; includes link to useful introductory article, "Towards an Appreciation of Javanese Gamelan," by Hardja Susilo.

- Indonesian Music: http://trumpet.sdsu.edu/M151/Indonesian_Music1a.html
  General introductory material on Javanese and Balinese gamelan music.

- Krakatau: http://www.krakatau.net
  In English; official Web site of Indonesian fusion group Krakatau, led by Dwiki Dharmawan.

- Musik Indonesia: http://www.edvos.demon.nl/midi-indonesia
  Links to various kinds of popular music in Indonesia.

- Northern Illinois University SEASite, Arts and Culture: http://www.seasite.niu.edu/Indonesian/Budaya_Bangsa
  Javanese *gamelan* and shadow puppetry.

- Tembang: http://www.tembang.com/
  Links to various kinds of music in Indonesia, mostly pop.

Latin America/Chile, Bolivia, Ecuador, Peru

John M. Schechter

Latin America is a kaleidoscope of cultural and ecological patterns, producing many distinctive regional lifeways. A continent and a half, it has more than twenty different countries in which Spanish, Portuguese, French, and dozens of Native American languages in hundreds of dialects are spoken. It is at once the majestic, beautiful Andes Mountains, the endless emptiness of the Peruvian-Chilean desert, and the lush rain forests of the huge Amazonian basin. Native American cultures that were not eradicated by Europeans and their diseases have in many cases retained certain distinctive languages, belief systems, dress, musical forms, and music rituals. Most Latin American cultures, though, share a common heritage of Spanish or Portuguese colonialism and American and European cultural influences. For instance, several ports in Colombia and Brazil served as major colonial centers for the importation of black slaves; Latin America remains a rich repository of African and African American music-cultural traditions, including rituals, musical forms and practices, and types of musical instruments.

In Latin American culture, mixture is the norm, not the exception. When you walk through the countryside of northern Andean Ecuador, for example, you hear a Spanish dialect borrowing many words from Quichua (*kee*-chooa), the regional Native American language. The local Quichua dialect, conversely, uses many Spanish words. South of Ecuador, in the high mountain regions of Peru, the harp is considered an indigenous instrument, although European missionaries and others in fact brought it to Peru. In rural areas of Atlantic coastal Colombia, musicians sing songs in Spanish, using Spanish literary forms, but these are accompanied by African-style drums and rhythms and by Amerindian flutes and rattles. In northern highland Ecuador, African-Ecuadorians perform the *bomba* (*bom*-ba), a type of song that features African American rhythms, Quichua Indian melodic and harmonic features, and Spanish language—with sometimes one or two Quichua words. Overall, it is hard to maintain strict cultural divisions because the intermingling of Iberian (Spanish and Portuguese), African, and Native American strains is so profound in the Latin American experience.

Salient Characteristics of Latin America ♪♪♪

- A continent and a half of more than twenty different countries with dozens of different languages, including Native American dialects.
- A diverse geography that includes the Andes Mountains, the Amazon basin, and the Peruvian-Chilean deserts.
- Merging cultures of Iberian (Spanish and Portuguese), African, and Native American cultures.
- A common heritage among Latin American cultures of Spanish/Portuguese colonialism, along with U.S., European, and Native American influences.
- Diversity and heritage reflected in enormous variety of regional and local musics.

When you first think of Latin American music, you might hear in your mind's ear the vibrancy of the rhythms in salsa. There is an enormous variety of beaten and shaken rhythm instruments, such as claves, bongos, congas, and maracas, both in salsa and throughout Latin America. In distinctive sizes and shapes, the guitar figures prominently in Latin American folk music. In Peru and Bolivia, for example, a type of guitar called the *charango* (cha-*ran*-go) may have as its body the shell of an armadillo. There are other types of Latin American music with which you might also be familiar, including bossa nova, calypso, and tango.

In this chapter, we take a close look at musics of four Latin American countries: Chile, Bolivia, Ecuador, and Peru. We shall study songs in both the Spanish language and the Quichua (or, Quechua) language—an indigenous tongue of the Andes, spoken by some six to eight million people in Bolivia, Peru, Ecuador, and Argentina. We shall listen to pieces by two duos and several ensembles, musics that are either notably traditional or markedly contemporary. The seven pieces speak eloquently, though, to their own cultures' political concerns, to their "social" forms of music making (Andean panpipe playing), to their histories and ecologies, or, in one case, to the composer's autobiography. A central theme in three instances is that of praise and esteem for one's beloved.

Chilean Nueva Canción: Víctor Jara / Inti Illimani

Víctor Jara was a great figure in the modern song movement, *Nueva Canción* (nu-*e*-va kan-*syon*), or "New Song," of Chile and, sometimes with different names, of all Latin America. *Nueva Canción* is a song movement through which people stand up for their own culture—for themselves as a people—in the face of oppression by a totalitarian government or in the face of cultural imperialism from abroad, notably the United States and Europe. It developed first in the Southern Cone of South America— Argentina, Chile, and Uruguay—during the 1950s and 1960s, and it has since spread throughout Latin America. As we know from our own history, the 1960s in particular witnessed violent upheavals. Latin America echoed the assassinations and urban violence in the United States: Nearly every country in South America, as well as Cuba and the Dominican Republic in the Caribbean, saw revolution, massacre, underground warfare, or other forms of violent social and political confrontation at that time. For a fuller discussion of the philosophy, political contexts, songs, composers, and ensembles of *Nueva Canción,* see Schechter 1999b:425–37. For now, let us look closely at one of Víctor Jara's most well-known compositions, "El aparecido" (1967), **CD 2, Track 7,** as interpreted here by the noted Chilean *Nueva Canción* ensemble, Inti Illimani (Quechua: "sun"; name of a mountain in Bolivia). The listening chart provides the full text of "El aparecido" (ehl a-pa-reh-*see*-doh) and illustrates the formal structure of this modern-day, composed Chilean *cueca* (*kweh*-ka).

When you listen to "El aparecido," you may be wondering about the metrical rhythm of the piece (recall the discussion of rhythm and meter, in Chapter 1). You may think that you hear the music at one moment in moderate 3/4 meter, *1-2-3, 1-2-3*—but at the next moment, in lively 6/8 meter, *1-2-3-4-5-6, 1-2-3-4-5-6.* This version of a traditional Chilean rhythm known as the *cueca* in fact juxtaposes both of those types of metrical rhythm, at the same time. When this occurs—and it happens in many types of Latin American folksong, musics heard from Mexico all the way down to Chile and in many countries in-between—it is referred to as *sesquialtera* metrical rhythm: roughly, the simultaneous feeling of 3/4 and 6/8 meters. This metrical-rhythmical ambiguity is the heart and soul of much, though not all, Hispanic-derived Latin American regional folk music. You'll hear it in Mexican *son huasteco,* in Colombian *bambuco,* in Ecuadorian *albazo,* in Peruvian *marinera,* in Argentinian *chacarera,* in Chilean/Bolivian *cueca,* and in many other genres as well.

When you look at the listening chart you may also wonder about the words major and minor key (or scale). Chapter 1 explained the concept of the major scale, with the example of the C Major scale built on the consecutive white keys of the piano. Specifically, it noted that the interval between each pitch is not the same. It spoke of this Euro-American major scale, but also of the Javanese *sléndro* and *pélog* scales and the Japanese *in* and *yo* scales. Different scale types reflect different organizing principles behind the relationships and sequence of their constituent pitches.

"El aparecido" uses variants of the minor scale as well as the major scale. The vocal stanzas and instrumental sections use two forms of the minor scale, while the refrain moves into different major keys, only to conclude on the minor home key. One will often encounter this mix of scales in traditional musics of the Andes region, including Chilean folk music; when Chilean *Nueva Canción* musicians compose contemporary interpretations of traditional musics, they reflect that cultural sensitivity to major and minor keys.

Note that in the listening chart the word *counterpoint* refers to combining two or more melodic parts. On the repeat of the fourth stanza ("*Hijo de la rebeldía*"), the voices divide, so that one group seems to "follow" the other, with the same text fragments, yet different melodic fragments; thus, we have an example of counterpoint—contrapuntal, or polyphonic, texture.

As you can see, the lyrics of "El aparecido" reflect the turbulence of the times. Written by Víctor Jara in 1967, "El aparecido" was dedicated "to

CD 2:7

"El aparecido" ("The Apparition") (3:34). Inti Illimani ensemble: Max Berrú, Horacio Durán, Jorge Coulon, José Miguel Camus, José Seves, Horacio Salinas. Monitor Presents *Inti-Illimani 2: La Nueva Cancion Chilena.* 1991.

Close Listening

"El aparecido" ("The Apparition")—Chilean *cueca*

Counter Number	Commentary
Introduction	
0:00	Ensemble enters in the song's minor home key, 6/8 meter. *Kena* (flute) plays melody and suggests the shape of the vocal stanzas to come.
1st stanza	
0:10	*Sesquialtera* meter. *Kena* "tail" repeats opening segment of the introduction. *Abre sendas por los cerros / Deja su huella en el viento,* He opens pathways through the mountains, / Leaves his mark on the wind, *El águila le da el vuelo / Y lo cobija el silencio.* The eagle gives him flight / And silence envelops him.
2nd stanza	
0:36	*Nunca se quejó del frío / Nunca se quejó del sueño.* Never has he complained of the cold, / Never has he complained of lack of sleep. *El pobre siente su paso / Y lo sigue como ciego.* The poor man senses his step / And follows him like a blind man.
Refrain	
0:58	Melody changes to a major key; concludes in minor. *¡Córrele, córrele, correlá, / Por aquí, por aquí, por allá.* Run, run, run, / Here, here, over there. *¡Córrele, córrele, correlá, / Córrele, que te van a matar,* Run, run, run, / Run or they'll kill you, *Córrele, córrele, correlá, / Córrele, que te van a matar,* Run, run, run, / Run or they'll kill you, *Córrele, córrele, correlá!* Run, run, run!
Instrumental interlude	
1:18	*Kena* repeats melody of introduction with first three pitches an octave higher.
3rd stanza	
1:29	Minor key. *Kena* "tail." *Su cabeza es rematada / Por cuervos con garra de oro:* His head is finished off / By ravens with talons of gold: *Como lo ha crucificado / La furia del poderoso.* Like the fury of the powerful has crucified him.
4th stanza	
1:57	Minor key. *Hijo de la rebeldía / Lo siguen veinte más veinte.* Son of rebellion / Twenty, and twenty more pursue him. *Porque regala su vida / Ellos le quieren dar muerte.* Because he offers his life / They want his death.

Counter Number	Commentary
Refrain	
2:17	Melody changes to major key; concludes in minor home key.
Instrumental interlude	
2:37	Minor key. *Kena* repeats melody of Introduction with first three pitches an octave higher.
4th stanza repeats	
2:48	Background voices sing stanza in counterpoint with soloist.
Refrain	
3:09	Major key. Concludes in the minor home key.

E.(Ch.)G."—Ernesto Che Guevara. Now famous in this interpretation by Inti Illimani, the piece speaks of this revolutionary figure's eluding his pursuers; the music reaching a climactic point in its chorus: "*¡Córrele, córrele, córrela; córrele, que te van a matar; córrele, córrele, córrela!*" ("Run, run, run; run, for they are going to kill you; run, run, run!") (Schechter 1999b:428–29).

As we have noted elsewhere, the 1950s to 1970s in Latin America was a period of violent upheaval, witnessing the Plaza de Mayo massacre in Buenos Aires, and subsequently the fall of Perón in Argentina (1955); the fall of Cuba's Batista government and the victorious Cuban Revolution (1959); the fall of the João Goulart government in Brazil (1964), beginning a fifteen-year hard-line era; the U.S. intervention in Santo Domingo (1965); an increase in guerrilla activity in Peru, Colombia, and Bolivia; the death of Ernesto Che Guevara in Bolivia (1967); the subsequent spread of guerrilla fighting in Central America and Venezuela, and the Tlatelolco massacre in Mexico (1968); and the victory of the Unidad Popular in Chile (1970), initiating three years of government under Salvador Allende, followed by the 1973 military coup (Schechter 1999b:428, citing Carrasco Pirard 1982:604).

Metaphor plays a major role in *Nueva Canción*. So, here, in "El aparecido," Guevara is depicted as a mythological figure ("*Abre sendas . . . en el viento*"), one of great power and respect ("*El águila le da el vuelo*"); one of mystery ("*lo cobija el silencio*"); and one pursued by many ("*Lo siguen veinte más veinte*") of the powerful, of the wealthy ("*Su cabeza es rematada / Por cuervos con garra de oro*"). "El aparecido" falls within an established Latin American tradition of praising in song individuals—often being pursued—whom some might consider outlaws, others heroes. Among the protagonists of the Mexico-Texas border *corrido* (ballad) tradition (pronounced ko-*rree*-do), one could point to "Gregorio Cortez," and to two songs about "Robin Hood" figures, "Joaquín Murieta" and "Heráclio Bernal" (Schechter 1999a:8–10); a Robin Hood figure of twentieth-century Argentina is Juan Bautista Bairoleto (Moreno Chá 1999:267–70).

Because of their political stance, Inti Illimani at one point had to leave Chile. They returned from Italy in 1988, after fifteen years in exile. In February 1994 they performed at the University of California at Berkeley. This concert showed how much the ensemble had evolved since a group of Santiago university students had created it in 1967. In addition to the familiar *Nueva Canción* panpipes, *charango,* and *kena* (Andean vertical notched flute; pronounced *ke*-na), the seven-member aggregate now incorporated instruments not native to Chile or to the Andes: hammered dulcimer and soprano saxophone. The ensemble's multi-instrumentalists now performed sophisticated, tailored arrangements, featuring contemporary, highly coloristic harmonizations of traditional Andean and Caribbean genres. To these points, Inti Illimani musicians have remarked that the ensemble's extended years in exile—half their total years of existence—have led them to more universal creative roots (González 1989:272–73). The group's repertoire in this highly polished performance was remarkably varied, showcasing the breadth of Latin American (if elaborately disguised) forms: hocketing panpipes (see the discussion of Bolivian *k'antu* next, in this chapter), Peruvian *wayno* (see the discussion of Peruvian *wayno* later in this chapter), Venezuelan *joropo* (see Schechter 2002:387–88), Chilean *cueca,* Ecuadorian *sanjuán* (see the discussion of Ecuadorian *sanjuán* later, in this chapter), "El aparecido," Cuban *son,* and Mexican *ranchera.* Inti Illimani toured the United States in fall 1995, performing in Nebraska, Michigan, Wisconsin, Missouri, Illinois, and Washington, D.C. In 2001–2002, the ensemble toured Italy, Spain, South America, Mexico, and North America.

Nueva Canción lives on as an international movement. It has traditional and regional roots but a modern and socially conscious musical style and message. It seeks to draw attention to the people—often the forgotten people—and to their struggles for human dignity.

Bolivian K'antu

Certain *Nueva Canción* performers such as Inti Illimani chose the *zampoña* (sam-*pon*-ya), or panpipes, among other traditional instruments, to symbolize their esteem for the native traditions of the Andes and neighboring regions. It is true that panpipes are widely known outside South America. Nevertheless, the depth of the panpipe tradition in South America is remarkable. Today, we can find a huge number of named varieties of panpipes among native peoples from Panama down to Peru, Bolivia, and Chile. In Peru and Bolivia, cultures dating back fifteen centuries knew and played panpipes of bamboo or clay.

Listen to "Kutirimunapaq" (koo-tee-ree-moo-*na*-pakh) (**CD 2, Track 8**) as performed by Ruphay, a Bolivian ensemble. They are playing *k'antu* (k-*an*-tu), a type of ceremonial panpipe music from the *altiplano,* or high plateau, of Peru-Bolivia. The word *k'antu* might be related to a widely known flower of Bolivia, the *kantuta,* or it might be derived from the Spanish word for song, *canto.* The listening guide provides the full text of "Kutirimunapaq" and illustrates the formal structure of this Bolivian *k'antu.*

CD 2:8

"Kutirimunapaq" (~"So That We Can Return") (3:51). *K'antu* of Bolivia. Performed by Ruphay. *Ruphay. Jach'a Marka,* 1982. Discos Heriba SLP 2212. Heriba Ltda. La Paz, Bolivia.

Close Listening

"Kutirimunapaq" (~"So That We Can Return")—Bolivian *k'antu*

Counter Number	Commentary

Introduction

0:00	*Wankaras* (drums) and *ch'inisku* (triangle) only enter. Unmetered, gradually increasing tempo that tapers off.

1st full cycle—A section

0:10	Full ensemble (multiple *zampoñas, wankaras; ch'inisku*).
0:26	Repeat.
	Characteristic rhythmic break just before cadence and start of repeat each time through.

B section

0:37	Full ensemble
	Characteristic rhythmic break just before cadence.
0:53	Repeat.
1:06	Cadence, moves directly into C section.

C section

1:07	Full ensemble.
1:12	Cadence (no break beforehand).
1:13	Immediate repeat.
1:19	Characteristic break at cadence, leading right back to beginning of A section and 2nd full cycle.

2nd full cycle—A section

1:20	Full ensemble (multiple *zampoñas, wankaras, ch'inisku*).
1:33	Characteristic rhythmic break just before cadence.
1:34	Repeat.

B section

1:47	Full ensemble.
2:01	Characteristic rhythmic break just before cadence.
2:02	Repeat.
2:16	Cadence moving directly into C section.

C section

2:16	Full ensemble.
2:21	Cadence (no rhythmic break beforehand) and immediate repeat.
2:27	Characteristic break at cadence, leading right back to beginning of A section and 3rd full cycle.

Third full cycle of A–C

2:29	A section.
2:55	B section.
3:25	C section.
3:31	Repeat.
3:38	Final cadence: *Wankaras* and *ch'inisku* play unmetered/accelerando motif similar to outset.

The entire piece is played three times. Sing some of the melody to get a feel for the rhythm and flow of this *zampoña* music. On a second hearing, the sound may seem richer to you than on the first; you hear a panpipe ensemble playing what seems to be the same melody at various pitch levels, one at an octave below the original pitch level, another a perfect fourth above that lower octave (a perfect fifth below the original octave).

"Kutirimunapaq" (Quechua: roughly, "so that we can return") is music of the Kallawaya people, who live on the eastern slope of the Bolivian Andes, north of Lake Titicaca, close to the Peruvian border. (In Peru and Bolivia the language is called Quechua; in Ecuador the dialects are called Quichua.) The Kallawaya *campesinos* (farmers, peasants; pronounced kam-pe-*see*-nos) live at different altitudes in the Charazani Valley—from 9,000 to 16,000 feet above sea level. Those at the lower elevations speak Quechua and cultivate potatoes, barley, and beans; at the upper elevations they speak Aymara and keep llamas, alpacas, and sheep. The Inkas adopted Quechua as their official language and spread it with them throughout their empire (1200–1533 C.E.). "Kutiri-munapaq" is a *k'antu* from the community of Niñokorin, at 11,000 feet.

The *k'antu* ensembles, for which the Charazani region is famous, each comprise twenty to thirty *zampoña*-playing dancers, who move in a circular pattern. Some of them simultaneously beat a large, double-headed drum called a *wankara*. The triangle (in Quechua, *ch'inisku*), which we hear in this example, is often present as well.

The Kallawaya play the panpipes in their dry season, which lasts roughly from June to September; during the rainy season, which lasts from November to at least late February, they play transverse flutes (played horizontally, like the Western silver flute) or duct flutes (played vertically; constructed like a recorder). The preference on the altiplano for duct flutes during the rainy season may be related to the belief that their clear sound attracts rain and prevents frost, which are both necessary for growing crops.

Our ensemble consists of *zampoñas* of different sizes but with the same basic construction, in terms of numbers of tubes. Each musical register is represented by one named pair of panpipes, consisting of an *ira* (*ee*-ra) set of pipes (considered in the Bolivian altiplano to embody the male principle, and serving as the leader) and an *arca* (*ar*-ka) set of pipes (considered to embody the female principle and serving as the follower), which together form a single instrument. In our context, the *ira* set has six pipes and the *arca* set has seven; we may refer to this type as 6/7-tubed. The different-sized instruments play the same melody, which results in the rich musical fabric of parallel octaves, fifths, and fourths.

There are at least two especially interesting aspects of this music. One is the doubling of the melodic line; the other is the way a melody is produced. Doubling the melody at a fixed interval has occurred at other times, in other places. One was in Europe, during the Middle Ages. There, by the ninth century C.E., one-line Christian liturgical chant was being accompanied either by one lower part at the octave below or by a lower part at the fourth or fifth below. Another alternative augmented the two-voice complex to three or four voices by doubling one or both lines at the octave. Thus, early medieval Europe had musical textures with parallel octaves, fourths, and fifths very similar in intervallic structure (if not in rhythm) to what we hear in twentieth-century Bolivian *k'antu.* In twentieth-century Africa, songs in parallel fourths and fifths are found among groups that have the tradition of pentatonic, or five-pitch, songs, such as the Gogo people of Tanzania (Nketia 1974:163).

Many peoples have used, and continue to use, the performance practice of hocketing, whereby the melody is dispersed among two or more voices or instruments—that is, when one sounds, the others do not. Performing music in hocket is a uniquely communal way of making music: You cannot play the entire melody yourself—you need one or more partners to do it with you. In Africa the hocketing technique appears, among instrumental traditions, in the flute parts of Ghanaian Kasena *jongo* dance music, in the *akadinda* xylophone music of the Baganda of Uganda, and in several flute and gourd-trumpet traditions elsewhere in East Africa and in Southern Africa; for vocal traditions, hocketing can be heard in the singing of the San (Bushmen) of Southern Africa (Cooke 1998:601; Kaemmer 1998:703, 705; Koetting 1992:94–97). Certain European music of the thirteenth and fourteenth centuries had several parts but used notes and rests in a way that effectively divided the melody line between two voice parts: as one sounded, the other was silent. A hiccup effect was thus created (*hoquetus* is Latin for hiccup and the likely derivation of the term). Hocketing with panpipes appears closer in time and space to our modern Bolivian music. In Panama, the Kuna Indians play six-tubed *guli* panpipes. Each person holds one tube, with the melody distributed among all six players. The Kuna also play *gammu burui* panpipes. Each fourteen-tube set is bound into two groups, or rafts, of seven tubes (two rafts of four-tube and three-tube size, held side by side), with the melody distributed between the two seven-tube players in hocket technique (Smith 1984: 156–59, 167–72).

As among the Kuna, in Bolivian *k'antu* the hocket procedure is integral to the overall musical fabric. In fact, hocketing is actually required by the way these panpipes are constructed. Although there are types of altiplano panpipes with from three to seventeen tubes, a widely used type is 6/7-tubed, discussed earlier. This panpipe type can be tuned in e minor (or in another perspective, G major); this type of *zampoña* accommodates European-derived scales. Not all *zampoñas* of the altiplano are tuned in this diatonic manner; many have different scales. This basic tuning is nonetheless widely found among both Quechua-speaking and Aymara-speaking peoples.

As pointed out in the listening chart, the formal structure of this performance of "Kutirimunapaq" is ABC, each section being repeated, then the entire piece repeated twice, for a total of three times. This is a characteristic structure for the Bolivian *k'antu,* accommodating the continuous dancing that goes with the music making. Counting the number of different notes that sound in this particular *k'antu* we find that, within the octave, five notes predominate: C#, E, F#, G#, and B. Then, the C# and E come back in the upper octave. Note that C#, not E, serves as the tonic pitch in this case. There is one more note used (D#), but this comes in only at the end of sections A, B, and C—once each time, just prior to the final cadence, or stopping point, itself marked by a rhythmic "break," in "Kutirimunapaq."

This *k'antu* is primarily five-pitch, or pentatonic. Many traditional dance musics in the Andes region are similarly pentatonic, though certainly not all of them. "Kutirimunapaq" is strongly rhythmic, with the steady pound of the *wankara* supporting the beat. Andean dance music, from Bolivia up to Ecuador, has this powerful rhythmic cast, underscoring its dance function.

Hocketing panpipes, with rhythmic melodies played in parallel fifths and octaves and with strong, steady rhythm on a large drum, begin to distinguish this Bolivian altiplano stream of Latin American music. In turn, the evocation of Native American cultures such as this high-Andean one, through use of Andean instruments, begins to demarcate *Nueva Canción*. As we have seen, New Song is not only nostalgic but also politically committed and international. Above all, it speaks of and on behalf of the people—characteristically, the forgotten people. We now turn our attention north of Chile, Bolivia, and Peru to a nation of many other unsung (or less-sung) individuals and peoples, a country itself frequently overlooked in discussions of Latin America: Ecuador.

The Quichua of the Northern Andes of Ecuador

We can best appreciate the traditional nature of northern Ecuadorian Quichua music by knowing something of the traditional setting in which Quichua live. The musicians we shall be listening to have traditionally lived in *comunas* (ko-*mu*-nas), or small clusters of houses, on the slopes of Mount Cotacachi, one of several volcanoes in the Ecuadorian Andes. These *comunas* lie outside the town of Cotacachi, in Imbabura Province (see the map at the beginning of the chapter). The Quichua spoken in Cotacachi-area *comunas* was spoken there four hundred years ago. Today in Ecuador more than one million people speak the language.

The agriculture and material culture of the Andes around Cotacachi are also traditional. In this rich green countryside dotted with tall eucalyptus, at 8,300 to 9,700 feet above sea level, maize has been the principal cultivated crop for hundreds of years. Quichua homes typically have one room, often with a covered patio, both with dirt floor (Figure 8.1). Regional Quichua homes have been constructed this way for four hundred years. Today, homes made of concrete block are replacing the older type of dwelling.

Salient Characteristics of the Quichua and their Music

- A traditional people who share a common language, agricultural life, and similar material culture.
- Live in small clusters of houses (*comunas*) on the slopes of the northern Andes of Ecuador.
- The importance of walking is both real (a vital communication and physical link) and symbolic in the culture, as reflected in song texts.
- *Sanjuanes*: the traditional song of harpists and musical timekeepers; played inside and out of Quichua communities at weddings, private Masses, and children's wakes.

John M. Schechter

Figure 8.1
Home of Mama Ramona and Miguel Armando in the *comuna* of Tikulla, outside Cotacachi. May 1980.

Styles of dress have also remained basically the same since the sixteenth century. Everyone covers his or her head to protect it from the intense heat and light of the near-vertical sun at midday (Cotacachi is almost precisely on the Equator). Women wear cloths, and men wear hats. Quichua women wear embroidered blouses, over which they drape shawls (in Quichua, *fachalina*). They secure their two skirts, one blue and one white, with two woven belts: a wider, inner belt, called the *mama chumbi* (mother belt) and a narrower, outer belt, called the *wawa chumbi* (child belt). Designed in this region, these belts were traditionally woven on home back-strap looms by Quichua families in various *comunas,* and they usually carried the names of Imbabura towns. Men and boys have traditionally worn a white or blue shirt, white pants, and dark *poncho,* though today in Imbabura you will see Quichua teenagers wearing English-language sweatshirts and jeans. Any large gathering of Quichua, such as for Saturday market or Palm Sunday processions, is still largely a sea of blue and white. In Figure 8.2 we see three generations within the same family. The grandfather wears traditional dress; his adult son retains the white sandals, white shirt, pants, and hat; his grandson wears Western-influenced clothes.

Among Cotacachi Quichua, a strong sense of community arises from a common and regional dialect, a common dress, and common aspects of material culture. Quichua eat the same diet of beans and potatoes, grown in their own plots. They gather together regularly for weekly markets, for periodic community work projects (*mingas*), and for fiestas—such as a child's wake (Schechter 1983, 1994a) or a wedding (Andrade Albuja and Schechter 2004).

In 1980 few Cotacachi Quichua owned vehicles; by 1990 a few community leaders possessed new pickup trucks. In any case, Quichua homes on Cotacachi's slopes are for the most part not located on roads but interspersed along a network of footpaths called *chaki ñanes* (*cha*-ki *nyan*-es).

Figure 8.2
Three generations of Quichua men.
May 1980.

Without telephones, Quichua families have traditionally communicated only by foot, along *chaki ñanes;* these paths bear the weight of Quichua women carrying infants, brush, and food to and from market, and of Quichua men carrying potatoes, milled grain, or perhaps a harp (see Figure 8.3). For all Quichua, the way around the slopes on *chaki ñanes* is second nature.

The Musical Tradition: *Sanjuán*

The common language, dress, material culture, and daily labor all find a musical echo in *sanjuán.* The term *sanjuán* (san-*hooan*) arose at least as early as 1860. At that time, it referred to either a type of song played at the festival

Figure 8.3
Chaki ñan (Ecuadorian footpath).
May 1980.

Figure 8.4
Harpist Raúl, playing his Imbabura harp. Ecuador, March 1980.

John M. Schechter

of St. John (San Juan) the Baptist held in June or a type of dance performed at that festival. Today, the instrument that Cotacachi Quichua often use to perform *sanjuán* is the harp without pedals, often referred to in English as the diatonic harp because it is usually tuned to one particular scale and cannot be changed quickly to another. Reflecting their other deep-rooted traditions, Quichua have been playing the harp in the Ecuadorian highlands for hundreds of years; in the eighteenth century, it was the most common instrument in the region (Recio [1773] 1947:426). The harp's popularity in the Andes is not limited to Ecuador; recall that in the Peruvian highlands, it is so widespread among Quechua that it is considered a native instrument. Brought from Europe initially by several different groups of missionaries, especially the Jesuits, and even by the first conquistadors, the harp has been in Latin America for more than four hundred years.

The Imbabura harp is common only in Imbabura Province (Figure 8.4). It appears as an oddity among harpists in central highland Ecuador, where musicians play a larger instrument. The type of harp Raúl plays in Figure 8.4 is made of cedar and uses wooden nails. The sound emanates through three circular holes on the top of the soundbox; they are consistently found in the pattern shown in Figure 8.5, on either side of the column, or pole, that connects the neck to the soundbox.

Looking at Raúl's harp, you may think that the instrument has an unusual shape, compared with Western harps with which you may be familiar. The Imbabura harp's column is straight but short, giving the instrument a low "head," or top. Its soundbox is distinctively arched, wide, and deep. On older harps in this region, bull's-hoof glue was used. The tuning pegs are made of iron or wood. The single line of strings is typically a combination

Figure 8.5
Schematic diagram showing position of sound holes in an Imbabura harp.

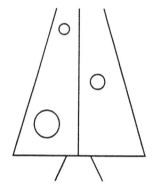

CD 2:9

"Muyu muyari warmigu" ("Please Return, Dear Woman") (4:20). Performed by Efraín, harp; Rafael, voice and golpe. Field recording by John M. Schechter, inside a schoolhouse in a *comuna* on the slopes of Mt. Cotacachi, October 13, 1990.

of gut, possibly nylon, and steel. The gut strings—used for the bass and middle registers—used to be made by the Quichua themselves from the cut, washed, dried, and twisted intestinal fibers of sheep, dogs, cats, or goats. Sometimes musicians use nylon strings for the middle register, or range, of notes. The steel strings, closest to the performer, play the treble register, in which the melody line is articulated. Once again relying on their environment for necessary materials, Quichua musicians may use the leg bone of the sheep (Quichua: *tullu*, "bone") to turn the tuning pegs on the harp neck. This Imbabura harp is a descendant of sixteenth- and seventeenth-century Spanish harps, as shown by shared features of tuning, construction, configuration, and stringing. The Imbabura harp has remained essentially unchanged in appearance for one hundred to two hundred years, and possibly longer (Schechter 1992).

Let us now look at **CD 2, Track 9**: the *sanjuán* "Muyu muyari warmigu" ("Please Return, Dear Woman"; pronounced *moo*-yoo moo-*yah*-ree war-*mee*-goo), sometimes referred to as "Chayamuyari warmigu" ("Come Here, Indeed, Dear Woman"). This performance is by the highly esteemed Cotacachi-area harpist, Efraín, together with one of his favored singers, Rafael. Having worked with Efraín ten years earlier, in the environs of Cotacachi, I was pleased to renew our acquaintanceship in 1990. We met to plan the recording session, which would be held in a classroom of the same primary school on Cotacachi's slopes at which my wife and I had resided, from October 1979 through April 1980; this stereo recording of "Muyu" and other pieces for harp and voice took place on October 13, 1990.

Harpists play the higher, or treble strings (treble clef part) with their stronger hand; the lower, or bass, strings (bass clef part) with their weaker hand. Efraín, left-handed, plays treble with the left hand, bass with the right hand (Figure 8.6).

In general, the form of "Muyu muyari warmigu" is typical of Cotacachi Quichua *sanjuanes*. It is fundamentally a repetitive form, in which one or two different phrases are perhaps irregularly inserted into an otherwise similar phrase pattern. In *sanjuán*, the main motive predominates; this is the one you hear the most, which I refer to as A phrases in "Muyu." These main motives are the melodies one identifies with particular *sanjuanes*. The *sanjuán* phrase often lasts eight beats, and the rhythm of the first half of the

John M. Schechter

Figure 8.6
Rafael (tapping the *golpe*) and Efraín (playing the Imbabura harp), during the recording (CD 2, Track 9). Mt. Cotacachi, Ecuador, 1990.

phrase is often identical, or nearly identical, to the rhythm of the second half; we can call this phrase structure, then, isorhythmic—meaning "equal rhythm," or the "same rhythm." In "Muyu" the rhythm of the first half of the A phrase is Ta Ta Ta-Ta, Ta Ta Ta Ta; and the rhythm of the second half of the phrase is exactly the same. The listening guide provides the full text of "Muyu" and illustrates the formal structure. *Sanjuanes* are most often in double-couplets: one two-line verse is stated, then immediately repeated; then comes either another double-couplet or a harp interlude.

Close Listening

CD 2:9

"Muyu muyari warmigu" *("Please Return, Dear Woman")*—Ecuadorian highland Quichua *sanjuán*

Counter Number	Commentary

Introduction

| 0:00 | Harp plays seven A phrases, then two B phrases. |

1st double-couplet

0:44	Vocal and harp.
	Muyu muyari warmigu / Muyu muyari payagu.
	Please return, dear woman / Please return, dear "old lady."
	Muyu muyari warmigu / Muyu muyari payagu.
	Please return, dear woman / Please return, dear "old lady."

2nd double-couplet

0:52	Vocal and harp.
	Kambaj shayashka puistuka / Sisagullami viñashka.
	The place in which you've stood / Just a dear flower has grown.
	(Couplet repeats.)

Instrumental Interlude

| 1:01 | Harp plays six A phrases, then two B phrases. |

1st double-couplet repeats

| 1:37 | Vocal and harp. |

2nd double-couplet repeats, modified

1:45	Vocal and harp.
	Kambaj shayashka puistupi / Sisagullami viñashka.
	The place in which you've stood / Just a dear flower has grown.
	(Couplet repeats.)

Instrumental interlude

| 1:54 | Harp plays five A phrases, then two B phrases, then one A phrase. |

3rd double-couplet

2:30	Vocal and harp.
	Llakiwanguichu warmigu / Juyawanguichu warmigu?
	Will you be sad, to me, dear woman? / Or will you be loving, to me, dear woman?
	(Couplet repeats.)

2nd double-couplet repeats, modified

2:38	Vocal and harp.
	Kambaj shayashka puistupi / Sisagullami viñashka.
	The place in which you've stood / Just a dear flower has grown.
	(Couplet repeats.)

Counter Number	Commentary

Instrumental interlude

2:47	Harp plays two A phrases, then two B phrases, then six A phrases, then two B phrases.

1st double-couplet repeats, modified

3:41	Vocal and harp. *Muyu muyari warmigu / Muyu muyari urpigu.* Please return, dear woman / Please return, dear turtle dove. (Couplet repeats.)

2nd double-couplet, modified

3:50	Vocal and harp. *Kambaj shayashka puistupi / Sisagullami viñashka.* The place in which you've stood / Just a dear flower has grown. (Couplet repeats.)

Instrumental ending

3:59	Harp plays three A phrases leading to final chord. Words spoken at end by John Schechter: "*Diusílupagui, maistrugukuna; Alimi llujshirka; disílupa'i.*" "Thank you, esteemed maestros; it came out well; thank you."

As you can hear and see on the chart, the A phrase predominates in this song. The consecutive A phrases (by harp alone and by harp and voice) are varied by two B phrases and harp interludes. Most *sanjuanes* follow this general pattern, although perhaps less regularly, with A phrases predominating and sometimes without any B phrases at all. The A phrases are supported largely by the major chord, while concluding on its relative minor. This scheme of harmony—notably the "bimodality" of a constant alternation between the major and its relative minor key—is characteristic of northern Ecuadorian highland *sanjuán,* as well as many other Andean traditional musics. The isorhythm we spoke of earlier is a regular feature of northern highland Ecuadorian Quichua *sanjuanes.* Some combination of sixteenth-eighth-sixteenth, and two eighths is characteristic of most *sanjuanes.* In the "Muyu" rhythm, Ta Ta Ta-Ta, Ta Ta Ta Ta, the first two Ta syllables correspond to two eighth-notes, the Ta-Ta to sixteenth-eighth, and the next Ta to another sixteenth—while the last three Ta's correspond to two eighths, then a quarter-note. Thus, the careful listener can often identify a Quichua *sanjuán* by the presence of these rhythm-kernels.

It is always interesting to observe how oral tradition works in traditional cultures. Here you will find three comparable segments of "Muyu," all performed by regional Quichua musicians. The first was recorded on December 28, 1979, by the solo singer, César, who was then twelve years old. The second was recorded on September 16, 1990, eleven years later, by the singer-guitarist, Segundo "Galo" Maigua Pillajo, the composer of the *sanjuán* "Ilumán tiyu," which we discuss next in this chapter. Finally, the third is our "Muyu," performed on October 13, 1990. Musically, all three performances share roughly the same A phrase with which we are now familiar. However, textually, the first and second double-couplets show some interesting variations, as follows:

December 28, 1979 version:

Chayamuyari warmiku	Come here, indeed, dear woman (or, wife)
Chayamuyari warmiku,	Come here, indeed, dear woman,
Chayamuyari warmiku	Come here, indeed, dear woman
Chayamuyari warmiku,	Come here, indeed, dear woman,
Kampak purishka llaktaka	The community you've walked
Sumakllamari rikurin,	Appears just beautiful, indeed,
Kampak purishka llaktaka	The community you've walked
Sumakllamari rikurin,	Appears just beautiful, indeed,

September 16, 1990 version:

Kampak shayashka pushtuka	The place in which you've stood
Sumbrallamari rikurin,	Appears just shady, indeed,
Kampak shayashka pushtuka	The place in which you've stood
Sumbrallamari rikurin,	Appears just shady, indeed,
Muyu muyari nigragu	Please return, dear dark woman
Muyu muyari payagu,	Please return, dear "old lady,"
Muyu muyari nigragu	Please return, dear dark woman
Muyu muyari payagu,	Please return, dear "old lady,"

October 13, 1990 version:

Muyu muyari warmigu	Please return, dear woman
Muyu muyari payagu,	Please return, dear "old lady,"
Muyu muyari warmigu	Please return, dear woman
Muyu muyari payagu,	Please return, dear "old lady,"
Kambaj shayashka puistuka	The place in which you've stood
Sisagullami viñashka,	Just a dear flower has grown,
Kambaj shayashka puistuka	The place in which you've stood
Sisagullami viñashka,	Just a dear flower has grown,

We can see several interesting things here. First, every line is eight syllables long, a form the performers must traditionally follow. Quichua performers of *sanjuán* operate under this oral-traditional principle, known as *formulaic expression,* or "a group of words which is regularly employed under the same metrical conditions to express a given essential idea." (Lord [1960]1978:4, quoted in Schechter 1996:248). Second, each double-couplet equates to eight musical (quarter-note) beats. The melody proceeds sequentially, the first 4 beats—corresponding to one eight-syllable line—winding down to the fifth scale degree, or step, of the minor key, in our "Muyu" version falling on the "-gu" of "warmigu," the last 4 beats continuing the twisting descent to take the next eight-syllable line down to the lower home-note of the key, falling on the "-gu" of "payagu." Finally, the lyrics reflect what we call semantic parallelism: That is, a couplet like this one often has the two lines nearly identical, with only a small word-shift, in the second line. For example, "Please return, dear woman" is followed by "Please return, dear 'old lady.'" Ballad scholars call this incremental repetition; such repetition facilitates transmission via oral tradition, because the near-repetition of a line means that one does have to remember so much. Young César's version actually has identical lines in the first couplet.

This is also a love song; a major theme of all the lyrics is praise for one's beloved. Many traditional songs throughout Latin America speak to the beauty of, and general admiration for, the women of a man's home region (for more, see Schechter 1999a:4–7). Hence, in "Muyu," we read, basically: that place in which you've stood/walked—been, appears beautiful/shady/produces a flower. Finally, we can substitute the verbs for each other, as in: come here (*chayamuyari*) and return (*muyu muyari*). In short, we have, in "Muyu," a carefully structured, entirely traditional, package of oral tradition: it is comprised of rather strict rules having to do with the song's subject matter, number of syllables, verb interchangeability, musical isorhythm in an eight-beat phrase, and parallelism in the text.

A Classic *Sanjuán*

At least one Imbabura Quichua *sanjuán* is a classic in its highland region: "Ilumán tiyu" ("Man from Ilumán"; pronounced ee-lu-*mahn tee*-yoo). This popular *sanjuán* was composed by Segundo "Galo" Maigua Pillajo, a Quichua composer-guitarist-singer of the Imbabura village of Ilumán. Galo Maigua's *sanjuán* compositions are often motivated by autobiographical forces. His fame among Imbabura Quichua is attested to by wide acknowledgment of his highly popular *sanjuanes;* by the high local demand for his ensemble, Conjunto Ilumán; and by their having produced, by 1990, a commercial cassette.

My fieldwork in 1990 in Imbabura brought to light the fact that *sanjuán* often takes on the nature of a ballad, even in instances where that fact is not immediately obvious. The thoughts of a *sanjuán* text typically express the essence of a large story, making the *sanjuán* a highly distilled ballad form, the synoptic character of the text being in keeping with the elliptical character of Andean poetry dating back to the times of the Inkas. The ballad nature of "Ilumán tiyu"—the story behind the *sanjuán*—is not at all obvious. We'll go into this enigma a bit later, but for now, let us listen to "Ilumán tiyu." In the village of Ilumán, in the home of a local policeman, I recorded the composer, Galo Maigua (Figure 8.7), singing "Ilumán tiyu" and playing guitar together with his Conjunto Ilumán, on October 27, 1990 **(CD 2, Track 10)**. The listening chart provides the full text of "Ilumán tiyu" and illustrates the formal structure. Note that "AI" means the instrumental playing of the A phrase and "AV" means the vocal version; "II" signifies Introduction, or Interlude, on the home chord.

CD 2:10

"Ilumán tiyu" ("Man from Ilumán") (3:18). Composed by Segundo "Galo" Maigua Pillajo. *Sanjuán* of Ecuador. Performed by "Galo," guitar and vocal, with the Quichua ensemble Conjunto Ilumán. Field recording by John Schechter at the home of a local policeman, village of Ilumán, Imbabura, Ecuador, October 1990.

Figure 8.7

Members of the Quichua ensemble Conjunto Ilumán. Ilumán, Imbabura Province, Ecuador, 1990. Composer Galo Maigua, with guitar, stands at the far right.

John M. Schechter

The symmetries/balance, here, are prodigious: three vocal statements and three B statements; four Intro/Interludes and four instrumental statements; the consecutive pattern, AV-B-AI enunciated three times; the consecutive, overlapping larger pattern, II-AV-B-AI-II occurring twice—within itself being framed by the II statements. In sum, one finds a distinctive cohesiveness—strongly reinforced by the Ta-Ta, Ta Ta Ta Ta Ta Ta; Ta-Ta, Ta Ta Ta Ta Ta Ta eight-beat isorhythm, and by the rising, then falling (archlike), melodic shape to the eight-beat A phrase.

What had never been comprehensible since my 1980 research, when I recorded numerous versions of "Ilumán tiyu" in the environs of Cotacachi, was the significance of the lyrics. When I was informed that Galo Maigua was in fact the composer of this *sanjuán*, I tried, during a visit to his Ilumán home on September 30, 1990, to learn what might lie behind words that seem merely a statement that the man singing and speaking is an *indígena* from Ilumán.

Galo Maigua described the tale behind the text. He told me that before he composed "Ilumán tiyu" he had become extremely ill with tuberculosis; the condition of his lungs had deteriorated, and he believed he was about to die. Although during 1972–1973 wanderings through the *comunas* around Cotacachi he had sung the melody to a variety of words (Galo says he composes by first hearing a melody and later setting a text), he now determined that he would like everyone—be they young woman or old woman, for example—to dance to this, his song, after his death. In effect, "Ilumán tiyu" became Galo's final statement of his identity to posterity: "I"—the man singing, speaking—am a man from Ilumán; remember me by remembering my music: "Dance to my song." In sum, what appeared to the uninformed listener to be innocuous words came, on greater understanding, to have profound import for a composer believing himself to be on his deathbed.

Close Listening   CD 2:10

"Ilumán tiyu" ("Man from Ilumán")—Quichua *sanjuán*

Counter Number	Commentary	Form
Introduction		
0:00	Violin outlines home chord four times.	II
0:09	*Kenas* and violin play the principal melody of "Ilumán tiyu"—four A phrases.	AI
0:27	Violin outlines home chord four times.	II
Quichua language double-couplets		
0:36	Vocalists sing the two double-couplets to four A phrases. Violin plays in harmony.	AV
	A *Ilumán tiyu cantanmi, / Ilumán tiyu nijunmi.*	
	The man [not uncle] from Ilumán sings, / The man from Ilumán is saying.	
	A *Ilumán tiyu cantanmi, / Ilumán tiyu nijunmi.*	
	The man from Ilumán sings, / The man from Ilumán is saying.	
	A *Sultira kashpa paya kashpa, / Ñuka tunupi bailapai.*	
	Being a young [unmarried] woman, [or an] old woman, Dance to my song.	
	A *Sultira kashpa paya kashpa, / Ñuka tunupi bailapai.*	
	Being a young woman, old woman, / Dance to my song.	
Interlude		
0:55	*Kenas* and violin play two B phrases.	B
1:04	Violin plays two A phrases.	AI
1:13	*Kenas* and violin play two A phrases.	AI
1:23	Violin outlines tonic chord, four times.	II
	Musician shouts, *"Kushi, kushiguta!"* ("Real happy!").	
The Spanish-language double-couplets		
1:32	Vocalists sing the two Spanish-language double-couplets to four A phrases. Violin plays in harmony.	AV
	A *Este es el indio de Ilumán, / El que canta (canto)* sanjuanito,*	
	This is the indígena of Ilumán, / He who sings sanjuán,	
	A *Este es el indio de Ilumán, / El que canta (canto)* sanjuanito,*	
	This is the indígena of Ilumán, / He who sings sanjuán,	
	A *Para que bailen toditos, / Para que bailen toditas.*	
	So that all men might dance, / So that all women might dance.	
	A *Para que bailen toditos, / Para que bailen toditas.*	
	So that all men might dance, / So that all women might dance.	
	**I sing, meaning the composer	
Interlude		
1:50	Violin plays two B phrases.	B
2:00	*Kenas* and violin play the principal melody of "Ilumán tiyu"—four A phrases.	AI
2:18	Violin outlines home chord four times. ("¡Ahora, tshhh!")	II
Repeat Quichua language double-couplets		
2:27	Double-couplets sung to four A phrases, the violin playing in harmony.	AV
Conclusion		
2:46	*Kenas* and violin play two B phrases.	B
2:55	*Kenas* and violin play the principal melody of "Ilumán tiyu"—four A phrases.	AI

If, as we have noted, II stands for Introduction/Interlude, AI for A phrase played by instruments, AV for A phrase vocalized by the ensemble, and B for B phrase, the formal structure of Galo Maigua's composition, "Ilumán tiyu," comes out to be as follows:

II / AI / II / AV / B / AI / II / AV / B / AI / II / AV / B / AI

Used with permission of Galo Maigua.

Spanish speakers will note that the intermingling of Spanish and Quichua words appears prominently in this *sanjuán.* Moreover, the verse *"Este es el indio de Ilumán, / El que canta sanjuanito"* is a rough translation of the first, critically important, verse; Galo Maigua commented to me that a major area radio station had prompted him to produce the parallel text in Spanish. Some of his other *sanjuanes,* such as "Antonio Mocho" and "Rusita Andranga," share the distilled-ballad character of "Ilumán tiyu." Both of these *sanjuanes,* along with "Ilumán tiyu," appear on the commercial cassette *Elenita Conde,* by Conjunto Ilumán; the cassette was mastered in Otavalo and mass-produced in Bogotá, Colombia, somewhat prior to 1990.

Efraín and Rafael, Segundo "Galo" Maigua Pillajo and his Conjunto Ilumán colleagues, and hundreds of other Quichua musicians in the Otavalo Valley, Imbabura Province, are not the only regional stakeholders in the genre that is northern Ecuadorian highland *sanjuán. Sanjuán* can also be heard in area mestizo households, and, a few hours up the Pan American highway towards the Colombia border, in African-Ecuadorian gatherings. The lesson here, is that a prominent regional music can trump racial and cultural barriers, establishing itself firmly in a region with different cultural signatures therein. Let us take a closer look at the musicians up the road, in Chota.

African-Ecuadorian Music of the Chota River Valley

On October 27, 1979, I met Germán Congo, the excellent lead guitarist of the ensemble Conjunto Rondador (the *rondador* is a single-rank panpipe of Ecuador) at one of their performances in Ibarra, the capital of Imbabura Province. Germán invited me to visit him and his musician-brothers in the Chota Valley. On March 1, 1980, my friend Don Valerio, my wife, Janis, and I journeyed to Chota. This was the first of several visits to Chota and Ibarra, in 1980 and again in 1990, in which my research focused on the musical artistry of the Congo brothers, their colleague Milton Tadeo, and their fellow Chota musicians (Schechter 1994b).

When we think of Latin American regions that have large populations of African Americans, Ecuador does not usually come to mind. Yet as much as 25 percent of the country's population is African Ecuadorian. They are heavily concentrated in coastal Esmeraldas Province, which neighbors Imbabura Province. The first Africans arrived in Ecuador in the sixteenth century, after which Jesuit missionaries brought in large numbers of African slaves to work on plantations both on the coast and in the central highlands: Indigenous laborers were hard to find in some areas and unwilling to serve as slaves in others. The relatively small pocket of approximately fifteen thousand African Ecuadorians in the Chota Valley, comprising ten to fifteen small villages, has an uncertain origin. The most widely accepted view is that the African Ecuadorians of the Chota Valley are descended from slaves held by the Jesuits on their plantations in the highlands (Lipski 1987:157–58).

The best-known musicians in the Chota Valley, in the 1980s and 1990s, were the guitarist-composer-singers Germán, Fabián, and Eleuterio Congo and their colleague Milton Tadeo. Twenty-five years ago they played mostly around their home village of Carpuela; by 1990 they were regional celebrities with regular weekend performances in local villages, on the coast, and in

Figure 8.8
Grupo Ecuador de los Hermanos Congo y Milton Tadeo. Germán Congo plays *requinto* guitar, Fabián Congo and Milton Tadeo guitars, Eleuterio Congo the *bomba* drum, and Ermundo Mendes León the metal *güiro*. Imbabura, Ecuador, 1990.

nearby Colombia. As of October 1990 they had recorded six long-playing records within seven years. The Congo brothers are the third generation of composer-performers in their family.

On October 21, 1990—more than ten years after I had first worked with them, Fabián, Germán, and Eleuterio Congo, together with Milton Tadeo and colleague Ermundo Mendes León, performed "Me gusta la leche" ("I Like Milk"; pronounced meh *goo*-sta la *leh*-cheh), heard here on **CD 2, Track 11**. At this time, the full ensemble identified themselves as "Grupo Ecuador de los Hermanos Congo y Milton Tadeo" (Ecuador Ensemble of the Congo Brothers and Milton Tadeo). We made the stereo recording in a community house near Germán's home, close by the Imbabura Provincial capital, Ibarra. Germán played lead guitar (*requinto* guitar), Fabián and Milton both played guitar and sang in duet, Eleuterio played the *bomba* (the Chota-area double-headed drum held between the knees and played with the hands), and Ermundo Mendes León played the *güiro*, a scraper (see Figures 8.8 and 8.9). The listening chart provides the full text of "Me gusta la leche" and illustrates the formal structure of this highland African-Ecuadorian *sanjuán*.

 CD 2:11

"Me gusta la leche" ("I Like Milk") (2:32). Performed by Germán Congo, lead guitar (*requinto*); Fabián Congo and Milton Tadeo, vocals and guitars; Ermundo Mendes León, *güiro*. Field Recording by John M. Schechter, outside Ibarra, Imbabura, Ecuador, October 21, 1990.

Figure 8.9
(Left to right) Eleuterio Congo, Milton Tadeo, Fabián Congo, John Schechter, Germán Congo, and Ermundo Mendes León. Outside the house of Germán Congo, Imbabura, Ecuador, 1990.

John M. Schechter

Photo courtesy of Germán Congo's family

"Me gusta la leche" ("I Like Milk")—African-Ecuadorian *sanjuán*

Counter Number	Commentary
Introduction	
0:00	*Requinto* guitar plays introductory motive *a* (twice), then
0:10	introductory motive *b* (twice), then
0:20	introductory motive *c* (twice).
	Each motive is eight quarter-note beats long.
1st stanza (double-couplet)—A phrase	
0:29	Vocals on the A phrase, the principal melody of the *sanjuán*.
	Me gusta la leche, me gusta el café, / Pero más me gusta lo que tiene Usted.
	Me gusta la leche, me gusta el café, / Pero más me gusta lo que tiene Usted.
	I like milk, I like coffee, / But I like what you have better.
	I like milk, I like coffee, / But I like what you have better.
2nd stanza (double-couplet)—A phrase	
0:38	*Requinto* counterpoint added to vocal melody in A phrase (principal melody).
	Así negra linda de mi corazón, / Cuando yo te veo, me muero de ilusión.
	Así negra linda de mi corazón, / Cuando yo te veo, me muero de ilusión.
	So, beautiful black woman of my heart, / When I see you, I'm filled with anticipation.
	So, beautiful black woman of my heart, / When I see you, I'm filled with anticipation.
***Requinto* interlude**	
0:48	Lead guitar and ensemble. Lead plays *c* motive from introduction twice.
3rd stanza (double-couplet)—A phrase	
0:58	*Requinto* counterpoint added to vocal melody in A phrase (principal melody).
	En esta cuaresma no me confesé / Porque en viernes santo yo me enamoré.
	En esta cuaresma no me confesé / Porque en viernes santo yo me enamoré.
	During this Lent I did not go to confession, / Because, on Good Friday, I fell in love,
	During this Lent I did not go to confession, / Because, on Good Friday, I fell in love.
2nd stanza repeat	
1:08	Vocals with *requinto* counterpoint
Instrumental interlude	
1:18	Ensemble plays two new B phrases.
1:27	Germán's *requinto* guitar repeats the introduction motives.
3rd stanza repeat	
1:57	Vocals return with *requinto* counterpoint.
2nd stanza repeat	
2:06	Vocals with *requinto* counterpoint.

Counter Number	Commentary
***Requinto* interlude repeat**	
2:16	Lead guitar and ensemble. Lead guitar plays *c* motive from introduction twice.
Final cadence	
2:26	Ensemble with lead guitar playing melodic riff (in the minor home-key). Spoken at end by John Schechter: *Gracias*.

In this *sanjuán* we see the same 8-beat phrases and double-couplet structure of text that we saw in "Muyu muyari warmigu," a Quichua *sanjuán* that would in 1990 have been performed in the Otavalo Valley, a couple of hours down the highway from the Chota River Valley, site of the Congos' home village of Carpuela. However, despite the double-couplet construction and comparable tempo of the music (one can easily dance Quichua *sanjuán* to "Me gusta la leche"), this is not Quichua *sanjuán*, though it is *sanjuán*. In the first place, we do not have clear phrase isorhythm: The second 4 beats are not identical, here, to the first 4 beats, as in Quichua *sanjuán*. Looking at the first stanza ("*Me gusta la leche*"), we see this pattern:

- First 4 beats: four sixteenth-notes, two eighth-notes, four sixteenth-notes, quarter-note
- Second 4 beats: four sixteenth-notes, sixteenth-note, eighth-note, sixteenth-note, eighth-note, two sixteenth-notes, quarter-note

This is quite fascinating. In this musical genre "shared" between two neighboring cultures, Quichua and African-Ecuadorian, there is a suggestion of isorhythm in that beat 5 is the same as beat 1 (four sixteenth-notes), and beat 8 is the same as beat 4 (quarter-note); the divergence comes with beats 6 and 7. Beat 6 is sixteenth-eighth-sixteenth. The sharp-eared among you will recall that this small rhythmic fragment—sixteenth-eighth-sixteenth— was a rhythmic marker for Quichua *sanjuán*. Here it is again, in neighboring African-Ecuadorian *sanjuán*. Beat 7, eighth and two sixteenths, is close to beat 3 (four sixteenths), yet also different. In the third stanza ("*En esta cuaresma*"), the "noteworthy" beat 6 now gives us a syncopation, accenting the fourth sixteenth-note—a weak beat—thus providing increased rhythmic drive. Quichua *sanjuán* almost never utilizes such weak-beat accent and syncopation. We also have the wonderful counterpoint (independent melody and rhythm) of Germán's lead (*requinto*) guitar, which provides a remarkable texture, depth, and richness to the music—something Chota musicians often refer to as *dulzura*, or sweetness (Schechter 1994b:293).

"Me gusta la leche" is a rich musical expression of a border region: African Ecuadorian, close to a major Quichua cultural zone, within a Spanish-speaking nation. It therefore demonstrates hybrid traits: a genre (*sanjuán*) native to the neighboring Quichua indigenous people, yet here borrowed and—with phrasing twists, rhythmic variance and nuance, and *requinto dulzura*—made unique to Chota.

The Andean Ensemble Phenomenon: Going Abroad

By 1990, the reputation of the Congo brothers and Milton Tadeo had enabled them to travel throughout Ecuador and into Colombia, playing for substantial fees, and on television (Schechter 1994b:288). Galo Maigua and his Quichua colleagues have played in Europe. Conjunto Ilumán in particular represents a now-broad phenomenon, both in the Andes and beyond: the itinerant Andean ensemble and the globalization of Andean musics. Other Ecuadorian ensembles focusing on Quichua or *Nueva Canción* musics over the last twenty years have included Ñanda Mañachi (Quichua: "Lend me the way"; 1977, 1979, 1983); Conjunto Indígena "Peguche" (Spanish: *indígena* ensemble from the village of Peguche [near Otavalo]; 1977); and Jatari (Quichua: "Get up!"; 1978). The carefully and elaborately produced albums of Ñanda Mañachi, in particular, are notably evocative of the Quichua music-culture of Imbabura.

In the Otavalo Valley of Imbabura, Quichua ensembles date back at least to the 1940s and 1950s and began to proliferate in the 1970s (Meisch 1997:200–201). The groups mentioned earlier, such as Ñanda Mañachi and Conjunto Indígena Peguche, emphasized in their album liner notes the central role of "music as an expression of indigenous values and its role in [the 1970s Indigenous Quichua] cultural resurgence" (Meisch 1997:201). The Otavalo Quichua musical-ensemble renaissance is evident from Lynn Meisch's listing of numerous long-playing records recorded from 1970 to 1986—nearly all of which were recorded in Ecuador and contained only Ecuadorian music (Meisch 1997:205–6).

In 1990, in this same broad, green valley, teenagers and young men were actively engaged in music making. In Imbabura, one radio station had an annual festival of musical ensembles, in which any and all area village ensembles could participate, each playing perhaps two songs on the radio. In July 1990 this village ensemble marathon featured enough groups to last twelve hours. Music making provides an important means of socialization among Quichua youths who have long since ceased attending school and who find few community activities available to them, except for volleyball, which is pursued with a vengeance in the village plazas and *comunas* of Imbabura. You will hear Quichua teenagers rehearsing diligently on weekends at an ensemble member's home, performing a few traditional *sanjuanes* and, like their counterparts in the United States, often experimenting with their own compositions.

The 1990s witnessed an explosion of this music as Otavalenian musicians left their homeland to seek larger audiences throughout the world. As Lynn Meisch noted, "Otavalo music [performed by Quichua indigenous musicians] has now become globalized, part of the world music beat influencing the music made by others, with Sanjuanitos seen as emblematic of Ecuadorian music" (1997:217). Motivated by potential economic rewards, many Imbabura Quichua ensemble members have, in effect, become "transnational migrants" (Meisch 1997:218) or "immigrants who develop and maintain multiple relationships—familial, economic, social, organizational, religious, and political—that span borders . . . [creating a] multiplicity of involvements . . . in both home and host societies" (Basch, Schiller, and Blanc 1994:7). Today's

Quichua musicians are recording CDs, not LPs; those CDs are most often produced outside of Ecuador, and they include ample proportions of non-Ecuadorian, as well as Ecuadorian, Andean songs (Meisch 1997:253–55).

Not surprisingly, as the Bolivian ethnomusicologist Gilka Wara Céspedes says, "The Andean Sound is becoming a part of the sonic scene from Europe to Japan" (1993:53). Further, "Otavalo [Quichua] musicians are everywhere, playing in malls, on street corners, at music festivals, and in concert halls and clubs on six continents, and recording and selling their music at locales around the world" (Meisch 1997:243). Where Ecuadorian Andean *indígena* textile manufacturers have for some fifty years traveled the international byways, selling their home-woven ponchos, blankets, and scarves, today the entrepreneurial instinct remains intact but the product has changed: from bulky woolens to featherweight cassettes and CDs, and delicate bamboo *zampoñas* and *kenas*. As one Otavalenian musician told Meisch in 1994, "'We have two ways to earn a living in whatever locale: music and the sales of *artesanías* [arts and crafts]'" (1997:187). Specifically, Otavalo Quichua ensembles have appeared at First Peoples powwows in Canada and the United States, in folk festivals in Poland and Washington, D.C., and on street corners, tourist thoroughfares, and subway stations in Quito, New York, San Francisco, Florence, Moscow, Montreal, Paris, Sevilla, Córdoba, and Madrid, among numerous other places (1997:243).

The United States unquestionably plays a vital role in this international Andean sonic scene. As of about ten years ago, Amauta, based in Seattle, comprised Chilean and Bolivian musicians playing traditional Andean instruments; they had appeared at the Seattle Northwest Regional Folklife Festival. Condor, out of Corvallis, Oregon, was an ensemble of five professional, college-educated musicians from Argentina, Peru, and Mexico; the group focused on traditional Andean musics. Andanzas (Spanish: "wanderings") performed music from a variety of Latin American and Caribbean traditions; this widely traveled, four-member ensemble included musicians from Argentina, Bolivia, and Mexico, as well as a classically trained U.S. harpist. Andesmanta (Quichua: "from the Andes"), an ensemble of Ecuadorian musicians playing traditional highland Ecuadorian musics—including *sanjuanes*—as well as other South American folk musics, had performed at Carnegie Hall and the Metropolitan Museum of Art. Among the most well-established of U.S.-based Andean groups is Sukay (Quechua: "to work furrows in straight lines" or "to whistle musically"); this group formed originally in 1974, then recorded eight albums by 1994 and gave performances at Lincoln Center and major folk music festivals (Ross 1994: 19–24). (A list of selected recordings by these and other Andean Ensembles can be found in Ross 1994:27 and, for Ecuadorian Andean ensembles, in Meisch 1997:357–65.)

Chaskinakuy

One of the cofounders of Sukay was the Swiss multi-instrumentalist and instrument-craftsman Edmond Badoux. In 1985, with the flautist-percussionist

Figure 8.10
Duo Chaskinakuy. June 1992.

© Irene Young. Used by permission.

Francy Vidal (self-described as "an 8th-generation 'Californiana' with roots in Mexico and in Europe"), he formed the gifted California-based duo, Chaskinakuy (Quechua: "to give and receive, hand to hand, among many"; see Figure 8.10). Chaskinakuy's husband-and-wife members, Edmond and Francy, characterize themselves as "dedicated revivalists." The two musicians sing in Quechua/Quichua and Spanish, and they play more than twenty-five native Andean instruments, some rarely heard outside their highland Andean contexts: Peruvian harp (Edmond even plays this instrument, on occasion, upside-down, in accordance with the Peruvian harp's unique processioning posture), pelican-bone flute, long straight trumpet, condor-feathered *zampoña,* and *pututu* (Quechua conch trumpet). Chaskinakuy now performs often with violinist-guitarist-mandolinist Daniel Zamalloa, though not on the song studied here, "Amor imposible" (ah-*mor* eem-poh-*see*-bleh).

Chaskinakuy [info@chaskinakuy.com] has appeared in concerts, festivals, university lecture series, and schools in eighteen U.S. states, in Canada, and in Switzerland. They have three times received the Multi-Cultural Grant from the California Arts Council and for six seasons were picked for the Council's Touring and Presenting Program. Chaskinakuy has three recordings on their own label: *A Flor de tierra* (2002), *Cosecha* (1993), and *Music of the Andes* (1988). They return frequently to the Andes to sustain their performance research into traditional village musics and festivals. Their renditions of Andean musics reflect the musicians' wonderful blend when singing and their remarkably close attention to every stylistic detail appropriate to the particular regional music: harmonic underpinnings, melodic lines and inflections, vocal tone qualities, phrasing, and rhythmic accentuations. Now listen to Chaskinakuy's rendition of the Peruvian *wayno (wahy-no)*, "Amor imposible" **(CD 2, Track 12)**.

 CD 2:12

"Amor imposible" ("Impossible Love") (2:32). Traditional Peruvian *wayno.* Performed by Chaskinakuy. *Chaskinakuy, Music of the Andes: Cosecha.* CD engineered and mixed by Joe Hoffmann and remastered by Brian Walder at Hoffmann Studios. Occidental, California, 1991.

As you listen to your second Latin American "harp-country genre" (the first being Ecuadorian *sanjuán,* and now Peruvian *wayno*), you will probably note four prominent similarities to the "Muyu muyari warmigu" *sanjuán* of Efraín and Rafael. First, we see the use of the harp—now as accompaniment to the lively south-Andean *wayno,* then as accompaniment to its lively north-Andean cousin, the *sanjuán.* Second, we hear the now-familiar Andean bimodality, the use of the minor and its relative major—here, b minor/D major. Moreover, where the B phrases of Efraín and Rafael's "Muyu" explored the region of the subdominant of the relative major, likewise Edmond and Francy's "Amor imposible" employs also G major, the subdominant of its relative major—D. Third, those with keen ears will remark that the rhythm is not beaten on a drum, but rather—as in "Muyu"—on the harp soundbox; this type of percussive *golpe,* or *cajoneo,* on the harp soundbox can be heard in several Latin American countries, including Peru. Lastly, each has a distinctive rhythmic motif. Recall that the rhythmic motifs of Ecuadorian *sanjuanes* revolve around sixteenth-eighth-sixteenth notes. In Peruvian *wayno* the *golpe* involves something close to one eighth and two sixteenths; this pattern, sometimes close to three triplets, is the near-invariant rhythmic signature of the *wayno.* (You can find a substantial discussion of the history, regional varieties, other musical traits, and poetic substance of the *wayno* in Romero 1999:388–89).

Again, this performance of "Amor imposible" proves particularly compelling because Edmond captures the distinctive character of Peruvian harp accompanimental style, and Francy grasps the distinctive melodic turns of phrase, characteristic portamento, and distinctly focused and clear vocal quality of the female Peruvian singer of *wayno.* The listening chart provides the full text of "Amor imposible" and illustrates the formal structure of this Peruvian *wayno.*

As you can see from the lyrics, "Amor imposible" offers one example of the poetic character of this genre: "Most waynos . . . are of an amorous nature. Despite the immense variety of waynos, many depict nostalgia for a lost love" (Romero 1999:389). The theme of nostalgia runs powerfully throughout songs that have emerged through the ages in Latin America (Schechter 1999a:2–7).

Each stanza has four lines. The first three stanzas all have eleven-syllable lines, while the fourth stanza has the syllable-pattern 6-5-6-5, as does the last stanza. The formal structure of the music of "Amor imposible" is as follows: Intro-AA-A-A-A-B-B-CC'-DD'-EE'-EE'.

Raúl Romero (1999:388–90, 414–15) discusses the character and formal structure of the Peruvian *wayno.* One of the possible formal structures, he notes, is roughly AABB (1999:414). What we hear in "Amor imposible" is an expansion, an extrapolation, of that form: Much of the song is occupied with the A phrase—which correlates with the eleven-syllable stanzas, with lesser emphasis being given to the B phrase—which correlates with the 6-5-6-5 stanzas. Then, Edmond's C phrase explores the subdominant key, which lasts into the D phrase; the concluding E phrase dwells on the fifth scale degree, prolonging the final arrival to the home-note, the first scale degree.

Counter Number	Commentary

Introduction

0:00	Harp enters.
0:05	*Golpe* enters emphasizing long-short-short rhythmic pattern.

1st stanza—A phrase

0:13	Harp and *golpe* play main melody.
	Vocal style with distinctive phrasing and characteristic portamento of the *wayno*.
	Es imposible dejar de quererte, / Es imposible dejar de amarte,
	Este cariño que yo a tí te tengo / Es un cariño puro y verdadero.
	It's impossible to stop loving you, / It's impossible to stop loving you,
	This affection that I have for you / Is an affection pure and true.

1st stanza repeat—A phrase

0:28	Harp and *golpe*.

Harp interlude, "Arpita!"—A phrase

0:43	Harp.

2nd stanza—A phrase

0:58	Harp and *golpe* play main melody.
	¡Cómo quisiera que venga la muerte! / ¡Cómo quisiera morir en tus brazos!
	Quizás así podría olvidarte / Porque, en mi vida, todo es imposible.
	How so, would I like death to come! / How so, would I like to die in your arms!
	Perhaps that way, I could forget you / Because, in my life, everything is impossible.

3rd stanza—A phrase

1:14	Harp and *golpe* play main melody.
	Ay, cruceñito, amorcito mío / Este cariño te traigo y te digo
	Aunque mi cuerpo quede sepultado / Queda mi nombre grabado en tu pecho.
	Ay, dear man from [Santa] Cruz, my dear love / This affection I offer you and tell you of
	Even though my body might be buried / My name remains engraved in your breast.

4th stanza—B phrase

1:29	Harp and *golpe* play contrasting melody.
	Dicen con la muerte / Se llega a olvidar,
	Quizás en la tumba / Más nos amamos.
	They say that, with death, / One comes to forget,
	Perhaps in the grave / We'll love one another more.

5th stanza—B phrase

1:37	Harp and *golpe* play contrasting melody.
	Si muero primero / Yo allá te espero,
	Así para amarnos / Eternamente.
	Should I die first, / I'll wait for you, over there,
	In that way, to remain loving one another / Eternally.

Counter Number	Commentary
Harp interlude—CC'–DD'–EE'–EE'	
1:46–1:56	Harp plays new C phrase twice.
1:57–2:06	Harp plays new D phrase twice.
2:07–2:27	Harp plays new E phrase four times.
2:28	Final cadence.

Other Groups

Both the *waynos* and *sanjuanes* of Andean ensembles—as well as *Nueva Canción* musics—have taken root in U.S. universities. For example, the University of Texas at Austin for some years maintained an Andean ensemble, among their other Latin American groups. This began in 1976 with the *Nueva Canción* ensemble, Toqui Amaru (Mapuche and Quechua: "chief serpent"), founded by Renato Espinoza of Chile, with Guillermo Delgado-P. and Enrique Cuevas of Bolivia, Néstor Lugones of Argentina, and Alejandro Cardona of the United States. At the University of California, Santa Cruz, students perform in intermediate and advanced-level Andean ensembles called Voces (Spanish: "voices") and Taki Ñan (Quichua: "song path"), respectively.

Taki Ñan, which recorded an in-house cassette in 1992 and an in-house CD in 1998, focuses on traditional Andean musics in Spanish and Quichua/Quechua, as well as on *Nueva Canción* musics. Starting out with a single, ten-student Latin American ensemble in 1986 that focused on Ecuadorian genres, Voces and Taki Ñan became independent of each other in 1991. Over the years, Taki Ñan has tended to follow two approaches: focusing its repertory or presenting a more varied program. When focusing in depth, during one particular quarter of study, the group emphasizes, for example, Colombian musics, Argentinean musics, Afro–South American musics; in fall 1992 they prepared six different field-recorded versions of "Ilumán tiyu." Taki Ñan has also presented programs with a variety of traditional and *Nueva Canción* musics. In nearly every one of these programs, from 1989 to the present, both Taki Ñan and Voces have performed south-Andean *zampoña* musics—including the *k'antu* "Kutirimunapaq." Over these years Taki Ñan has benefited enormously from the musical and linguistic assistance of Guillermo Delgado-P., as well as from workshops offered by Chaskinakuy and by the Peruvian musician Héctor Zapana. (A full account of the evolution of Taki Ñan appears in Schechter 2003.) Aconcagua, at Florida State University, performs a variety of Andean musics and has been directed by an alumna of Taki Ñan. Viento, in Berkeley, California, is directed by Chaskinakuy and comprises Berkeley-resident students and community members. Frequently performing at the La Peña Cultural Center in Berkeley, Viento focuses on traditional south-Andean musics for *zampoña* and *tarqa* (wooden duct flute). Lydia Mills, another Taki Ñan alumna, for years directed Los Mapaches, an ensemble of about thirty-five schoolchildren from the Berkwood Hedge School, in Berkeley, who performed Andean musics—on *zampoñas* and other instruments—locally, in concert.

Afro-Peruvian Music: A Landó

The interpretations and reinterpretations of traditional South American musics take place, of course, not only abroad but on the continent itself. One prominent instance of the reconstruction of an imagined music of the past occurs with today's Afro-Peruvian music. Peru was a major nucleus of African slavery in the colonial era; a substantial part of eighteenth-century Lima, Peru, was black (Romero 1994:307). At the same time, the disappearance in that same century of the African marimba and African drum types marked the diminution of African-related musical practice. By the outset of the twentieth century, songs and choreographies with African provenience were entering a clouded past (Romero 1994:313–14). By 1940 blacks represented a mere 0.47 percent of the population of Peru (Feldman 2003:156). Against these demographic and cultural trends, a revival of Afro-Peruvian traditions took place. Raúl Romero, a Peruvian ethnomusicologist, summarizes the mid-twentieth-century revival movement as follows:

> The revival and reconstruction of ancient and almost forgotten "Afro-Peruvian" song-genres began in the late 1950s. Rather than originating in a popular spontaneous movement, this was initiated by local intellectuals interested in the revival and recognition of the contribution of blacks to Peruvian culture. The late historian José Durand (1935–1990), along with Nicomedes Santa Cruz (1925–1992) and his sister Victoria Santa Cruz (1992) were the main collectors, producers, and promoters of black performances during this period. (1994:314)

Heidi Feldman notes that there was originally a tie between a 1960s black Peruvian political movement (roughly simultaneous with the U.S. Civil Rights Movement) and the Afro-Peruvian musical revival. Lately, though, that link to political agendas has been weakened; Afro-Peruvian music making in its home country now is serving to divert tourists (2003:156–57). Among the musical genres and dance-plays considered Afro-Peruvian are the *landó,* the *son de los diablos,* the *festejo,* and the *ingá* (Romero 1994:318; see also Tompkins 1998).

Let us study, then, an Afro-Peruvian *landó* (lan-*do*)—a reconstructed genre (Feldman 2003:156; Romero 1994:318)—written by Daniel "Kiri" Escobar and performed in this rendition with the soloist Eva Ayllón **(CD 2, Track 13)**. The recording appears on *The Soul of Black Peru,* "the first recording of Afro-Peruvian music widely available in the United States" (Feldman 2003:157). The listening guide provides the full text of "Azúcar de caña" (ah-*soo*-kar deh *kah*-nyah) and illustrates the formal structure of this Afro-Peruvian *landó.*

Here, we are impressed by the rhythmic subtleties of Eva Ayllón's singing, how she declaims the text so expressively, with a distinct sensuality: The song incorporates several terms of flirtation and eroticism. Scarcely acknowledged in the 1970s, Eva Ayllón by the mid-1980s was among the most esteemed of Afro-Peruvian singing artists (Martínez and

CD 2:13

"Azúcar de caña" ("Sugar Cane") (4:21). Performed by Eva Ayllón and ensemble. The Soul of Black Peru/El Alma Del Peru Negro/Afro-Peruvian Classics, 1995.

Close Listening   CD 2:13

"Azúcar de caña" ("Sugar Cane")—Afro-Peruvian *landó*

Counter Number	Commentary

Introduction

0:00	Ensemble with vocal solo.
0:02	Distinctive *quijada* sound.
	¡Aha! ¡Vamos temple! !Si!
	Aha! Let's go in [musical] harmony! Yes!

1st stanza

0:10	Vocal solo: expressive singing style.
	Salgo de mañana, a tumbar la caña, / Salgo de mañana, a tumbar la caña,
	Lucero del alba siempre me acompaña. / Lucero del alba siempre me acompaña.
	I go out in the morning, to cut sugar cane, / I go out in the morning, to cut sugar cane,
	The morning star always accompanies me. / The morning star always accompanies me.

2nd stanza

0:31	Vocal solo.
	Machete en la mano, corazón de vino, / Machete en la mano, corazón de vino,
	El río, mi hermano, zafra mi destino. / El río, mi hermano, zafra mi destino.
	Machete in hand, heart of wine, / Machete in hand, heart of wine,
	The river, my brother, the sugar-cane harvest my destiny. / The river, my brother, the sugar-cane harvest my destiny.

1st interlude

0:52	Music reinforces relative minor key.
	Sale el sol tras la montaña, / Sale el sol tras la montaña, / Sale el sol tras la montaña,
	The sun rises behind the mountain, / The sun rises behind the mountain, / The sun rises behind the mountain,
1:06	*E, inundando todo el valle con aromas de la caña.*
	And, flooding the whole valley with the aroma of the sugar cane.

2nd interlude

1:14	Relative minor key again reinforced.
	Esta noche en mi cabaña, / Esta noche en mi cabaña, / Esta noche en mi cabaña,
	Tonight in my cabin, / Tonight in my cabin, / Tonight in my cabin,
1:27	One-line connector produces tonal instability and introduces text of vocal choral echo.
	Voy a bailar coba coba con mi mochera,* esta saña.[†]
	I'm going to dance body to body with my *mochera,** this dance.[†]
	**mochera/mochero*: woman/man from the Moche region of coastal Peru.
	[†]*Saña* is also a coastal district, in the Peruvian provinces of Lambayeque and Chiclayo; it has been influenced by older Afro-Peruvian traditions (Casas Roque 1993:299–300, 331).

Choral echo with Ayllón interjections

1:32	*—con mi mo-chera, esta saña, / —con mi mo-chera, esta saña,*
	—con mi mo-chera, esta saña, / —con mi mo-chera—
	("*Je-ye, esta saña, señores; ¡pata en el suelo!*")
	—with my mochera, this dance, / —with my mochera, this dance,
	—with my mochera, this dance, / —with my mochera—
	("Yes, yes, this dance, folks; feet to the floor!")

(continued)

"Azúcar de caña"("Sugar Cane")—Afro-Peruvian *landó*

Multipart chorus

1:42	Chorus with Eva Ayllón and male-voice interjections.
	Azúcar de caña, / Sombrero de paja, / Mula resongona, / Juguito guarapo.
	Azúcar de caña, / Sombrero de paja, / Mula resongona, / Juguito guarapo.
	("¡Toma! ¡De la negra! ¡Así! ¡Eso es!")
	Sugar cane, / Straw hat, / Whining mule, / Sugar-cane liquor.
	Sugar cane, / Straw hat, / Whining mule, / Sugar-cane liquor.
	("Drink! My woman's! Like that! That's it!")

Vocal solo

2:03	*Azúcar, azúcar, / Azúcar, azúcar,*
	Sugar-, sugar-, / Sugar-, sugar-,

Instrumental interlude

2:09	Transition to 3rd stanza.

3rd stanza

2:14	Vocal solo.
	Roncan los trapiches, moliendo la caña, / Roncan los trapiches, moliendo la caña,
	Juguito guarapo, quémame el entraña. / Juguito guarapo, quéma mis entrañas.
	("¡Rico!")
	The sugar mills roar, grinding the sugar cane, / The sugar mills roar, grinding the sugar cane,
	Sugar-cane liquor, burn my innards. / Sugar-cane liquor, burn my innards.
	("Delicious!")

4th stanza

2:35	Vocal solo.
	Noche de la zafra, luna de cañero, / Noche de la zafra, luna de cañero,
	¿Cuándo será mío, mi valle, mochero? / ¿Cuándo será mío, mi valle, mochero?
	Night of the sugar-cane harvest, moon of the sugar-cane worker, / Night of the sugar-cane harvest, moon of the sugar-cane worker,
	When will my valley be mine, *mochero?* / When will my valley be mine, *mochero?*

Repeat from 1st interlude through multipart chorus and subsequent vocal solo

2:57–4:13	Vocal solo and call-and-response texture.
4:13	Reprise of multipart chorus, and fade out.

Jarque 1995). We hear the distinctive buzz of the *quijada* (kee-*ha*-da), a traditional instrument dating back in Peru to the eighteenth century and made of a donkey, horse, or cow jawbone (for an eighteenth-century drawing, see Casas Roque 1993:308; see also Romero 1994:312–13). Known as *carraca llanera* in the Plains of Colombia, this percussive instrument is struck; the animal's molars, when loosened by exposure to the elements, produce a clear dry crack when hit with the fist. In some ensembles of Colombia, the molars may be scraped with a stick. We also hear an exchange between the solo vocalist Ayllón and the chorus; this creates the feeling of a call-and-response texture, something that we typically associate with an African or African-derived music.

The lyrics throughout the entire piece resound with the culture and ecology of the song's home region. First the Moche culture (*mochera/mochero*) existed prior to the time of the Inkas in north-coastal Peru. Still today, one can observe remnants of the Moche culture, both in the physical features of the inhabitants of this coastal zone and in their surnames and place-names (Casas Roque 1993:299). Second, the song oozes with the harvest, milling, aroma, and drink of the *caña*—sugar cane, grown in lowland areas. *Guarapo* is an alcoholic beverage made from the cane—a *licor* that can burn one's insides. *Trapiches,* or sugar mills, process the *caña. Trapiche* and *caña* emerge in music not only along the Peruvian coast but also to the north in Ecuador and Colombia. In an interview with Milton Tadeo and Ermundo Mendes León (October 31, 1990), these Chota Valley musicians told me that the *bomba,* a traditional—really emblematic—genre of Chota, had actually emanated from the *trapiche* culture of the older generations of Chota. Jesuit missionaries derived a degree of wealth, up to the eighteenth century in Ecuador, through, among other things, several sugar plantations located near today's Carpuela, the Congo brothers' home village. Milton recounted to me one traditional *bomba* text that goes like this: "'A la culebra verde, negrita, no hagas caso, mete *caña* al trapiche, chupa y bota gabazo.' (Don't pay attention to the green snake, dear woman; put cane to the sugar mill, suck on it, and throw away the waste pulp.)" (Schechter 1994b:288–89). Farther north, in Colombia, we find a lively and raucous festive *bambuco* titled "El Guaro." William Gradante notes, "The terms *guaro* and *guarapo* refer to the sugary juice squeezed from sugar cane—in this case in its fermented, highly intoxicating, homemade form" (1999:341). This upbeat *sesquialtera* folk song, made famous in an interpretation by the renowned Colombian duo of Garzón y Collazos, speaks of the same joy of the *caña* that we have seen in Peru and Ecuador: "De la *caña* sale el *guaro*—¡Qué caramba!—Sí la *caña* es buena fruta. Si la *caña* se machaca—¡Qué caramba!— El *guaro* también se chupa. [*Guaro* comes from sugar cane—Whew!—Sugar cane sure is great. If the cane is squeezed—Whew!—Then you can even drink it.]" (Gradante 1999:347).

Despedida, or Farewell

We began with the comment that Latin America was a kaleidoscope of cultural patterns, and we explored the musical manifestation of several of these. We have sensed the urgency of a *Nueva Canción* song of Víctor Jara, as performed by Inti Illimani; the power and impact of Bolivian *zampoña*-ensemble music making; the isorhythm and thematic continuity of the Ecuadorian Quichua *sanjuán,* "Muyu muyari, warmigu"; the symmetries, balance, and autobiographical intent of "Galo" Maigua's "Ilumán tiyu"; the way neighboring Chota Valley musicians mold the *sanjuán* to certain of their own musical priorities of phrase, rhythm, and guitar counterpoint; the manner in which non-Andeans such as Edmond Badoux and Francy Vidal of Chaskinakuy, in the context of the globalization of Andean ensemble music, can capture exquisitely the musical essence of a Peruvian *wayno*—its instrument, formal structure, rhythm, and harp and vocal performance practices;

and finally, the suave Afro-Peruvian *landó,* highlighting the local coastal *caña* life and culture. We can begin to appreciate—in our *despedida,* or farewell, to Latin American music-culture—the richness of ensemble music making in Latin America: These *Nueva Canción* songs, *zampoña* pieces, *sanjuanes, waynos,* and *landós* speak to deeply felt political concerns; deep-rooted musical forms of expression; detailed and attentive attempts, from afar, to capture the overall character of an Andean song-dance type; and dedicated efforts to recreate local musical style. From "El aparecido" and "Muyu," to "Amor imposible" and "Azúcar de caña," we have feasted on a substantial buffet, one that I hope will entice you to savor the many other pungent and satisfying flavors of Latin American music.

Study Questions

1. What is the song "El aparecido" about, and how does it fit both within the *Nueva Canción* movement in Latin America and within larger traditions of Latin American song?

2. What are two particularly interesting aspects of the Bolivian *k'antu* "Kutirimu-napaq"?

3. What are some traditional aspects of northern Ecuadorian highland Quichua material culture and music culture?

4. Using "Muyu muyari warmigu" as an example, can you discuss characteristics of northern Ecuadorian highland Quichua *sanjuán,* mentioning aspects of phrase structure, rhythm, and verse structure?

5. What is the Quichua *sanjuán* "Ilumán tiyu" really about?

6. How is the African-Ecuadorian *sanjuán* "Me gusta la leche" actually an example of a hybrid music?

7. How is the Andean music ensemble now truly an international phenomenon?

8. What are some features of the Peruvian *wayno,* and how is it that Chaskinakuy captures its character so well in their rendition of "Amor imposible"?

9. How do the lyrics of the Afro-Peruvian *landó* "Azúcar de caña" reflect the ecology and culture of its home region?

10. What are two examples, discussed in this chapter, of the revival/reinterpretation/transplantation of traditional Latin American musics?

11. What are two musical instruments, mentioned and heard in this chapter, whose "ancestors" go back at least two hundred years, in the Andes of South America?

Glossary

"Amor imposible" (ah-*mor* eem-poh-*see*-bleh) Peruvian *wayno,* performed by the ensemble Chaskinakuy (Edmond Badoux and Francy Vidal).

arca (*ar*-ka) A second rank, or line, of south-Andean panpipes; represents, on the Bolivian high plateau (altiplano), the female principle; serves as the "follower." Shares the full melody, with the *ira* rank of pipes, playing in hocket (see glossary for hocketing, *ira*).

"Azúcar de caña" (ah-*soo*-kar deh *kah*-nyah) Afro-Peruvian *landó,* composed by Felipe Daniel Escobar Rivero, performed here by Eva Ayllón and the ensemble, Perú Negro.

bomba (*bom*-ba) In the context of African Ecuadorians living in the Chota river valley of northern highland Ecuador, a double-headed drum held between the knees and played with the hands. Also used to describe a traditional musical genre, of this same cultural region, in *sesquialtera* meter (see glossary). (Also a name for a genre of African-derived traditional dance music in Puerto Rico, and for drum types used in those ensembles.)

campesinos (kam-pe-*see*-nos) Peasants, farmers. In the south-Andean context (Peru, Bolivia), specifically, one who speaks either the Quechua or Aymara language.

chaki ñan (*cha*-ki *nyan*) In Northern Andean Ecuador, a mountain footpath alongside agricultural plots.

charango (cha-*ran*-go) A small, fretted guitarlike instrument of Andean Bolivia, Peru, and northern Argentina, often with ten strings in five pairs, and used in peasant (Quechua-speaking First Peoples) and mestizo music in courting, festival, and/or ensemble (stage) contexts. May have a flat or a round back made of either wood or armadillo shell.

comunas (ko-*mu*-nas) Small clusters of nonadjacent houses in which the Quichua of the northern Ecuadorian highlands (the Otavalo valley) have traditionally lived.

corrido (ko-*rree*-do) A ballad genre from the Mexico-Texas border region, characteristically performed by a male duo self-accompanied on guitars and often containing formulaic elements and a characteristic opening and closing; often addresses the exploits of heroic figures, migration experiences, romance, or tragedy.

counterpoint Combining two or more melodic parts.

cueca (*kweh*-ka) *Sesquialtera* dance music genre of Chile, Bolivia, and Argentina, in moderate tempo.

"El aparecido" (ehl a-pa-reh-*see*-doh) Song by Víctor Jara, performed here by Inti Illimani.

hocketing Dispersing the tones of the melody among several voices and/or instruments, which play it in alternation or sequence rather than simultaneously; the traditional performance practice for south-Andean panpipe music, such as "Kutirimunapaq."

"Ilumán tiyu" (ee-lu-*mahn tee*-yoo) Ecuadorian Andean *sanjuán* in Quichua and in Spanish, performed by the ensemble Conjunto Ilumán.

ira (*ee*-ra) One rank, or line, of south-Andean panpipes; represents, on the Bolivian high plateau (altiplano), the male principle; serves as the "leader." Shares the full melody, with the *arca* rank of pipes, playing in hocket (see glossary for *arca*, hocketing).

isorhythm Equal rhythm, the same rhythm. Applies to northern Ecuadorian highland Quichua *sanjuán*, in which the rhythm of the first half of the phrase is characteristically identical or nearly so to the rhythm of the second half.

k'antu (k-*an*-tu) A type of ceremonial panpipe music from the altiplano, or high plateau, of Peru-Bolivia. The word *k'antu* might be related to a widely known flower of Bolivia, the *kantuta*, or it might be derived from the Spanish word for song, *canto*.

kena (*ke*-na) An Andean vertical notched flute.

"Kutirimunapaq" (koo-tee-ree-moo-*na*-pakh) Piece for Andean hocketing panpipes, by the Bolivian ensemble Ruphay.

landó (lan-*do*) Reconstructed genre of Afro-Peruvian music. An example is "Azúcar de caña."

metaphor An assertion that one thing is also something else; a comparison of analogous qualities, often involving similarities that are not immediately obvious, a comparison that typically enhances meaning.

"Me gusta la leche" (meh *goo*-sta la *leh*-cheh) African-Ecuadorian highland *sanjuán,* performed by Grupo Ecuador de los Hermanos Congo y Milton Tadeo.

mode The organization of scale steps (whole and half) in an octave. For example, if you play just the white keys on the piano in the octave from D to d, you have the Dorian mode; from G to g yields the Mixolydian mode; from A to a the Aeolian mode. The major scale, which you will hear if you play the white keys from C to c, is called the Ionian mode.

"Muyu muyari warmigu" (*moo*-yoo moo-*yah*-ree war-*mee*-goo) Ecuadorian Andean *sanjuán* in Quichua, performed by Efraín, harp, and Rafael, vocals.

Nueva Canción (nu-*e*-va kan-*syon*) Lit., "New Song." A political song movement through which people stand up for themselves in the face of oppression by a totalitarian government or in the face of cultural imperialism from abroad. It developed first in the Southern Cone of South America—Argentina, Chile, and Uruguay—during the 1950s and 1960s, and it has since spread throughout Latin America.

Quichua (or Quechua) (*kee*-chooa) (*keh*-chooa) Dating back to the Inka civilization, a language spoken by up to eight million First Peoples (Native Americans) in the Andes region of South America, including Ecuador, Peru, Bolivia, Argentina, and Colombia. Heard in both "Muyu muyari warmigu" and "Ilumán tiyu."

quijada (kee-*ha*-da) Dating back in Peru to the eighteenth century, a percussive instrument made from the jawbone of a donkey, horse, or cow; the animal's molars, when loosened by exposure to the elements, produce a clear dry crack when struck with the fist. Used today in Afro-Peruvian musics.

sanjuán (san-*hooan*) Originally (c. 1860) either a type of song played at the festival of St. John (San Juan) the Baptist held in June or a type of dance performed at that festival. Today it is a northern Ecuadorian highland Quichua genre that displays an isorhythmic 8-beat two-part phrase structure characterized by related melodic patterns. Lyrics, in repeated couplets, may display features of semantic parallelism and/or distilled balladry. An example is "Muyu muyari warmigu." *Sanjuán* is also performed by African Ecuadorian musicians in an adjacent highland region; an example is "Me gusta la leche."

sesquialtera **metrical rhythm** Music that can be felt in both 3/4 and 6/8 metrical rhythm—either simultaneously or alternatively. This metrical-rhythmic ambiguity is the heart and soul of much, though not all, Hispanic-derived Latin American regional folk music.

transnational migrant musicians Musician-members of a particular ethnic group residing—at different moments in time—both in their home territory and in different nations. Here, it applies specifically to Quichua musicians of the Otavalo valley, northern highland Ecuador, and their social networks both in that valley and abroad.

wayno (*wahy*-no) Known by various regional names, a deeply rooted, lively musical genre native to the south-Andean region of Peru and Bolivia. Texts may speak to a lost love; musically characterized by duple—or a combination of duple and triple—meter, and bimodality (minor, together with relative major). An example is "Amor imposible."

zampoña (sam-*pon*-ya) In Andean South America, refers to panpipes, a set of end-blown bamboo tubes lashed together, each tube producing a particular pitch. In the southern Andes (Peru and Bolivia), *zampoñas* are in two ranks, or lines, of pipes and, in traditional performance format, are played in hocket (see glossary), with the two ranks being divided between two different performers. The south-Andean *zampoñas* are traditionally played in large ensembles, accompanied by drums.

Resources

References

Andrade Albuja, Enrique, and John M. Schechter. 2004. "'*Kunan punlla rimagrinchi. . . .*': Wit and Didactics in the Quichua Rhetorical Style of Señor Enrique Andrade Albuja, Husbandman-Ethnographer of Cotacachi, Imbabura [Ecuador]." Pp. 311–36 in *Quechua Verbal Artistry: The Inscription of Andean Voices/Arte Verbal Quechua: La Inscripción de Voces Andinas,* edited by Guillermo Delgado-P. and John M. Schechter. Bonn: Bonner Amerikanistische Studien (BAS, Volume 38); Aachen: Shaker Verlag.

Basch, Linda, Nina Glick Schiller, and Christina Szanton Blanc. 1994. *Nations Unbound: Transnational Projects, Postcolonial Predicaments and Deterritorialized Nation-States.* Langhome, Pa.: Gordon and Breach Science Publishers.

Carrasco Pirard, Eduardo. 1982. "The Nueva Canción in Latin America." *International Social Science Journal* 94 (34:4): 599–623.

Casas Roque, Leonidas. 1993. "Fiestas, danzas y música de la costa de Lambayeque." Pp. 299–337 in *Música, Danzas y Máscaras en los Andes,* edited by Raúl R. Romero. Lima: Pontificia Universidad Católica del Perú, Instituto Riva-Agüero.

Céspedes, Gilka Wara. 1993. "Huayño, Saya, and Chuntunqui: Bolivian Identity in the Music of 'Los Kjarkas.'" *Revista de Música Latinoamericana/Latin American Music Review* 14(1): 52–101.

Chaskinakuy. 1988. *Music of the Andes.* CHASKINAKUY CHA-001. Cassette.

———. 1993. *Cosecha.* CHASKINAKUY CHA-002. CD.

———. 2002. *A Flor de tierra.* CHASKINAKUY CHA-003. CD. Eleven pages of liner notes.

Conjunto Ilumán. n.d. *Elenita Conde.* Ensemble directed by Segundo "Galo" Maigua Pillajo of Ilumán, Ecuador. Pre-1990. Cassette.

Conjunto Indígena "Peguche" [Ecuador]. 1977. *Folklore de mi tierra.* Orion 330-0063. Industria Fonográfica Ecuatoriana (IFESA). Guayaquil, Ecuador. Distributed by Emporio Musical S.A., Guayaquil and Psje. Amador, Quito.

Cooke, Peter. 1998. "East Africa: An Introduction." Pp. 598–609 in *Africa: The Garland Encyclopedia of World Music,* vol. 1, edited by Ruth M. Stone. New York: Garland.

Feldman, Heidi. 2003. "The International Soul of Black Peru." Pp. 155–61 in *Musical Cultures of Latin America: Global Effects, Past and Present: UCLA Selected Reports XI,* edited by Steven Loza. Los Angeles: University of California–Los Angeles Department of Ethnomusicology and Systematic Musicology.

González, Juan Pablo. 1989. "'Inti-Illimani' and the Artistic Treatment of Folklore." *Revista de Música Latinoamericana/Latin American Music Review* 10(2): 267–86.

Gradante, William J. 1999. "Andean Colombia." Pp. 302–82 in *Music in Latin American Culture: Regional Traditions,* edited by John M. Schechter. New York: Schirmer Books.

Jatari. 1978. *Jatari!! 4.* Fadisa (Fábrica de Discos S.A.). Quito, Ecuador. 710129.

Kaemmer, John E. 1998. "Southern Africa: An Introduction." Pp. 700–21 in *Africa: The Garland Encyclopedia of World Music,* vol. 1, edited by Ruth M. Stone. New York: Garland.

Koetting, James T. 1992. "Africa/Ghana." Pp. 67–105 in *Worlds of Music: An Introduction to the Music of the World's Peoples,* 2nd ed., edited by Jeff Todd Titon. New York: Schirmer Books.

Lipski, John M. 1987. "The Chota Valley: Afro-Hispanic Language in Highland Ecuador." *Latin American Research Review* 22(1): 155–70.

Lord, Albert. [1960] 1978. *The Singer of Tales.* New York: Atheneum.

Martínez, Gregorio and Fietta Jarque. 1995. Liner notes to cassette, *The Soul of Black Peru/Afro-Peruvian Classics/El Alma del Perú Negro.* Compiled by David Byrne and Yale Evelev. Warner Bros Records Inc. 9 45878-4.

Meisch, Lynn A. 1997. "Transnational Communities, Transnational Lives: Coping with Globalization in Otavalo, Ecuador." Ph.D. diss., Stanford Univ.

Moreno Chá, Ercilia. 1999. "Music in the Southern Cone: Chile, Argentina, and Uruguay." Pp. 236–301 in *Music in Latin American Culture: Regional Traditions,* edited by John M. Schechter. New York: Schirmer Books.

Morris, Nancy. 1986. "Canto porque es necesario cantar: The New Song Movement in Chile, 1973–1983." *Latin American Research Review* 21(2): 117–36.

Ñanda mañachi 1 (Préstame el camino). 1977. Produced by Jean Chopin Thermes. Llaquiclla. IFESA (Industria Fonográfica Ecuatoriana S.A.) 339-0501. Guayaquil, Ecuador. Recorded in Ibarra, Ecuador.

Ñanda mañachi 2 (Préstame el camino). 1979. Produced by Jean Chopin Thermes. Llaquiclla. IFESA (Industria Fonográfica Ecuatoriana S.A.) 339-0502. Guayaquil, Ecuador. Recorded in Ibarra, Ecuador.

Ñanda mañachi/Boliviamanta: Préstame el camino desde Bolivia. Música quichua del equinoccio Andino. Churay, Churay! 1983. Llaquiclla. Fediscos. Guayaquil, Ecuador. Onix L.P. 59003.

Nketia, J. H. Kwabena. 1974. *The Music of Africa.* New York: Norton.

Recio, P. Bernardo. [1773] 1947. *Compendiosa relación de la cristiandad (en el reino) de Quito.* Madrid: Consejo Superior de Investigaciones Científicas, Instituto Santo Toribio de Mogrovejo.

Romero, Raúl R. 1994. "Black Music and Identity in Peru: Reconstruction and Revival of Afro-Peruvian Musical Traditions." Pp. 307–30 in *Music and Black Ethnicity: The Caribbean and South America,* edited by Gerard H. Béhague. Coral Gables: Univ. of Miami North-South Center/Transaction.

———. 1999. "Andean Peru." Pp. 383–423 in *Music in Latin American Culture: Regional Traditions,* edited by John M. Schechter. New York: Schirmer Books.

Ross, Joe. 1994. "Music of the Andes." *Acoustic Musician,* June, pp. 18–27.

Schechter, John M. 1983. "*Corona y baile*: Music in the Child's Wake of Ecuador and Hispanic South America, Past and Present." *Latin American Music Review/Revista de Música Latinoamericana* 4(1): 1–80.

———. 1992. *The Indispensable Harp: Historical Development, Modern Roles, Configurations, and Performance Practices in Ecuador and Latin America.* Kent, Ohio: Kent State Univ. Press.

———. 1994a. "Divergent Perspectives on the *velorio del angelito*: Ritual Imagery, Artistic Condemnation, and Ethnographic Value." *Journal of Ritual Studies* 8(2): 43–84.

———. 1994b. "Los Hermanos Congo y Milton Tadeo Ten Years Later: Evolution of an African-Ecuadorian Tradition of the Valle del Chota, Highland Ecuador." Pp. 285–305 in *Music and Black Ethnicity: The Caribbean and South America,* edited by Gerard H. Béhague. Coral Gables, Fla.: Univ. of Miami North-South Center/Transaction.

———. 1996. "Tradition and Dynamism in Ecuadorian Andean Quichua *Sanjuán*: Macrocosm in Formulaic Expression, Microcosm in Ritual Absorption." Pp. 247–67 in *Cosmología y Música en los Andes,* edited by Max Peter Baumann. Frankfurt am Main: Vervuert; Madrid: Iberoamericana.

———. 1999a. "Themes in Latin American Music Culture." Pp. 1–33 in *Music in Latin American Culture: Regional Traditions,* edited by John M. Schechter. New York: Schirmer Books.

———. 1999b. "Beyond Region: Transnational and Transcultural Traditions." Pp. 424–57 in *Music in Latin American Culture: Regional Traditions,* edited by John M. Schechter. New York: Schirmer Books.

———. 2002. "Latin America/Ecuador." Pp. 385–446 in *Worlds of Music: An Introduction to the Music of the World's Peoples,* 4th ed., edited by Jeff Todd Titon. Belmont, CA: Schirmer.

———. 2003. "Taki Ñan: South American Affinity Interculture in Santa Cruz, California." Pp. 271–84 in *Musical Cultures of Latin America: Global Effects, Past and Present: UCLA Selected Reports XI,* edited by Steven Loza. Los Angeles: University of California–Los Angeles Department of Ethnomusicology and Systematic Musicology.

Smith, Sandra. 1984. "Panpipes for Power, Panpipes for Play: The Social Management of Cultural Expression in Kuna Society." Ph.D. diss., Univ. of California, Berkeley.

Tompkins, William David. 1998. "Afro-Peruvian Traditions." Pp. 491–502 in *The Garland Encyclopedia of World Music:* Vol. 2. *South America, Mexico, Central America, and the Caribbean,* edited by Dale A. Olsen and Daniel E. Sheehy. New York: Garland.

Vidal, Francy. 2004. April 17. Available: http://www.chaskinakuy.com/biography.htm.

Additional Reading

Aretz, Isabel. 1967. *Instrumentos musicales de Venezuela.* Cumaná, Venezuela: Editorial Universitaria de Oriente.

———. 1991. *Historia de la Etnomusicología en América Latina (desde la época pre-colombina hasta nuestros días).* Caracas: Ediciones FUNDEF – CONAC – OEA.

———, relater. 1977. *América Latina en su música.* México, D.F.: Siglo Veintiuno Editores.16.

Aretz, Isabel, Gérard Béhague, and Robert Stevenson. 1980. "Latin America." Pp. 505–34 in *The New Grove Dictionary of Music and Musicians,* vol. 10, edited by Stanley Sadie. London: Macmillan.

Averill, Gage. 1997. *A Day for the Hunter, A Day for the Prey: Popular Music and Power in Haiti.* Chicago: University of Chicago Press.

Baumann, Max Peter. 1985. "The Kantu Ensemble of the Kallawaya at Charazani (Bolivia)." *Yearbook for Traditional Music* 17:146–66.

———, recopilado y editado. 1983. *Sojta Chunka Qheshwa Takis Bolivia Llajtamanta: Sesenta Canciones del Quechua Boliviano.* Cochabamba, Bolivia: Centro Pedagógico y Cultural de Portales.

Béhague, Gérard. 1979. *Music in Latin America: An Introduction.* Englewood Cliffs, N.J.: Prentice-Hall.

———. 1984. "Patterns of Candomblé Music Performance: An Afro-Brazilian Religious Setting." Pp. 222–54 in *Performance Practice: Ethnomusicological Perspectives,* edited by G. Béhague. Westport, Conn.: Greenwood Press.

———. 1990. "Latin American Folk Music." Pp. 185–228 in *Folk and Traditional Music of the Western Continents,* 3rd ed., edited by Bruno Nettl; revised and edited by Valerie Woodring Goertzen. Englewood Cliffs, N.J.: Prentice-Hall.

———, ed. 1994. *Music and Black Ethnicity: The Caribbean and South America.* Coral Gables, Fla.: Univ. of Miami North-South Center/Transaction.

Bigenho, Michelle. 2002. *Sounding Indigenous: Authenticity in Bolivian Music Performance.* New York: Palgrave Macmillan.

Carvalho-Neto, Paulo de. 1964. *Diccionario del folklore ecuatoriano.* Tratado del Folklore Ecuatoriano 1. Quito: Editorial Casa de la Cultura Ecuatoriana.

Cavour, Ernesto. c. 1974. *La zampoña, aerófono boliviano: Método audiovisual.* [La Paz?]: Ediciones Tatu.

Dicks, Ted, ed. 1976. *Victor Jara: His Life and Songs.* London: Elm Tree Books.

Fairley, Jan. 1985. "Annotated Bibliography of Latin-American Popular Music with Particular Reference to Chile and to Nueva Canción." Pp. 305–56 in *Popular Music:* Vol. 5. *Continuity and Change.* Cambridge, England: Cambridge Univ. Press.

Fuks, Victor. 1988. "Music, Dance, and Beer in an Amazonian Indian Community." *Revista de Música Latinoamericana/Latin American Music Review* 9 (2): 151–86.

Grebe, María Ester. 1973. "El Kultrun mapuche: Un microcosmo simbólico." *Revista Musical Chilena* 27 (123–24): 3–42.

Hurtado Suárez, Wilfredo. 1995. *Chicha peruana: Música de los nuevos migrantes.* [Lima, Perú?]: Grupo de Investigaciones Económicas ECO.

List, George. 1983. *Music and Poetry in a Colombian Village: A Tri-Cultural Heritage.* Bloomington: Indiana Univ. Press.

Mendoza, Zoila S. 2000. *Shaping Society through Dance: Mestizo Ritual Performance in the Peruvian Andes.* Chicago Studies in Ethnomusicology. Chicago: Univ. of Chicago Press.

Mendoza de Arce, Daniel. 2001. *Music in Ibero-America to 1850: A Historical Survey.* Lanham, Md.: Scarecrow Press.

Olsen, Dale A. 1980. "Folk Music of South America: A Musical Mosaic." Pp. 386–425 in *Musics of Many Cultures: An Introduction,* edited by E. May. Berkeley: Univ. of California Press.

———. 1986–1987. "The Peruvian Folk Harp Tradition: Determinants of Style." *Folk Harp Journal* 53:48–54; 54:41–58; 55:55–59; 56:57–60.

———. 1996. *Music of the Warao of Venezuela: Song People of the Rain Forest.* Gainesville: University Press of Florida.

Olsen, Dale A., and Daniel E. Sheehy, eds. 1998. *Garland Encyclopedia of World Music:* Vol. 2. *South America, Mexico, Central America, and the Caribbean.* New York: Garland Reference Library of the Humanities, vol. 1193.

Parra, Isabel. 1985. *El libro mayor de Violeta Parra.* Madrid: Ediciones Michay.

Parra, Violeta. 1970. *Décimas: Autobiografía en versos chilenos.* Santiago de Chile: Ediciones Nueva Universidad, Universidad Católica de Chile, Editorial Pomaire.

Ramón y Rivera, Luis Felipe. 1969. *La música folklórica de Venezuela.* Caracas: Monte Avila Editores.

Robertson, Carol E. 1979. "'Pulling the Ancestors': Performance Practice and Praxis in Mapuche Ordering." *Ethnomusicology* 23 (3): 395–416.

Roel Pineda, Josafat. 1959. "El Wayno del Cuzco." *Folklore Americano* 6–7:129–246.

Romero, Raúl, ed. 1993. *Música, danzas y máscaras en los Andes.* Lima: Pontificia Universidad Católica del Perú: Instituto Riva-Agüero.

Schechter, John M. 1987. "Quechua *Sanjuán* in Northern Highland Ecuador: Harp Music as Structural Metaphor on *Purina.*" *Journal of Latin American Lore* 13 (1): 27–46.

———, ed. 1999. *Music in Latin American Culture: Regional Traditions.* New York: Schirmer Books.

Seeger, Anthony. 1979. "What Can We Learn When They Sing? Vocal Genres of the Suya Indians of Central Brazil." *Ethnomusicology* 23 (3): 373–94.

———. 1987. *Why Suyá Sing: A Musical Anthropology of an Amazonian People.* Cambridge, England: Cambridge Univ. Press.

Stevenson, Robert. 1968. *Music in Aztec and Inca Territory.* Berkeley: Univ. of California Press.

Stuempfle, Stephen. 1995. *The Steelband Movement: The Forging of a National Art in Trinidad and Tobago*. Philadelphia: Univ. of Pennsylvania Press.

Turino, Thomas. 1983. "The Charango and the Sirena: Music, Magic, and the Power of Love." *Revista de Música Latinoamericana/Latin American Music Review* 4 (1): 81–119.

———. 1989. "The Coherence of Social Style and Musical Creation among the Aymara in Southern Peru." *Ethnomusicology* 33 (1): 1–30.

———. 1993. *Moving away from Silence: Music of the Peruvian Altiplano and the Experience of Urban Migration*. Chicago: Univ. of Chicago Press.

Valencia Chacón, Américo. 1989. *El siku o zampoña: Perspectivas de un legado musical preincaico y sus aplicaciones en en desarrollo de la música peruana/The Altiplano Bipolar Siku: Study and Projection of Peruvian Panpipe Orchestras*. Ed. bilingue/ Bilingual ed. Lima: Centro de Investigación y Dessarrollo [*sic*] de la Música Peruana: Artex Editores.

Additional Listening

Afro-Hispanic Music from Western Colombia and Ecuador. 1967. Recorded and edited by Norman E. Whitten, Jr. Folkways FE 4376.

BOLIVIAMANTA: Wiñayataqui. Musique traditionnelle des Andes. 1989. ©A.S.P.I.C. [Association pour la Sauvegarde du Patrimoine et de l'Indépendance Culturelle] Editions, Suisse. A.S.P.I.C. X 55501. CD.

El cancionero noble de Colombia. 1962. Recorded by Joaquín Piñeros Corpas. Bogotá: Ministerio de Educación-Editorial Antares-Fontón. 3 discs, 36 pp. text.

Cantan Garzón y Collazos [Colombia]. n.d. (pre-1970). Industria Electro-Sonora, Medellín, Colombia. Sonolux LP 12-104/IES-1.

Chaskinakuy. 1991. *Music of the Andes: Cosecha*. Produced by Edmond Badoux and Francy Vidal. Cassette. Also recorded at Hoffmann Studios, Occidental, California, 1993. CD. All arrangements are by Chaskinakuy.

Clásicas de la canción paraguaya: Alfredo Rolando Ortiz, arpa. n.d. (pre-1980). Quito, Ecuador: Industrias Famoso LDF-1015.

Colombia: La Ceiba. 1989. ©A.S.P.I.C. [Association pour la Sauvegarde du Patrimoine et de l'Indépendance Culturelle] Editions, Suisse. A.S.P.I.C. X 55504. CD.

Harpe Paraguayenne/Paraguayan Harp. 1993. © J.P. Tzaud. Playa Sound PS 65128. Made in France. CD.

Harpes du Venezuela/Harps of Venezuela. 1991. © Discos Top Hits. Playa Sound PS 65083. Made in France. CD.

The Inca Harp: Laments and Dances of the Tawantinsuyu, the Inca Empire [Peru]. 1982. Recorded by Ronald Wright. Lyrichord LLST 7359.

Indian Music of Mexico. 1952, 1962. Recorded by Henrietta Yurchenko. Ethnic Folkways Library FE-4413. 4 pp. notes by Gordon F. Ekholm and Henrietta Yurchenko.

Mountain Music of Peru. 1966. Recorded by John Cohen. Folkways FE 4539.

Mushuc huaira huacamujun: Conjunto indígena "Peguche" [Ecuador]. 1979. Guayaquil, Ecuador: IFESA (Industria Fonográfica Ecuatoriana S.A.). Runa Causay. 339-0651.

Music of the Jívaro of Ecuador. 1972. Recorded and edited by Michael J. Harner. Ethnic Folkways Library FE 4386.

Música andina de Bolivia. 1980. Recorded with commmentary by Max Peter Baumann. Lauro Records LPLI/S-062. 36 pp. booklet.

Música folklórica de Venezuela. n.d. (post-1968). Recorded by Isabel Aretz, Luis Felipe Ramón y Rivera, and Álvaro Fernaud. International Folk Music Council, Anthologie de la Musique Populaire. Ocora OCR 78.

Perou: Julio Benavente Diaz: "Le charango du Cuzco." 1985. Recorded by Rafael Parejo and Regina Baldini. Ocora. Musiques traditionnelles vivantes. Sacem. 558 647.

Pre-Columbian Instruments: Aerophone [Mexico]. 1972. Produced by Lilian Mendelssohn, with Pablo Castellanos. Played by Jorge Daher. Ethnic Folkways Library FE 4177.

Taki Ñan 1998. 1998. Recorded June 10 and June 18, 1998, at the Music Center, Univ. of California, Santa Cruz, Santa Cruz, California. Ensemble Director: John M. Schechter. Recording Engineers: Richard Karst and Mike Jerugim. CD.

Viewing

Argentinísima I. 1972. Video. In Spanish, without subtitles. Directed by Fernando Ayala and Héctor Olivera. Featured performers: Atahualpa Yupanqui, Ariel Ramírez, Los Chalchaleros, Mercedes Sosa, and Astor Piazzolla. Media Home Entertainment, Inc., 510 W. 6th St., Suite 1032, Los Angeles, Calif. 90014.

El canto cuenta su historia. 1976. Film/video. In Spanish, without subtitles. Directed by Fernando Ayala and Héctor Olivera. Featured performers: Cayetano Daglio, Ángel Villoldo, Francisco Canaro, Carlos Gardel, Rosita Quiroga, Ignacio Corsini, Ada Falcón, Agustín Magaldi and Pedro Noda, Marta de los Ríos, Margarita Palacios, Eduardo Falú, Los Cantores de Quilla Huasi, Jorge Cafrune, Amelita Baltar, and Hermanos Abalos. Condor Video (A Heron International Company), c/o Jason Films, 2825 Wilcrest, Suite 670, Houston, Tex. 77042. Aries Cinematográfica, Argentina.

Disappearing World: Umbanda: The Problem Solver. 1977. Video. In English and in Portuguese with English subtitles. Directed by Stephen Cross. Narrated by Peter Fry. Brian Moser, series editor. Public Media Video, 5547 N. Ravenswood Ave., Chicago, Ill. 60640-1199; Granada Colour Production, Granada UK.

Folklórico: Ballet Folklórico de México. 1989. Video. In Spanish, without subtitles. Directed by Amalia Hernández. Featured performers: Ballet Folklórico de México. Madera Cinevideo, 525 E. Yosemite Ave., Madera, Calif. 93638.

The Incas. 1980. Video. Produced by Anna Benson-Gyles. Narrated by Tony Kahn. Michael Ambrosino, executive producer. Odyssey Series. For Odyssey: Marian White, producer; David Berenson, editor. Co-production of British Broadcasting Corporation (BBC) and Public Broadcasting Associates, Inc., Boston, Mass. Incas/Odyssey Series/Box 1000, Boston, Mass. 02118. PBS Video, 1320 Braddock Pl., Alexandria, Va. 22314.

Mountain Music of Peru. 1984. 16mm film/video, 60 min. Color. Directed by John Cohen. Berkeley: University of California, Extension Center For Media and Independent Learning, 2000 Center St., 4th floor, Berkeley, Calif. 94704.

Plena Is Work, Plena Is Song. 1989. 16mm film/video. Directed by Pedro A. Rivera and Susan Zeig. Cinema Guild, Inc.: 1697 Broadway, Suite 506, New York, N.Y. 10019-5904.

Q'eros: The Shape of Survival. 1979. 16mm film/video, 53 min. Color. Directed by John Cohen. Berkeley: University of California, Extension Center for Media and Independent Learning, 2000 Center St., 4th floor, Berkeley, Calif. 94704.

Schaeffer, Nancy. 1995. "Directory of Latin American Films and Videos: Music, Dance, Mask, and Ritual." *Revista de Música Latinoamericana/Latin American Music Review* 16(2): 221–41.

What's Cuba Playing At? (¿Qué se toca en Cuba?) 1985. Video, 72 min. In Spanish, with subtitles. Directed by Michael Dibb. BBC TV Production, in association with Cuban Television. Center for Cuban Studies, 124 W. 23rd St., New York, N.Y. 10011.

Web Resources

- Chaskinakuy
  http://www.chaskinakuy.com
  http://www.chaskinakuy.com/recording.htm
  http://www.chaskinakuy.com/biography.htm

- Chapter Author, John M. Schechter
  http://arts.ucsc.edu/faculty/schechter/

- Florida State University School of Music Center for Music of the Americas
  http://www.music.fsu.edu/ctr-americas.htm
      The Center for Music of the Americas was established in 1985 to create
  and enhance understanding among the peoples of North, South, and
  Central America and the Caribbean through music and its related arts and
  folkways. It forms an integral part of the Florida State University School of
  Music. The center oversees numerous world music performance groups,
  within the School of Music, and it seeks to support any and all activities
  related to music in the Americas. The center is closely related to the
  disciplines of Ethnomusicology, Historical Musicology, and Multicultural
  Music Education.

- Latin American Music Center, Indiana University School of Music
  http://www.music.indiana.edu/som/lamc/
      A major research center for the study of Latin American music. This Web
  site includes a link to "Online Resources."

- LAMC-L: Academic Discussion of Latin American Music
  http://www.music.indiana.edu/som/lamc/edusearch/lamc-l/
      At the Latin American Music Center, Indiana University School of
  Music. LAMC-L is an e-mail discussion list and file server for the Latin
  American Music Center at the School of Music, Indiana University,
  Bloomington. This list provides subscribers with an avenue for exchanging
  news about work-in-progress; for posing questions of general interest
  about Latin American music; for announcing conferences, festivals,
  concerts, recordings, and publications; and for engaging in the serious
  discussion of issues pertaining to Latin American music.

- *Latin American Music Review/Revista de Música Latinoamericana*
  http://www.utexas.edu/utpress/journals/jlamr.html
      This journal, published by University of Texas Press, explores the
  historical, ethnographic, and sociocultural dimensions of Latin American
  music in Latin American social groups, including the Puerto Rican,
  Mexican, Cuban, and Portuguese populations in the United States. Articles
  are written in English, Spanish, or Portuguese.

- *Revista Musical Chilena*
  http://www.scielo.cl/scielo.php?script=sci_serial&pid=0716-2790&lng=
  en&nrm=iso
      Published by the Universidad de Chile, Facultad de Artes. One of the
  major musicology/ethnomusicology journals published in Latin America.

CHAPTER

9

Discovering and Documenting a World of Music

Jeff Todd Titon and David B. Reck

All of us are familiar with the tale (or movie) of Dorothy and her adventures with the Tin Man, the Lion, and the Scarecrow in the fantastic land of Oz. But most of us have forgotten Dorothy's startling discovery once she got back to Kansas: Home was where her heart was, a fascinating world of people, family, neighbors, and friends—of things that before her adventures she had overlooked. This is a familiar theme in literature the world over. The hero (representing us) travels to faraway places, sees and does fabulous things, meets incredible people, searches for marvelous treasures. But invariably the rainbow leads home; the pot of gold is buried in one's own backyard; the princess is none other than the girl next door.

In our explorations of the world's musics we—both students and scholars—are fascinated by cultures and peoples greatly separated from us by geography or time, in sound and style, in ways of making and doing music. In a sense, for every one of us there is an Oz. But there is also a music-culture surrounding us, one that we see and hear only partially because it is too close to us, because we take it for granted, as fish do water. Our musical environment is held both within us—in our thoughts—and outside us—by other members of our community. It expands out from us (and contracts into us) in a series of circles that may include family, ethnic groups, regional styles, geographical location, and cultural roots (Western Europe, Africa, Asia, and so on). It is available to us live or mechanically reproduced. It comes to us out of history (the classical masterworks, old-time fiddle tunes, bebop jazz) or from the here and now (the latest hit on the music charts or the avant-garde "new thing").

Music in Our Own Backyards

This chapter is all about gathering reliable information on today's music. We encourage you to seek out a nearby musical world, to observe it in person, to talk with the people involved in it, to document it with recordings and photographs, and to present the information in a project that will contribute to knowledge about today's musical activities. If this research project is part of a course, you should check with your instructor for specific directions. What follows is a general guide, based on the experience we and our students have had with similar projects at our colleges and universities.

Selecting a subject for your research is the first step in the project. Songs and instrumental music serve a great many purposes and occur in a wide variety of contexts, from singing in the shower to the Metropolitan Opera, from the high school marching band to the rock festival, from the lullaby to the television commercial, and from music videos to computer music via the Internet. Whether trivial or profound, it is all meaningful. To help you select a subject, we shall consider a few organizing principles: family, generation and gender, leisure, religion, ethnicity, regionalism, nationalism, and commercialization. As you read through the following brief survey, you will be led to or reminded of some subjects that interest you. Here we focus on North American examples, but if you are using this book elsewhere you should apply these (and perhaps other) organizing principles to examples you think of from your own music-culture. Later we shall give you some specific suggestions on how to move from a subject to a topic, and how best to proceed from there to gather the information.

Family

As is true of all cultures, most North Americans first hear music in family life (Figure 9.1). Much of that music comes from the CD player, radio, television, or computer. People often say they were very strongly influenced by the kind of music they heard before they were old enough to have their own albums. Families also usually provide some live music. Many mothers and grandmothers sing lullabies, for example. Sometimes lullabies are the only songs in a foreign language that North American children with strong ethnic backgrounds hear, because people (particularly grandparents) often fall back on old, familiar languages for intimate songs.

In short, most North Americans have an early layer of songs learned in childhood in a family setting. Often they are just songs for entertaining children, with no deep cultural message to impart. What they do teach are the musical tastes of the particular group, whether rural Quebecois, California suburban, Illinois heartland, Appalachian mountain, or New York inner-city. Children then work in harmony with (or against) this basic musical background as a part of growing up and finding their identity.

Generation and Gender

Much North American music making is organized along age-group or generational lines. Schools, church classes, scouting groups, children's sidewalk games, college singing groups, and many other musical situations include people of about the same age. Songs learned by these groups may stay with them as they grow older.

Walker Evans. Courtesy of Library of Congress.

Figure 9.1
A sharecropper family sings hymns in front of their home. Hale County, Alabama, 1936.

Yet, under the influence of television and recordings, the amount of generational mixing in North American musical life has grown. For example, much of the music thought to belong only to the young in the 1960s, such as Beatles' music, appealed to older generations as well. And today's youngsters like their parents' music better than their parents liked that of their own parents. In ethnic musics too, young people have taken to learning traditional songs from their grandmothers instead of laughing at the old folks' songs as they might have one or two generations ago.

There are fewer gender differences regarding music today than there used to be. Just as women now take up sports like race-car driving and become professional jockeys, so more women play instruments, such as the drums and saxophone, that used to be largely limited to men (Figure 9.2). A whole genre that used to be exclusively male—barbershop quartet singing—now has a parallel female style, exhibited by groups such as the Sweet Adelines. One women's bluegrass group years ago called themselves the All Girl Boys, while a new generation of bluegrass stars includes Alison Krauss, Rhonda Vincent, and Laurie Lewis. Even so, gender differences remain important, as many of today's musical groups, like other North American social groups, are organized along gender lines.

Leisure

Music as a recreational leisure activity is an important part of North American life. For example, one barbershop quartet program listed the wives of the singers as "Thursday Night Widows"—perhaps one reason for the formation of women's quartets. Many North Americans feel the need for a strong group pastime, and of course some of this impulse is channeled into musical organizations. A local American Legion Post, or an ethnic group such as the Polish Falcons, may have a band; here the music making affirms group

Figure 9.2

"The boys in the band." Grove Lake Concert Band, a brass band from Oregon, 1911. (Photographer unknown.)

solidarity. Fielding a band for the local parade or festival brings the group visibility and pride. Individual members may find performing in a fife-and-drum corps or the Governor's Footguard Band (to use Connecticut examples) a satisfying way to spend leisure time. Black youngsters in high school and college form extracurricular, informal hip-hop or gospel groups; sometimes these groups become semiprofessional or even fully professional. Most high schools and colleges can boast a few rock bands and possibly even a jazz group, as well as cocktail pianists, folksinging guitarists, and chamber music ensembles.

Religion

Religion is one of the better-documented areas of North American musical life. Scholars know about music's role in many religious movements, ranging from the eighteenth-century Moravians through the revival movements of the nineteenth century and the founding of sects such as the Mormons or Pentecostals. Much has been written about the appropriateness of certain types of music making in religious settings, such as organ playing in the Jewish synagogue or the introduction of folk and jazz elements to church services. Scholarly study focuses on the Negro spiritual, while the tent revival preacher, the snake handler, and the old-time churches also receive attention (see Figure 9.3). But the musical activities of contemporary, mainline middle-class churches, synagogues, and mosques offer equal interest, though few people study them. The songs of new religious movements,

Figure 9.3
Music almost always accompanies formal rites of passage, such as this old-time baptism. Eastern Kentucky, 1990.

Jeff Todd Titon

such as small meditation groups based on Christian or Eastern religious thinking, also deserve attention. These groups work to encourage solidarity and teach their message, but they have no traditional music. Often they change the words of well-known songs as a way of starting, just as Martin Luther changed the words of German drinking songs 450 years ago to create a body of sacred songs we know as Protestant chorales. The new groups may also work hard on developing an "inner music" of their members, through which the believer reaches the desired state of tranquility.

Ethnicity

Ethnicity is the oldest consideration in the study of the North American music-culture in the sense that the United States is usually regarded as a nation of immigrants. It is also one of the newest considerations because of the current interest in ethnic identity, a trend that has gathered force since the late 1960s (Figure 9.4).

Ethnicity has always played a major role in North American musical history. An *ethnic group* is a population that has a sense of solidarity among its members. That sense of solidarity arises from shared memories of a common past, and often from the idea of a common homeland; from the idea that way back in time the group had a common ancestry, which gives them all a feeling of kinship; and from elements of common culture, such as religion or language. Whether in the dialect and songs of the French Acadians in New Brunswick, the heroic *corrido* ballads sung along the Rio Grande by Mexican Americans, the ballad of hard-hearted Barbara Allen sung by British Americans , or a Yiddish lullaby in a Brooklyn tenement, North Americans have built and maintained ethnic boundaries through music. Music's function as a sign of group solidarity and common ancestry is nowhere clearer than in the variety of songs, dances, and instrumental

Figure 9.4
Alan Shavarsh Bardezbanian plays the oud with his Middle Eastern Ensemble. National Folk Festival, Bangor, Maine, 2003.

Jeff Todd Titon

tunes that characterize the North American ethnic mosaic. Students in the United States whose parents or grandparents stopped public singing of Old World songs on their way to becoming "one-hundred-percent Americans" now become enthusiastic about joining ethnic music groups or studying their group's heritage. Other parents and grandparents, of course, never stopped singing their native songs.

North American ethnic music has always involved transcontinental exchange. On the one hand, Greek Americans are influenced by new developments in popular music in Athens, while on the other, Polish American records find great favor among farmers in far-off mountain villages in Poland. American jazz and country music have spread around the world, from Holland to Russia and Japan. A complicated interplay goes on between black music in North America, Africa, and the Caribbean (Figure 9.5). A single song may embody layer upon layer of musical travel. Reggae developed in Jamaica, where it represented a blend of Afro-Caribbean and black U.S. soul music. This already complicated style came to America from England, where pop groups repackaged it and exported it, and the cycle continues: Reggae is now popular in some parts of Africa; indeed, in many parts of the world.

In today's world, family- and community-based musics have become markers of ethnic identity and an older way of life. At the same time they are packaged, bought, and sold in the marketplace; this encourages originality and virtuosity, qualities that may not have been important in the musics' traditional contexts.

Jeff Todd Titon

Figure 9.5
One of Boston's Caribbean steel-drum bands performs at a women's prison. 1979.

Regionalism

Regionalism in North America is thought to have declined with the spread of the interstate highway system, chains of fast-food restaurants, and the spread of television, all of which began in the 1950s. But just as ethnic groups never really dissolved into the so-called melting pot, so ways of life still differ according to region: speech, food, music, and so forth. Regionalism crops up in the names of styles, such as the Chicago blues sound and the Detroit "Motown" soul sound, or even within ethnic styles, as in the different sounds of Polish polka bands in the Midwest versus the Northeast. The crisp bowing, downbeat accents, and up-tempo performance of a fiddle tune in the Northeast (Figure 9.6) bears little resemblance to the same tune's performance in the Southwest, with its smooth bowing and more relaxed beat. The same hymn tune shows considerable variation even within the same denomination in different parts of the country. One Indiana Primitive Baptist was overheard to comment on the slow, highly decorated tunes of Primitive Baptists in North Carolina: "They take ten minutes just to get through 'Amazing Grace!'"

Like ethnicity, regionalism is coming back into fashion. There are now so many local festivals that books of listings are published. Some locales host mock battles, which are fought again and again for throngs of tourists to appropriate live or recorded music. One highly visible regional music performance is the singing of "My Old Kentucky Home" at the May running of the Kentucky Derby. In a recent year 150 thousand spectators joined in, and millions of television viewers were on hand to link the song and event to the region of its origin.

In summary, even if it sometimes seems the result of shrewd marketing to promote local cultures, regional musical diversity has not yet given way to a one-size-fits-all music. North America is still too large and diverse to

Figure 9.6
Fiddler Ed Larkin. Tunbridge, Vermont, 1941.

Jack Delano. Courtesy of Library of Congress.

turn all music into brand names or to have the entire population respond equally to all music, and the search for revival or for novelty continues.

Nationalism

As a colony that declared its independence and fought a war to preserve it, the United States long ago began seeking ways to establish a national musical identity. Popular national sentiment was evoked by the frequent performance of patriotic songs, a tradition that has declined only in recent decades. Official music plays less of a part in U.S. life now than when John Philip Sousa's band and its imitators played flag-waving tunes on the bandstand for Sunday promenaders, or when schoolchildren knew all the verses of the national anthem. President Jimmy Carter's musical foray into jazz—he sang "Salt Peanuts" with the composer and trumpeter Dizzy Gillespie—was a media event. President Bill Clinton's saxophone playing reflected the musical tastes of the Vietnam generation, for whom patriotic music rang hollow.

Perhaps our most obvious repertory of national music consists of Christmas songs such as "Jingle Bells," "White Christmas," and "Rudolph the Red-Nosed Reindeer." During the holiday season it is almost impossible to escape them. The curmudgeon who shoos away carolers from his front yard is said to lack the Christmas spirit, and he soon gains a neighborhood reputation as a Scrooge. Other examples include patriotic songs learned in public school, songs like "The Star-Spangled Banner," "America the Beautiful," and "My Country 'Tis of Thee." "Take Me out to the Ballgame" and "God Bless America" represent songs that began life in musical theatre or on recordings but that have now become part of the national repertory.

Commercial Music

Much of the music in North American culture is supplied by paid professionals. It is remarkable that this complex culture carries musical events also typical of non- or preindustrial societies. Though some genres, such as the funeral lament, have largely disappeared in the United States, rituals like weddings and initiations (bar mitzvahs, debutante parties, senior proms) that mark a change of life still demand solemnization by music. A wedding may take place in a park with an ice cream truck, balloons, and jeans instead of in a formal church setting, yet music remains indispensable even if it consists of pop tunes instead of an official wedding march. Elegant yacht clubs tend to schedule dances during full-moon evenings, continuing a practice of certain ancient cultures.

A great deal of the commercial music North Americans come into daily contact with may be described as "disembodied"—that is, the listener does not feel the physical presence of the performer and many times cannot even see the original musical situation (as in Figure 9.7). Some of this music can be partially controlled by the listener, who selects recordings from his or her collection to suit a mood. Although the listener can imagine the original musical situation—concert or recording studio—there is no possibility of interaction with the performers, and the music is the same each time it is heard.

"What instrument do you play?" begins an old joke. The reply: "Just the stereo." Ethnomusicologists pay attention to how people use music in their daily lives. Many young people today have become active consumers who not only select music but engineer and package it for themselves and their friends. The models for this kind of musical activity were the "Deadheads" who recorded and traded tapes of live Grateful Dead concerts. Long before the Deadheads, jazz buffs were recording after-hours jam sessions and trading the results. Today, the person who downloads commercial music from the Internet, edits it, and burns custom CDs or stores the music on an iPod plays quite an active role in choosing music to suit a lifestyle. Music making on the computer does not require singing or playing a traditional instrument; instead, the computer becomes both the instrument and the recording studio.

Figure 9.7
Dancing to records on a jukebox. West Virginia, 1942.

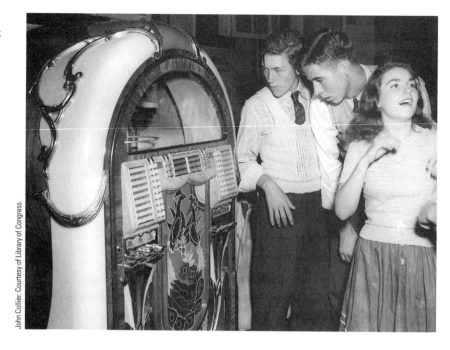

John Collier. Courtesy of Library of Congress.

One of the most significant recent developments in commercial music is the rise of the format called MP3 (now being replaced by AAC) and the distribution of music in this format over the Internet. Musicians who think that the music industry takes too much of the profits from album sales have been able to market their recordings directly to consumers via the World Wide Web. Consumers flock to Web sites where they can download music, often for free.

At the opposite end of the spectrum from disembodied commercial music is public background music. Unlike listening to music of one's own choice in one's own room on a computer, there is no logical connection between buying groceries and hearing piped music in a supermarket. In offices and factories, the employer may choose to have background music that is manufactured and programmed to increase worker productivity. This of course represents a particularly powerful type of unrequested music. Some do not even notice it.

This brief survey should help you select a subject for your project: a nearby musical world that you're interested in, have access to, and can gather information about.

Doing Musical Ethnography

Your aim in discovering and documenting a world of music is a *musical ethnography*—a written representation, description, and interpretation of some aspect of a music-culture, organized from the standpoint of a particular topic. Your writing may be accompanied by photographs, recordings, or even videotapes that you make while documenting the music-culture. A major goal in doing musical ethnography is to understand a music-culture or some part of it from a native's or insider's point of view. What does that point of view encompass? Recall how in Chapter 1 we divided a music-culture into four components: ideas, activities, repertories, and material culture. Approaching a music-culture for the first time, you may feel overwhelmed, but if you use Table 1.1 (p. 17) to organize your thinking about what you see and hear, you will be able to see how you might go about gathering information on specific aspects of it.

The music in the repertory can be recorded for later study and analysis. Much of social organization and material culture can be observed. By listening to musicians talk with each other, and by talking to them, you can begin to understand their ideas about music; through interviews you can learn more about those ideas, the repertory, musical activities, and material culture. (After all, conversations and interviews formed the basis for the musicians' life histories in this book.) But discovering and documenting a world of music is not like examining an amoeba under a microscope. People will differ in how they behave, what they believe, and what they say to you. Different people will sing "the same tune" differently. Under these conditions, accurately representing and describing a music-culture, even a single aspect of it, in a musical ethnography is a complex and subtle undertaking.

Selecting a Subject: Some Practical Suggestions

It is obvious that your project requires you to collect, understand, and organize information about music in order to present it. It differs from the usual school research paper in that it focuses on a musical situation that you seek out directly from people rather than from books in a library. In ethnomusicology, as in anthropology and folklore, this in-person witnessing, observing, questioning, tape recording, photographing, and in some cases performing is called *fieldwork:* work "in the field" rather than the laboratory or library. This is not to say that library research is useless or should be avoided. You might find background information on your topic in the library, and you should not overlook the opportunity to do so. But most of your project takes you into the field, where you will obtain your most valuable and original information.

Collecting, understanding, and organizing information about music are, of course, interrelated. You will begin with certain insights about the information you collect. As you organize it, you will gain new insights. After you organize it, you will be able to describe it and move toward an interpretation of it.

You can approach the choice of a research subject in different ways. First, you might try to chart the music you hear daily:

1. Keep a log or journal of all the music you hear over three or four days or a week. Note the context, style, and purpose of the music. Calculate how much of your day is spent with music of some sort.

2. Record, videotape, or simply describe in words several television commercials that employ music. Note the style of the music and the image it attempts to project. How is the music integrated into the message of the advertisement? Is it successful? Offensive? Both?

3. Map the uses of music in various movies or television shows as you watch them. For contrast, select a daytime serial and a crime-fighting show, or a situation comedy and a popular dramatic series, for example.

4. Survey the uses of background music in local stores. Interview salespeople, managers, owners, customers (always obtaining their permission). See what they say about music and sales.

A second approach is to examine the music in your own background. Explore your memory of songs and music. Note how your religious and ethnic heritage influenced the music you heard and your current musical interests. How has your musical taste changed as you have grown older? Survey the contents of your CD collection or your preferences in listening to music on the radio, television, or the Internet. The same questions can be asked of your friends and family.

A third approach is to explore music in your community—your school community or your hometown. Here you can interview people, listen to musical performances and possibly take part in them yourself, and gather quite a lot of information. Here are several possible subject headings:

Ethnic groups
Piano teachers
Private instrumental instruction (music stores, private lessons in the home)
Choir directors
Church organists, pianists, and so on
School music (elementary, junior high, high school)
Music stores
Musical instrument makers
Background music in public places
The club scene (bars, coffeehouses, restaurants, clubs)
Musical organizations (community choral groups, bands, barbershop quartets, and so forth)
Part-time (weekend) musicians
Professional or semiprofessional bands (rock, pop, jazz, rhythm and blues, country, gospel, and so forth)
Chamber music groups
Parades and music
Disc jockeys
Symphony orchestras

A fourth approach narrows the subject and concentrates on an individual musician's life, opinions, and music. Often we focus our attention on the musical superstars, but in the process we forget the many fine and sensitive musicians, many of them amateurs, who live in our communities. Senior citizens, teachers, owners of record or music stores, or tradespeople like the local barber, school custodian, or factory worker have

Jeff Todd Titon

Figure 9.8
Nathan, Chris, and Robin Sockalexis, Penobscot Nation, Old Town, Maine, singing and drumming. Bangor, Maine, 2003.

sometimes had rich musical experiences as professional or part-time musicians. To search out such people is not always easy. Try the musicians' union, ethnic organizations, word of mouth, school or college music teachers, radio station disc jockeys, the clergy, club owners, newspaper columnists and feature story writers, or even local police stations and fire departments. Musicians can be approached directly at fairs, contests, festivals, concerts, and dances (Figure 9.8). Many colleges and universities have foreign student associations that include amateur musicians, and they can tell you about others in the area. Ethnic specialty restaurants and grocery stores are another resource.

The musical world that surrounds you is so diverse that you may feel swamped, unable to focus your energy. But when it finally comes down to deciding on a subject for your project, two guiding principles will help you out: *Choose something you are interested in, and choose something you have access to.* It will be hard to succeed if you are not curious about the music you examine, and you will have to be close to it to look at it carefully.

Collecting Information

Once you have chosen a subject, your next move is to immerse yourself in the musical situation, consider what aspects of it interest you, and select a topic. Then you need to plan how to collect information—what questions to ask when you talk to the musicians or others involved, what performances to record, and so forth. Almost always you will need time and the flexibility to revise your plans as you collect the information you need. For that reason you should get started as early in the term as possible. Most people will be happy to tell you about their involvement with music as long as you show them you really are interested.

Gaining Entry

Musical activities usually have a public (performance) side and a private (rehearsal) side. The performance is the tip of the iceberg; you will want to understand what lies beneath, and that is best learned by talking to the people involved. If you must approach a stranger, you may want to arrange an introduction, either by a mutual friend or by a person in authority. If, for example, you want to talk with musicians in an ethnic organization, it is wise to approach the president of the organization and seek his or her advice first. This allows you not only to get good information but also to share your plans with the president, who needs to know what is going on in the group. In other situations it is best to let the people in authority know what you intend to do, and why, but to avoid having them introduce you, particularly if their authority is legal only and they do not belong to the same ethnic group as the people whose music you will be studying.

The first contact is especially important because the way you present yourself establishes your identity and role. That is one reason why you must take the time to be honest with yourself and others about your interest in their music and the purpose of your project. If you are a college student, you may find yourself being assigned the role of the expert. But this is a role to avoid. Tell the people who give you information that they are the experts and that you are the student who wants to learn from them—that otherwise you would not seek their help. Let them know that you hope they will be willing to let you talk with them, observe them, and, if appropriate, participate in the music.

Selecting a Topic

Usually your subject takes in several music situations, and you will find yourself having to choose among them so as not to undertake a larger project than you can accomplish. If, for example, you want to learn about Irish American music in your community, you may find that there is so much going on that a survey of it all will be superficial. It will be easier to discover a topic if you decide to concentrate on one aspect of it, perhaps the musical tradition of one family, or the musical scene in a particular club. Remember once again to choose something you are interested in and have access to.

After you have narrowed your subject, you face the next step, which is one of the most difficult: selecting a topic. A *topic* is more than just a subject. It is a subject viewed from a particular angle, from a certain perspective, and with a limited goal in mind. For example, "the Jewish cantor" is a subject, something to investigate. "Musical education of Jewish cantors in New York City" is a topic. The cantor is viewed from a special perspective: education. You want to understand what the education of a cantor consists of and what the results are. Another example of a subject is "the Outlaws, a local country music band." A topic that involves the band might be "gender and gender roles in the music of the Outlaws, a local country music band." Here the focus is on the band members' attitudes, interactions, lyrics, social scene, and so forth, as they relate to gender. By themselves, subjects cover too much ground. Topics focus your attention on specific questions that will help you organize the information you collect.

The process of refining a topic is gradual and involves a lot of thought. To begin, go back to Chapter 1 and use the music-culture model to select aspects of your subject that you are interested in. Do you want to focus on conceptions of music, activities involving music, repertories, or material culture? Of course, these aspects are interrelated, and it will be difficult to ignore any of them completely; nevertheless, concentrating most of your attention on one of them will help you select a topic you can manage. It will also give you some initial ideas to think about as you gather your information. While doing field research you will find that some areas of your topic yield better information than others. As you assess the results of your research-in-progress, you should be able to refine and refocus your topic to take advantage of the good information you have gathered, while you may have to deemphasize, or possibly even discard, other aspects of your topic that you have found difficult to research.

Your instructor can help you move from a subject to a topic. Many teachers ask students to begin their field research early in the term and to make a short, written proposal in which they describe their subject and their topic. Instructor feedback at this point can save you a lot of time later. For example, many students at first choose topics that are too broad, given the limitations on their time and the instructor's guidelines for the paper's length. Another common difficulty is a topic that is too vague. You can sharpen up your topic if you formulate it as a question or series of questions. Interpretation—figuring out what your documentation means—always goes in the direction of answering questions about your topic. If you have decided to focus on one band's repertory, a topic like "the repertory of the Accidental Tourists, a campus rock band" should be made more precise with questions like "How does the band choose, learn, arrange, and maintain songs for their repertory?" A series of questions like this can help you focus your observations and interviews. In this case you would want to ask the band members these questions and to attend some rehearsals and see how the band chooses, learns, and arranges their songs. Formulating a topic as a series of questions will help you organize your project around those questions. When it comes time to write your project up, the answers to those questions, and how the answers are related, will lead you to your overall interpretation of the topic and the main point you want to make.

In other words, gathering information is not simply a matter of recording it as a sponge soaks up water. You will want to be selective in what you document, because after documentation you will need to interpret your material. Say that your subject is music on the school radio station, and your topic has to do with the radio station's attitude toward women's hip-hop groups. You decide to interview some of the people who work at the station, and in the interviews you try to figure out a way to approach your topic. One deejay might play a lot of women's music on a particular show, and you might find out something about this deejay's attitude by asking.

As you gather information, you try to estimate how well theory is put into practice—the station people say they are in favor of women's music, but you find that overall they don't play very much of it. You wonder why. Do the station people think the audience does not want to hear it? What does the audience want to hear, how do they know, and should they play what the audience wants to hear, anyway?

Questions like these will arise during the course of your research. They can help you to select the kind of documentation that you will do—whether, for example, to survey the recordings in the radio station's library—and help you to focus your interpretation so that by the end of your project you will have some answers to your questions. You will not merely be gathering material but focusing that material on a topic; the heart of your project is your own interpretation of the material in light of the topic you have chosen.

Library and Internet Research

Depending on the topic you have selected, you may want to visit the library and the Internet at this point to see if anyone has published research on your topic. Try your library's collection first. The electronic card catalog will be helpful; look under such headings as "music," "folk music," "popular music," and whatever categories and keywords are closely related to your subject. It might be useful to spend a couple of hours in the library stacks, looking at books on the shelves and opening any on your subject, for it is almost impossible to know where to look for everything in the card catalog alone. One reference work that you may find useful is *American Musical Traditions*, edited by Jeff Todd Titon and Bob Carlin (Titon and Carlin, 2002).

If your library subscribes to *Ethnomusicology*, the journal of the Society for Ethnomusicology, you will find in each of its three yearly issues an invaluable guide to published research in the "Current Bibliography, Discography and Filmography" section. The most recent years' entries are available on the Society for Ethnomusicology's Web site: http://www.indiana.edu/~ethmusic/. Another useful resource is *Ethnomusicology OnLine*, at http://research.umbc.edu/efhm/eol.html.

The American Folklife Center, at the Library of Congress, and the Smithsonian Institution's Center for Folklife and Heritage, both of which have extensive collections of recorded sound, can be accessed on the Internet via the following addresses:

http://lcweb.loc.gov/folklife/
http://www.folklife.si.edu/

You may find some of the following additional periodicals helpful:

American Music
Asian Music
Black Music Research Journal
The Black Perspective in Music

Bluegrass Unlimited
Journal of American Folklore
Journal of Country Music
Journal of Jazz Studies
Journal of Popular Culture
Journal of Popular Music and Society
Latin American Music Review
Living Blues
Music Educators' Journal
The Old-Time Herald
Popular Music
Southern Exposure
Western Folklore
World of Music
Yearbook of the International Council for Traditional Music

Look in the reference section of your library or on the Internet for such bibliographies as the Music Index and RILM, as well as specialized bibliographies and reference works, such as the earlier mentioned *American Musical Traditions* (Titon and Carlin 2002). There may also be discographies of recordings in music in the area you are researching. For example, Richard Spottswood's *Ethnic Music on Records: A Discography of Ethnic Recordings Produced in the United States, 1893 to 1942* is a five-volume work that lists 78-rpm recordings made during that period (Spottswood 1990). If your research topic involves a U.S. ethnic music, then this could be a valuable resource for you. The bibliographies will point you toward books and articles on your subject. The reference librarian can help you find these. Many of these music-related bibliographies and discographies are now available electronically. Some are on the Internet and others are available on CD-ROM.

The Internet has become a vast resource for information about music. Try searching the Internet for keywords that surround your topic. You will probably find that you have to refine your search greatly in order to make it efficient. You should also realize that some of the information you find on people's Web sites, such as their opinions about music, does not carry the authority of a scholarly book. Nevertheless some of these specialized Web sites offer a good deal of useful information that you may not be able to find in books.

The Internet is particularly good in gathering groups of people together to discuss a subject of common interest and share insights. For example, numerous bluegrass Web sites reflect how bluegrass fans think and talk about their music. A bluegrass list, or discussion group, Bluegrass-L, is open to subscribers and might even be a good place to do research. Other interest groups involving music abound on the Internet. Look in the newsgroups listed under Rec.Music. Several discussion lists focus on musics in India, for example; there is an Arab music list, and so forth. Of course, the Internet also has a great deal of music, now available in MP3 and other audio formats, as well as in streaming audio and video.

Another good reason for visiting the library early in your project is that you may find a reference to a promising article or book that you will need to request on interlibrary loan. But avoid the temptation to read everything that looks as if it might somehow be relevant. The Internet can also take up a lot more time than it should. Remember that you will gather most of your information directly by observing a music-culture in action and by speaking with people who participate in the music-culture. Library and Internet research merely provides background information, and sometimes it cannot even do that—your subject may not have had attention in print, or the little that has been written may not be useful. But if research on your topic has been published, you will be able to undertake a better project if you are familiar with this research. Further, the people whose music you are studying can often suggest good books and articles for you to read, saving you time in your search.

Participation and Observation

Doing research in the field requires a basic plan of action. Which people should you talk with? Which performances should you witness? Should you go to rehearsals? What about a visit to a recording studio? If you are studying a music teacher, should you watch a private lesson? Should the teacher teach you? Will you take photographs? Videotape? What kind of recording equipment can you get? Who will pay for it? You have probably been thinking about these and many similar questions. One more that you should pay attention to at this time regards your personal relationship to the people whose music you will study. Should you act as an observer, as a detached, objective reporter? Or should you, in addition to observing, also participate in the musical activity if you can?

Participating as well as observing can be useful (and quite enjoyable). You hope to learn the music "from the inside." Rather than hanging around the edges of the action, depending on others to explain all the rules, you will come to know some of the musical belief system intuitively.

But participating has its drawbacks. The problem with being a participant-observer is that you sometimes know too much. It is like not knowing the forest for the trees: The closer you are to a situation, the less of an overall view you have, and in order to address your project to an outside reader, you will need to imagine yourself an outsider, too. We tend to filter out the regularities of our lives. If every time we met a stranger we had to stop and think about whether our culture says we should shake hands, rub noses, or bow, we would be in constant panic; if we had to think hard whether red means stop or go, driving would be impossible. This filtering process means that we take the most basic aspects of a situation for granted. So if you are participating as well as observing, you must make a special effort to be an outsider and take nothing for granted. This dual perspective, the view of the participant-observer, is not difficult to maintain while you are learning how to participate in the musical situation. In fact, when you are learning, the dual perspective is forced on you. The trouble is that after you have learned, you can forget what it was like to be an outside observer. Therefore it is quite important to keep a record of your changing perspective as you move from outsider to participant. This record should be written in your field notes or spoken into your tape recorder as your perspective changes.

In fact, you may already be a full participant in the music-culture you intend to study. Writing a musical ethnography about a music-culture in which you have been involved for some time may seem quite appealing. Although this kind of research appears easy, it is not. Your knowledge usually is too specialized for general readers. Further, the issues that matter to you as a member of the music-culture may not interest the general reader. You may feel that because of the depth of your knowledge, you do not need to interview any other members of the music-culture, but this is not so. Other participants' perspectives will be different from yours, and equally important. You may find, also, that in writing about a music-culture in which you are a full participant, you are anxious to express a particular point of view as if it is a generally accepted truth rather than a bias coming from inside the music-culture.

What if you work as an observer only and forego participation? There are some advantages to doing so. It saves time. You can put all your energy into watching and trying to understand how what people tell you is going on matches what you can actually see and hear going on. You can follow both sides of "what I say" and "what I do" more easily when you are merely observing as opposed to participating. On the other hand, you do not achieve objectivity by keeping yourself out of the action. Your very presence as an observer alters the musical situation, particularly if you are photographing or tape-recording. In many situations you will actually cause less interference if you participate rather than intrude as a neutral and unresponsive observer. If you are studying dance music, for example, it is a good idea to dance, thereby blending in (Figure 9.9).

Ethics

Doing fieldwork involves important ethical considerations. Most colleges and universities have a policy designed to prevent people from being harmed by research. Be sure to find out from your instructor if your project is bound by your institution's human subjects research policy and whether you need to get it reviewed and approved by your institution. Be sure, also, to discuss the ethics of the project with your teacher before you begin and, if things change, as you proceed. Whether your project is part of a course or not, think carefully about the impact of what you propose to do. *Always* ask permission. Understand that people have legal rights to privacy and to how they look, what they say, and what they sing, even after you have recorded it. Be honest with yourself and with the people you study about your interest in their music and the purposes of your project. Tell them right from the start that you are interested in researching and documenting their music. If you like their music, say so. If the project is something for you to learn

Figure 9.9
Fiddler and guitarist at Fiesta. Taos, New Mexico, 1940.

Russell Lee. Courtesy of Library of Congress.

from, say so. Explain what will happen to the project after you finish it. Is it all right with them if you keep the photographs and tapes you make? Would they like a copy of the project? (If so, make one at your expense.) Is it all right if the project is deposited in the college or university archive? Most archives have a form that the people (yourself included) will sign, indicating that you are donating the project to the archive and that it will be used only for research purposes. If this project is not merely a contribution to knowledge but also to your career (as a student or otherwise), admit it and realize that you have a stake in its outcome. Ask the people whose music you are studying why they are cooperating with you and what they hope to achieve from the project, and bear that in mind throughout. Never observe, interview, make recordings, or take photographs without their knowledge and permission.

Today many ethnomusicologists believe that simply going into a musical situation and documenting it is not enough. The fieldworker must give something back to the people who have been generous with their thoughts, music, and time. In some cultures, people expect money and should be paid. Fieldworkers sometimes act not simply as reporters, or analysts, but also as cultural and musical advocates, doing whatever they can to help the music and musical communities they are studying flourish. This application of knowledge to the needs of music-cultures is termed *applied ethnomusicology*. Some ethnomusicologists in the United States work for arts councils, humanities councils, and other public agencies where they are expected to identify, document, and present family and community-based arts to the public. Many taxpayers believe that if the government supports the fine arts, it should also support folk and ethnic arts. In fact, most European governments do more than the United States and Canada to preserve and promote their folk and ethnic music. Ethnomusicologists hear a similar kind of commercial popular music throughout the world, and many conclude that local musics—of which there are a great variety—are endangered. It is to humankind's advantage to have many different kinds of music, they believe. For that reason, they think advocacy and support are necessary in the face of all the forces that would make music sound alike the world over. This argument may at first seem remote to your project, but not when you think about your own involvement with the people and music you are studying.

Field Gear: Notebook, Recorder, Camera

The perfect fieldworker has all-seeing eyes, all-hearing ears, and total recall. Because none of us is so well equipped, you must rely on the written notes, recordings, and photographs that you make in the field. These documents serve two purposes: They enable you to reexamine at leisure your field experiences when you write up your project, and they may be included in the final form your project takes, because they are accurate records of performances, interviews, and observations. On the other hand, field equipment presents certain difficulties: It costs money, you need to know how to work it properly, and you may have to resist the temptation to spend your time fiddling with your gear when you should be watching, thinking, and listening instead.

Fifty years ago, fieldworkers relied primarily on note taking, and today it is still necessary. No matter how sophisticated your gear is, you should carry a small pocket notebook. It will be useful for writing down names and addresses, directions, observations, and thoughts while in the field. In the days before sound recording, music was taken by dictation in notebooks. While this is still possible, it is not advisable except when performances are very brief and you have the required dictation skills. Dictating a song puts the performer in an unnatural context and changes the performance. However, notebooks are especially useful for preserving information learned in interviews, particularly if a tape recorder is unavailable or awkward in the interviewing situation. In addition, you should try to write down your detailed impressions of the following:

- The overall field situation: your plans, questions, any difficulties you find
- As complete a description as possible of the musical situation itself, including the setting, the performers, the audience, and the musical event from start to finish
- Your reactions and responses to the field experience

Your field notebook becomes a journal (and in some instances also a diary) that you address to yourself for use when you write up your project. As such, it is useful to write in it daily.

Most university music departments and many university libraries now loan inexpensive portable recorders to students for use in fieldwork projects. Whether you use a recorder, and if so what type it is (microcassette, portable cassette, mini-disc, CD, DAT, and so forth), largely depends on the nature of your project and your instructor's expectations. Although they may be adequate for some interview situations, microcassette recorders do not record music well enough for documentation purposes. The inexpensive, portable, full-sized cassette tape recorders are best suited to recording speech (interviews, for example). Although they come with built-in microphones, the sound quality can be improved dramatically if you use an inexpensive external microphone plugged into the recorder's microphone input jack. So equipped, a portable cassette tape recorder may be adequate for recording music. Of course you need to be thoroughly familiar with its operation—before you go into the field—in order to make accurate recordings. But the portable cassette recorder is mechanically simple, and anyone can learn to operate it in just a few minutes. Digital mini-disc and CD recorders are more expensive but make higher quality recordings. Digital audiotape (DAT) recorders are even more expensive and the sound is better yet, but these lie beyond the reach of most students. One thing to remember about cassette and DAT tape is that it does not age well. The useful life of a cassette tape may be as short as ten years, while a DAT or videotape may not last longer than five, depending on storage conditions. Transferred to CD-R or DVD format and stored in a dark place in a protected climate, a tape recording should have a much longer archival life.

The best way for beginners to improve the sound of a recording is to place the microphone in a good spot. If the sound is soft or moderate and it comes from a small area (a solo singer, a lesson on a musical instrument, or an interview, for example), place the microphone in close and in the middle of the sounds. If the sounds are loud and widely spread out (a rock band or a symphony orchestra, for example), search out "the best seat in the house" and place or hold the microphone there. Make a practice recording for a few seconds and play it back immediately to check microphone placement and to make certain the equipment is working properly (Figure 9.10). Take along spare batteries and blank tapes.

If properly used, even the simplest cameras take adequate pictures of musical performances. A picture may not be worth a thousand words, but it goes a long way toward capturing the human impact of a musical event.

Figure 9.10
A chief checks the quality of a recording of his musicians. Kasena-Nankani Traditional Area, Ghana.

James T. Koetting

A digital camera is especially useful because it allows you to see the photograph immediately and correct mistakes (such as standing too far from the action) at once. Digital pictures have another advantage: You can give copies easily to the people you photograph.

Using a video camcorder to document a musical event offers the advantage of sound combined with a moving picture. It may be possible to focus selectively on certain aspects of the musical event, such as dancers or particular musicians, so that they can be seen as well as heard in action. Videotape footage accompanying your project should be edited down to a manageable size, and it should reveal those aspects of the music-culture that are related directly to your topic. Video formats are changing rapidly, while the quality available at a particular price point keeps improving.

Americans are in love with technology, even technology to get away from technology (backpacking equipment, for example). If you already know a lot about recording and photography, and you own or can borrow high-quality equipment, by all means use it. Some of the photographs in this book and the accompanying recordings were made by the authors using professional equipment; after all, fieldwork is a part of our profession. But the more sophisticated our equipment is, the more difficult it is to use it to its full potential. Consider the true story of a photographer who went to a rock music festival and brought only his pocket camera. In the photographer's pit in front of the stage, he had maneuvered himself into the best position and was standing there taking pictures when a professional nudged him, saying, "Get out of here with that little toy!" The pro stood there with cameras hanging from his neck and shoulders, covering his body like baby opossums. "Well," said the amateur, yielding his position with a smile, "I guess if you need all of that equipment, you need to stand in the right spot, too!"

Interviewing

Interviews with people whose music you are studying can help you get basic information and feedback on your own ideas. Ethnomusicologists used to call such people *informants* but today they are usually called *consultants*. Be careful not to put words in your consultants' mouths and impose your ideas. The first step in understanding a world of music is to understand it as much as possible in your consultants' own terms. Later you can bring your own perspective to bear on the musical situation. Remember that much of their knowledge is intuitive; you will have to draw it out by asking questions.

Come into the interview with a list of questions, but be prepared to let the talk flow in the direction your consultant takes it. In his 1957 preface to *Primitive Man as Philosopher* Paul Radin distinguished between two procedures for obtaining information: question-and-answer and "letting the native philosopher expound his ideas with as few interruptions as possible" ([1927] 1957). Your consultants may not be philosophers, but they should be given the chance to say what they mean. Some people are by nature talkative, but others need to be put at ease. Let the person know in advance what sorts of questions you will be asking, what kind of information you need, and why. Often you will get important information in casual conversations rather than formal interviews; be ready to write down the information in your field notebook. Some people are by nature silent and guarded; despite your best intentions, they will not really open up to you. If you encounter that sort of person, respect his or her wishes and make the interview brief.

Beginning fieldworkers commonly make two mistakes when interviewing. First, they worry too much about the tape recorder, and their nervousness can carry over to the person they interview. If you have already gotten the person's consent to be interviewed, however, it should not be hard to get permission to tape the interview. One fieldworker always carries her tape recorder and camera so they are visible from the moment she enters the door. Then she nonchalantly sets the tape recorder down in a prominent spot and ignores it, letting the person being interviewed understand that the tape recorder is a natural and normal part of the interview. Still ignoring the recorder, she starts off with the small talk that usually begins such a visit. Eventually the other person says something like, "Oh, I see you're going to tape-record this." "Sure," she says steadily. "I brought along this tape recorder just to make sure I get down everything you say. I can always edit out any mistakes, and you can always change your mind. This is just to help me understand you better the first time." She says that once they have agreed to be interviewed, nobody has ever refused her tape recorder. But she adds that if anyone told her to keep the recorder shut off, she would certainly do so.

A second problem is that beginning fieldworkers often ask leading questions. A *leading question* is one that suggests or implies (that is, it leads or points to) one particular answer. Leading questions make the information obtained unreliable. In other words, it is not clear whether the person being interviewed is expressing his or her own thoughts or just being agreeable and giving the answer the consultant thinks the interviewer wants. In addition, leading questions usually result in short, uninteresting answers. Study this first dialogue to see how not to interview:

FIELDWORKER 1:   Did you get your first flute when you were a girl?

CONSULTANT: Yeah.

FIELDWORKER 1:   What was the name of your teacher?

CONSULTANT: Ah, I studied with Janice Sullivan.

FIELDWORKER 1:   When was that?

CONSULTANT: In college.

FIELDWORKER 1:   I'll bet you hated the flute when you first started. I can remember hating my first piano lessons.

CONSULTANT: Yeah.

The trouble here is that the consultant gives the kinds of answers she thinks are expected of her. She is just agreeing and not necessarily telling the fieldworker what she thinks. She is not even giving the conversation much thought. The fieldworker has asked the wrong kind of questions. Now look what happens when another fieldworker questions the same person.

FIELDWORKER 2:   Can you remember when you got your first flute?

CONSULTANT: Yeah.

FIELDWORKER 2:   Could you tell me about it?

CONSULTANT: Sure. My first flute—well, I don't know if this counts, but I fell in love with the flute when I was in grade school, and I remember going down to a music store and trying one out while my father looked on, but I couldn't make a sound, you know!

FIELDWORKER 2:   Sure.

CONSULTANT: So I was really disappointed, but then I remember learn-
                ing to play the recorder in, I think it was third grade, and I
                really loved that, but I didn't stick with it. Then in college
                I said to myself, I'm going to take music lessons and I'm
                going to learn the flute.

FIELDWORKER 2: Tell me about that.

CONSULTANT: Well, I had this great teacher, Janice Sullivan, and first she
                taught me how to get a sound out of it. I was really frus-
                trated at first, but after a while I got the hang of it, and she
                would always tell me to think of the beautiful sounds I
                knew a flute could make. I used to think a flute could
                make a sound like water, like the wind. Well, not exactly,
                but sort of. And then Mrs. Sullivan let me borrow a tape
                of *shakuhachi* music—you know, the Japanese flute?—
                and I heard different kinds of water, different kinds of
                wind! I knew then that I would play the flute for the rest
                of my life.

Compare the two fieldworkers' questions: "Did you get your first flute
when you were a girl?" is a leading question because it leads to the answer,
"Yes, I got my first flute when I was a girl." What is more, fieldworker 1
implies that most people get their first flutes when they are girls, so the consultant probably thinks she should answer yes. By contrast, the question
of fieldworker 2—"Can you remember when you got your first flute?"—is
open-ended and invites reflection, perhaps a story. When the consultant
says "Yeah," fieldworker 2 asks for a story and gets a much better—and
different—answer than does fieldworker 1. Go over the rest of the first
interview to see how fieldworker 1 injects her opinions into the dialogue
("I'll bet you hated the flute when you first started") and fails to draw out
the consultant's real feelings about her lessons, whereas fieldworker 2
establishes better rapport, is a better listener, asks nondirective questions,
and gets much fuller and truer answers.

If your project concentrates on a single consultant, you may want to
obtain his or her life story (Titon 1980). In this case you truly need a recorder
to get the story accurately. Because the way your consultants view their
lives can be as important as the factual information they give, you should
try to get the life story in their own words as much as possible. This means
refraining from questions that direct the story as you think it should go. What
matters is how your consultant wants it to go. Come back later, in another
interview, to draw out specific facts and fill in gaps by direct questioning. In
the initial interview, begin by explaining that you would like your consultant
to tell you about his or her life as a musician (or whatever is appropriate—
composer, disc jockey, and so forth) from the beginning until now. Once
begun, allow plenty of time for silences to let your consultant gather thoughts.
If he or she looks up at you expectantly, nod your head in agreement and
repeat what has just been said to show that you understand it. Resist any

impulse to ask direct questions. Write them down instead, and say you will come back to ask questions later—for now you want the story to continue.

Not everyone will be able to tell you his or her musical autobiography, but if you are fortunate enough to find someone who can, it may turn out to be the most important part of your project. On the other hand, if your consultant's life story is a necessary part of your project, but you cannot obtain it except by direct and frequent questioning, you should certainly ask the questions. If you get good answers, the result will be your consultant's life history, a collaborative biography rather than an autobiography.

Interviews, then, with the people whose music you are studying (and perhaps with their audience) help you obtain factual information and test your ideas. They also help you begin to comprehend the musical situation from their point of view: their beliefs, their intentions, their training, their feelings, their evaluations of musical performance, and their understanding of what they are doing—what it is all about. Ultimately, because this is your project, you will combine their ideas with your own interpretations when you write the project up, using the information you have collected.

Other Means of Collecting Information

Another technique, often used in social science research, is the questionnaire. Although its role in studying music is limited, and it should never be substituted for interviewing, a questionnaire can help you map out the general nature of a situation before moving into a specific sub-area to focus on. For example, to begin exploring the meaning of pop songs in students' lives, you may want to circulate a questionnaire to uncover the eventual sample you will study intensively. Questionnaires work best in studies of musical attitudes. To find out how shoppers react to supermarket background music, it would be hard to set up interviews but easy, if the store manager agrees, to distribute a questionnaire.

Aside from questionnaires, which seek out information, you might find information already gathered: autobiographical manuscripts, diaries, photos and recordings made by consultants for themselves. Clubs, fraternities, schools, churches, and various organizations often store away old materials that shed light on musical activities. At concerts, the programs handed out may be rich in information, ranging from description of the music to the type of advertisers that support the concerts. Membership lists and patrons' lists may be included as well.

Newspapers are enormously helpful. Hardly a day passes without journalistic commentary on the musical environment—in news stories, reviews, and advertisements. Feature stories provide up-to-date information on current concerts, trends, and musical attitudes, both local and national, while advertising can furnish insights into the ideals of the U.S. musical world projected by the media, ideals that influence most of us one way or another. For example, an ad for an expensive home entertainment system offers a direct connection between musical style and the rooms of the house: "101 Strings in the greenhouse, Bach in the bedroom, Frank Sinatra in the living room, Gershwin in the den, the Boston Pops on the patio, the Rolling Stones outside by the pool." What better brief description of middle-aged, middle-class musical taste could be found?

Finishing the Project

As you do all the hard work of organizing and collecting information, always think ahead to what you will do with it. As you go along, return to the list of questions you formulated in relation to your topic—the questions you wanted to ask about the musical situation. As you gather more information you will have formulated more questions. These questions and the information you have gathered are related, and they offer a natural organization for your project. Remember that the point of your project is to document some aspect of a nearby music-culture and to interpret it based on the topic you have chosen. More advice on how to write it up and what form to present it in will be available from your instructor.

Be sure to keep in mind that you are not the only one affected by your finished project. Other people's feelings and, on occasion, social position are reflected in your work. Be clear in what you say about the people you worked with. Confidentiality may be important; if people asked you not to use their names or repeat what they said to you, respect their wishes. As is customary in many anthropological works, you may decide to change names of people or places to make certain no one is identified who does not want to be. Imagine the problems created for the member of a band who criticizes the leader if word gets back to the group, or for a school music teacher if he criticizes the school board to you in private and you quote him.

If you need to clear up research questions, check back with your consultants. As you interview, collect information, and think about the musical situation you study, new questions always will occur to you. It is no different when you write up your project; you will probably find it helpful to get back in touch with your consultants and ask a few final questions so that you will be satisfied with your project when you have finished it.

The authors of this book hope, as the Preface put it, that our readers will experience "what it is like to be an ethnomusicologist puzzling out his or her way toward understanding an unfamiliar music." A good field project inevitably provides just that experience. Valuable and enjoyable in and of itself, discovery and documentation of a world of music takes on added significance, because even the smallest project illuminates our understanding of music as human expression.

Study Questions

1. What are the organizing principles that help ethnomusicologists study music-cultures? Choose two and explain why they are important.

2. What four approaches can you take to narrow the subject of your music study down to a topic?

3. How do you find information on music-cultures? What are the main kinds of sources for this information?

4. In a field study, what are the pros and cons of participating and observing?

5. What ethical issues might arise in ethnomusicologists' fieldwork?

6. What gear does an ethnomusicologist need? Why?

7. What makes an interview good or bad?

Glossary

consultants People interviewed by ethnomusicologists in order to obtain information about a music-culture. Formerly known as informants.

fieldwork In ethnomusicology, as in anthropology and folklore, the in-person witnessing, observing, questioning, tape recording, photographing, and in some cases performing; work "in the field" rather than the laboratory or library.

human subjects research policy The policy of an institution that defines the rules for ethical conduct when one researches human beings. This almost always includes causing no harm, voluntary participation by the subjects (permission), permissions, and legal privacy issues.

leading question In interviewing, a question by the interviewer that suggests or implies a particular answer, thereby making the information obtained unreliable.

musical ethnography A written representation, description, and interpretation of some aspect of a music-culture, organized from the standpoint of a particular topic.

participant-observer A person who studies a culture by joining in its activities as well as by observing it from an outside perspective.

topic A subject viewed from a particular angle, from a certain perspective, and with a limited goal in mind.

Resources

References

Radin, Paul. [1927] 1957. *Primitive Man as Philosopher.* New York: Dover.

Spottswood, Richard. 1990. *Ethnic Music on Records: a Discography of Ethnic Recordings Produced in the United States, 1893 to 1942.* 5 vols. Urbana: Univ. of Illinois Press.

Titon, Jeff Todd. 1980. "The Life Story." *Journal of American Folklore* 93:276–92.

———. and Bob Carlin, eds. 2002. *American Musical Traditions.* New York: Gale Research.

Additional Reading

Barz, Gregory F., and Timothy J. Cooley. 1997. *Shadows in the Field: New Perspectives for Fieldwork in Ethnomusicology.* New York: Oxford Univ. Press.

Collier, John, Jr., and Malcolm Collier. 1986. *Visual Anthropology: Photography as a Research Method.* Albuquerque: Univ. of New Mexico Press.

Emerson, Robert M., Rachel I. Fretz, and Linda L. Shaw. 1995. *Writing Ethnographic Fieldnotes.* Chicago: University of Chicago Press.

Ethnomusicology 36 (2). 1992. [Special issue on fieldwork in the public interest]

Georges, Robert A., and Michael O. Jones. 1980. *People Studying People.* Berkeley: Univ. of California Press.

Golde, Peggy, ed. 1986. *Women in the Field: Anthropological Experiences.* 2nd ed. Berkeley: Univ. of California Press.

Herndon, Marcia, and Norma McLeod. 1983. *Field Manual for Ethnomusicology.* Norwood, Pa.: Norwood Editions.

Hood, Mantle. 1982. *The Ethnomusicologist,* chaps. 4 and 5. 2nd ed. Kent, Ohio: Kent State Univ. Press.

Horenstein, Henry. 1983. *Black and White Photography.* Rev. ed. New York: Little, Brown.

Ives, Edward D. 1980. *The Tape-Recorded Interview: A Manual for Fieldworkers in Folklore and Oral History.* Knoxville: Univ. of Tennessee Press.

Jackson, Bruce. 1987. *Fieldwork.* Urbana: Univ. of Illinois Press.

Lornell, Kip, and Anne K. Rasmussen. 1997. *Musics of Multicultural America.* New York: Schirmer Books.

Rabinow, Paul. 1977. *Reflections on Fieldwork in Morocco.* Berkeley: Univ. of California Press.

Sanjek, Roger, ed. 1990. *Fieldnotes: The Makings of Anthropology.* Ithaca, N.Y.: Cornell Univ. Press.

Spradley, James P. 1979. *The Ethnographic Interview.* New York: Holt, Rinehart, & Winston.

Van Maanen, John. 1988. *Tales of the Field: On Writing Ethnography.* Chicago: Univ. of Chicago Press.

Wax, Rosalie. 1971. *Doing Fieldwork: Warnings and Advice.* Chicago: Univ. of Chicago Press.

Wengle, John L. 1988. *Ethnographers in the Field: The Psychology of Research.* Tuscaloosa: Univ. of Alabama Press.

Web Resources

- American Folklife Center
  http://lcweb.loc.gov/folklife/

- *Ethnomusicology OnLine*
  http://research.umbc.edu/efhm/eol.html

- Smithsonian Center for Folklife and Heritage
  http://www.folklife.si.edu/

- Society for Ethnomusicology
  http://www.indiana.edu/~ethmusic/

Index

Italic page references denote glossary entries.